COASTAL NAVIGATION STEP BY STEP

COASTAL NAVIGATION STEP BY STEP

by Warren Norville

INTERNATIONAL MARINE PUBLISHING COMPANY
CAMDEN, MAINE

To my wife, Harriet

CONTENTS

PREFACE

What does a navigator need to know to conduct safely the passage of a vessel of any size in pilot waters? What knowledge and what skills will he use when he is navigating a ship or boat on soundings?

What kind of knowledge and what "tricks of the trade" particularly lend themselves to the needs of the small vessel operator, whether he is a fisherman, tugboatman, crewboat skipper, or yachtsman? These people frequently find themselves alone on watch. As the only watch standers on deck, they are required simultaneously to do the work of helmsman, lookout, and navigator. Often they do not have the instruments for taking bearings, the devices for measuring speed, or the sophisticated electronic gear found on larger vessels. They must depend on more simple ways to get this information. I remember well my own dilemma when, as a new returnee from being a watch officer on naval and other large vessels, I tried to apply some of the techniques I used so easily on a destroyer to the navigation of a small cruising sloop. The man alone at the helm of a little ship needs accurate navigation as much as anyone. If time or circumstances prevent him from getting an accurate fix he must at least have some means of knowing when he is standing into danger or when he is proceeding safely. The means he uses to do this must be the same means he can literally "bet his life on."

What must be covered in a work such as this to give these small vessel navigators something more substantial than mere seat-of-the-pants navigation?

These are the questions I asked as I prepared to write this book. Whether you are the master or mate of a supertanker or skipper of a shrimpboat, this book should have useful information for you.

This work is the result, in part, of the classes I taught in piloting and dead reckoning at the University of South Alabama. Much that is presented here is also the result of my experience in teaching people, from all walks of life, who wanted to sit for a Coast Guard license. And last, as implied above, much of the material consists of those things I have found useful to me when cruising in my own little sloop, piloting a tug and tow, or coasting along a foreign shore as master or navigator of someone else's vessel.

I am not implying that this book alone will make you a good pilot or prepare you to sit for any specific examination. But I do say that if you master the topics in this work, and reinforce this knowledge with a proper amount of experience, you should then have the ability to take a vessel along any coast, with care, but also with confidence.

This book is about piloting and about dead reckoning. These two parts of the study of navigation do not excite the imagination like celestial navigation or loran. We will study the use of loran in this book. Yet piloting and dead reckoning are two parts of the art and science of navigation that must be mastered before you can call yourself a competent navigator.

Dead reckoning is the basic technique of the navigator. The only purpose of piloting, celestial navigation, loran, or the more exotic systems of electronic navigation is to check the accuracy of the dead reckoning plot.

Piloting is essential because without a mastery of the skills involved you cannot make a landfall, enter a harbor, or conduct a vessel along a coast safely. Because piloting is practiced in confined waters, beset by the hazards of shoals, tides, rocks, currents, and other dangers, the utmost skill and attention is required of the navigator. Being a good pilot is the highest attainment of the navigator's art. Never is a vessel more exposed to dangers than when she is in pilot waters. Piloting is a skill, however, that anyone who will make the effort can learn. Application and study are the keys to mastering this art, along with no little amount of experience.

Just a few generations ago all the seaman's arts were learned at sea. But as available knowledge increased, more and more information was presented in the classroom. Time, and often too severe a lesson, have always made learning by experience a costly affair. But when experience can be coupled with education, the benefits of both are enhanced beyond comparison, and the time required to attain a useful degree of skill is greatly reduced — to say nothing of also reducing the wear and tear on people and property. So practice what you study here. Whenever you have the opportunity, carry this book aboard ship with you, whether it be for an afternoon pleasure cruise or a trip you make in pursuit of your living. Practice in familiar waters will build the confidence you will need to pilot with confidence in strange seas.

This book is intended to take you step by step and show you, as if you were at sea, what the navigator does in pilot waters. To accomplish this I have divided the book into a number of short chapters. Each chapter tells you how to do a specific thing. Whenever possible, I have avoided theory, but I have not turned stern-to and run when a little explanation of the theory might help. You will find some discussion of the ways and whyfores of variation and deviation, but if you simply want to correct your compass course, the text will tell you how to do it. If you have forgotten how to work a bow and beam bearing, or if you never knew before, you will find a chapter on this type of problem, and on nothing else. If you are a beginner or if you want to refresh your knowledge of piloting, study the entire book.

Warren Norville

ACKNOWLEDGEMENTS

A book, like a work in architecture, may originate in the mind of its creator, but no work was ever completed without the help of many whose special talents make it possible for the concept to evolve into a finished piece. This work was my concept originally, but many others contributed their essential talents to make its completion possible. Many I have not named specifically, yet I recognize and appreciate the help they gave me.

This work may have never been completed without the help of such people as my good friends and jovial students, Lawrence Gamotis and Roby Bevan. It was with Lawrence and Roby that I made my research cruise from Mobile to Panama City, in my sloop *Li'l Tiger*, photographing and checking aids to navigation during a memorable four days of hard running, hard work, fair and foul weather, but always good companionship.

I am grateful to my cousin, Rachel Mason, for her help as chief mate on several weekends around Saint Andrews Bay, Florida, as we checked out the problems and examples that were set in this area in the beginning of our hypothetical voyage of *War Hat*. And to Rachel too, for typing so many pages of the final draft of this manuscript.

It was Carolyn Smith and my daughter, Mary Jane Norville, who contributed their talents as crew in *Li'l Tiger* on the leg of the coasting voyage from Panama City to Mobile Bay, checking out along the coast the simulated situations used in this book. It was Carolyn Smith, again, who sailed with me on the final passage from Mobile Bay Entrance to Gulfport as we continued to make in fact our hypothetical voyage of *War Hat*. And when all this was done, it was Carolyn who typed the last few hundred pages of the finished manuscript.

I am especially indebted to Mr. Hiram Hamilton Maxim of Farmington and Old Lyme, Connecticut, for his invaluable assistance with the chapter on radio navigation. Many of the good ideas and special little "tricks of the trade" expressed in this chapter are Mr. Maxim's. Not only did he permit me to use freely so many of his ideas, but also he gave me invaluable assistance by critiquing so thoroughly this part of the manuscript.

And most of all, my wife, Harriet, "Li'l Tiger", who, despite her thinking that boats look best with barnacles on their cabin tops and fish swimming through their portholes, puts up with my mess and clutter when I turn her house into an author's study; for keeping a candle in the window while I am away at sea; and, in this case specifically, for rescuing my aged Volkswagen and my young orange-and-white kitten from the high water of the unprogrammed and unpredicted cyclone that battered our coast during our first voyage to Panama City.

1 WHAT IT IS ALL ABOUT

This chapter could have been called "How To Plan a Coastal Passage." What is involved in the work of a pilot getting ready to go "a-coasting?" What is he required to do before he goes to sea? How does a navigator plan a coasting voyage? And after he is at sea what is he required to do? When you can answer all these questions, and do the work they require, you can call yourself a good pilot.

Many of the topics taken up in this chapter will be discussed much more fully in later chapters. Here, we are introducing you to much of the pilot's work; later, we will explain the techniques thoroughly.

When planning a passage, the first and most important step is for the navigator to garner all the information available concerning things of interest to navigation along the way of the intended voyage. The best source of this information is often local knowledge. But local knowledge for safe navigation can take a lifetime, or at best years, to acquire. For the stranger or others less familiar with an area, the main source of information is from the charts of an area.

As navigator you should have a complete chart portfolio of the waters you may be in. This portfolio should consist of a small-scale chart covering the entire passage if the voyage is a long one. This chart will give you "the big picture." From it you can see the general lay of the coast and surmise a reasonable idea of the problems involved in the intended passage. For the actual day's work of navigating the vessel, you will need a series of coastal charts, overlapping in areas covered, encompassing the entire passage. These charts must be large enough in scale, and sufficient enough in detail, to show all the hazards and available aids to navigation along your course as well as depict any other items of interest. And most important, you should secure the even larger scale harbor charts of every harbor your vessel *can* get into as well as harbor charts of those ports you plan to enter. In the event of bad weather or other mishap, it is nice to have adequate charts of the nearest port of refuge. Many a prudent sailor has spent a quiet night in his bunk, with a good anchor out, simply because he had the foresight to equip himself with a chart of every port of refuge he might need to seek. His less prudent fellows have been compelled to spend an unpleasant night clawing off a lee shore. We all know the alternative to a safe harbor is sea room, and don't cut it too fine. Make your decision to get offshore or seek harbor while the option is still open. The right charts can help you make this decision.

I cannot take you with me on a cruise, but with very little make-believe I can have you work each of the types of problems you would be likely to encounter on a coasting voyage. A lot of our time we will be in the Gulf of Mexico, on a coastal passage from Panama City, Florida, to Gulfport, Mississippi. But we may suddenly find ourselves off the coast of Africa or Central America taking vertical sextant angles off a mountain peak, since there are no mountains along the Gulf coast.

As navigator you must know the characteristics of your vessel. For purposes of illustration in this book, consider her to be a small schooner about forty-five feet overall. Her normal cruising speed under power is ten knots. Her draft is six feet. Her name is *War Hat*.

For the passage along the Gulf Coast you will require charts. The planning chart or sailing chart for this area is National Ocean Survey Chart No. 1115. The National Ocean Survey was formerly the Coast and Geodetic Survey, and its charts are still referred to as Coast and Geodetic Survey charts also, or simply as C&GS charts. C&GS Chart No. 1115 is a small-scale sailing chart designed for offshore sailing or offshore coasting. This chart covers the whole route of your intended passage along the Gulf Coast. For the precise navigation required to take us safely along this coast, you will need the larger scale coasting

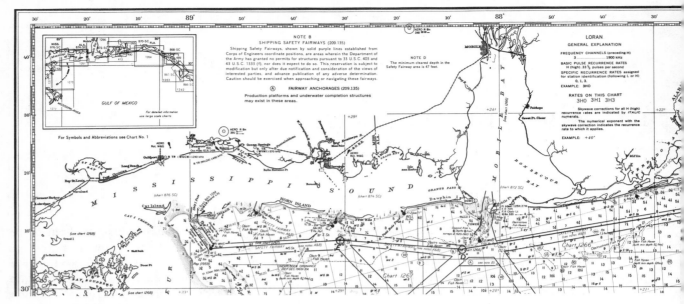

Figure 1-1. Courses for an entire passage plotted on Ocean Survey Chart No. 1115. Points *A*, *B*, *C*, *D*, and *E* are points arbitrarily selected by the navigator to fit the requirement that the vessel hold approximately five miles offshore in the safety fairways, and then hold the north side of the safety fairways to the Gulfport seabuoy. The area covered by this section of the chart lies between approximately latitudes 30⁰ 00′N and 30⁰ 45′N, and longitudes 85⁰ 00′W and 89⁰ 00′W.

charts. You can get the numbers of these charts by close inspection of Chart No. 1115. You can also get the numbers of these charts from the chart catalog at your chart agent's store. Most of the larger marine stores are agents of the Defense Mapping Agency and the National Ocean Survey and are referred to generally as chart agents. If there is no chart agent in your area, you may order charts by mail from the following agencies:

Defense Mapping Agency
Hydrographic Center
Washington, D.C. 20390

National Ocean Survey (NOAA)
Distribution Division C-44
Riverdale, Maryland 20840

Select the charts you will need for this passage. The charts are C&GS Charts Nos. 1263, 1264, 1265, 1266, and 1267. Larger scale charts are available for precise navigation within the harbors you may visit. These charts can be obtained through the same sources and should be included in your portfolio. They are also listed in the catalogs. Had you been planning a passage along another coast, you would have selected your charts in precisely the same way,

but of course you would have selected the numbers for those charts of the area of your intended passage. You could obtain and refer to your own copy of *Nautical Chart Catalog 1* (United States Atlantic and Gulf Coasts), published by the National Ocean Survey, and select the charts you would need for your passage. Similar catalogs are published for other regions by NOS, as appropriate.

To benefit from this book, you will not need to buy the charts listed above. As required, sections of each chart listed will be used to illustrate specific items or examples.

You are to be the navigator. To plot you must have a good set of parallel rulers along with a sharp, medium-hard pencil. A pair of dividers is a must. If you prefer, a course protractor or other instrument may be substituted for the parallel rulers.

You would not attempt this voyage without a current *Light List*, CG-160, for this area, published by the U.S. Coast Guard. *Tide* and *Current Tables* for the year are a must also. Your date of departure is 21 October 1972. Copies of pages from the *Light List* and of pages of the *Tide Tables* and the *Current Tables* are included in the text where appropriate.

Another publication you must have is *The American Practical Navigator*, originally by Nathaniel Bowditch, now HO Publication Number 9, but known to navigators and seamen simply as *Bowditch*.

Bowditch is the epitome of navigation references for North American navigators. No navigator can truly practice his skills without access to the tables in this remarkable publication. When you reach the point where you can read and understand all the material in *Bowditch,* you can consider yourself an authority on navigation. Although any properly equipped vessel going to sea will have a ship's copy of *Bowditch* on board, this book is so important and useful that many navigators carry their personal copies with them. This work contains page excerpts of the necessary tables required to work or follow the problems and examples in the text. Nevertheless, if you are seriously interested in becoming a good navigator, you should get yourself a copy of *Bowditch.* You can buy the tables from *Bowditch,* in a separate edition, but for the difference in price I suggest you go ahead and buy the entire book.

There is always essential information a pilot will need concerning an area that cannot be handily put on a chart. A supplementary publication is issued by the agency issuing the chart to cover this need. In the continental United States and territories, these publications are called *Coast Pilots* and are issued by the National Ocean Survey. For foreign coasts, a similar publication is issued by the Defense Mapping Agency, and this publication is called *Sailing Directions.* You should have on board a current issue of the *Coast Pilot* covering that stretch of coast you expect to sail, which in our case is the Gulf Coast of the United States, which is covered by volume number 5.

There are other publications you can use. HO 117 lists the radio aids to navigation and the other radio services available to the navigator. HO 117A is the

publication covering the Atlantic, Mediterranean, Caribbean, and Gulf areas. HO 117B covers the Pacific Ocean and contiguous areas. An *International Code of Signals* (HO Pub. No. 103) is a good investment. Admittedly, if you run up a flag hoist or flash a light at a lot of our seagoing compatriots, they will think you have sprung something in your tophamper, but the real professionals know what you are doing. With the international signal book, you can communicate with a Greek, and not know a word of his language.

If you were really going to make this passage, after you gathered all the charts and publications together, you could begin your voyage. So as you read into this book pretend you are at sea. Refer to the various pages reproduced in this book as if you were actually referring to the particular publication required. You can merely read this book, and you may get something out of it, but you certainly won't get as much from reading it as you will from working your way through it. If you will work as you go, I believe you will have a delightful experience, in that you will soon see there is really nothing mysterious about any kind of navigation, including piloting. It will be a fruitful experience because of this. It will be the next best thing to being at sea and having the boat roll and pitch under you.

Break out Chart No. 1115 (or refer to Figure 1-1 as appropriate). Chart No. 1115 is the small-scale sailing chart that covers the route of the entire passage. On this chart lay out a course, or a series of courses in fact, to conform to your route. Study the chart carefully, and decide how far off shore you want to be enroute. You could go straight across,

3

DEPARTED: PANAMA CITY, BUOY #1 _____ ZT SPEED: 10 KNOTS

FROM	TO	COURSE TRUE	COURSE COMPASS	DIST.	ETE	ETA ORIG.	REV.	ATA
PC#1	SEA BUOY	233°	238°	2.2 mi.	0ʰ 13ᵐ			
SEA BUOY	"A"	233°	238°	2.1 mi.	0ʰ 13ᵐ			
"A"	"B"	297°	298°	22.7 mi.	2ʰ 16ᵐ			
"B"	"C"	277°	279°	27.5 mi.	2ʰ 45ᵐ			
"C"	"D"	261°	264°	73.7 mi.	7ʰ 22ᵐ			
"D"	"E"	276°	280°	20.4 mi.	2ʰ 03ᵐ			
"E"	SHIP I.P.	266°	269°	21.15 mi.	2ʰ 09ᵐ			
TOTALS				168.75	17ʰ 02ᵐ			

Figure 1-2. A table of courses and estimated arrivals for the navigator's notebook.

mostly out of sight of land, to Ship Island, but you decide to hold an average of five miles off shore. At this distance you will be far enough out to have good water. You will be close enough to the beach to see any navigational aids that may be there. Since it is impossible to hold exactly five miles off without steering a constantly curving course, there is a need for a bit of judgement here. Your plot should look something like the one shown in Figure 1-1. As you plot your courses, watch carefully to see that you will clear all obstructions, hazards, restricted areas, and any other such places it would not be prudent for your vessel to be. After you have plotted the courses for the passage, check again to see that you have not overlooked any of these things you should avoid. Notice, too, the shipping fairways beginning at Pensacola and running west. You should vary your distance off shore to conform to these shipping fairways, holding to the right, or north side when westbound.

After you have plotted these courses measure the distance between each point where you intend to change course. On a Mercator chart, you measure distances on the latitude scale between the parallels of latitude in which your course lies. A minute of latitude equals one nautical mile. It is a good idea to make up a table showing the courses for each leg, both true courses and compass courses, the distance between points, the estimated time enroute (ETE), the estimated time of arrival at each point (ETA), and leave a blank column in the table to record the actual time of arrival (ATA) at each point. The ETA column should be divided into two sub-columns to show the ETA of the original planning, and a revised ETA as the voyage progresses. The revised ETA sub-column and the ATA column are left blank at this time, and filled in with the appropriate data as you proceed along the coast. This table need not be any-

thing fancy, but can be neatly written in longhand in your navigator's notebook. The complete table for your passage from Panama City to Ship Island Pass is shown in Figure 1-2.

I am not going to tell you that making this table is absolutely necessary, but think a minute. You now have in a brief outline the entire voyage. If at any point a large variation in time enroute or course to steer presents itself, you will have an immediate indication that something is awry. By totaling up the times, ETEs, you know how long the voyage should take. Total up the distances for each leg, and you will know how far you must sail. Keep your ETAs and ATAs up to date as you go. You will have to revise constantly your original ETAs due to the unforeseeable effects of wind and current on your speed. But by keeping this information as current as possible, you will always be better prepared to act if any emergency should arise.

About the navigator's notebook I just mentioned — as navigator you should keep such a notebook. The navigator's notebook is a workbook, and as such it should contain all the observations and calculations you employed in the navigation of your vessel. You should also include a narrative account of your "day's work" to record anything of interest to you as navigator or events of general interest to the ship. If all goes well, your navigator's notebook makes a nice keepsake of the voyage. If disaster strikes, you have an excellent record of the navigator's work leading up to the moment of trouble. This record could well exonerate you, provided of course you did not goof. Any kind of blank book will do for a navigator's notebook. Just be sure it is big enough. Many navigators like the standard stenographer's notebook for this purpose. The important thing for you to do is keep a navigator's notebook. Keep it up to date. Keep it complete. And keep it neat!

The table you made, shown in Figure 1-2, is part of your preliminary planning. It is now time to break out your larger scale charts. These are the charts you should keep your navigational plot on. You must lay out your course again on these larger scale charts. You could lay out these courses on each chart as you progress along your passage. By laying the courses on each chart as you progress, you can plot your courses to conform to changes caused by conditions you encounter enroute. On the other hand it is essential that you plot your various points to change course by transferring these points from your sailing chart.

On all charts it is a good idea to label your courses. Courses are labeled by writing the true course and compass course above the rhumb line. Put the true

4

course first and compass course last. If your courses are 261° true and 267° compass, write them like this: 261°T/267°C. Under the course line put the speed, S 10 knots. As you plot these courses again on the larger scale coasting charts, watch for dangers, things to avoid, and aids to navigation or other things of interest to the safety of your vessel. The larger scale of these charts will make such things easier to spot. If you find you must make changes in the courses you planned, be sure to revise accordingly the table you made from your planning chart. The closer resolution you can obtain from the larger scale charts will almost certainly require some small revisions to this table, particularly for distances.

Careful study of any chart is absolutely essential. You must be aware of all hazards in the area you are to traverse. You must also be aware of all the aids to navigation you may be able to use along the way. You must be aware of any and all things that can affect the safety of your vessel. The chart is your prime source of this information.

Getting underway: As navigator, before casting off your moorings or weighing anchor, locate your position precisely on the largest scale chart of the harbor or anchorage you are in. For Panama City this will be Chart No. CS 489. Actually Chart No. CS 489 (National Ocean Survey) is a larger scale harbor chart, but Chart No. 1263 provides all the detail required to traverse safely from your anchorage to the marked channel, and then to sea in a vessel the size of *War Hat*. Had you planned extensive maneuvers in the harbor, Chart No. CS 489 would have been required. But by using Chart No. 1263 you are able to plot both your course from your anchorage to sea, and continue your plot along the coast after clearing the seabuoy on this same chart. So break out Chart No. 1263. (Look ahead to Figure 7-8).

Lay out a safe course from your berth or anchorage to the marked channel. To begin your voyage, assume you are anchored in 42 feet of water, on a soft mud bottom, in the bay at Panama City, just far enough north of the flashing red light at Palmetto Point to swing safely. From this anchorage the course to black can buoy "21" is 304°T to pass this buoy close aboard on your starboard hand. Because this course takes you close to the bank on the north side of the channel, you would tell your helmsman to "steer nothing to the right of 304°," or whatever compass course you figured would give you a true course of 304°.

When black buoy "21" is abeam, change course to 307° to pass red buoy "20" abeam to port. Be sure to "uncorrect" these true courses to compass courses so you will know the course to steer. (Correcting and

uncorrecting the compass are explained in Chapter 5. For now just keep in mind these things must be done.)

The buoys you will be passing as you turn to stand out to sea are of special interest. They are dual purpose buoys in that they mark both the upper reaches of the main ship channel into Panama City and the Gulf Intracoastal Waterway (ICW) at this point. Furthermore, these buoys are opposed as to the direction of "standing in," as the ICW is assumed to be standing in going west along the coast here, and inbound vessels in the main ship channel are proceeding easterly. As the main ship channel is the primary waterway, this buoy is black, odd numbered, and a can buoy. As its identification as a marker for the Intracoastal Waterway, it will have a yellow triangle painted on it. This indicates that the black can buoy number 15 is to be considered a red nun buoy for the purpose of ICW marking. For the details of the buoyage system used in the United States, please refer to Chapter 10 of this work and Coast Guard publication CG-193, *Aids to Navigation.*

You are now ready to sail. Heave around and, when the anchor is home in the hawsepipe, proceed to sea. Standing out of Panama City, you will find that the channel is well marked. You can easily steer safely by heading between the buoys and beacons. Keep the black buoys or beacons to starboard. Easy isn't it? So easy it would be silly to plot a course for each reach of the channel. Or would it be silly? Suppose fog, rain, or other factors reduced your visibility. If you had your course laid out, you would not need to be hanging over a chart table when your eyes should be out on stems trying to see through the fog. Buoys also have a way of drifting or being dragged off station. If the charted course to steer doesn't jibe with the course you must hold to fetch a buoy, you know something is wrong. This is how complete, early planning can contribute so much to the safety of a voyage.

When you reach the seabuoy, set your course for the point at which you wish to make your first course change. From the table you made up earlier, you can see this course is 233°T/236°C. The point you will be heading for is point *A*. Navigators speak of this type of designation as "point Alpha." The next point is *B*, Bravo, *C*, Charlie and so on. Note the exact time you passed the seabuoy, and set your course. This is the time of your departure. Be sure to steer the *compass* course!

From now on until your vessel is moored in a safe harbor, you must keep an accurate account of her position to keep her out of danger. The main secret of a good navigator's skill is never to lose track of his vessel's position. To keep this accurate account of your vessel's position you first must keep an accurate dead reckoning or DR track. But wind and currents will make your DR wrong sooner or later. To correct your DR you must establish your position as accurately as possible from time to time. How often will depend on several things, such as the speed of your ship, the state of the weather, and how close you may have to pass dangers or other things you want to avoid. The means you use to find or fix your position will depend on personal preference to some extent, but mostly you will be governed by what aids to navigation are available, and what instruments are on hand to make your observations with. On a large, deep-draft vessel, operating at fast speeds close to the beach, this fixing of the vessel's position can be a continuous evolution of bearings, plots, sextant angles, and other observations. On a smaller boat, such as a yacht or fishing vessel, it may be satisfactory to get a fix only at set intervals. The important thing is to make your observations often enough to get an early indication if you are being set off course.

Then you can take corrective action before your vessel is in trouble. It will be a test of your judgement as navigator how often this should be. In strange waters, with sufficient searoom, the maximum time between fixes should not exceed fifteen minutes, and, in close quarters, fixing your vessel's position, regardless of her size, can resolve into a continuous series of taking and plotting bearings.

As you progress you should make any course changes necessary to keep your vessel heading toward her destination and out of danger. By timing your runs between fixes, you can get a true indication of your speed.

In a nutshell this is what piloting and dead reckoning is all about. You get underway and stand out to sea. When clear of the seabuoy you set your course. By using your speed, time, and the direction you go, your course, you maintain your DR plot. By the use of various means, you frequently check the accuracy of your DR plot. In coastal or inland waters these methods are summed up as piloting. The remainder of this book tells you how all this is done.

2 DEFINITIONS, OR WHAT THE WORDS MEAN

Whenever I start with a new group of beginning navigation students, whether it is piloting or celestial navigation, my first plea is, "please do not let the new words you encounter throw you." There is nothing hard or profound about either of these phases of navigation. Navigation, like any other study, must have its special terms to describe its special character. Unfortunately, a lot of people are frightened away from learning navigation by a few unfamiliar words. This is as true of the professional as it is of the amateur. Those who persevere through the first few exposures necessary to gain a working familiarity with these words go on to success.

Please hang in there!

Most of the new words you encounter in this work will be defined as they come into use in the text. In most cases the meaning of these words will be obvious in their context, even if they are words you have not been using every day. Some words I have already used will be defined specifically so you will have the exact nautical definition firm in your mind. This way I hope to avoid drowning you in a mass of verbiage before you are well into your study of navigation. There are some words, however, that do require special explanation. Regrettably the explanations may sound almost as foreign as the words themselves. You will also be surprised at the number of words the navigator uses that you already know. All of these words are ones you will use every day in your study and practice of navigation. Bear in mind my definitions are slanted in relation to the use of the word as it applies to navigation. Hence a definition of a certain word or expression may not be the common definition, but it is the definition practical navigators use.

DEGREES

The earth, for all practical purposes to the navigator, is a sphere. Any time you go from one place to another on the surface of the earth, you travel in a circle or at least in a curved path. If you go the shortest distance between two points on the earth's surface, you go by what sailors term the *great circle course*. Your course traverses an arc of this great circle. If you go another route, such as along a parallel of latitude, your course traverses an arc of a small circle. *Small circle* and *great circle* are terms I will define in a few more paragraphs. All I want you to think of now is that, in both of these cases, your courses will traverse arcs of circles. All circles have circumferences of 360 degrees. This is true of circles one inch in diameter or of circles 6,888 miles in diameter, the diameter of the earth. From this it is obvious that degrees cannot be general units of linear measurement. Degrees are measurements of *arc*. An arc of a circle is a part of the circumference of a circle. Thus degrees are measurements of the number of fractional parts, expressed as a fraction whose denominator is 360, in a part of the circumference of a circle. This is understood, and for this reason navigators do not say turn 90/360ths to the right when a right turn of this amount is required. They simply say come right 90 degrees.

ANGLES

Two straight lines, radii, extending from the center of a circle to each end of an arc of a circle subtend *angles*. An arc of a circle that covers one-eighth of a circle is an arc of 45 degrees. One-eighth of 360 is 45. Two radii from the center of this circle to each end of this arc make an angle of 45 degrees. Angles are measured in degrees too. Now, if you take the intersection of any two lines as the center of a circle, you can enscribe an arc to cross these lines. The number of degrees in this arc measures the angle at which these lines cross. So two lines crossing form an angle that can be measured in degrees. The term forty-five degrees is usually written as 45°. Degrees and decimal fractions of a degree, such as forty-five and seven tenths degrees, are written 45⁰ 7. Note the placement of the degree symbol in relation to the decimal.

MINUTES

Degrees are divided into smaller units called *minutes.* Unless there can be no chance of confusion, a navigator is careful to say "minutes of arc" to distinguish from minutes of time. A minute of arc is one sixtieth of a degree. There are 60 minutes of arc to a degree. The term forty-five minutes is usually written 45'. Forty-five and seven tenths minutes would be written 45'.7.

SECONDS

Minutes of arc can be divided into smaller units called *seconds.* These are seconds of arc. There are 60 seconds of arc to a minute of arc. The term forty-five seconds of arc is written as 45". Forty-five and seven tenths seconds is written 45".7. In navigation most measurement of arc on the earth's surface is to the nearest tenth of a minute. Measurement to the nearest second is reserved for only the most precise work or for plotting on very large-scale charts. A second of arc on a great circle of the earth is approximately 101 feet.

Depending on the diameter of a circle, the actual linear size of a degree, minute, or second will vary. On a circle twelve inches in diameter, a degree will measure a little over one inch. On a great circle of the earth, a degree equals sixty miles: one minute of arc of a great circle of the earth equals one mile.

GREAT CIRCLES

If you do not already know, by now you ought to be curious as to just what a great circle is. In the theoretical world of the geometricians, any time a plane is passed through a sphere, the points where the surface of the sphere touch the plane will make a circle on the plane. This is what your high school geometry teacher meant when he said: "The locus of the points at which a plane passing through a sphere contacts the surface of the sphere will enscribe a circle on the plane." What your teacher meant is illustrated by slicing an orange in two. The flat sides of the two pieces make a circle. The path of the knife blade passing through the orange is analogous to the plane passing through the sphere. If this plane passes through the center of the sphere, the circle enscribed will be a *great circle.* Now, I have been saying "enscribes a circle on the plane." Obviously, as this circle is at the point of contact between the plane and the sphere, the knife blade and the orange, the circle is also enscribed on the

sphere. In navigation, circles on spheres are what interest us. Since the plane must pass through the center of the sphere to enscribe a great circle on the sphere, the diameter of this great circle is the same as the diameter of the sphere. As no circle can be enscribed, *drawn* if you prefer, on the surface of a sphere, the diameter of which circle is greater than the diameter of the sphere, a great circle is the largest circle that can be enscribed on a sphere. The shortest distance between two points on the surface of a sphere is the shorter arc of a great circle that passes through these two points. This is why, when wind, weather, currents, and other things permit, a great circle course is the best course to steer on a long passage. Regrettably, these factors usually do not encourage great circle sailing.

SMALL CIRCLES

Circles on the surface of a sphere whose centers are not at the center of the sphere are *small circles.* Any circle on the surface of a sphere that is not a great circle is a small circle. The diameter of a small circle is always less than the diameter of the sphere it is on.

NAUTICAL MILE

Ask anyone who has read any history of the age of exploration what a mile is. He or she will reply with: "What kind of mile? An English mile? A Roman mile? A Dutch mile?" When you consider a Roman mile is 4,260 feet, an English statute mile 5,280 feet, and a Dutch mile over 24,000 feet, you can see these are fair questions. Imagine the confusion this difference in meaning of the same term, as used in different countries, brought to the early explorers. Our British cousins followed the Dutch explorers to the Pacific Ocean. When an Englishman wanted to follow a side route the Dutchman said covered 30 miles, the Englishman probably packed enough lunch for a day, not realizing he really had 120 English nautical miles to go!

The mile navigators use, almost exclusively, is the *nautical mile.* The nautical mile is defined by geographers as one minute of arc on the earth's equator. Navigators just say a nautical mile is one minute of arc on any great circle of the earth. A minute of latitude, by the navigator's definition, equals a nautical mile. A nautical mile is 6,080 feet. Whenever the word mile is used in this book, it means nautical mile. If another type of mile is intended, it will be specifically stated. You will find distances measured in statute miles on our rivers and on the Great Lakes. The Corps of Engineers uses the statute mile to measure distances on the Intracoastal Waterway.

LATITUDE

Latitude measures angular distances north or south of the *equator*. Latitude is measured in degrees or parts of a degree. The equator is a great circle perpendicular to the axis of rotation of the earth. The axis of rotation of the earth passes through the earth's geographic poles. From our definition of a great circle, the equator is a circle whose center is concentric with the earth's center. The only place a great circle can be in accord with both of these requirements, concentricity and perpendicularity to the poles, is at a locus of points of equal distance from both poles. Hence the term equator. The equator is at zero degrees latitude. Latitude increases as *north latitude* northward from the equator to 90°N at the north pole, and as *south latitude* southward from the equator to 90°S at the south pole. Degrees of latitude are represented on the chart or globe by lines parallel to the equator. These lines are drawn due east and west. Because they are parallel to the equator, lines representing latitude are called *parallels of latitude*. Parallels of latitude enscribe small circles on the earth's surface.

To determine the latitude of a place on the earth's surface, determine how many degrees, minutes, and tenths of a minute the place is north or south of the equator. For example, the latitude of Sand Island Light at the mouth of Mobile Bay is thirty degrees, eleven and three tenths minutes north. Navigators write this as 30° 11'.3N. Had you been measuring this latitude on a larger scale chart, you would have found the latitude of Sand Island Light to be more precisely at 30° 11' 16".8N. As I said before, however, measurement to the nearest tenth of a minute suffices for most purposes of navigation. But what you have expressed by these figures, no matter what fineness of resolution you employ, is simply that Sand Island Light is so many degrees and parts of a degree of arc north of the equator. Latitude is measured *along* meridians of longitude north or south of the equator as appropriate.

GEOGRAPHIC POLES

If you read carefully the previous paragraph on latitude, you found the meaning of the term *geographic poles*. The earth's geographic poles, or simply the poles, are the points on the earth's surface at which the axis of rotation of the earth and the surface of the earth coincide. The north pole is at 90° north latitude, and is the basic reference point for compass directions. The south pole is at 90° south latitude.

LONGITUDE

Longitude measures the angular distance, in degrees, minutes, and tenths of a minute, or seconds if required, east or west of a point of beginning on the earth's surface. We can define latitude easily because, even though the earth is a sphere, the poles give us reference points from which to locate zero degrees of latitude, the equator. There is no naturally defined geographic point from which to measure angular distances east or west. An arbitrary point must be chosen. Most west European countries and the United States use the meridian of Greenwich, England, as the zero meridian. Navigators call the Greenwich meridian the *prime meridian*. Since there are 360° to a circle, longitude west of Greenwich is measured from 0° at Greenwich to 180° west longitude (180° is one-half of 360°), and longitude east of Greenwich is measured from 0° at Greenwich to 180° east longitude. Meridians of longitude are great circles that converge at the poles. For this reason a degree of longitude will equal sixty miles at the equator, 46.1 miles at 40° north or south latitude, and zero miles at 90° north or south latitude, the poles. You *cannot* measure distances by using the longitude scale of your chart. The only exception to this would be the longitude scale of a chart at the equator. From the things I have told you in this paragraph, this should be obvious. Longitude is measured east and west *along* parallels of latitude.

On a chart the latitude scale is on either side of the chart. In north latitude, latitude increases from the bottom or lower edge of the chart as you move *up* the chart. In south latitude, latitude increases as you go *down* from the top of the chart. On a Mercator chart, the *latitude scale* is the scale you must use to measure distances. One degree of latitude equals sixty miles. One minute of latitude is one mile. Remember to measure distances between the parallels you are working in. (I discuss this further in the next chapter).

The longitude scale is at the top and bottom of the chart. Again I say, you *cannot* use the longitude scale to measure distances. In west longitude, longitude increases from the right-hand side of the chart as you move to the left. In east longitude, longitude increases from the left-hand side of the chart as you move across the chart to the right. To orient yourself on a chart, keep in mind the top of the chart is north, the right side of the chart is east, the bottom edge of the chart is south, and the left side of the chart is west.

With latitude and longitude you can locate any spot on the earth. If you know exactly how many degrees, minutes, and tenths of a degree a place is north of the equator, and you know exactly how many degrees, minutes, and tenths of a minute a place is west or east of Greenwich, you can locate that place precisely on any chart or map.

BEARING

The direction in which an object lies from you is its *bearing*. A bearing is the line of sight along which you must look to see an object. The measurement of the direction of a bearing, or simply the measurement of bearings, is reckoned by measuring the angle the line of bearing makes, in a clockwise or easterly direction, with the meridian from north. As in all measurement of angles and arc, this value is expressed in degrees from $000°$, north, through $360°$.

COURSE

The direction in which you intend to go is the *course*. Courses are measured by the angle the direction of your intended travel makes, when reckoned in a clockwise direction from the north pole, with the meridian of your position. The term *course made good* is the course your vessel actually traveled, as a result of the effects of set, drift, and leeway, instead of the course or direction you intended to travel.

POSITION

The actual geographic location of your boat is her *position*. Positions may be expressed as coordinates of latitude and longitude or as the bearing and distance from an object whose position is known.

LINE OF POSITION

A line at any point on which a vessel may be is a *line of position*. For example, if your boat is on a bearing from a lighthouse, you know your boat is somewhere on a line along that bearing. Lines of bearing are straight lines of position. If you can establish the distance your boat is off the lighthouse, you will not only know that you are on that line, but also exactly where you are on that line. You will have established a *fix*. This fix will give you your position. Two straight lines of position will give you a fix at their point of intersection. Lines of position can also be circles. If you know the exact distance you are from the lighthouse, you know your boat is somewhere on a circle whose center is at the lighthouse and whose radius is the distance you are off the lighthouse. You can also get a good fix from circular lines of position plotted as the distance off two different objects. A more detailed explanation will be given in the chapter on fixes and running fixes.

RHUMB LINE

A rhumb line is a line that crosses all meridians at the same angle. On great circle charts, such a line would be a curved line. But as we are confining our navigation to Mercator charts, we can define a rhumb line as a straight line on a Mercator chart. On a Mercator chart a straight line does cross all the meridians at the same angle because Mercator distortion causes the meridians to project as parallel lines on a Mercator chart. On a Mercator chart your course is a rhumb line. This one fact is the characteristic that makes the Mercator chart the most popular type of chart for marine navigation. In the rare event you do find yourself plotting the great circle course between two distant points on a Mercator projection, you will see that a great circle course plots as a curve, convex toward the elevated pole, on the Mercator chart.

For a complete reference for the meanings of navigational terms, see the glossary appearing in the 1962 edition of *Bowditch* as Appendix C, or the *Navigation Dictionary* (HO Publication 220).

3 CHARTS AND CHART PROJECTIONS

If you open *Bowditch* to the chapter on charts, you will see that there are many different ways a chart can be made. Each of these methods of making charts has its merits that make it best for charts intended for certain uses, and each method has certain disadvantages that limit it. A problem common to making any chart, regardless of the method, is that all charts are projections of the features of a spherical surface, the earth, onto a plane surface, the piece of paper the chart is printed on. This causes the areas depicted to be distorted. It is impossible to portray an exact picture of the surface of a sphere, such as the earth, on any flat or plane surface no matter what method of projection you use. As a navigator you must be aware of the limitations imposed on the chart you are using as a result of this distortion.

Almost all surface navigation is done today on Mercator charts. A Mercator chart is one made by a Mercator projection. Even the navigation for long ocean passages is done almost exclusively on Mercator charts. Some navigators still use great circle charts to plan long passages, but great circle routes are often deferred in favor of a route selected because of more favorable winds, weather, and currents. I will bet my bones you could sail around the world and never use any chart but a Mercator.

The big advantage of a Mercator chart is that a straight line, such as your course, crosses all the meridians of longitude on the chart at the same angle. Such a straight line is called a *rhumb line*, and this one characteristic of the Mercator chart makes quick, easy plotting possible. The big disadvantage of the Mercator chart is extreme distortion in higher latitudes. To understand why this is so, you must understand how a Mercator chart is made. Imagine a large sheet of rectangular, and flat, paper sensitized like photographic paper. Imagine also a transparent globe representing the earth. This globe should have all the usual features found on a globe printed on its

surface. In the center of this globe provide a light source. Wrap the globe up in this piece of sensitized paper so that the paper forms a tube or cylinder the same diameter as the globe. In the Standard Mercator* projection, this paper will touch the globe at the equator, all around. Now flash the light in the center of the globe long enough to expose the sensitized paper. Develop this paper, and you have a Mercator projection of the earth. Your set-up for this would look like the arrangement shown in Figure 3-1.

In Figure 3-1 the horizontal lines indicate parallels of latitude. For this illustration the parallels of latitude are drawn in at 20-degree intervals. On the globe these parallels are an equal distance apart because, on the circumference of a circle or a sphere, any even increment of degrees will graph an equal distance apart. These parallels of latitude will project as horizontal, parallel lines on the chart too. But when projected on the surface of the cylinder, which is the Mercator chart, the distance between these parallels, as projected, increases as the latitude moves away from the equator, until at just about 80^0, in the illustration, the parallels of latitude are no longer projected onto the paper. From this illustration it is apparent why the distortion on a Mercator chart is extreme in high latitudes and least near the equator. As the projected distance between each parallel of latitude progressively increases as latitude increases from the equator, the amount of distortion between any two parallels is not the same.

---

*In this text, unless specifically stated otherwise, the term *Mercator projection* will mean *Standard Mercator projection*. As explained in *Bowditch*, another type of projection, called the *Oblique Mercator projection*, is sometimes used in chart making. The Oblique Mercator projection is made as if the roll of paper or cylinder touched the earth at some point besides the equator.

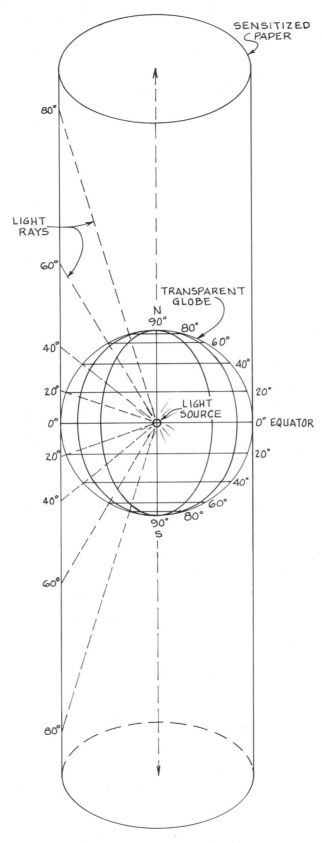

Figure 3-1. The Mercator projection in theory.

For this reason the projected dimensions of areas in high latitudes on a Mercator chart appear much larger than actual size.

The curved lines on the globe that converge at the poles, which are latitude 90° north and 90° south, represent meridians of longitude. For reasons of geometry, although less obvious in the illustration, these meridians will project as parallel lines on the chart also. The meridians will project as vertical lines, however. That these lines project as parallel lines, when in fact they converge, causes extreme distortion in the east-west dimension of areas in high latitudes. Figure 3-2 illustrates, in perspective, how your Mercator projection actually looks when the paper is again flattened out. For an even better concept of the distortion in a Mercator chart, put a globe and a Mercator chart of the world side by side. Select an area of the earth near the equator, and select an area of similar shape and size in a high latitude. Compare the relative sizes of these two areas as depicted on the globe and as depicted on the Mercator chart. On the globe, the area in a high latitude will be depicted as about the same actual size as the area near the equator. On the Mercator chart, the area in the high latitude will appear much larger than the area near the equator, even though both areas are actually about the same size. This apparent difference in size of the two areas on the Mercator chart is due to Mercator distortion.

This is the story of Mercator distortion. It is important that you remember the effects of Mercator distortion whenever you are using a Mercator chart. Otherwise, in taking distances off Mercator charts, you will fall victim of those errors that have been the undoing of many navigators. Always measure distances between the parallels of latitude bracketing your position or the area in which you are working. Remember, one minute of latitude equals one nautical mile, but because Mercator distortion causes the parallels of latitude to be printed farther apart as you move away from the equator, the actual linear distance on the chart paper representing a minute of latitude increases as you move toward the pole. Hence you must always measure distances on the latitude scale lying between the parallels of latitude bracketing your position. If your track covers several parallels of latitude, reset your dividers to match the scale between these several parallels and measure your distance in these increments. For general planning purposes, when your course lies between several parallels of latitude, it is permissible to use the scale of the latitude lying halfway between the two extremes of latitude. This halfway latitude is known as the *middle latitude.*

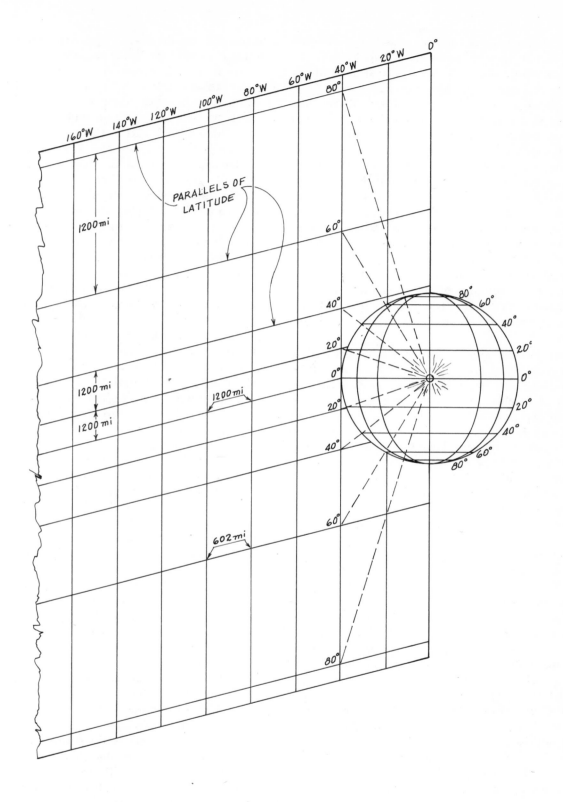

Figure 3-2. The Mercator projection rolled out flat after being exposed and developed. Mercator distortion makes the distance between parallels of latitude seem greater as you move toward the poles, and makes meridians of longitude appear parallel when they actually converge at the poles.

The charts you will use for precise navigation will cover much smaller areas than our hypothetical mappemonde*, and consequently these charts will be of a much larger scale. Mercator distortion will not be as apparent, but it will still be there. To convince yourself that this distortion does exist, take a chart such as C&GS Chart No. 1115 and measure the actual distance between two adjacent parallels of latitude near the top of the chart. Then measure the distance between two adjacent parallels of latitude near the bottom of the chart. Use a pair of dividers, and measure 60 minutes of arc, 60 miles, from the latitude scale near the top of the chart, and then measure 60 minutes of arc, again 60 miles, from the latitude scale near the bottom of the chart. You will notice that you had to change the spread of your dividers even though you were measuring 60 miles on the same chart, but in two different places. This is Mercator distortion. If you are not careful, it can foul you up!

Despite their limitations, charts are essential to safe navigation. A good up-to-date chart can tell you many things. A chart is a veritable lodestone of information, both written and symbolic. To be useful and dependable, however, it is an absolute must for the chart to be up to date. Old information can be misleading and very dangerous if it is no longer according to fact. Handling charts on a small vessel can be a problem to the point of being ludicrous, especially when the wind gets to them. I tell my students to fold their charts. I tell them not only does this make the chart manageable in size but also it soon ruins the chart. "Ruins it?" they say. "Why?" Well if you handle charts enough to ruin them at not too long intervals, this is a backhanded way of assuring they will be replaced from time to time. Of course an orderly system of periodic checking of the dates on your charts is much better. Charts should be replaced before they get too old. Meanwhile, current corrections should be entered on your charts while they are in service. The usual source of chart corrections is the *Local Notices to Mariners*, which is free for the asking. Just write the commander of your Coast Guard District, attention Aids to Navigation Section, and the Coast Guard will be glad to send these notices to you. The addresses of the several Coast Guard districts appear in the accompanying table. All the Coast Guard asks in return is that you help them out by reporting any aids out of place,

*Mappemonde — this word is one I first saw used by Dr. Samuel Eliot Morison in his *Northern Voyages.* I have borrowed it because it is so descriptive. The meaning? World map or map de monde.

damaged, or destroyed, and that you report any other matters of interest to the safety of navigation.

Much of the information on a chart is in the symbols used to depict different things. The general meaning of many of these symbols is obvious. For those symbols you do not understand, or do not understand fully, C&GS Chart No. 1 or Defense Mapping Agency Chart No. 1 will give you a full explanation. If you ask for this chart by either title you will get the same chart. This chart is a joint publication of both agencies and can be purchased from any Hydrographic Office Agent. (The U. S. Navy Hydrographic Office has undergone several name changes in the past few years, and is now integrated into the Department of Defense, Defense Mapping Agency, as the Hydrographic Center. But to save rattling off this jawbreaker, all concerned still call it the Hydrographic Office.) Chart No. 1 is also reproduced in *Dutton's Navigation and Piloting* by Shufeldt and Dunlap, and extracts of Chart No. 1 are reproduced on page 983 of the 1962 edition of *Bowditch.* Both of these works should be in the library of any serious navigator.

Responsibility for compiling and publishing navigation charts is primarily divided between the National Ocean Survey, formerly the Coast and Geodetic Survey, a function of the National Oceanic and Atmospheric Administration in the Department of Commerce, and the Defense Mapping Agency, formerly the Hydrographic Office. The National Ocean Survey charts, still called C&GS charts, cover coastal areas of the United States and her territories. Oceanographic charts, still called HO charts, cover foreign countries and the oceans of the world. Obviously there must be considerable overlap in areas covered when charts are made by both offices of areas adjacent to or contiguous with the United States or her territories. Charts of inland rivers, waterways, and the Great Lakes are published by the U. S. Army, Corps of Engineers. Charts of the Mississippi River are published by the Mississippi Commission. Most of these charts can be obtained from the same source. Your Oceanographic Office agent (HO charts) is almost always an agent for the other chart publishing offices too.

The best way to get familiar with a chart is to use it and study it. Studying one chart will go a long way to familiarizing you with the way all charts are arranged. Spread Chart No. 1115 on your chart table. Study the information on this chart. See what the chart tells you. Chart No. 1115 is a typical chart of this scale.

To begin with, the information in the masthead of the chart tells you it is a chart of the Gulf Coast of

COAST GUARD DISTRICTS AND ADDRESSES OF DISTRICT COMMANDERS

NO.	ADDRESS	WATERS OF JURISDICTION
FIRST.............	J. F. Kennedy Federal Building, Government Center, Boston, Mass. 02203 PHONE: 617-223-3632 .	Maine, New Hampshire, Massachusetts, and Rhode Island to Watch Hill.
SECOND.........	Federal Bldg., 1520 Market Street, St. Louis, Mo. 63103 PHONE: 314-622-4600.	Mississippi River System, except that portion of the Mississippi River south of Baton Rouge, Louisiana, and the Illinois River north of Joliet, Illinois.
THIRD.	Governors Island, New York, N. Y. 10004 PHONE: 212-262-4800.	Rhode Island from Watch Hill, Connecticut, New York, New Jersey, Pennsylvania, and Delaware, not including the Chesapeake and Delaware Canal.
FIFTH	Federal Building, 431 Crawford Street, Portsmouth, Virginia. 23705 PHONE: 703-393-9611.	Maryland, Virginia, North Carolina, District of Columbia, and the Chesapeake and Delaware Canal.
SEVENTH	51 Southwest First Avenue. Miami, Florida 33130 PHONE: 305-350-5621. Commander, Greater Antilles Section, U.S. Coast Guard, San Juan, Puerto Rico. 00903. PHONE: 725-5761	South Carolina, Georgia, Florida to 83°50′ W., and Puerto Rico adjacent islands of the United States. Immediate jurisdiction of waters of Puerto Rico and adjacent islands of the United States.
EIGHTH	Room 328, Customhouse, New Orleans, La. 70130. PHONE: 504-527-6234.	Florida from 83°50′ W. thence westward Alabama, Mississippi, Louisiana, and Texas.
NINTH	New Federal Office Building, 1240 East 9th Street, Cleveland, Ohio 44199 PHONE: 216-522-3131.	Grear Lakes and St. Lawrence River above St. Regis River.
ELEVENTH.......	Heartwell Building, 19 Pine Avenue, Long Beach, Calif. 90802. PHONE: 213-590-2311.	California, south of latitude 34°58′ N.
TWELFTH........	Appraisers Building, 630 Sansome St., San Francisco, Calif. 94126. PHONE: 415-556-2560.	California, north of latitude 34°58′ N.
THIRTEENTH	618 Second Avenue, Seattle, Wash. 98104. PHONE: 206-624-2230.	Oregon, Washington, and Idaho.
FOURTEENTH	677 Ala Moana Blvd., Honolulu, Hawaii. 96813 PHONE: 808-546-5840.	Hawaii and the Pacific Islands belonging to the United States west of longitude 140° W. and south of latitude 42° N.
SEVENTEENTH	P. O. Box 3-5000, Juneau, Alaska. 99801. PHONE: 907-586-2680.	Alaska.

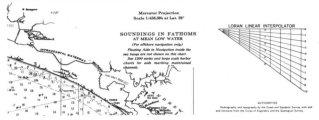

CAPE ST.GEORGE TO MISSISSIPPI PASSES

Figure 3-3. The masthead of Chart No. 1115.

the United States of America (see Figure 3-3). In the boldest type anywhere on the chart it tells you this is a chart of the Gulf Coast between Cape St. George and the Mississippi Passes. In relatively small print beneath this headline, you are informed the chart is a Mercator projection. The scale of the chart is also given. Except to indicate to you that the chart is a large scale, small scale, or intermediate scale, the exact scale is not too important for ordinary purposes of navigation. Knowing whether the scale is sufficiently large to show all necessary details is of prime importance to the navigator, however.

Large scale charts cover smaller water areas, and can thus show much more detail on a given size sheet of chart paper. Consequently large scale charts are absolutely necessary for the precise navigation required in restricted waters. On the other hand, small scale charts depict a much larger area on a piece of chart paper the same size, with a resultant loss of detail. For this reason small scale charts are used for offshore navigation and planning long passages.

There are actually several scales used in the making of charts. These scales are strictly linear scales. The smallest scales used by the Hydrographic Center are 1:600,000; sometimes smaller ones are used on sailing charts. The next scale is that of the general charts used for coastal navigation outside of outlying reefs and shoals. The scale of these charts ranges between 1:100,000 and 1:600,000. The coastal charts, such as the 1200 series *War Hat* will be plotting her passage on, are intended for close-in coastal navigation. The scale of these coastal charts ranges from 1:50,000 to 1:100,000. Harbor charts will have a scale of 1:50,000 or less.

What do these ratios, such as 1:50,000 mean? All they indicate is that one inch in actual measure-

ment on the chart equals 50,000 inches on the earth's surface. A scale of 1:600,000 means that one inch on the chart depicts 600,000 inches on the surface of the earth. See *Bowditch*, article 504, page 104, the 1962 edition.

Carefully look over the untinted portions of the chart. It is covered with numbers, printed in black ink, and spaced about an inch apart. These numbers are the soundings at the location at which they appear. They indicate the depth of the water at that spot. Soundings on United States charts are presently given in feet or fathoms. A fathom is six feet. To find whether these numbers represent fathoms or feet of depth, refer to the masthead of the chart. Below the statement that the chart is a Mercator chart, you will see the legend "Soundings in Fathoms at Mean Low Water"*. This same information regarding soundings also appears in the margin at the bottom of the chart. The word "mean" is used here as average. As a rule, small-scale charts covering deep ocean areas give depths in fathoms. Larger scale charts of inshore coastal areas, bays, sounds, and harbors give soundings in feet. Occasionally, in areas of great depth range, soundings are given in feet for the inshore and shallower areas, and in fathoms in the areas of great depth. In parts of the world, particularly on charts published by foreign countries, depths are given in meters or other units of measure. (See page 999 of the 1962 edition of *Bowditch*.)

In this untinted area of the chart, you will see black lines made up of different combinations of dots and dashes (see Figure 3-4). Each of these different combinations of dots and dashes is reserved to mark the lines of demarcation between different depths. There is a set of dots and dashes comprised of one dot, one dash, one dot, one dash repeatedly. The line made by these dots and dashes curves along a course more or less approximating the coastline. This particular line on the chart marks a series of points where the depth of the water is 10 fathoms from datum. Seamen refer to a line such as this as the 10-fathom curve. Another line consisting of two dots and one dash is next seaward from this 10-fathom curve. This second line marks a locus of soundings of 20 fathoms, and is referred to as the 20-fathom curve. Note carefully the soundings on

*"Mean Low Water" is the reference point or datum for soundings on the Atlantic and Gulf Coasts of the United States. Mean Low Low Water is the datum for soundings on the Pacific Coast. For datum in other parts of the world see pages 1000 and 1001 of the 1962 edition of *Bowditch*.

the shore side of the 10-fathom curve. These soundings will all be 10 fathoms or less than 10 fathoms. The soundings shoreward or inside of the 20-fathom curve will all be 20 fathoms or less than 20 fathoms. Soundings outside the respective curves or seaward of the respective curves will exceed the depths indicated by the fathom curve. Lines of three dots and one dash mark the 30-fathom curve, four dots and one dash the 40-fathom curve, and five dashes the 50-fathom curve. A line of continuous dashes marks the 100-fathom curve. From the hundred fathom curve the sounding curves are simply marked by a series of dashes in groups equal in number to the number of hundreds of fathoms marked by the curve, so a series of dashes of two dashes to the group marks the 200-fathom curve, three dash groups the 300-fathom curve, and so on until at 500 fathoms, five dashes to the group marks the 500-fathom curve. Nine fine dots and a dash mark the 1,000-fathom curve. Fifteen hundred fathoms are marked by another line of continuous dashes. When you study your chart, learn the symbols or combinations of dots, dashes, or dots and dashes that mark each sounding curve on the chart.

Fathom curves are given for each set increment in depth up to the maximum depth on the chart. The combination of dots and dashes is varied to assist the navigator in identifying the depth curve of the ship's position. These fathom curves give an accurate outline of the topography of the bottom. Charts with soundings in feet have similar lines to mark the contours of the bottom in multiples of the depth of the water in feet. You will see the importance of these curves when you begin to use soundings as an aid in determining your position. Soundings are an important tool to the pilot, so much so that some describe piloting simply as navigating a vessel "on soundings." A vessel is said to be on soundings when she crosses inside the 100-fathom curve. I hope I do not have to explain to you the value of knowing the depth of the water in relation to your vessel's draft.

As you read down the heading of Chart No. 1115, just beneath the information concerning soundings you will find a statement, in parentheses, that this chart is for offshore navigation only. You are told to see the 1200 series and larger scale charts for aids marking channels. Glance along the coastal areas of this chart, Chart No. 1115, and you will see notes such as "(Chart 870 SC)", printed in magenta ink, in Choctawhatchee Bay. This note tells you that, if you want to navigate in Choctawhatchee Bay, you should use Chart No. 870 SC published by the National Ocean Survey. Along the coast, the areas covered by the 1200 series of charts are outlined by

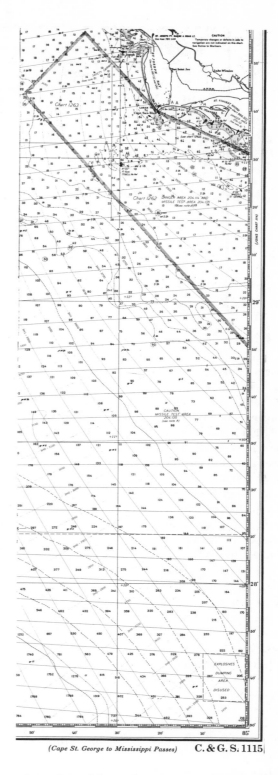

(Cape St. George to Mississippi Passes)   C. & G. S. 1115

Figure 3-4. Cut-out from Chart No. 1115 showing sounding curves. The cut-out is from the extreme eastern or right-hand edge of the chart. The soundings shown range from zero fathoms at Cape San Blas to 1,768 fathoms (10,608 feet!) in the lower left-hand corner. Note the different combinations of dots and dashes on each curve.

17

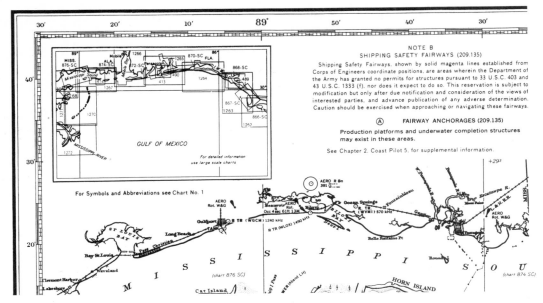

Figure 3-5. Cut-out of Chart No. 1115 showing the catalog section and Note B.

magenta lines. You will note these areas overlap. Each area is also marked by the appropriate number of the chart of that area. This number is printed in magenta too. In the upper left-hand corner of Chart No. 1115 is a box, with a very small-scale chart of the entire area of Chart No. 1115 inside, which gives the numbers and outlines the areas covered by all of the large-scale charts of any place you might want to go between Cape St. George and the Mississippi Passes (see Figure 3-5). Chart No. 1115 serves quite well as a catalog of the charts you will need to navigate in this area.

Keep on studying Chart No. 1115. This is the only way to become familiar with any chart. When you learn to get the maximum information from a particular chart, you will be well on your way to being able to read any chart. Chart No. 1115 is as good a chart as any to begin with. Off the east end of Santa Rosa Sound is a restricted area (see Figure 3-6). A legend in magenta ink refers you to Note A. Note A, printed on the chart in an otherwise blank space representing land areas, too far from the coast to interest the navigator, refers you to Chapter 2 of *Coast Pilot 5*, and to other sources of information concerning regulations regarding this restricted area.

In the water areas along the coast are double, bold magenta lines labeled "SAFETY FAIRWAYS (See Note B)". They appear in Figure 3-5. Note B explains the meaning of safety fairways, and the meaning of the fairway anchorage symbols. Again you are referred to *Coast Pilot 5*, Chapter 2 for supplemental

NOTE A

Navigation regulations are published in Chapter 2, Coast Pilot 5, or subsequent yearly supplements and weekly Notices to Mariners. Copies of the regulations may be obtained at the office of the District Engineer, Corps of Engineers in Mobile, Ala.

Anchorage Regulations may be obtained at the office of the Commander, 8th Coast Guard District in New Orleans, La.

Refer to section numbers shown with area designation.

LIGHT VISIBILITY

The shorter of either the nominal or the geographic range is charted. See U.S. Coast Guard Light List for additional information.

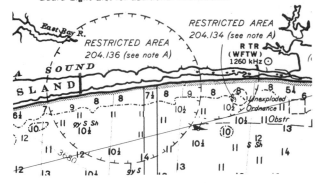

Figure 3-6. The restricted area and Note A on Chart No. 1115.

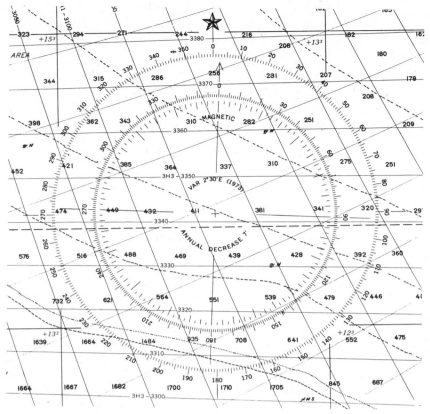

Figure 3-7. A compass rose.

information. The basic fact that these lines enclose areas in which no permits for the location of structures are issued is given right on the chart.

Caution notes, also printed in magenta ink, appear in several places on the chart. These notes give information concerning submerged pipelines and cables.

A note explaining how the visibility of lights is charted appears just above the restricted area at Santa Rosa Sound (see Figure 3-6). This note refers you to the U. S. Coast Guard *Light List* for more information. From these notes alone you can see how useful related publications such as the *Coast Pilot* and the *Light List* are.

There are other notes. One cautions you about calibration and location of radio stations for direction-finding purposes. Other notes concern storm warnings, temporary changes in aids to navigation, plus additional information.

An absolutely essential feature of any chart appears in three different places on Chart No. 1115. This is the compass rose. There are three compass roses on Chart No. 1115. In each of these roses there is an inside and an outside rose. The inner rose gives magnetic north and directions related to the magnetic pole (see Chapter 4). The outer rose gives true

north and directions related to true north. In the center of the rose is a note stating the variation and the year the variation was determined along with the annual change in variation.

Chart No. 1115 is a loran chart too. A general explanation of the loran characteristics of Chart No. 1115 is given in a note just east of Mobile Bay. In the upper right-hand corner of the chart, just to the right of the title, is a loran linear interpolater (see Figure 3-3). This mysterious triangular-shaped thing looks like a graph. It is. On the water areas of the chart are faint lines of different pastel colors. These colors correspond to the color of loran rates given in the note east of Mobile Bay (see Figure 1-1). The use of these pastel lines and the linear interpolater will be explained when you study radio navigation in Chapter 21.

I have mentioned many things you will find on a chart. There are many more items. To learn to use charts, you must study them every chance you get. Provide yourself with several charts of different scales covering the areas you are most likely to cruise in your boat. Nothing can be more useful than closely screening all the charts of an area you plan to make a passage through. It can save you all kinds of grief, and if you are a true sailor, it can be fun, too.

4 THE MAGNETIC COMPASS AND COMPASS ERROR

Woodsmen, hunters, and outdoorsmen have found it convenient to think of a magnetic compass as an instrument that always points to true north. I hope I do not shock you too much, but nothing can be farther from the truth. A magnetic compass almost never points to true north! A magnetic compass may, and usually will, give an indication of the general direction of true north, but two magnetic compasses on two vessels moored side by side will not give the same indication of the direction of north. For that matter, two magnetic compasses on the same boat will not either. The difference in the direction the compass points to and indicates to be north and what is actually true north is the *compass error*. In the magnetic compass, the compass error comes from several sources.

One reason the magnetic compass does not point to true north is that a magnetic compass really should *not* point to true north. Why? Because the earth is a magnet, and the essential direction device in a magnetic compass is a magnet. According to the physical laws governing a magnet, opposite poles of magnets attract each other. For this reason the south pole of the magnet in your compass ought to seek the earth's north magnetic pole. Unfortunately, the earth's north magnetic pole is not located in the same place as the earth's north geographic pole. Nor is the earth's south geographic pole at the same place as the earth's south magnetic pole. To make the matter even worse, the earth's magnetic poles do not stay put, but wander leisurely around. The center of magnetic attraction of the earth's north magnetic pole is somewhere in northeastern Canada. This magnetic north pole is what your magnetic compass should point to, and does point to if it is not affected by other magnetic influences.

Let's see what this difference in location between the earth's geographic pole and the earth's magnetic pole does to your compass. I mean, of course, your magnetic compass, but from now on, unless I specifically designate otherwise, when I say compass I mean *magnetic compass*. Your compass points to northeastern Canada because that is where the earth's north magnetic pole is. Where is true north? True north is the earth's north geographic pole. Depending on where you are on the surface of the earth, this difference in direction between magnetic north and true north will vary. It is easy to see, then, why it is called *variation*. Variation is the first error you will be concerned with. The variation for an area is found on the nautical charts of that area.

You now know the first error affecting your compass is variation, and you know variation is caused by the difference in location between the earth's geographic poles and the earth's magnetic poles. The next and most important question for a practical navigator is what to do about variation? This question can be answered directly by giving you a set of rules to go by. If you will remember these rules and apply these rules correctly, you cannot go wrong. You will remember these rules better, though, if you understand exactly how variation affects your compass. When you understand how variation affects your compass you can figure out what to do to correct it.

If you know the compass is not pointing true north, you can begin by asking yourself what direction your compass is pointing. Suppose you know the variation in your area is 5° east. There is a rule that says to get a true course from a compass course you must always *add easterly error*. If you are steering a course of 000°, which is due north, by compass, what is your true course? If you are steering 000° compass, and you must add easterly error to correct a compass course to a true course, you must be steering 005° true. Let me emphasize, adding easterly variation to a compass course to get a true course only applies when there are no other sources of magnetic influence affecting your compass. As you will see later, this is seldom the case.

If the proper way to determine the true course when you are steering 000° compass, which from now on will be written 000°C, is to add easterly error, it would seem that, conversely, you should *subtract* westerly error. And indeed you should. If you are steering a course of 000°C in an area in which the variation is 5°W, you must be on a true course of 355°. This course is written as 355°T. Again, no other magnetic influences are assumed to be about.

Maybe if I draw you a picture, you can understand why you must add easterly error to a compass course, and subtract westerly error from a compass course, to get a true course. Study Figure 4-1 carefully.

The diagram is a polar diagram; in other words, you are looking down on the north pole. The effects of variation are very much simplified for the sake of illustration. The center of the circle, P_g, is the north geographic pole. The magnetic north pole is at P_m. The radials extending out from P_g represent meridians of longitude. The rim of the outer circle represents the equator. There are five boats illustrated in the diagram: *A, B, C, D,* and *E*. Each boat is heading 000°T. The arrow on each boat indicates the direction the compass on the particular boat says is north. The arrows point to magnetic north, P_m. The angle each arrow makes with the meridian is the variation. This angle is measured from 000° clockwise to the arrow for easterly variation and counter-clockwise for westerly variation. True course is the angle a vessel's direction of travel makes with the meridian when reckoned in a clockwise direction, through 360°, from the north geographic pole. More simply stated, the true course of a vessel is the angle her course makes with 000°T when measured clockwise to her course. As this angle between the true courses of vessels *A, B, C, D,* and *E* is zero degrees, the true course of each boat must be 000°T.

Notice you always write courses with three integers. Thus north is written either as 000° or 360°. Five degrees east of north is written as 005°, and is spoken of as zero zero five degrees. Forty-five degrees east of north is written 045°, and is spoken as zero four five degrees. Southeast is 135°, and is spoken as one three five degrees. A course of 45 degrees west of north is northwest, and is written as 315° and spoken as three one five degrees. And so on around the compass, because courses are reckoned from north clockwise through 360°. After each course, such as 135°, you must always say if the course is true, magnetic, or compass by putting the capital letters T, M, or C immediately following the degree sign. Thus each boat in the diagram is steering 000°T. Boat *A* is steering 350°M.

What do these terms True, Magnetic and Com-

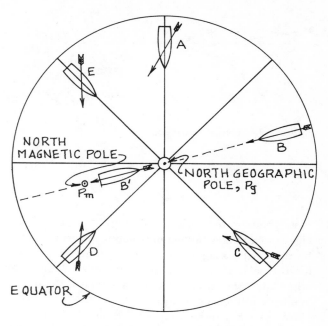

Figure 4-1. A polar diagram showing compass error.

pass, abbreviated T, M, and C, mean when used with a course? A true course is the angle, reckoned clockwise, that the direction your boat is going makes with the meridian. The direction of the north geographic pole is the zero reference point. If this true course makes an angle of 135° to the right or clockwise with the meridian, you would say your boat is steering 135° true, and you would write this as 135°T.

A magnetic course is the angle, measured clockwise, that the course your vessel is steering makes with the direction of the earth's magnetic pole. If the variation in the area your boat is in is 5°E, your course will make an angle of 130° with the direction of the earth's north magnetic pole from her position. Your course will be 130° magnetic. You would write this 130°M.

A compass course is the angle, measured clockwise, from the direction your boat's compass *says* is north. And unless you have one of those rare vessels where there is no magnetic influence aboard, the direction your compass *says* is north will be neither true north nor magnetic north, but some other direction resulting from the combined effects of the earth's magnetism and the magnetism in your boat. Since you steer by the compass, the compass course you steer must be corrected for both these errors. If inherent magnetism causes your compass to have an additional error of 5°E, your compass would say you were steering 125°. You would write this as 125°C. It is

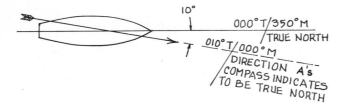

Figure 4-2. Boat *A*'s variation.

best, though, to learn new things one at a time. Hence we are now talking only about the error caused by the earth's magnetism. We are going to assume, for the sake of our diagram, that boat *A* and the other boats shown are of that rare type without any magnetic influences aboard.

Now back to the diagram. Boat *A* is steering 000°T. She has no magnetic influences around her except the earth's magnetism, which causes the variation for the part of the world she is in. If the variation for the part of the world boat *A* is in is 10°, the arrow representing the compass makes an angle of 10° with the meridian she is on (see Figure 4-2). You can see this arrow is deflected to the right of boat *A*'s heading. When facing north, things to your right are east of you. Consequently boat *A*'s variation is east, and, since the variation is 10°, you would say the variation in the part of the world boat *A* is in is 10 degrees east. You would write boat *A*'s variation as 10°E.

The next question is what course does the lubber's line on boat *A*'s compass indicate she is steering? Since the 000° mark of her compass card is 10 degrees to the right of her heading, the lubber's line of her compass must indicate she is steering 350°. This is her course in relation to the earth's magnetic pole. She is steering 350°M, pronounced three five zero degrees magnetic.

As helmsman aboard boat *A*, you can tell your magnetic course by looking at your compass. You can tell what your variation is by looking at your chart. If you are going to do any navigating, you must know your true course. But the course you are steering is 350°M, and your variation is 10°E. If you add the 10° easterly variation to your magnetic course, you get a course of 360°T, which is the same as 000°T. From Figures 4-2 and 4-3, you true course is 000°. Therefore, to correct a magnetic course to a true course, you must add easterly error.

Go back to Figure 4-1 and look at boat *C*. The compass card of boat *C* is deflected to the left or west

22

of true north, because Pm is west of true north at boat *C*'s position. Boat *C* is actually steering 000°T. But if the variation in this area deflects boat *C*'s compass card to the left or west of 000°T, the variation in this area must be west. If the amount of this variation is 10°, the compass card on boat *C* will indicate she is steering 010°. As there is no other error affecting the compass of boat *C*, this is a magnetic course, and also her compass course. As navigator of boat *C*, to find the true course boat *C* is steering, you must subtract your variation of 10°W to get your true course of 000°. To find true course when variation is west, you must subtract this westerly variation from your magnetic course. By extension, we can say to correct a compass course to true you must always subtract westerly error.

These are our rules. When a compass course is known, to find the equivalent true course, you must add easterly variation and subtract westerly variation. The same rules can be applied to any compass error. Regardless of cause, when a magnetic force deflects the compass card to the right of true north, the force induces an easterly error, and if a force deflects a compass to the left of true, this force induces westerly error. When the value or amount of the deflection these forces cause is known in degrees, you can apply these factors to correct your compass by adding easterly error, and subtracting westerly error.

Converting or correcting a known compass course steered to a true course is called "correcting" the compass. These rules of adding easterly error and subtracting westerly error apply when the compass is "corrected." When a true course is known, the process of finding a compass course is termed "uncorrecting." "Uncorrecting" is a reversal of "correcting," and for this reason the rules of adding easterly and subtracting westerly error are reversed when "uncorrecting." The process of correcting and uncorrecting the compass is explained in the next chapter. At this point it is only necessary that you understand why these rules apply in converting from a compass course to a true course.

Look now at boat *D*. Her compass is deflected to the west of true north also. This deflection causes westerly variation, too. But since *D* is at a different place than boat *C* in relation to the earth's magnetic pole, Pm, the amount of this deflection is not the same at boat *D* as it is at boat *C*. The variation depends on the location of the boat on the earth's surface, and the amount of variation may vary even though the direction of the compass card's deflection is the same. The variation at boat *A* and boat *E* is east, but the amounts differ. If you look at boat *A* and boat *D*, not only is the amount of variation different, but also at boat *A* the variation is east and at boat *D* the variation is west. At boat *B* and boat *B'* the variation is zero.

On large-scale charts and coastal charts, the variation for an area is found near the center of the compass rose on the chart. Be careful to use the compass rose nearest your position, as the variation will usually be different between two separate roses even on the same chart. On small-scale charts, covering large areas, such as the sailing charts, the variation is shown by drawing magenta lines connecting areas of equal variation. These lines are called *isogonic lines*. A heavier line connects areas of no variation, and such lines are called *agonic lines*. Isogonic lines and agonic lines tend generally north and south, and approximate the magnetic meridians. If you consult a sailing chart, however, you will notice these lines do not run straight and true as the geographic meridians, but wave a bit. This waving is due to various factors including local magnetism within the earth.

I have oversimplified my description of variation by attributing it entirely to the earth's magnetic pole being non-coincidental with the earth's geographic pole. Local magnetism in some areas will have an effect on your magnetic compass. This local magnetism not only can be considerable, but also can be variable enough over short periods of time to cause a navigator a lot of grief. Punta Malo, just above Balboa on the Gulf of Panama, is such an area. Magnetic disturbances within the earth are also prevalent around the Canary Islands. There are many other places on the earth that experience such things. These areas are described in the *Coast Pilot* and *Sailing Directions*. They are also noted on some charts.

The important things to remember about variation are: (1) variation is an external influence on your boat's compass; and (2) the amount and quality, east or west, of the variation affecting your compass is found on the nautical charts of the area you are in.

Up to now, in explaining variation, I have only hinted at other sources of compass error, and specifically stipulated that our vessels *A,B,C,D,* and *E* had no other magnetic influences affecting their compasses. Unfortunately this is almost never the case. Some fiberglass sailboats with small engines may not have enough ferrous metal in them to affect the compass. I sailed across the Atlantic in a 52-foot ketch built of cupra-nickle. She had no detectable magnetism around her binnacle either. Unless you can afford cupra-nickle or like to row rather than motor when there is no wind, you can expect your boat to have some magnetism inherent in her. This

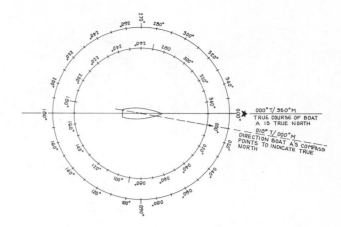

Figure 4-3. A drawing similar to the compass rose on a large-scale chart. The outer circle is the true rose, and the star indicates the direction of true north. The inner circle is the magnetic rose, but, as Boat *A* has been placed in the center of the rose, this inner rose could also be the compass card of Boat *A*. From this it is easy to see just how your compass would point if you were steering Boat *A* in an area where the variation was 10ºE.

magnetism, which is inside your boat, causes an error known as *deviation*.

An analysis of the nature of this magnetism within a vessel, its effect on a vessel, how it tends to arrange itself in steel vessels depending on their heading when built, are all matters far beyond the scope of this book. If you want to study these phenomena in depth, *Bowditch* covers the subject well. All you will need to know, as a practical navigator, in most cases, is that deviation does exist, and how to determine the amount of deviation affecting the compass on your boat. I intend to explain this much of the matter of deviation to you, and again, for the purpose of clarity, I am going to use a little license, and oversimplify my explanation.

Let us begin by considering your own boat as a magnet. In the simplest arrangement, the bow of your boat will be one pole of the magnet, and her stern will be the other pole. In actual situations this is seldom the case (see *Bowditch*), but as we proceed you will see why this assumption lends itself so well to the purpose of explanation.

Along with the fact that deviation is due to the magnetism within a vessel is the even more important fact that the amount and direction of deviation will change as the heading of the boat changes. On one heading your boat may have a deviation error of 9ºE, and on another heading she may have a devia-

23

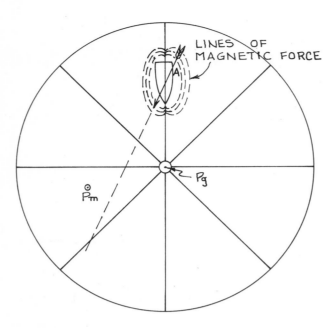

LINES OF MAGNETIC FORCE

Figure 4-4. A polar diagram showing Boat *A* still on a course of due north, 000°T. But now Boat *A* is herself a magnet, with magnetic lines of force surrounding her.

tion error of 7°W. Figure 4-4 explains why this is so.

Look at the diagram in Figure 4-4 carefully. As helmsman of boat *A*, you can see your compass now doesn't even point to magnetic north! Your compass points somewhere between magnetic north and true north. How do you know just where you are going?

This is a good question, because, if you intend to navigate from one place to another, it sure helps to know the direction you are going. Before answering this question, though, let's first reason why the compass is again deflected. Remember, I said for the purpose of illustration, the bow of your boat will be one pole of the boat's magnetism, and her stern the other pole. From the diagram, the bow of boat *A* must be a pole of north magnetic polarity, and is thus attracting the north-seeking south magnetic pole of the compass needle. The compass is deflected to the left so the error induced is westerly. As the needle is also pointing nearer to true north, the total compass error is less. This conforms completely with our rules of adding easterly and subtracting westerly error to correct the compass, because in the illustration variation is east. Subtracting a westerly deviation from an easterly variation will reduce the total compass error.

I still have not shown you why deviation changes with each change of heading. Let's take the same diagram we used in Figure 4-4, but change the true course of boat *A* to 090°T. See Figure 4-5.

The magnetic lines of force around your boat have completely changed their orientation to the earth's magnetic field. Your compass still does not point to true north or magnetic north, but now points even more to the east because the magnetic north pole of your boat is east of the earth's magnetic north pole. Your compass is deflected even more to the right. Now your deviation is east too.

For every different heading your boat takes, her magnetic field will vary in its orientation to the earth's magnetic field. Also the relationship of the magnetic poles in your boat will vary in their relationship or orientation to the earth's magnetic poles. Consequently, the resultant deviation of your compass will change with every heading of your boat.

Since deviation is caused by the magnetism in a vessel, any time you change the magnetism of your boat, her deviation will change. On any boat, if you move a lot of iron or steel around, you will certainly disturb her magnetic qualities. It is especially important not to put any iron or steel objects near the compass. Even putting aboard stores, if in large enough quantities, can change the magnetic qualities of a boat. I was victim of an extreme case involving both of these faults. Six of us left Dauphin Island on a yacht for an extended weekend cruise. We sailed after dark. The day before the owner of the yacht had taken her out, and ran a complete new deviation card for her. Then he brought her back to her berth, and loaded stores for our four-day weekend cruise. A lot of these stores consisted of canned goods to feed six hungry people. Her pantry was right under her binnacle! As if this was not enough, someone put the dinghy anchor on the console next to the binnacle, and casually threw a jacket over it. We cleared the marked channel by visual reference and did not take time to check the compass. This was our next mistake. It wasn't long after getting into the sound before we became painfully aware things were not right. After getting more and more confused we did the best thing. We anchored to wait for daylight so we could see what in the Hell was wrong with our compass.

On a commercial vessel every time you load or discharge cargo, especially if the cargo contains ferrous metals, the deviation of the vessel will change. I complained once to the captain of a tug I was in because her compass was so far off. When I asked him why the compass was not compensated, the captain of the tug told me it was useless to do so. The deviation of the tug's compass changed every time she made up to a barge.

When a vessel stays on a steady course for several days, her deviation may change. This is particularly true of power vessels, because the vibration of a power vessel's machinery will accelerate a realignment of the molecules of the metal in her hull, and thus change her magnetic quality.

From all this it should be obvious that deviation can be the more difficult of the factors involved in compass error. Not only is deviation an important factor, it is a changing factor. Deviation varies with each change of heading. Deviation will also vary with time. A deviation card you make for your boat today may be totally incorrect several months from now.

How do you determine the amount and direction of your vessel's deviation? You get this information from the deviation card or other deviation record of your vessel. You should have a deviation card for each compass used aboard your boat. Where do you get a deviation card? You can make up your own or you can have a professional compass adjuster do it. If the deviation error in your boat's compass is very large, you should have your compass compensated. You compensate a compass by placing magnets in or near the binnacle, which is the place where the compass is housed, in such a way as to offset, balance, or *compensate* for the magnetism within the boat. This is a job for a professional compass adjuster. When the compass adjuster compensates your compass he will also make up a deviation card in the process.

For those of you who cannot get the services of a professional compass adjuster, and those of you who carry such varied cargoes each trip it isn't feasible to

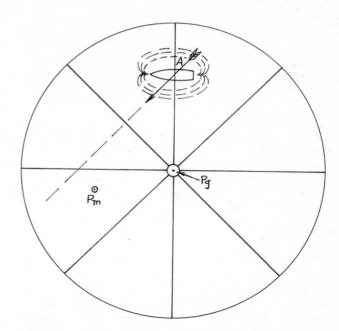

Figure 4-5. Boat *A* on a course of 090°T.

get a professional adjuster to work up a deviation card, there is hope too. I will put you on to a few tricks as to how to find your deviation, and even tell you how to make up your own deviation card. But before I can do this I must teach you how to apply the compass error.

5   HOW TO APPLY THE COMPASS ERROR

The traditional approach to applying the compass error is to determine a true course when the compass course is known. Seamen call this "correcting" the compass. The origin of this approach dates back to the days of sail. Sailing vessels depend on the wind to move, and they can only go in the directions the wind permits. This is not to say sailing vessels cannot go into the wind, but no sailing ship can go into the eyes of the wind. Wind ships must beat to windward, and, by keeping close hauled, with the wind on their bows, they make their way to windward, changing course from tack to tack as necessary to keep near their rhumb line or avoid dangers. How close a sailing vessel can sail on the wind depends on her rig and the strength of the wind. When a sailing vessel was bound for a port to windward, she was sailed as close on the wind as she could properly sail. When searoom was sufficient, the helmsman held her as close into the wind as he could without luffing. The compass course was noted, and recorded on a slate or traverse table. If the wind freshened or backed or veered so she could come up more on her rhumb line, the new course was noted. At the end of the watch the mate corrected these compass courses to true courses by applying the compass error. With the true courses steered, along with the time and speed run on each course, the mate could work up his reckoning for his watch. To do this he had to know the true courses steered.

Even today with powerful steamers, as well as smaller power vessels, it is not always possible to go directly into the wind and sea without risking unacceptable damage to the vessel. When these conditions exist, vessels steer a course as near their rhumb line as conditions permit. Often the course to be steered is found by trial and error until a course as near as possible to the rhumb line is found on which the vessel does not labor too badly. When a compromise course like this is steered, the navigator must take the compass course steered and convert it to a true course to work up his dead reckoning. The ability of a powered vessel to go dead to windward in most cases still has not eliminated the need to know how to correct the compass course to a true course.

How is the compass error applied to find a true course? The answer is best given by an example. Suppose you want to take your boat to a port that is dead to windward on a rhumb line course of 135°T. You find the best course she will lay on the starboard tack is 096°C. From the chart you notice the variation in the locality of your position is 3° 45'E. Compass corrections are customarily worked to the nearest half of a degree on large vessels, and to the nearest whole degree on small vessels. Call this variation 4°E. From the deviation table of your vessel, you find the deviation for this compass course to be 9°W.

You now have all the information necessary to correct your compass course to a true course. The difference between your compass course and your magnetic course is due to your vessel's deviation. For this reason it is logical first to correct your compass course to a magnetic course. Apply your deviation of 9°W to your compass course. Remember, to correct the compass course you subtract westerly deviation. Subtract 9°W from 096°, and you get your magnetic course of 087°.

The next step is to apply your variation. From the chart you found the variation to be 4°E. To correct a magnetic course to a true course you add easterly variation. Add 4°E to 087°M, and you get your true course of 091°.

From this you can see that to correct a compass course to a true course you must take your compass course, apply deviation to get the magnetic course, and then apply variation to get your true course. The sequence is compass, deviation, magnetic, variation, true. This can be abbreviated as simply C,D,M,V, T. Some folks have trouble remembering this sequence, but sailors are a worldly lot. They have a memory aid to help recall the first letters of the sequence. The memory aid is *Can Dead Men Vote Twice*. Again C,D,M,V,T. To facilitate the addition and subtraction, these letters are written in a vertical column:

C		Compass		Can
D		Deviation		Dead
M	for	Magnetic	or	Men
V		Variation		Vote
T		True		Twice

The figures you have been working with in the example you just completed can now be put next to the appropriate letters as follows:

C	096°
D	-9°W
M	087°
V	+4°E
T	091°

The lines and the symbols + and − are usually omitted, but I have put them here to show the arithmetic involved. This is all there is to correcting the compass. Yet to some people, this is one of the most difficult parts of the study of navigation to master. I believe these people must be determined to make compass correction a big mystery.

In case you still have doubts about how easy correcting the compass can be, let's work another problem. We will work this problem step by step. You put your boat about, and fair away on the other tack, close hauled. You find she will lay a course of 173° compass. Because your DR shows you to be nearer another compass rose on your chart, you see the variation is now 3° 12′ east. From your deviation table you find your deviation is 11°E. What true course are you steering?

STEP 1

Write down your correction formula in a vertical column.

STEP 2

Add the information you have opposite the appropriate letter in the column. Opposite C put 173°, opposite D, 11°E.

STEP 3

You add easterly error to correct a compass course, so add the deviation of 11°E to the compass course of 173°, and get your magnetic course of 184°. To help remember the rules to add easterly error and subtract westerly error, it is a good idea to jot down E+ W− to the right of the column.

STEP 4

Your variation is 3°12′E. Round this figure off to 3°E as the variation to the nearest half degree, and put 3°E opposite V.

STEP 5

Add the variation of 3°E to the magnetic course of 184°. Your true course is 187°.

C	173°	E+ W−
D	11°E	
M	184°	
V	3°E	
T	187°	

What is hard about that? The course of 187°T is the course you must use to plot your DR. As in all things, practice makes perfect. To help you get this practice you are urged to work the compass correcting problems at the end of this chapter.

Another problem regarding the application of the compass error is the problem of finding the course to steer, or compass course, when the true course is known. This is just the reverse of the type of problem you just finished working. Since finding the true course when the compass course is known is called *correcting* the compass course, sailors call finding the compass course when the true course is known *uncorrecting*.

You must always uncorrect a true course to find the compass course to steer. An example will clarify what I mean. When you departed point *A* off St. Andrews Bay seabuoy, you plotted a true course to point *B* to be 297°. You determined the compass course you must steer to be 298°. How did you do this? You uncorrected your true course of 297° to get 298°C. You reversed the sequence of correcting a compass course. You started with the true course, applied variation to get the magnetic course, and then applied deviation to get the compass course. The order in which you did this was true, variation, magnetic, deviation, compass. This is written T, V, M, D, C, and, if you have trouble remembering these letters, sailors have another memory aid that again proves sailors do other things besides splice, paint, chip rust, and play politics. The memory aid is *True Virgins Make Dull Companions*. T, V, M, D, C. Write these letters in a vertical column:

T		True		True
V		Variation		Virgins
M	for	Magnetic	or	Make
D		Deviation		Dull
C		Compass		Companions

After you laid down the true course from point *A* to point *B*, you uncorrected this true course step by step to find the compass course you needed to steer. The steps were:

STEP 1

Write down the letters T, V, M, D, C in a vertical column.

STEP 2

Write in the information you have opposite the appropriate letter. Opposite T put 297°. Opposite V put 3°E. Again you can put E and W to the right of your column to help you recall whether to add or subtract, but remember this time the signs are reversed. E is -, and W is +. You are uncorrecting. If you must add easterly error and subtract westerly error to correct the compass, isn't it logical to subtract easterly and add westerly error to uncorrect?

STEP 3

Apply your variation of 3°E. Your magnetic course is 294°.

STEP 4

From the deviation card of your boat, you find the deviation to be 4°W for a magnetic course of 294°. As you are uncorrecting, add 4° to the magnetic course. Your compass course is 298°.

T	297°	E- W +
V	3°E	
M	294°	
D	4°W	
C	298°	

There are several things that will keep you out of trouble in applying the compass error. They are:

1. If you will always write down the letters C, D, M, V, T in a vertical column when you are *correcting* a compass course, and the letters T, V, M, D, C in a vertical column when you are *uncorrecting*, and then put the Information you have opposite the correct letters, you can hardly go wrong. Of course you must apply the error correctly.

2. When *correcting*, which is coming from a known compass course to find a true course, you must always add easterly error and subtract westerly error.

3. When *uncorrecting*, which is coming from a known true course to find a compass course, you

must always subtract easterly error and add westerly error.

4. You *correct* a compass course you have been steering to find your true course so you can plot or otherwise reckon your DR. You always plot true courses on charts, and you always use true courses to compute your DR by the sailings, which are a means to determine by mathematics instead of plotting the true course and distance to begin a passage between two points, when the positions of both points are known.

5. You *uncorrect* a true course to find the compass course you must steer to make a true course. You first get the true course between two points by laying a course on your chart by drawing a line between the first point, which is your departure, and the second point, which is your destination. On a Mercator chart this course is a rhumb line. You then measure the true direction of this course with your parallel rulers or plotter. Then *uncorrect* this true course to find the compass course you must steer.

Work the problems at the end of this chapter. The practice these problems will give you should help you master the technique of applying the compass error.

PRACTICE PROBLEMS IN APPLYING THE COMPASS ERROR.

General Problems

1. You are steering a course of 298°C. Variation in the area is 8°W. Your deviation card shows your deviation to be 12°W for this heading. What is the true course you are steering?

2. The true course from Sand Island Light to the place you want to fish is 169°. Variation in this area is 4°E. Deviation for a magnetic heading of 173° is 9°W, and deviation for a heading of 165° is 6°W. What course must you steer to go to your fishing grounds?

3. You have been able to lay a course of 197°C for three hours. Your variation shown on the chart is 3°W. Deviation for your heading is 4°E. What is the true course you are laying?

4. You cross a range that is aligned on a line 297°T. You observe the range to be 284° on your compass. The chart shows the variation in the area to be 3°E. What is your compass deviation for the heading you are on?

5. The compass course you are steering is 247° in problem number 4. What is your true course?

Problems to be worked using the table in Figure 6-4 of Chapter 6.

6. You want to make good a course of 085°T from the beacon at the east end of the Dauphin Island channel. Variation at this point is 4°E. What is the compass course you should steer?

7. You are offshore in the Gulf of Mexico steering a course of 317°C. Your chart shows the variation to be 5° 19′ E in the area. What is your true course?

8. You are on a heading of 136°C. You observe a beacon to bear 296° by your compass. Variation at your position is 3° 11′ E. What is the true bearing of the beacon?

9. You get a loran fix and plot your course from the fix to the Panama City seabuoy to be 032°T. Variation from the chart at your position is 3° 12′ E. What course must you steer to lay Panama City seabuoy?

10. You spot smoke on the horizon and turn to head for it on a course of 212°C. Variation at your position is 5°E. After 30 minutes on course, you determine no assistance is required from you. You change course to the reciprocal of the true course you were steering. What is the compass course you would steer?

Solutions

1.	C	298°		2.	T	169°
	D	12°W			V	4°E
	M	286°			M	165°
	V	8°W			D	6°W
	T	278° Ans.			C	171° Ans.

3.	C	197°		4.	T	297°
	D	4°E			V	3°E
	M	201°			M	294°
	V	3°W			D	10°E Ans.
	T	198° Ans.			C	284°

5.	C	247°		6.	T	085°
	D	10°E			V	4°E
	M	257°			M	081°
	V	3°E			D	3°E
	T	260° Ans.			C	078° Ans.

7.	C	317°		8.	C	296°
	D	2°W			D	1°W
	M	315°			M	295°
	V	5°.5E			V	3°E
	T	320° Ans.			T	298° Ans.*

9.	T	032°		10.	C	212°
	V	3°E			D	6°W
	M	029°			M	206°
	D	7°E			V	5°E
	C	022° Ans.			T	211°
						−180°
					T	031°
					V	5°E
					M	026°
					D	8°E
					C	018° Ans.

*In problem number 8, the deviation is dependent on the compass course of the boat, and *not* the bearing. Thus the correct deviation to use is based on a course of 136°C.

6   HOW TO FIND YOUR DEVIATION

You now should understand the errors of deviation and variation well enough to use these errors in correcting and uncorrecting your compass. You know you find the variation in an area by consulting the charts of that area. You know you find the deviation for your boat's heading by consulting her deviation card. How do you make up her deviation card?

If you can afford the time and the expense, the best way to get an accurate deviation card for your boat is to hire a good, professional compass adjuster. A good compass adjuster will remove as much of the deviation error as possible by placing compensating magnets around the binnacle. After this he will then make up a deviation card for your boat.

What do you do if you cannot find a compass adjuster? You make up your own deviation card. There are several ways you can do this; each way depends on making a comparison between a compass course or bearing and a magnetic course or bearing.

A commonly used practice to determine deviation is to run a range. A range is a line of bearing made by two fixed objects. A range usually consists of two specially constructed aids to navigation so aligned as to indicate the center of a channel or an approach to an anchorage or mooring. To run a range you should select a suitable range on a chart of your area. If no established ranges are available, it may be possible to select two objects you can line up on a suitable bearing. This bearing, from any range, established or otherwise selected, should pass through an area which will provide sufficient searoom to maneuver.

STEP 1
Find an established range on a chart of your area or select two objects to give you a suitable range. If you can use an established range, put there as an aid to navigation, this will be your best choice. Almost any harbor chart or coastal chart will have a suitable range charted on it. There are several ranges on

Chart No. 1266. An excellent one is just east of Dauphin Island Bridge, the bridge that connects Dauphin Island with the mainland. This range is established to aid westbound vessels approaching the bridge to keep in the channel. The entrance to the approach channel is only two miles or so southeast of the first structure of the range. This makes it possible to see the range well before you enter the channel. Southeast of the entrance to the channel, and on the range, are several square miles of fairly deep, open water. You should have ample searoom. Figure 6-1 is a section taken from Chart No. 1266 showing this range and the surrounding area. Let's assume you select this range to determine your deviation.

STEP 2
Find the magnetic bearing of the range you select. You do this by simply lining up your parallel rulers, or whatever plotting instrument you prefer to use, to pass through the charted positions of the two structures of the range. The true heading or bearing of the range in Figure 6-1 is 287°. The magnetic bearing of this range is 283°.

STEP 3
The next step is to make up a work table. From this work table you will extract your deviation table. This work table should have columns headed *M Brng* for the magnetic bearing of the range, *C Brng* for the compass bearing of the range, *D* for deviation, *C Course* for compass course, and *M Course* for magnetic course. Figure 6-2 is an example of such a work table.

The magnetic bearing of the range, 283°, is a constant, and should be put into the table when you make it up. You can also put in your compass courses at the same time. You should cross the range at 15° increments of change in your course. At the head of the compass course column begin with 000°, then 015°, and so on as shown in Figure 6-2. This can all

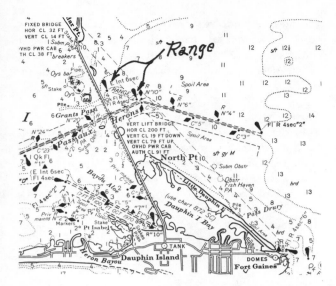

Figure 6-1. A cut-out of Chart No. 1266 showing the range aligning the channel approaching Dauphin Island Bridge, westbound. This is an excellent range for checking a compass because of the deep water and open area east of the red beacon number 2.

M BRNG	C BRNG	D	C COURSE	M COURSE
283°			000°	
"			015°	
"			030°	
"			045°	
"			060°	
"			075°	
"			090°	
"			105°	
"			120°	
"			135°	
"			150°	
"			165°	
"			180°	
"			195°	
"			210°	
"			225°	
"			240°	
"			255°	
"			270°	
"			285°	
"			300°	
"			315°	
"			330°	
"			345°	

Figure 6-2. A work table from which a deviation table can be extracted.

be done ahead of time; when the table is completed to the point shown in Figure 6-2 you are ready to run the range.

STEP 4

Get your boat underway and proceed to any point in the open water southeast of the approach channel, but close enough to keep the range well in sight. Proceed until you can put your boat on a compass course of 000°, and cross the range. Be sure to steer a steady course. At the instant you cross the range, observe the compass bearing of the range. It is best to have an assistant do this so you can watch the compass to see that the boat doesn't fall off course. Enter this compass bearing of the range in the work table under the column headed *C Brng* on the same line as your compass course of 000°. Now come around to a course of 180°C. Again, as you cross the range, have your assistant note the compass bearing, and put this bearing in the *C Brng* column opposite your compass course of 180°. Careful steering and careful observation are essential if you want good results. Come around again, and steady on 015°C. As you cross the range, have your assistant observe the compass bearing of the range, and note it as before. Continue changing course by 15-degree increments until you have crossed the range, and noted the bearing for each compass course in the table. The compass bearing column, *C Brng*, of the work table should now be filled in as shown in Figure 6-3.

M BRNG	C BRNG	D	C COURSE	M COURSE
283°	274°	9° E	000°	009°
"	275°	8° E	015°	023°
"	276°	7° E	030°	037°
"	278°	5° E	045°	050°
"	279°	4° E	060°	064°
"	280°	3° E	075°	078°
"	282°	1° E	090°	091°
"	283°	0° E	105°	105°
"	284°	1° W	120°	119°
"	284°	1° W	135°	134°
"	286°	3° W	150°	147°
"	286°	3° W	165°	162°
"	287°	4° W	180°	176°
"	288°	5° W	195°	190°
"	289°	6° W	210°	204°
"	290°	7° W	225°	218°
"	291°	8° W	240°	232°
"	292°	9° W	255°	246°
"	290°	7° W	270°	263°
"	288°	5° W	285°	280°
"	287°	4° W	300°	296°
"	285°	2° W	315°	313°
"	280°	3° E	330°	333°
"	277°	6° E	345°	351°

Figure 6-3. A completed work table.

DEVIATION TABLE

VESSEL: SCHOONER WAR HAT   DATE 14/6/72

C COURSE	DEV.	M COURSE
000°	9° E	009°
015°	8° E	023°
030°	7° E	037°
045°	5° E	050°
060°	4° E	064°
075°	3° E	078°
090°	1° E	091°
105°	0° E	105°
120°	1° W	119°
135°	1° W	134°
150°	3° W	147°
165°	3° W	162°
180°	4° W	176°
195°	5° W	190°
210°	6° W	204°
225°	7° W	218
240°	8° W	232°
255°	9° W	246°
270°	7° W	263°
285°	5° W	280°
300°	4° W	296°
315°	2° W	313°
330°	3° E	333°
345°	6° E	351°

Figure 6-4. War Hat's deviation table.

STEP 5

By taking the difference between the magnetic bearing of the range, a constant of 283°, and the compass bearing observed for each compass course on which you crossed the range, you can determine the amount of deviation for that compass course. You can determine the direction of this deviation by observing if the compass bearing of the range, when on the range, is greater than the magnetic bearing or less than the magnetic bearing. If the compass bearing is less than the magnetic bearing, the deviation is *east*. If the compass bearing is greater than the magnetic bearing, the deviation is *west*. Find the difference between the magnetic and compass bearings of the range for each course and bearing in the work table. The deviation, *D*, column in the work table

32

will now be complete. See Figure 6-3. You will know your deviation for each 15-degree increment of compass course you may steer from 000°C. You can now correct any compass course to a magnetic course.

STEP 6

Your deviation table must also give you the deviation for a magnetic course so you can use the table to un-correct as well as correct courses. To find the magnetic course corresponding to each value of deviation, simply correct the compass course in the work table by applying the deviation you determined for that course, and put the results in the proper places in the magnetic course, *M Course*, column. The *M Course* column should now be filled in as in Figure 6-3.

STEP 7

You are ready to write or type your smooth deviation table. You are finished with the magnetic bearing column and the compass bearing column. The information you will need is now all in the deviation, compass course, and magnetic course columns. These three columns will make up your deviation table, but change the sequence of these three columns to compass course, deviation, and magnetic course. Figure 6-4 shows how this finished deviation table should look. To get you familiar with the routine of consulting a deviation table, the one shown in Figure 6-4 will be the deviation table you should use to correct or uncorrect the compass as may be required to solve any problem given from now on in this study, unless otherwise specified.

The system of running a series of courses across a range should not require you to be underway for hours and hours. You will be surprised how quickly you can do it. You will do better if you can get a helper. There is no need to run "hooked up" (running at the fastest normal cruising speed), but, if you proceed slowly, you will be able to run much shorter legs on each course. Running much shorter legs will more than make up for the loss of speed. Of course you should go fast enough to have good rudder control. Each time you cross the range on an initial course, return on a reciprocal of that course. For example, you first crossed the range on a course of 000°C. You should turn and re-cross the range on a course of 180°C. Turn then to a course of 015°C, re-cross again on a course of 195°C, back across on a course 030°C, and return on a course of 210°C. Keep crossing and re-crossing the range until you have observed a compass bearing for each course in the work table.

Important. Any time you are working on or near an established range you are most likely working in a regularly traveled area. Always keep a sharp lookout. It is too easy to get engrossed in what you are doing and let another vessel get so close a collision may result. A half-finished deviation table for a sunken boat is not very useful.

A very similar procedure to running a range can be carried out if you can anchor on a range. Be sure you anchor so as not to obstruct or embarrass traffic using the channel or fairway the range is established for. After your anchor is down and holding, a small boat is used to pull or "swing" the larger vessel around in a circle. A work table exactly as used before is necessary. As the bow of the big vessel passes through each 15-degree heading, a compass bearing of the range is observed and noted in the work table. The calculations required are also the same as before. It is important that you be far enough away from the range so the length of your anchor cable does not allow you to swing off the range. This procedure is known as *swinging ship*. For that matter, any system of changing the heading of a vessel through a series of headings to determine deviation is called swinging ship.

Another method of finding the deviation is to turn your boat through a succession of different headings and observe the azimuth of a celestial body such as the sun. You must then compute the true azimuth of the body observed for the time the azimuth was taken. Uncorrect the true azimuth to the magnetic azimuth of the body. The difference between the magnetic azimuth and the azimuth you observed will be your boat's deviation for that heading. I will not explain how to compute a celestial azimuth as this is properly within the scope of celestial navigation. On the other hand celestial azimuths are frequently used by navigators, in pilot waters, to check their compass error.

There are several other methods of finding your boat's deviation. Your own ingenuity may tell you a way that best suits you. You may find yourself called on to take a boat or ship from one port to another, and there will be no deviation card on board. As you proceed down the marked channel from the mooring, you can get the true course required to conform to the channel from your chart. Uncorrect this true course to a magnetic course. Take the difference between this magnetic course and the compass course you must steer to keep in the channel. This difference will be your deviation for the compass or magnetic heading you are holding. Each time the course of the marked channel changes, repeat the procedure. Before you get to the seabuoy you should have computed your deviation for several compass courses. After you have left the marked channel, keep a sharp lookout for ranges. Each time you cross a range take a compass bearing and figure your deviation for the course you are on. Every time you stand in or out on a range note your compass course. From these observations you can figure your deviation. If you are making a sea passage offshore, as soon as you clear the seabuoy and fair away on course get a celestial azimuth if you can. From this azimuth compute the deviation for the course you are on. After awhile you should have the start of a fairly good deviation table without having gone to any extra effort.

Knowing your compass error is absolutely essential to safe navigation. How else can a navigator really know the true course his vessel is steering? If you as navigator do not know the true course you are steering, how can you know where you are going? People make unkind remarks about people who don't know where they are going. Navigators who don't know where they are going deserve the *most* unkind remarks.

Know your compass error! At sea or underway check your compass error at least once a day. Remember your boat's deviation will change.

And one more thing. Those binnacle lights. Check your compass with the binnacle lights off, then check your compass with the binnacle lights on. Sometimes the difference is startling. A properly wired binnacle should not affect the compass when the binnacle lights are turned on and off. It can be disastrous to work up a good deviation card in daylight and then go to sea at night, in ignorant bliss, thinking your compass error is well known and accounted for, when all the time those nasty little energized wires have negated all your hard work!

7   SPEED, TIME, DISTANCE, AND YOUR DR

DR means *dead reckoning*. Dead reckoning is the fundamental method of navigation. Every other method the navigator uses, whether it is piloting, celestial navigation, loran, or some other, is intended to correct the DR plot. If you cannot accurately work your dead reckoning, you cannot expect to be a competent navigator. With little more than good dead reckoning, you can sail around the world. Dead reckoning was the prime means of navigation in the early days of offshore sailing. Now, I do not recommend you try a circumnavigation using dead reckoning alone. Such a passage could be made, but it would not be safe, fun, or sensible.

As in other types of navigation, dead reckoning requires the proper tools. To plot departures, courses, distances, or anything else requires instruments such as parallel rulers and dividers, or some suitable substitute for these devices. Parallel rulers consist of two straight-edged rulers of equal length joined together by two or more movable connectors. These connectors are attached so that the rulers may be placed side by side with the edges touching, or they may be spread apart as far as the movement of the connectors will allow, but in any position the four edges of the two rulers will remain exactly parallel to each other. Thus by lining up one edge between two points, and then holding one rule firmly in place while moving the other, alternating between each rule with the movement, it is possible to "walk" the rulers across a chart and transfer a line parallel to another. The typical use of parallel rulers is to align an edge through your departure and destination, and then *carefully* walk the rulers over to the compass rose on the chart to read the course. See Figures 7-1 and 7-2. I emphasize *carefully* because, if you do not hold the stationary ruler firmly and move the other with care, the rulers may slip. If they slip enough for you to be aware of it, you may only need to cuss a little and start over. If the parallel rulers slip, and you do not notice it, you will read the wrong course off the compass rose. Wrong courses can be serious. This tendency to slip is the biggest disadvantage of parallel rulers. If you do hold the rulers firmly, move deliberately and carefully, without banging the edges together as you walk them, you can do very precise work with parallel rulers.

Parallel rulers come in various sizes, and they are made of various materials. You can buy parallel rulers from 8 inches long all the way up to 30 inches long. They may be made of clear plastic, ebony, brass, or any other suitable material. Some are very elaborate things with protractors and scales etched onto the rulers. My favorite pair is plain, black plastic, 24 inches long. When I go on a boat delivery trip, and must pack things in an attache case, I carry a pair of clear plastic parallel rulers 12 inches long. And on *Li'l Tiger*, my cruising sloop, I have an 18-inch ebony set. So suit yourself.

Some people prefer a protractor for plotting courses and the like. A protractor is a device for measuring angles. When using parallel rulers, the compass rose on the chart serves as a protractor. The trouble with the compass rose is that it is fixed in place on the chart. And herein lies the advantage of the protractor — it's not fixed in place. Some protractors are fitted with an arm or arms, or they are printed on a large sheet of clear plastic. See Figures 7-3 and 7-4. The essential feature of the protractor is an arc of a circle, usually of at least 180 degrees, graduated at least to the nearest degree, etched or printed on the instrument so that the instrument can be used to measure angles. To be used, the protractor must be oriented to a meridian, with the zero of the arc pointing to the north pole. Those protractors made especially for navigation are called course protractors, position plotters, plotters, or some other similar name. They are all very good instruments.

The drafting machine is really nothing more than a very sophisticated arrangement of the course pro-

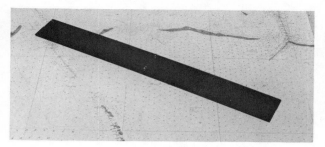

Figure 7-1. Parallel rulers in the closed position.

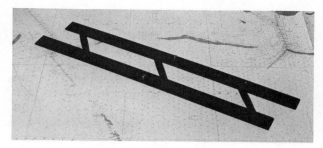

Figure 7-2. Parallel rulers in the open position.

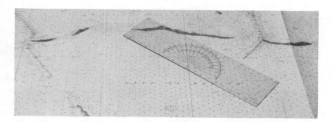

Figure 7-3. A protractor for plotting courses.

Figure 7-4. A protractor with a movable arm.

Figure 7-5. A pair of drafting triangles used for plotting courses.

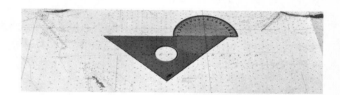

Figure 7-6. A protractor used in combination with a triangle.

tractor. The key components of a drafting machine are a protractor and an arm. The arm is attached to the protractor, and the protractor is on a movable extension that is attached to the base, and the whole lash-up is attached to the chart table at the base. The extension is made so that no matter how it is moved with the protractor about the chart table, the arm of the protractor keeps the exact orientation to which it is set. *Bowditch* points out that drafting machines are for big ships with big chart tables. This was the case, but now it is possible to buy small, inexpensive drafting machines designed especially for small vessel navigation.

A simple, versatile arrangement for plotting courses is a pair of drafting triangles (see Figure 7-5). With two clear plastic triangles, you are again married to the compass rose of the chart. With a dime store protractor and the triangles you are set

free again (see Figure 7-6). And, with at least one triangle with the protractor printed on it, you are set free from the need of the dime store protractor.

Dividers are instruments for measuring and transferring distances. Dividers are essentially no more than a draftsman's compass with a metal point on each leg. To measure the distance between two points, spread the dividers so the tip of one leg is at one point, and the tip of the other leg is on the other point. Be precise. Then, without changing the spread of the dividers, put the tip of one leg on the zero point of the scale. Read the distance at the point on the scale that the tip of the other leg touches. To lay a known distance off on a course line, reverse the process by measuring the distance off the scale and transferring it to the course line. If the distances involved exceed the spread of the dividers, go to the scale, and measure off a convenient distance. Then start from one end of the course, normally your departure or last fix, and step your dividers to the point whose distance away you are measuring. Count the steps and multiply by the spread of the dividers. For example: if you spread your dividers to 60 miles, 1° or 60′ of latitude on the latitude scale, and walked three steps, the distance measured would be 180 miles. Only by coincidence will even numbers of steps match the distance. After counting all the whole steps, measure any remaining distance and add this to the distance stepped off. Thus, if after stepping off 180 miles, you had 7 miles left over, the total distance will be 187 miles.

By its modern definition, dead reckoning depends on three things, and only three things — a *departure*, a *direction* or *course*, and a *distance*.

Departure, when used in terms of a DR plot, simply means you leave or depart from a known position at a known time and date. For example, on our hypothetical cruise, when we depart the seabuoy at Panama City, the first entry in your navigator's notebook would read: "1441, 21 October 1972, Schooner *War Hat* took her departure from the seabuoy, buoy number 1, Panama City ship channel, close aboard to starboard, and set her course 233°T/238°C bound on a coastal training cruise for Gulfport, Mississippi." Buoy number 1 is you departure point. (Look ahead to Figure 7-8.)

The direction your vessel travels is your true course. You always plot true courses. To lay your course, you plot a rhumb line course from your point of departure to your destination by simply taking your parallel rulers or plotter and drawing a line from your departure to your destination on the chart. Your first destination, for the purpose of course plotting, is point *A*. This is your point of first course change along the coast. You plotted point *A* when you planned your passage. Connect these two points, point *A* and buoy number 1, with a pencil line. This is your rhumb line. You are using a Mercator chart. This rhumb line from buoy number 1 to point *A* is your course.

When plotting on charts, it is very important to use the correct type of pencil. A medium pencil is best. I like a 2H or 3H, but some navigators insist a 6H is best. Make your own choice. The main thing is to keep your pencil sharp so as to make any line or mark well defined. Do not press too hard. You want to be able to erase.

After you have plotted the course, take your parallel rulers and measure this course. You measure the course by stepping your parallel rulers over to the nearest compass rose on the chart, and reading the

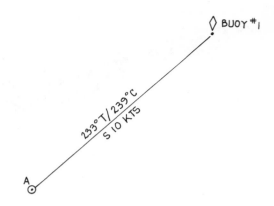

Figure 7-7. Labeling a course.

true course from the outer rose. If you are using a course protractor, you measure the course by determining the angle your course makes with the meridian, clockwise from 000°T. Be sure to keep in mind which way you are going or you may end up with a reciprocal course, which will take you in just the opposite direction from your destination.

You find the course to be 233°T. You then must uncorrect this course of 233°T to get your course to steer. You find you must steer a course of 239°C.

It is important that you label your course line. Over the line write "233°T/239°C". You are going to proceed at 10 knots, so beneath the course line write "S 10 kts." See Figure 7-7.

The true course of 233° is your direction for the first leg of your voyage. When you arrive at point *A*, you will need to change course to go on to point *B*. Point *B* is your next planned course change position. From point *A* draw a pencil line to point *B*. Point *B* is not on Chart No. 1263, but from your plot on Chart No. 1115 you know your course to be 297°T between point *A* and point *B*. Uncorrect this true course of 297°, and you find you must steer 298° by your compass. Label this new course in the same manner you labeled the course between your departure and point *A*.

Point *B* is now your destination for this leg of your passage, but *A* is *not* a new departure. You will estimate when you are at point *A* by dead reckoning. Thus point *A* is a pre-planned DR position. Your departure was buoy number 1 at Panama City. Until you get another position or fix, buoy number 1 will remain your point of departure. To know when you are at point *A*, you must know how long it will take you to run from buoy number 1 to point *A*. You know your speed; to find the time required for this run you must know your distance. Distance is the third component of your DR plot.

If a vessel takes her departure and steers a course for a specific time at a specific speed, the distance she will have run can be determined by the formula *distance equals speed multiplied by the time.* Expressed algebraically the formula is $D = ST$. D is the distance in miles. S is the vessel's speed in knots. T is the time the vessel has run, expressed in hours and fractions of an hour. This formula is called the *speed, time, distance formula.* In a three-part equation, if you know any two parts or factors in the equation, you can solve the equation for the third. Thus, in the formula $D = ST$, when speed is known and time is known, you solve for distance by multiplying the speed by the time.

If you know the distance you must run, and you know the speed your vessel will make, you can calculate the time needed to make the run by dividing the distance by the speed your vessel will make. In the formula this operation is expressed by transposing T. The formula then becomes $\frac{D}{S} = T$; or $T = \frac{D}{S}$. On your run from buoy number 1 to point A, you plan to make 10 knots. To know when you arrive at point A, you must know the time you will need to run at 10 knots to cover the distance from buoy number 1 to point A. T is your unknown. You have already measured the distance from buoy number 1 to point A; it is 4.3 miles. For your formula you have:

$D = 4.3$ miles

$S = 10$ knots

$T = ?$ (If you want to be really mathematical, write this as $T = x$.)

Your equation is $T = \frac{4.3}{10}$. T equals .43 hours.

The prevailing wind off Panama City is southeast. On your run out to point A, this will put you in a beam sea. If the cook asks you, as navigator, how long before you will come to a course on which he can expect a few things to stay on the galley range, you had better not reply "forty-three-hundredths of an hour." He will take after you with a meat cleaver. People express time in hours and minutes in these circumstances. The decimal expressions are reserved for mathematicians and navigators. You have to convert .43 hours to minutes. How do you do this? Multiply .43 hours by 60 because there are 60 minutes in an hour. The time it will take your boat to run from buoy number 1 to point A is 25.8 minutes. Round this figure off to 26 minutes. Tell the cook you will be on a much better course for him in about 26 minutes. You may get a good steak.

To convert decimal parts of an hour into minutes, multiply the decimal by 60. To convert any fractional part of an hour into minutes, multiply by 60.

Another application of the speed, time, distance formula is to find your speed when the time and distance run is known. You will see more of this when the effects of current are discussed. If $D = ST$; and $T = \frac{D}{S}$ then S will equal $\frac{D}{T}$.

Expressed in words this says: Speed in knots will equal the distance in miles divided by the time.

Suppose you are proceeding along the coast. Your log indicates you are making 10 knots. You get a pair of fixes 45 minutes apart that indicate you have gone 9 miles. What is the speed your boat is making good? As a sailor would say, what is your speed over the ground? Set up your formula. What information do you have to put into the formula? You have:

$D = 9$ miles

$T = 45$ minutes

$S = ?$

To solve this problem, the first thing you must do is convert 45 minutes into a fraction of an hour. To make this conversion divide 45 minutes by 60, which is .75 hours. You can now set up the problem as $S = \frac{9}{.75}$. Divide this out, and you get a speed made good of 12.0 knots. You know from your log you are making 10 knots through the water. You must be getting an assist of 2.0 knots from the current.

The several solutions to the speed, time, distance formula can be summed up by expressing each arrangement of the formula as a rule, and then as a formula:

1. When you want to find the distance run, and speed and time are known, multiply the speed in knots by the time in hours. The formula is:

$$D = ST.$$

2. When you want to know the time it will take to run a known distance, and you know your speed also, divide the distance by the speed. The formula is:

$$T = \frac{D}{S}$$

3. If you know the time it took you to go a known distance, and you want to know the speed you are making good, divide the distance run by the time. The formula is:

$$S = \frac{D}{T}$$

With the information I have given you in this lesson, let's work a DR position. At 1700 you wish to make a position report to the beach. A DR position will be satisfactory. What will be your 1700 DR?

You have already determined that the distance from your point of departure to point A is 4.3 miles, and you have determined that the time you should be at point A is 1507. You departed buoy number 1 at 1441, and must run for 26 minutes. At 1507 you reckoned your vessel to be at point A, and changed course to 297°T. Your question now is how far will you run from point A at 10 knots between 1507 and 1700. You can solve this problem step by step.

STEP 1

Find the time interval between 1507 and 1700. To do this subtract 1507 from 1700. Remember you are subtracting hours and minutes from hours and minutes. Your problem looks like this:

$$\begin{array}{r} 1700 \\ -1507 \\ \hline 0153 \end{array}$$

If you are among the many who have trouble subtracting hours and minutes write the problem down like this:

$$\begin{array}{r} 16^h\ 60^m \\ -15^h\ 07^m \\ \hline 01^h\ 53^m \end{array}$$

(16 hours and 60 minutes is 17 hours and 00 minutes)

You must run one hour and fifty-three minutes from point A to your 1700 DR Time, T, is 1^h and 53^m.

STEP 2

You must use hours or fractions of an hour to solve the speed, time, distance formula. Convert 53 minutes to a fraction of an hour. To do this, divide 53 minutes by 60 minutes, which is .88 hours. Add the whole hour of time remaining from Step 1. Time, T, is 1.88 hours.

STEP 3

List the information you have for the formula.

$$D = ?$$
$$S = 10 \text{ knots}$$
$$T = 1.88 \text{ hours}$$

STEP 4

Write your formula in the correct arrangement to solve for distance, D:

$$D = S \times T$$
$$D = 10 \times 1.88$$
$$D = 18.8 \text{ miles.}$$

STEP 5

With your dividers, measure 18.8 miles on the latitude scale of Chart No. 1263. You see immediately

you will run off the chart. If you want a quick solution for your 1700 DR, transfer your plot to Chart No. 1115. The plot is already laid out on this chart as a result of your earlier planning. See how helpful this early planning can be?

When you measure the distance, 18.8 miles, be sure you measure this distance on that part of the latitude scale that lies between latitude 30° 00'.0 N and latitude 30° 30'.0 N because your position will be between these parallels of latitude, and your course lies between these parallels.

STEP 6

After you have spread your dividers to a distance equal to 18.8 miles, handle them carefully so as not to change the spread accidentally. Put one point of your dividers on point A. Put the other point of the dividers on your 297°T course line. At this spot, where the second point touches the course, make a pencil mark. This mark should be as small as it possibly can be. To help you see this mark when you look for it again, draw a small circle around it. This marks your 1700 DR.

It is a good idea to repeat the process of measuring and marking the 18.8-mile distance from point A to be sure you have not made any error.

STEP 7

When you make your position report to the beach, you will state your position in terms of latitude and longitude. To find the latitude and longitude of your 1700 DR, you scale these coordinates off the chart. To measure the longitude, place your parallel rulers along a meridian. Meridians are the lines running north and south. Be sure the alignment of your parallel rulers is exactly along the meridian. Then step your parallel rulers over to your 1700 DR so an edge of the parallel rulers passes precisely through the 1700 DR. If your position is near enough to the edge of the chart, the end of the parallel rulers may extend across the longitude scale of the chart. In this case it will be possible to read the longitude directly from the chart. If the end of the parallel rulers does not extend to the longitude scale, it is then necessary to measure the distance from the edge of the parallel rulers passing through your 1700 DR to the nearest meridian with your dividers, and then to measure the longitude from the same meridian with your dividers on the longitude scale. The longitude of your 1700 DR is 86° 08'.0 W.

Latitude is measured in much the same way as longitude, except you align your parallel rulers precisely along a parallel of latitude. Parallels of

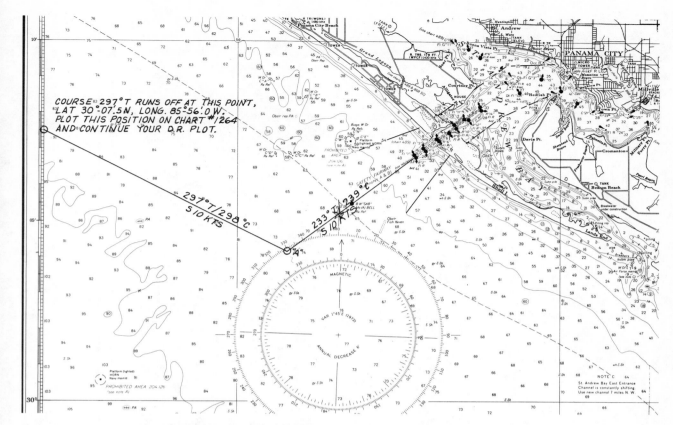

Figure 7-8. A cut-out of Chart No. 1263, showing the course steered after getting underway to the point where the DR is transferred to Chart No. 1264.

latitude are the lines running east and west on your chart. After aligning one edge of your parallel rulers with the nearest parallel of latitude, step your rulers over to your position so the edge of the parallel rulers passes through the exact point of your position. Again, if the end of the parallel ruler passes through the latitude scale of your chart, you can read your latitude directly from the chart. If your position is far from the edge of the chart, you must measure your latitude with your dividers. Your 1700 latitude is 30° 12'.5 N.

Your 1700 DR is latitude 30° 12'.5 N, longitude 86° 08'.0 W.

A comment is in order. In the above steps I assumed that you transferred your DR plot to Chart No. 1115. You could have transferred your DR plot to Chart No. 1264. You are going to have to use Chart No. 1264 anyway before you get to your 1700 DR. The reason you went back to Chart No. 1115 was in the interest of speed. Good practice would dictate that ultimately you would have worked up a DR for 1700 on Chart No. 1264.   It is not difficult to transfer the plot to Chart No. 1264. You already have a plot on Chart No. 1115. Let's see how you

would go about transferring your DR plot to the other chart. Your course of 297°T crosses the western edge of Chart No. 1263 at latitude 30° 07'.5 N, longitude 85° 56'.0 W. The eastern edge of Chart No. 1264 is at longitude 85° 55'.0 W. There is an overlap in longitude of one minute of arc between the two charts. This overlap is intended so you can transfer a plot from one chart to another. Here are the steps required to transfer your plot (refer to Figures 7-8 and 7-9):

STEP 1

Plot the position latitude 30° 07'.5 N, longitude 85° 56'.0 W on chart No. 1264. See Figure 7-9.

STEP 2

On Chart No. 1263 measure the distance from point *A* to the position latitude 30° 07'.5 N, longitude 85° 56'.0 W. See Figure 7-8. This is the position on the edge of Chart No. 1263 at which your course runs off the chart. You measure this distance with your dividers, and find it is 7.32 miles. If you subtract 7.32 miles from 18.8 miles you have remaining 11.48 miles. Do not round this off to 11.5 miles. On charts

39

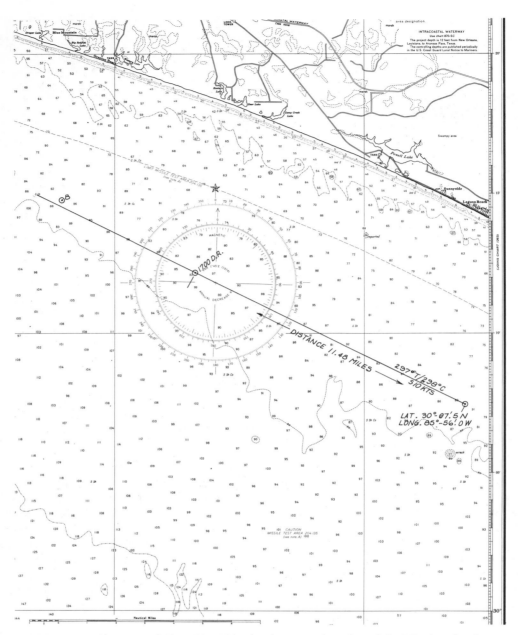

Figure 7-9. A cut-out of Chart No. 1264 showing a continuation of the DR plot after it was transferred from Chart No. 1263.

with scales as large as these two charts, it is possible to plot to this degree of resolution by estimating the hundredths position. You have 11.48 miles to run from the edge of Chart No. 1263 to your 1700 DR on Chart No. 1264.

STEP 3
From the position latitude 30° 07′.5 N, longitude 85° 56′.0 W, draw your course of 297°T. Properly stated in the seaman's vernacular, I should say

"lay" your course of 297°T. With your dividers measure a distance of 11.48 miles along your course. Mark this point with a small dot and circle it. This point, 11.48 miles on a course of 297°T from the above position is your 1700 DR plotted on Chart No. 1264; the coordinates are latitude 30° 12′.7 N, longitude 86° 07′.9 W. The slight difference between this position and your DR position plotted on Chart No. 1115 is due to the difference in scale. As Chart No. 1264 is a much larger scale chart, you should consider the DR plotted on Chart No. 1264 as the most exact.

Several plotting problems follow. Also included are several simple problems involving the speed, time, distance formula. Some of these plotting problems incorporate the need to correct the compass or uncorrect the compass. This is the way it is at sea.

PRACTICE PROBLEMS
Speed, Time, Distance

1. You make 7.5 knots for three hours. How far will you go?
2. You have a 71-mile run to make at 14.5 knots. What time will be required to make this run?
3. You ran 2 hours and 37 minutes at 17 knots. How far did you go?
4. Convert 2 hours and 22 minutes to hours and fractions of an hour.
5. You have gone 47 miles in 5 hours and 7 minutes. What is your speed?
6. You take your departure at 1743. The distance to your destination is 45 miles. You want to arrive at precisely 2300. What speed must you make?
7. You are making 9.5 knots. How long will it take you to go 23.4 miles?
8. You can make it from your anchorage to the seabuoy in 7 hours and 47 minutes if you sail at 6 knots. How far is the seabuoy from your anchorage?
9. You shove off at 0347 and run at 8 knots. What will be your distance run at 0627?
10. From your engine rpm's you think you are making 9 knots, but find you have gone 31 miles between 0847 and 1221. What is your speed over the ground?

Plotting (Use Chart No. 1264 or Figure 7-9)

11. At 1700 you receive a request for assistance from a vessel at latitude 30° 03'.4 N, longitude 86° 09'.6 W. What is the true course from your 1700 DR to the vessel's position?
12. What compass course would you steer to make your true course?
13. What distance must you run to reach the vessel requiring assistance?
14. At what time would you advise the distressed vessel you expected to reach her?
15. At 1734 you are advised that another vessel has taken the distressed vessel in tow and your assistance is no longer required. What course must you steer to return to your original track at point B?

Answers

1.	22.5 miles.	2.	4.9 hours.
3.	44.5 miles.	4.	2.37 hours.
5.	9.2 knots.	6.	8.5 hours.
7.	2ʰ 28ᵐ.	8.	46.8 miles.
9.	18.6 miles.	10.	8.7 knots.
11.	189°T.	12.	191°C.
13.	9.48 miles.	14.	1757.
15.	339°C.		

8   SOME TRICKS TO SOLVE THE SPEED, TIME, DISTANCE PROBLEM

Although using the speed, time, distance formula is not difficult, it does require some arithmetic. Converting minutes to fractions of an hour, and converting fractions of an hour to minutes requires figuring and takes time. Yet working the speed, time, distance formula is something any navigator must be able to do quickly and accurately. Developing this ability is not hard. As in anything else worth mastering, practice is the answer. As long as you navigate, you will not be able to avoid some calculations.

Nevertheless, several means of reducing this arithmetical burden, and also reducing the chance of error, have been devised. An excellent device for solving the speed, time, distance problem is the nautical slide rule. There are several different makes of nautical slide rule on the market; a typical one is illustrated in Figure 8-1. All nautical slide rules depend on the same basic principle. Most are circular, but I have seen some that were patterned after the standard straight slide rule. For that matter a good, simple, slide rule, with a C and D scale can be used very successfully for solving the speed, time, distance formula. Nautical slide rules are better, however, because they are labeled and calibrated especially to solve the speed, time, distance problem.

The nautical slide rule is very easy to operate. A set of instructions on the use of the nautical slide rule is usually included with every new one. For example, if you know your speed and the time you have been running, and want to know the distance run, dial in your speed on the speed scale with the proper pointer, and dial in your time, again with the proper pointer, on the time scale. You then read the distance run on the distance scale. In effect you dial in any two factors you know, and the answer is given automatically on the third factor scale or pointer.

There is a speed, time, distance table in *Bowditch*. See Figure 8-2. In the 1962 edition of *Bowditch* this table is Table 19, which gives the distance run at a

given speed for any time from one minute to sixty minutes. Speeds tabulated in Table 19 begin with 0.5 knot, and are given for each 0.5-knot increment of speed through 40 knots. The use of this table is extremely simple. Suppose you want to know the distance your boat will run at 13.5 knots in 47 minutes. Open *Bowditch* to the part of Table 19 that has the vertical column for 13.5 knots. This is page 1272 in the 1962 edition (see Figure 8-2). Run your eye down the minute column on the left- or right-hand side of the page until you come to the 47-minute line. Now run your eye across the page on this 47-minute line to the 13.5-knot speed column. The table tells you that your boat will run 10.6 miles in 47 minutes at 13.5 knots.

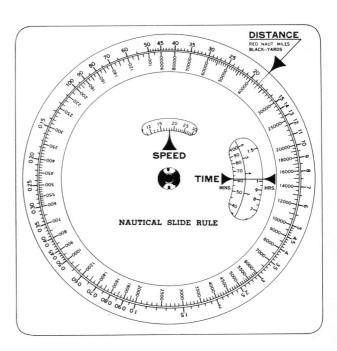

Figure 8-1. A nautical slide rule.

TABLE 19

Speed, Time, and Distance

Min-utes	8.5	9.0	9.5	10.0	10.5	11.0	11.5	12.0	12.5	13.0	13.5	14.0	14.5	15.0	15.5	16.0	Min-utes
	Miles	Miles	Miles	Miles	Miles	Miles	Miles	Miles	Miles	Miles	Miles	Miles	Miles	Miles	Miles	Miles	
1	0.1	0.2	0.2	0.2	0.2	0.2	0.2	0.2	0.2	0.2	0.2	0.2	0.2	0.2	0.3	0.3	1
2	0.3	0.3	0.3	0.3	0.4	0.4	0.4	0.4	0.4	0.4	0.4	0.5	0.5	0.5	0.5	0.5	2
3	0.4	0.4	0.5	0.5	0.5	0.6	0.6	0.6	0.6	0.6	0.7	0.7	0.7	0.8	0.8	0.8	3
4	0.6	0.6	0.6	0.7	0.7	0.7	0.8	0.8	0.8	0.9	0.9	0.9	1.0	1.0	1.0	1.1	4
5	0.7	0.8	0.8	0.8	0.9	0.9	1.0	1.0	1.0	1.1	1.1	1.2	1.2	1.2	1.3	1.3	5
6	0.8	0.9	1.0	1.0	1.0	1.1	1.2	1.2	1.2	1.3	1.4	1.4	1.4	1.5	1.6	1.6	6
7	1.0	1.0	1.1	1.2	1.2	1.3	1.3	1.4	1.5	1.5	1.6	1.6	1.7	1.8	1.8	1.9	7
8	1.1	1.2	1.3	1.3	1.4	1.5	1.5	1.6	1.7	1.7	1.8	1.9	1.9	2.0	2.1	2.1	8
9	1.3	1.4	1.4	1.5	1.6	1.6	1.7	1.8	1.9	2.0	2.0	2.1	2.2	2.2	2.3	2.4	9
10	1.4	1.5	1.6	1.7	1.8	1.8	1.9	2.0	2.1	2.2	2.2	2.3	2.4	2.5	2.6	2.7	10
11	1.6	1.6	1.7	1.8	1.9	2.0	2.1	2.2	2.3	2.4	2.5	2.6	2.7	2.8	2.8	2.9	11
12	1.7	1.8	1.9	2.0	2.1	2.2	2.3	2.4	2.5	2.6	2.7	2.8	2.9	3.0	3.1	3.2	12
13	1.8	2.0	2.1	2.2	2.3	2.4	2.5	2.6	2.7	2.8	2.9	3.0	3.1	3.2	3.4	3.5	13
14	2.0	2.1	2.2	2.3	2.4	2.6	2.7	2.8	2.9	3.0	3.2	3.3	3.4	3.5	3.6	3.7	14
15	2.1	2.2	2.4	2.5	2.6	2.8	2.9	3.0	3.1	3.2	3.4	3.5	3.6	3.8	3.9	4.0	15
16	2.3	2.4	2.5	2.7	2.8	2.9	3.1	3.2	3.3	3.5	3.6	3.7	3.9	4.0	4.1	4.3	16
17	2.4	2.6	2.7	2.8	3.0	3.1	3.3	3.4	3.5	3.7	3.8	4.0	4.1	4.2	4.4	4.5	17
18	2.6	2.7	2.8	3.0	3.2	3.3	3.4	3.6	3.8	3.9	4.0	4.2	4.4	4.5	4.6	4.8	18
19	2.7	2.8	3.0	3.2	3.3	3.5	3.6	3.8	4.0	4.1	4.3	4.4	4.6	4.8	4.9	5.1	19
20	2.8	3.0	3.2	3.3	3.5	3.7	3.8	4.0	4.2	4.3	4.5	4.7	4.8	5.0	5.2	5.3	20
21	3.0	3.2	3.3	3.5	3.7	3.8	4.0	4.2	4.4	4.6	4.7	4.9	5.1	5.2	5.4	5.6	21
22	3.1	3.3	3.5	3.7	3.8	4.0	4.2	4.4	4.6	4.8	5.0	5.1	5.3	5.5	5.7	5.9	22
23	3.3	3.4	3.6	3.8	4.0	4.2	4.4	4.6	4.8	5.0	5.2	5.4	5.6	5.8	5.9	6.1	23
24	3.4	3.6	3.8	4.0	4.2	4.4	4.6	4.8	5.0	5.2	5.4	5.6	5.8	6.0	6.2	6.4	24
25	3.5	3.8	4.0	4.2	4.4	4.6	4.8	5.0	5.2	5.4	5.6	5.8	6.0	6.2	6.5	6.7	25
26	3.7	3.9	4.1	4.3	4.6	4.8	5.0	5.2	5.4	5.6	5.8	6.1	6.3	6.5	6.7	6.9	26
27	3.8	4.0	4.3	4.5	4.7	5.0	5.2	5.4	5.6	5.8	6.1	6.3	6.5	6.8	7.0	7.2	27
28	4.0	4.2	4.4	4.7	4.9	5.1	5.4	5.6	5.8	6.1	6.3	6.5	6.8	7.0	7.2	7.5	28
29	4.1	4.4	4.6	4.8	5.1	5.3	5.6	5.8	6.0	6.3	6.5	6.8	7.0	7.2	7.5	7.7	29
30	4.2	4.5	4.8	5.0	5.2	5.5	5.8	6.0	6.2	6.5	6.8	7.0	7.2	7.5	7.8	8.0	30
31	4.4	4.6	4.9	5.2	5.4	5.7	5.9	6.2	6.5	6.7	7.0	7.2	7.5	7.8	8.0	8.3	31
32	4.5	4.8	5.1	5.3	5.6	5.9	6.1	6.4	6.7	6.9	7.2	7.5	7.7	8.0	8.3	8.5	32
33	4.7	5.0	5.2	5.5	5.8	6.0	6.3	6.6	6.9	7.2	7.4	7.7	8.0	8.2	8.5	8.8	33
34	4.8	5.1	5.4	5.7	6.0	6.2	6.5	6.8	7.1	7.4	7.6	7.9	8.2	8.5	8.8	9.1	34
35	5.0	5.2	5.5	5.8	6.1	6.4	6.7	7.0	7.3	7.6	7.9	8.2	8.5	8.8	9.0	9.3	35
36	5.1	5.4	5.7	6.0	6.3	6.6	6.9	7.2	7.5	7.8	8.1	8.4	8.7	9.0	9.3	9.6	36
37	5.2	5.6	5.9	6.2	6.5	6.8	7.1	7.4	7.7	8.0	8.3	8.6	8.9	9.2	9.6	9.9	37
38	5.4	5.7	6.0	6.3	6.6	7.0	7.3	7.6	7.9	8.2	8.6	8.9	9.2	9.5	9.8	10.1	38
39	5.5	5.8	6.2	6.5	6.8	7.2	7.5	7.8	8.1	8.4	8.8	9.1	9.4	9.8	10.1	10.4	39
40	5.7	6.0	6.3	6.7	7.0	7.3	7.7	8.0	8.3	8.7	9.0	9.3	9.7	10.0	10.3	10.7	40
41	5.8	6.2	6.5	6.8	7.2	7.5	7.9	8.2	8.5	8.9	9.2	9.6	9.9	10.2	10.6	10.9	41
42	6.0	6.3	6.6	7.0	7.4	7.7	8.0	8.4	8.8	9.1	9.4	9.8	10.2	10.5	10.8	11.2	42
43	6.1	6.4	6.8	7.2	7.5	7.9	8.2	8.6	9.0	9.3	9.7	10.0	10.4	10.8	11.1	11.5	43
44	6.2	6.6	7.0	7.3	7.7	8.1	8.4	8.8	9.2	9.5	9.9	10.3	10.6	11.0	11.4	11.7	44
45	6.4	6.8	7.1	7.5	7.9	8.2	8.6	9.0	9.4	9.8	10.1	10.5	10.9	11.2	11.6	12.0	45
46	6.5	6.9	7.3	7.7	8.0	8.4	8.8	9.2	9.6	10.0	10.4	10.7	11.1	11.5	11.9	12.3	46
47	6.7	7.0	7.4	7.8	8.2	8.6	9.0	9.4	9.8	10.2	10.6	11.0	11.4	11.8	12.1	12.5	47
48	6.8	7.2	7.6	8.0	8.4	8.8	9.2	9.6	10.0	10.4	10.8	11.2	11.6	12.0	12.4	12.8	48
49	6.9	7.4	7.8	8.2	8.6	9.0	9.4	9.8	10.2	10.6	11.0	11.4	11.8	12.2	12.7	13.1	49
50	7.1	7.5	7.9	8.3	8.8	9.2	9.6	10.0	10.4	10.8	11.2	11.7	12.1	12.5	12.9	13.3	50
51	7.2	7.6	8.1	8.5	8.9	9.4	9.8	10.2	10.6	11.0	11.5	11.9	12.3	12.8	13.2	13.6	51
52	7.4	7.8	8.2	8.7	9.1	9.5	10.0	10.4	10.8	11.3	11.7	12.1	12.6	13.0	13.4	13.9	52
53	7.5	8.0	8.4	8.8	9.3	9.7	10.2	10.6	11.1	11.5	11.9	12.4	12.8	13.2	13.7	14.1	53
54	7.6	8.1	8.6	9.0	9.4	9.9	10.4	10.8	11.2	11.7	12.2	12.6	13.0	13.5	14.0	14.4	54
55	7.8	8.2	8.7	9.2	9.6	10.1	10.5	11.0	11.5	11.9	12.4	12.8	13.3	13.8	14.2	14.7	55
56	7.9	8.4	8.9	9.3	9.8	10.3	10.7	11.2	11.7	12.1	12.6	13.1	13.5	14.0	14.5	14.9	56
57	8.1	8.6	9.0	9.5	10.0	10.4	10.9	11.4	11.9	12.4	12.8	13.3	13.8	14.2	14.7	15.2	57
58	8.2	8.7	9.2	9.7	10.2	10.6	11.1	11.6	12.1	12.6	13.0	13.5	14.0	14.5	15.0	15.5	58
59	8.4	8.8	9.3	9.8	10.3	10.8	11.3	11.8	12.3	12.8	13.3	13.8	14.3	14.8	15.2	15.7	59
60	8.5	9.0	9.5	10.0	10.5	11.0	11.5	12.0	12.5	13.0	13.5	14.0	14.5	15.0	15.5	16.0	60

Figure 8-2. A portion of Table 19 from *Bowditch.*

43

Suppose you had run for two hours and 47 minutes. How would you use Table 19 to know how far you had run? *Bowditch* assumes you can at least work speed, time, distance problems for whole hours without any special help. If you can't, you had better swallow the anchor and become a news commentator. If you ran for two hours and 47 minutes the solution to your speed, time, distance problem would look like this:

13.5 knots × 2 hours =   27.0 miles.
13.5 knots for 47 minutes from
    Table 19 =   10.6 miles.
Distance run in 2ʰ 47ᵐ   37.6 miles.

Speed, time, distance problems are best solved by use of Table 19 when distance run is required. Table 19 can be used, however, to solve for speed when time and distance is known, and to solve for time when speed and distance are known.

If you are the navigator of a fishing boat, a crew boat, or even a yacht, you may find yourself simultaneously holding down the job of officer of the watch, helmsman, lookout, radar operator, and navigator. Your official title is "that guy on watch." This case is the usual one for most people operating smaller vessels for profit. When you are wearing all these hats, you do not have a lot of time to do arithmetic or flip through tables if you are in pilot waters. At a time like this, it is a big help to be able to work speed, time, distance problems in your head. And if you cannot work these problems in your head, you should at least be able to work them with the minimum of figures on scratch paper without ever leaving the wheel. I am going to explain three methods of mentally solving the speed, time, distance problem.

The first method depends on the following facts: There are 6,080 feet in a nautical mile. For ease of mental calculations you can drop the 80 feet and say there are 6,000 feet without introducing serious error unless great distances are involved. There are 60 minutes in an hour. If you are making 10 knots, you will go 60,000 feet in one hour. If you divide 60,000 feet by 60 minutes you will see you will go 1,000 feet in one minute at 10 knots. If you run one hour at 5 knots you will go five miles. Five times 6,000 feet is 30,000 feet. Divide 30,000 feet by 60 minutes, and you will see you will go 500 feet in one minute at 5 knots. If you run one hour at 7 knots you will run 42,000 feet in one hour. Divide 42,000 feet by 60 minutes, and you find you will run 700 feet in one minute at 7 knots. No matter what speed you are making, if you multiply your speed in knots by 100 the product will be your speed in feet per minute. Thus, at 1 knot you will make 100 feet per minute. At 4 knots you will make 400 feet per minute. At 14

knots you will make 1,400 feet per minute. And even fractional speeds work, so that if you are only making ½ knot you will make 50 feet per minute. At 7¼ or 7.25 knots you would make 725 feet per minute.

With this rule in mind if you are at the wheel and you want to know how long it will take you to go 4 miles at 7 knots, you can solve the problem in your head as follows:

- 4 miles, 4 × 6,000, is 24,000 feet.
- You go 700 feet per minute at 7 knots.
- 700 divided into 24,000 equals 7 divided into 240.
- 7 divided into 240 equals 34 +. Forget the decimal.
- It will take you 34 minutes to go 4 miles at 7 knots.

See how easy this is? When you have time, and nothing else is on your mind, practice this type of problem and then use this method on watch. Your shipmates will think you are a genius.

This little gem of knowledge — speed in knots multiplied by 100 equals speed in feet per minute — is especially good for picking up an anchorage or finding your way from buoy to buoy in fog. For example, you pass red nun buoy number 6 close aboard to port, standing out. Unlighted red nun buoy number 8 is 3/4 miles from buoy number 6. You steer for buoy number 8. You are making 4 knots. At what time should you be at buoy number 8? You mentally work the problem in this manner:

- 3/4 of 6,000 feet is 4,500 feet.
- At 4 knots you are making 400 feet per minute.
- You will make 4,000 feet in 10 minutes plus another 400 feet in one more minute.
- You will make 4,400 feet in 11 minutes.
- Forget the extra 100 feet.
- At 4 knots you will make 100 feet in 15 seconds.
- You should be at buoy number 8 eleven minutes after you pass buoy number 6.

When running alone in fog or at night, or whenever visability of aids to navigation is limited, the need to know the time to run between buoys or other marks is nothing less than crucial. If alone on watch, as you may well be, this is an excellent way to solve the problem.

How do you use the fact that speed in knots multiplied by 100 equals the speed in feet per minute to pick up an anchorage? A typical example would be a situation like this: You are sneaking along at night, at 3 knots, in fog. You are eastbound in Mississippi Sound somewhere west of the Pascagoula ship channel. See Figure 8-3. You do not know exactly

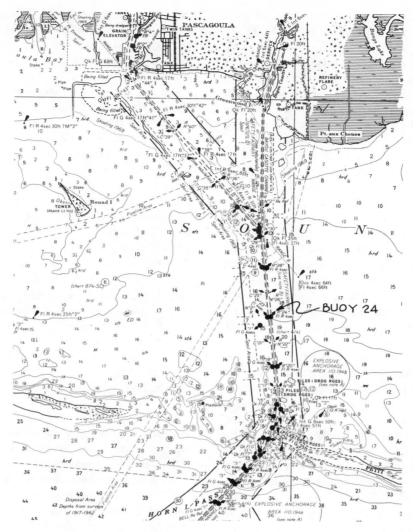

Figure 8-3. A cut-out of Chart No. 1267 showing the area around buoy 24 of the Pascagoula Ship Channel.

where you are. You want to anchor but must be certain that you will be well clear of the Pascagoula ship channel and the Intracoastal Waterway. You are watching your fathometer and also have a leadsman on the head of your lead barge. The depth of the water suddenly increases. You know you are crossing the Pascagoula ship channel. But where? Luckily you spot red buoy number 24 on your port bow, close aboard. You have an excellent fix now. You know you are at the junction of the Pascagoula ship channel and the Intracoastal Waterway. You sure can't anchor here! You turn to course 135°T. In seconds you are shrouded in fog again. As the deckhand said: "You can't see nothing." Your chart shows if you run on course 135°T from buoy number

24 for 4,500 feet you should be in safe water to anchor. You decide this is the thing to do. How long must you run on a course of 135°T to be at your selected anchorage?

- At 3 knots your boat is making 300 feet a minute. 4,500 divided by 300 is 15. The easy way to arrive at this is first to divide 4,500 by 100 and get 45, and divide 300 by 100 and get 3. Then you divide 45 by 3 and get 15.
- You tell yourself: "I will run 15 minutes. I should then be 4,500 feet southeast of buoy number 24, and well clear of any traffic. When the 15 minutes are up I will anchor."

Another handy way to work speed, time, distance problems in your head is by use of the six-minute run. To use the six-minute run, you time all your runs in intervals of six minutes or multiples of six minutes. Unlike the speed in feet per minute system just explained, the six-minute run method does not introduce any rounding-off error. The six-minute run is used by watch officers on larger vessels to solve all kinds of speed, time, distance problems, such as problems required by rapid radar plotting and distance-off problems. It will work well for you too.

Why use a six minute run? Because six minutes is one-tenth of an hour. For this reason, you can take the distance run in six minutes, multiply this distance by ten, and get your speed. For example, if you run 1.5 miles in six minutes you are making 15 knots. By the same token if you run for six minutes at 15 knots you will go 1.5 miles. If you run for 18 minutes at 15 knots you will go 4.5 miles, because 6 divided into 18 equals 3, and 1.5 multiplied by 3 equals 4.5.

Here are some practical examples of how the six-minute run method of solving speed, time, distance problems works. You are proceeding from your 1700 DR along the coast of Florida. You have 5.4 miles to go from your 1700 DR to point B. At point B you want to change course to 287°T/281°C. You are making 10 knots. At what time should you change course to 287°T? Here is your mental solution, using the six-minute run method:

- At 10 knots you will make 1 mile in six minutes.
- It will take you 5 times 6 minutes to make 5 miles. Thus you will make 5 miles in 30 minutes. $5 \times 6 = 30$.
- You still have 0.4 miles to go after the 30 minutes are up.
- $0.4 \times 6 = 2.4$.
- Time to run to point B from your 1700 DR is 32.4 minutes. Change course at 1732.

To solve this problem you did not have to leave the wheel.

Assume that after turning to your new course of 287°T you fixed your position, and 24 minutes later you fixed your position again. You find you have run 4.4 miles in 24 minutes. What speed are you making? Again the steps to a mental solution:

- 6 divided into 24 equals 4.
- There are 4 six-minute intervals in 24 minutes.
- 4 divided into 4.4 equals 1.1.
- You are making 1.1 miles every 6 minutes.
- You are making good a speed of 11 knots because $1.1 \times 10 = 11$.

Another excellent method for a quick mental solution to the speed, time, distance problem is found in the rule: "speed in knots multiplied by 100 equals the distance run in yards in 3 minutes." Why is this so? I have already shown that speed in knots multiplied by 100 equals the feet your boat will run in one minute. If you are making 6 knots, you are making 600 feet per minute. In three minutes you will run 1,800 feet. There are three feet in a yard. 1,800 feet equals 600 yards. Thus in three minutes you will run 600 yards. What makes this rule so good? Well, if we use 6,000 feet to equal a nautical mile, we can say 2,000 yards equals a nautical mile. So suppose you are bound east in the Intracoastal Waterway. Your boat is making seven knots. You are four and one half miles from a lock. The lockmaster calls you on the radio to ask when you expect to arrive at the lock. Tell him to "wait one," and think your answer out like this:

- $7 \times 100 = 700$ yards every 3 minutes.
- $3 \times 700 = 2,100$ yards.
- So, you will go 2,100 yards, 100 yards more than a mile in 3×3 minutes.
- 3×3 minutes = 9 minutes.
- Since you are using a rule of thumb solution, you can say 4.5 miles $\times$ 9 minutes = 40.5 minutes.
- Tell the lockmaster you will be at the lock in 40 minutes.

You could refine this to 38 or 39 minutes by taking into account the 450 yards you gained by ignoring the extra 100 yards in the $3 \times 700 = 2,100$ yards, but no one is going to check you to the minute.

I chose seven knots because seven is an odd number, and odd numbers are the hardest to use in mental arithmetic. Yet this was certainly easy enough. Let's take another example. Suppose your boat passed a mile marker and 18 minutes later she passed another point you know to be exactly one and one half miles from the mile marker. How fast are you going?

- 1.5 miles $\times$ 2,000 = 3,000 yards.
- 18 divided by 3 = 6.
- There are 6 three-minute runs in an 18-minute interval.
- As you made 3,000 yards in this 18-minute interval, divide 3,000 by 6.
- 3,000 divided by 6 = 500 yards.
- Your boat is making 500 yards every three minutes. $5 \times 100 = 500$, so you are making 5 knots.

You should make every effort to master the several methods of solving the speed, time, distance problem given in this chapter. The mental solutions explained here are one of the most useful tricks of the trade for small-craft navigators who often navigate and steer at the same time.

9   HOW TO DETERMINE YOUR SHIP'S SPEED

In this chapter I am not referring to finding your true speed by comparing your dead reckoning positions with a run of fixes. This will be covered in later chapters along with fixes and running fixes. Speed obtained by using the distance run and time between fixes is the true speed of your vessel over the ground, and is of utmost importance to the navigator. At this point, however, it is necessary for you to have a reasonably accurate way of determining your vessel's speed through the water in order to determine distance run to use in your DR plot. How do you know the speed your vessel is making through the water?

The speed of your boat in still water, unaffected by wind and current, would equal the speed of your boat over the bottom, or "over the ground." This is the geographic speed of your boat. For the purpose of keeping a DR plot, modern navigation disregards the effects of wind and current. Your speed through the water is the speed you must know to plot your DR accurately. (Positions involving the effects of wind and current are called *estimated positions* or EP's in modern navigation. This distinction is made because speed, time, and course are subject to precise measurement, whereas set, drift, and leeway, the effects of current and winds, are often the product of the navigator's judgement.)

Most larger vessels use a device called a *pitometer log*, or pit log, to determine speed. This device depends on a wand or extension that projects out of the bottom of the vessel into the water. The movement of the vessel through the water causes pressure on this extension. The greater the speed of the vessel, the greater the pressure. This pressure is translated by electrical and mechanical means to show the vessel's speed directly on a dial. Instruments based on this same principle are available for small vessels down to the size of outboard motorboats and day sailers. Depending on the preciseness of their location and calibration, these devices may be quite accurate even on small boats.

Another device for measuring a boat's speed through the water consists of a small propeller attached to the outside of the hull. As the boat moves through the water, the propeller spins and generates an electrical current. This current registers on a meter calibrated directly for speed. The speed at which the propeller turns depends on the speed of the boat through the water. The propeller speed determines the amount of electricity generated, so a direct measure of the boat's speed is possible. *Bowditch* calls these instruments *impeller logs*. Both the pit log and the impeller log, and any other speed measuring device attached to the bottom of the hull, must be located at a point on the hull where water turbulence is least. These devices must also be protected from fouling by marine growth and the occasional piece of weed or flotsam that may drape around the sensing mechanism. With few exceptions, too, a hole in the hull is required. And on sailing vessels these instruments may register differently on different tacks, even though the boat's speed is the same, because when a sailing vessel heels, the weather side is raised, and the log on the weather side is either not totally immersed or is operating in more turbulent water. This affects the accuracy of the log reading. For this reason many sailing yachts carry two such gizmos, one on each side of the bottom of the hull, to insure at least one instrument is properly immersed on either tack. The leeward log is the one to read on a given tack.

Another instrument is the *taffrail log*. The taffrail log is a distance-measuring instrument. Notice I said *distance*. Taffrail logs invariably record distance run much the same as the odometer on your car's speedometer, and not speed as pit logs and other logs do. You must compare readings at the beginning and at the end of a run to get the distance run by taffrail log. The taffrail log consists of three main elements: a registering gauge or dial, a log line, and a rotor. The gauge mounts on the stern of the vessel at the taffrail. Hence the name taffrail log. Attached to this gauge, by means of a geared swivel, is the log line,

TABLE 18
Speed Table for Measured Mile

Sec.	Minutes												Sec.
---	1	2	3	4	5	6	7	8	9	10	11	12	---
	Knots	*Knots*	*Knots*	*Knots*	*Knots*	*Knots*	*Knots*	*Knots*	*Knots*	*Knots*	*Knots*	*Knots*	
0	60.000	30.000	20.000	15.000	12.000	10.000	8.571	7.500	6.667	6.000	5.455	5.000	0
1	59.016	29.752	19.890	14.938	11.960	9.972	8.551	7.484	6.654	5.990	5.446	4.993	1
2	58.065	29.508	19.780	14.876	11.921	9.945	8.531	7.469	6.642	5.980	5.438	4.986	2
3	57.143	29.268	19.672	14.815	11.881	9.917	8.511	7.453	6.630	5.970	5.430	4.979	3
4	56.250	29.032	19.565	14.754	11.842	9.890	8.491	7.438	6.618	5.960	5.422	4.972	4
5	55.385	28.800	19.459	14.694	11.803	9.863	8.471	7.423	6.606	5.950	5.414	4.966	5
6	54.545	28.571	19.355	14.634	11.765	9.836	8.451	7.407	6.593	5.941	5.405	4.959	6
7	53.731	28.346	19.251	14.575	11.726	9.809	8.431	7.392	6.581	5.931	5.397	4.952	7
8	52.941	28.125	19.149	14.516	11.688	9.783	8.411	7.377	6.569	5.921	5.389	4.945	8
9	52.174	27.907	19.048	14.458	11.650	9.756	8.392	7.362	6.557	5.911	5.381	4.938	9
10	51.429	27.692	18.947	14.400	11.613	9.730	8.372	7.347	6.545	5.902	5.373	4.932	10
11	50.704	27.481	18.848	14.343	11.576	9.704	8.353	7.332	6.534	5.892	5.365	4.925	11
12	50.000	27.273	18.750	14.286	11.538	9.677	8.333	7.317	6.522	5.882	5.357	4.918	12
13	49.315	27.068	18.653	14.229	11.502	9.651	8.314	7.302	6.510	5.873	5.349	4.911	13
14	48.649	26.866	18.557	14.173	11.465	9.626	8.295	7.287	6.498	5.863	5.341	4.905	14
15	48.000	26.667	18.462	14.118	11.429	9.600	8.276	7.273	6.486	5.854	5.333	4.898	15
16	47.368	26.471	18.367	14.062	11.392	9.574	8.257	7.258	6.475	5.844	5.325	4.891	16
17	46.753	26.277	18.274	14.008	11.356	9.549	8.238	7.243	6.463	5.835	5.318	4.885	17
18	46.154	26.087	18.182	13.953	11.321	9.524	8.219	7.229	6.452	5.825	5.310	4.878	18
19	45.570	25.899	18.090	13.900	11.285	9.499	8.200	7.214	6.440	5.816	5.302	4.871	19
20	45.000	25.714	18.000	13.846	11.250	9.474	8.182	7.200	6.429	5.806	5.294	4.865	20
21	44.444	25.532	17.910	13.793	11.215	9.449	8.163	7.186	6.417	5.797	5.286	4.858	21
22	43.902	25.352	17.822	13.740	11.180	9.424	8.145	7.171	6.406	5.788	5.279	4.852	22
23	43.373	25.175	17.734	13.688	11.146	9.399	8.126	7.157	6.394	5.778	5.271	4.845	23
24	42.857	25.000	17.647	13.636	11.111	9.375	8.108	7.143	6.383	5.769	5.263	4.839	24
25	42.353	24.828	17.561	13.585	11.077	9.351	8.090	7.129	6.372	5.760	5.255	4.832	25
26	41.860	24.658	17.476	13.534	11.043	9.326	8.072	7.115	6.360	5.751	5.248	4.826	26
27	41.379	24.490	17.391	13.483	11.009	9.302	8.054	7.101	6.349	5.742	5.240	4.819	27
28	40.909	24.324	17.308	13.433	10.976	9.278	8.036	7.087	6.338	5.732	5.233	4.813	28
29	40.449	24.161	17.225	13.383	10.942	9.254	8.018	7.073	6.327	5.723	5.225	4.806	29
30	40.000	24.000	17.143	13.333	10.909	9.231	8.000	7.059	6.316	5.714	5.217	4.800	30
31	39.560	23.841	17.062	13.284	10.876	9.207	7.982	7.045	6.305	5.705	5.210	4.794	31
32	39.130	23.684	16.981	13.235	10.843	9.184	7.965	7.031	6.294	5.696	5.202	4.787	32
33	38.710	23.529	16.901	13.187	10.811	9.160	7.947	7.018	6.283	5.687	5.195	4.781	33
34	38.298	23.377	16.822	13.139	10.778	9.137	7.930	7.004	6.272	5.678	5.187	4.775	34
35	37.895	23.226	16.744	13.091	10.746	9.114	7.912	6.990	6.261	5.669	5.180	4.768	35
36	37.500	23.077	16.667	13.043	10.714	9.091	7.895	6.977	6.250	5.660	5.172	4.762	36
37	37.113	22.930	16.590	12.996	10.682	9.068	7.877	6.963	6.239	5.651	5.165	4.756	37
38	36.735	22.785	16.514	12.950	10.651	9.045	7.860	6.950	6.228	5.643	5.158	4.749	38
39	36.364	22.642	16.438	12.903	10.619	9.023	7.843	6.936	6.218	5.634	5.150	4.743	39
40	36.000	22.500	16.364	12.857	10.588	9.000	7.826	6.923	6.207	5.625	5.143	4.737	40
41	35.644	22.360	16.290	12.811	10.557	8.978	7.809	6.910	6.196	5.616	5.136	4.731	41
42	35.294	22.222	16.216	12.766	10.526	8.955	7.792	6.897	6.186	5.607	5.128	4.724	42
43	34.951	22.086	16.143	12.721	10.496	8.933	7.775	6.883	6.175	5.599	5.121	4.718	43
44	34.615	21.951	16.071	12.676	10.465	8.911	7.759	6.870	6.164	5.590	5.114	4.712	44
45	34.286	21.818	16.000	12.632	10.435	8.889	7.742	6.857	6.154	5.581	5.106	4.706	45
46	33.962	21.687	15.929	12.587	10.405	8.867	7.725	6.844	6.143	5.573	5.099	4.700	46
47	33.645	21.557	15.859	12.544	10.375	8.845	7.709	6.831	6.133	5.564	5.092	4.694	47
48	33.333	21.429	15.789	12.500	10.345	8.824	7.692	6.818	6.122	5.556	5.085	4.688	48
49	33.028	21.302	15.721	12.457	10.315	8.802	7.676	6.805	6.112	5.547	5.078	4.681	49
50	32.727	21.176	15.652	12.414	10.286	8.780	7.660	6.792	6.102	5.538	5.070	4.675	50
51	32.432	21.053	15.584	12.371	10.256	8.759	7.643	6.780	6.091	5.530	5.063	4.669	51
52	32.143	20.930	15.517	12.329	10.227	8.738	7.627	6.767	6.081	5.521	5.056	4.663	52
53	31.858	20.809	15.451	12.287	10.198	8.717	7.611	6.754	6.071	5.513	5.049	4.657	53
54	31.579	20.690	15.385	12.245	10.169	8.696	7.595	6.742	6.061	5.505	5.042	4.651	54
55	31.304	20.571	15.319	12.203	10.141	8.675	7.579	6.729	6.050	5.496	5.035	4.645	55
56	31.034	20.455	15.254	12.162	10.112	8.654	7.563	6.716	6.040	5.488	5.028	4.639	56
57	30.769	20.339	15.190	12.121	10.084	8.633	7.547	6.704	6.030	5.479	5.021	4.633	57
58	30.508	20.225	15.126	12.081	10.056	8.612	7.531	6.691	6.020	5.471	5.014	4.627	58
59	30.252	20.112	15.063	12.040	10.028	8.592	7.516	6.679	6.010	5.463	5.007	4.621	59
60	30.000	20.000	15.000	12.000	10.000	8.571	7.500	6.667	6.000	5.455	5.000	4.615	60
Sec.	1	2	3	4	5	6	7	8	9	10	11	12	Sec.

Figure 9-1. Table 18 from *Bowditch*.

and attached to the log line is the rotor, which is dragged astern. The log line should be long enough for the rotor to trail far enough astern to clear your wake turbulence. The movement of the boat through the water causes the rotor to turn. The turns of the rotor are transmitted through the log line to the gauge, by means of the geared swivel, and recorded as distance run. Taffrail logs are good instruments. They are simple enough to have few ills. They are not without some faults, however. Seaweed can, and will, foul the rotor and the log line. This fouling causes the rotor to quit turning or at least changes its rate of turn for a given speed. The result is an erroneous indication of distance run. Taffrail logs can be inaccurate in vessels running before a following sea. The rapid acceleration and deceleration as each sea passes under the boat can cause the log line to go slack and suddenly taut, making the dial register an erroneous run. Rotors and swivels do jam, and the log line can get kinked. I witnessed two hours of the most original cussing combined with dogged perseverance when a trolling line we were pulling fouled our log line on a yacht in mid-Atlantic. Most rotors are shiny brass. A coating of flat black paint on the rotor is a good investment. I am convinced the ocean bottom is covered with sharks, weighted down by the shiny brass rotors they have in their stomachs.

Marine stores and ship chandler's warehouses are loaded with shelves full of speed-measuring devices. Most of these items are very good, and they all cost money. If you are a racing yachtsman or commercial operator, these devices can be well worth their cost. If you have limited means, or if you are as most sailors are, you may prefer something less expensive or something your own ingenuity can provide.

On power vessels, and this includes everything from ocean liners to sailing auxiliaries under power only, a speed-power diagram or a speed-power table can give you a very accurate means of measuring your boat's speed through the water. Making a speed-power diagram or a speed-power table requires no more than the time to run a measured mile at various power settings, and the fuel you burn.

To make a speed-power table, first write down the different power settings at which you can run your engine. These power settings are tabulated as revolutions per minute (rpm's). For this reason it is essential your boat have a tachometer. Write the rpm's at which you can run in a vertical column on the left of a piece of paper. Begin with your slowest operating rpm's at the top of the column. These slow rpm's are very important, because in fog or other adverse conditions you are likely to run at very slow speeds, and an accurate knowledge of your speed is critical.

After you have tabulated the rpm's, find a measured mile on your local chart. If no official measured mile has been established, you may have to lay out your own measured mile from the landmarks and aids to navigation available. After you have located a measured mile, set your throttle to run your engine at the first rpm setting in your table. Start your run well enough away from the starting marker of the measured mile to fair up accurately on the measured mile course, and far enough away to insure your boat has reached her maximum speed for the power setting before the first mark comes abeam. At the instant you pass the starting mile marker abeam, start your stopwatch. When the finish mile marker is abeam, stop your stopwatch. Record the elapsed time. Now change course 180°, and run the measured mile again on the reverse course at the same power setting. Take you time again. Average your time for the two runs. The purpose of running the measured mile in both directions is to reduce the error due to wind, sea, and current. After you have run the measured mile in both directions at each power setting, compute your speed for each rpm run. The easiest way to compute your speed when the time required to run a measured mile is known is to refer to Table 18 of *Bowditch* (see Figure 9-1). This table consists of twelve columns of 61 lines each. Each column is a minute column beginning with one minute and continuing at one minute increments through twelve minutes. The horizontal lines of the table are for seconds of time, from zero seconds on the first line through 60 seconds on the bottom line. The use of Table 18 is simple. Suppose you ran a measured mile at 1,000 rpm's in 8 minutes and 42 seconds. To find the speed you were making enter the table at the 8-minute column. Go down the left-hand side of the page to the 42-second line, and read 6.897 knots. Round this figure off to 6.9 knots. At 1,000 rpm's your boat makes 6.9 knots.

After you have completed your rpm-speed table (see Figure 9-2), you may want to make an rpm-speed diagram or *speed-power curve* as most navigators call it. To make a speed-power curve you will need a piece of graph paper. On the graph paper let the vertical ordinate be the rpm ordinate, and let the horizontal ordinate be the speed. The zero-rpm, zero-speed point is at the intersection of these ordinates. Graph in the position for each speed and rpm setting in the speed-power table. When you have graphed a point for each speed-rpm, fair a line through each of these points. This faired line is your speed-power curve. The advantage of a speed-power curve is that you can get a direct indication of your speed for any power setting within the limits of the graph. See Figure 9-3.

SPEED POWER TABLE

YACHT WAR HAT   DATE 18 OCT. 1972

ENGINE RPM	SPEED KNOTS	ENGINE RPM	SPEED KNOTS
800	5.0	1400	8.4
900	6.3	1500	8.8
1000	6.9	1600	9.1
1100	7.2	1700	9.4
1200	7.6	1800	9.6
1300	8.0	1900	9.8
		2000	10.0

Figure 9-2. A hypothetical speed-power table. It is simple to understand—if your tachometer indicates your engine is turning 2,000 rpms, your boat should be making 10 knots through the water.

Up to now we have been talking about ways to measure the speed through the water of vessels that are large enough to have some kind of sophisticated gear, even if only a tachometer. What about the little guy who either can't, or doesn't want, to spend the money to buy this gear? Good precise navigation can be just as important to the navigator of small vessels as it is to the big boys. I can remember my own straits when I tried to transfer the good practices I learned as a navigator in the Navy to the navigation of small sailboats. It is good business to keep a DR plot on a small boat in strange waters, but when you have no pit log, no impeller log, and no tachometer, how can you know your speed? There are some very good methods, and you should know them even if your boat is equipped with all the latest electronic devices to measure speed. You carry a lead line, I hope, in case the fathometer goes out. Electronic and mechanical logs can quit too.

THE CHIP LOG

You can make your own chip log, and, if you do a passing good job, you can claim it was handed down to you by some seafaring ancestor. The chip log was the device our ancestors used to measure the speed of their vessels in the great days of sail. The traditional chip log consists of a spool, 150 fathoms of line plus the "stray" line, the chip, and a 28-second sand glass. The 28-second glass was the standard in the U. S. Navy. You may need 150 fathoms of line, but for the type of boat I am thinking of you most likely will not. With 150 fathoms of line, the log will measure speeds up to 18 knots. If you know the absolute maximum speed of your boat to be less than 18 knots you can reduce the amount of log line you need accordingly. The log line should be small enough in diameter to

spool easily, but large enough in diameter to resist tangling. It should be a type of line that will not stretch. Today, one-eighth-inch dacron makes a good log line.

To make the spool for your chip log is easy, even if you are not at all handy with tools. A wooden rolling pin is a good beginning, and one can be bought cheaply if you cannot steal one from the cook. Modify the rolling pin so the roller free-spools on the handles, and place wood or marine plywood disc flanges at each end of the roller to hold the line on the spool.

The chip is made from a thin piece of wood; a one-quarter-inch piece of marine plywood is excellent. From the plywood cut a quadrant of a circle on a radius of at least five inches. This is the chip. On the curved side of the chip put a piece of lead or other weight just heavy enough to cause the chip to float in a vertical position. At the three corners of the chip bore a hole just large enough to accommodate pieces of line the same size as the log line. To rig the chip you will need a socket and a peg. Cut a piece of dowel stock an inch or so in diameter and about four

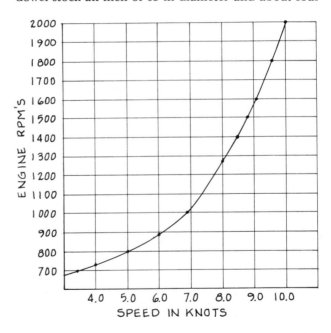

Figure 9-3. A hypothetical speed-power curve, which shows, for instance, that the speed of *War Hat* at a power setting of 1,640 rpms is 9.2 knots. Speed-power curves can give you a lot of information not as readily apparent from a speed-power table. This one indicates that, above 1,000 rpms, the increase in speed resulting from a given increase in rpm falls off until at a little above 2,000 rpms (not on the graph, as the highest rpm graphed is 2,000) the return in speed for increases in rpm will be zero. The speed curve becomes a vertical line at this point.

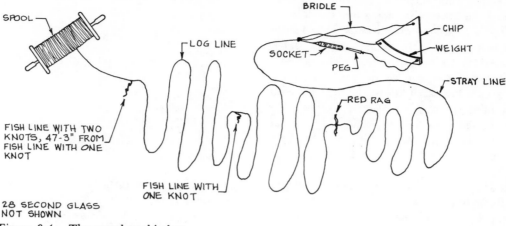

SPOOL

LOG LINE

BRIDLE

CHIP

WEIGHT

SOCKET

PEG

STRAY LINE

RED RAG

FISH LINE WITH TWO
KNOTS, 47-3" FROM
FISH LINE WITH ONE
KNOT

FISH LINE WITH
ONE KNOT

28 SECOND GLASS
NOT SHOWN

Figure 9-4. The complete chip log.

inches long, (an old broom or swab handle will do). In this piece of stock drill a hole, about one-half inch in diameter, lengthwise to make a wooden tube. This is the socket. Now fashion a peg from a piece of stock to fit this tube or socket just snug enough to require a hard jerk to snatch it from the socket. Bore a hole crossways through one end of the socket just large enough to receive a piece of the log line, and bore a hole crossways through the outside end of the peg just large enough to receive a piece of the log line. You are now ready to put the pieces together.

To rig your chip log, first wind the log line on the spool. When all the line is on the spool, reel off just enough to clear the wake of your boat. Mark this length with a piece of red rag. This first length of line is called the "stray line." Starting with the place where you put the piece of red rag, reel off 47 feet, 3 inches of log line, and place a piece of fish line with one knot in it through the strands of the log line at exactly this point. From this piece of fish line, measure out another 47 feet, 3 inches of log line, and mark this with a fish line with two knots in it. Measure off a third 47 feet, 3 inches, and mark this with a piece of fish line with three knots in it. Continue to reel off 47-foot, 3-inch lengths of line, and add a knot to the fish line marker at each additional point until you have run off the entire 150 fathoms of line, if you use that much. Otherwise continue in this way until you have marked enough line to measure speeds exceeding the maximum speed of your boat. Now roll the log line back on the spool, and attach the chip.

By the way, the spacing of 47 feet 3 inches between marks on the log line is derived from the ratio $x:6,080 = 28:3,600$, where 6,080 is the number of

feet in a nautical mile, 28 seconds is the interval of time used to log speed, and 3,600 seconds is the number of seconds in an hour.

The chip is attached to the log line by means of a bridle, about three feet long. Make the bridle from the same type of line as the log line. The three warps of the bridle attach to the three corners of the chip through the small holes you bored. Cut one warp of the bridle in two, and fasten the socket to the end of the warp from the apex of the bridle. Fasten the peg to the end of the warp from the chip. Tie the after end of the stray line to the apex of the bridle. Your chip log is now ready to use. See Figure 9-4.

Using the chip log ordinarily requires at least two people. On the old square riggers, casting the log was a ceremony almost as sacred as the noon sight. The master and the mate went to the stern of the ship along with another hand to hold the spool. The first officer held the sand glass. When all was in readiness, the master gave the order to "cast," and the chip was cast over the stern. The log line ran out, pulled by the braking action of the bridled chip, and as the first mark, the piece of red rag, was coming off the spool, the warning "stand by" was given. At the instant the piece of red rag passed over the taffrail, the order "turn" was called and the sand glass was turned. At the exact instant all the sand ran out of the top of the glass the mate sang out "mark." The spool was stopped, and the number of knots at the last piece of fish-line marker was counted. This was the speed of the ship in "knots" or nautical miles per hour. The log line was further marked by pieces of white rag spaced to divide the distance between each piece of fish line marker into five even segments. Thus speed could be measured to the nearest two-tenths of a knot. If the ship happened to be going faster than the log could measure, and the "knots" all ran off before the 28 seconds were up, the log was cast again, and a 14-second glass was used. Twice the number of knots run off in 14 seconds gave the speed of the ship. Today we use a stopwatch instead of a sand glass, and the spool can be mounted on the rail so only one man is necessary to cast the log. After the knots are counted, the chip is reeled in. To break the drag of the bridled chip, before reeling in, give the log line a hard yank. This will pull the peg from the socket and upset the bridle so the chip will come in edgeways.

A modification of the chip log is the ground log. The ground log is used in shoal waters and differs from the chip log only in the respect that a weight which will sink to the bottom is used instead of the chip. Since the weight rests on the bottom (sailors call it the ground), the speed of the vessel is measured in reference to a stationary object. For this reason speed measured by ground log is speed over the ground, the true geographic speed of the vessel, and not speed through the water.

THE DUTCHMAN'S LOG

The very earliest method of measuring the speed of a vessel was to throw a wood chip, or any object that would float, overboard to leeward, and measure the time interval required for the boat to put the object abeam of two marks on deck. These two marks were a precomputed distance apart along a line parallel to the keel. This distance apart could vary depending on the size of the ship and the units in which speed was measured. Often seamen used the distance between two fittings along the deck without actually making any marks as such. The distance from the cutwater to the foremast might be used for instance. American and English seamen call this system of measuring the speed of a vessel a *Dutchman's log*. Despite all the modern mechanical and electronic gadgetry many boats carry today, the Dutchman's log is still a useful device. As I said previously, electronic and mechanical devices can get out of order. I was navigator in a yacht making a trade-wind passage once, and the surging caused by the following sea made our taffrail log useless. This fancy piece of gear was put to rest in its box under the chart-room table for the remainder of the voyage. We resorted to the Dutchman's log with much better results.

Anyone who ventures out to sea must be able to navigate competently when all the black boxes and other gizmos quit. The Dutchman's log will help you do just this. Wood chips are cheap, too. Navigators during the Age of Discovery relied on latitude, the lead line, and the Dutchman's log.

TIME IN SECONDS	SPEED IN KNOTS
1	10.0
2	5.0
3	3.4
4	2.5
5	2.0
6	1.7
7	1.5
8	1.3
9	1.1
10	1.0

Figure 9-5. Speed table for the Dutchman's log, marks 16.9 feet apart.

You can lay out a distance between two marks or points on the deck of your boat. The arithmetic involved works out like this: At one knot your boat will go 1.688 feet in one second, because your boat goes 6,080 feet, a nautical mile, in 3,600 seconds, one hour. At one knot your boat will go 16.88 feet in ten seconds. Your boat will go 33.76 feet in 20 seconds at one knot. You can round off 16.88 to 16.9. If your boat is over 16.9 feet in length, and less than 33.8 feet in length, lay off two points on deck, on a line parallel to the keel, 16.9 feet apart. Gather a supply of small wood chips. The next time you are underway and want to know your speed, throw a chip off the bow to leeward. As you throw this chip sing out "stand by." When the wood chip passes the forward mark sing out "start," and start your stopwatch. At the instant the chip is abeam of the second mark, an observer (usually the helmsman) should sing out "mark." At this instant stop your stopwatch. Note the number of seconds it took the chip to pass between the two marks.

The table in Figure 9-5 will tell you the speed your boat is making for any whole number of seconds it takes for the two marks on deck to pass the wood chip. This table is for marks 16.9 feet apart. The figures in the "speed in knots" column are rounded off to the nearest tenth. Theoretically, the Dutchman's log is quite accurate. In practice, this accuracy suffers because you usually use your seaman's eye to tell when the chip is passed by each mark. In addition, most small-craft navigators have learned to count seconds accurately enough for most purposes, and therefore they don't use a stopwatch. So their time count can be a little off too. Counting seconds is important, anyway, because stopwatches get out of order. All competent navigators can count seconds with a remarkable degree of accuracy.

TIME IN SECONDS	SPEED IN KNOTS
1.0	20.2
1.5	13.5
2.0	10.1
2.5	8.1
3.0	6.7
3.5	5.8
4.0	5.1
4.5	4.5
5.0	4.0
5.5	3.7
6.0	3.4
6.5	3.1
7.0	2.8
7.5	2.7
8.0	2.5
8.5	2.4
9.0	2.2
9.5	2.1
10.0	2.0

Figure 9-6. Speed table for the Dutchman's log, marks 33.8 feet apart.

On vessels 33.8 feet or more in length, greater accuracy can be obtained by making the distance between the marks on deck some multiple of 16.9 feet. A slight error in time will have less effect on the accuracy of your speed measurement if the marks are farther apart. Figure 9-6 gives the speed in knots a vessel is making for any number of seconds and half

seconds between 1 and 10 for a vessel big enough to accommodate marks on deck 33.8 feet apart.

Figure 9-5 gives speeds only up to 10 knots. That is about as fast as any small fishing or cruising boat is going to go. The Dutchman's log is not intended for short-range, high-speed boats. Figure 9-6 gives speeds ranging between 2.0 knots and 20.2 knots. This range more than covers the probable cruising speeds of larger yachts or commercial vessels.

Close inspection of the tables in Figures 9-5 and 9-6 will indicate that the Dutchman's log is best used for speeds under 9 knots. A graph of the information in these two tables will show you even more vividly what I mean. See Figures 9-7 and 9-8. Let me digress here a moment and beg you not to let things like graphs frighten you. Graphs are not devices to be used only by mathematicians; they are truly useful to the average person. So get a grip on yourself and study the graphs. From the curve graphed in Figure 9-7 and the curve graphed in Figure 9-8, it is apparent that a very little change in time, just a fraction of a second, represents a change of speed of several knots at a speed above 9 knots.

A graph of the information appearing in Figures 9-5 and 9-6 is more useful than the tabulated information for at least one reason. As you use the Dutchman's log to gauge your boat's speed, you will find you almost never stop your stopwatch on an even second or an even half second. How would you use the table in Figure 9-6 if the time required for the two marks on deck to pass the wood chip is 2.8 seconds? You may get usable results from interpolation, but if you consult the graph in Figure 9-8, you can read the results directly from the graph —

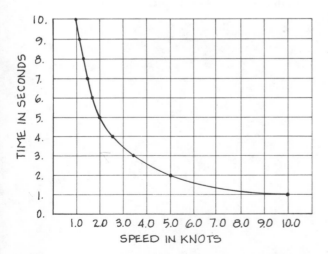

Figure 9-7. Time-speed curve for the Dutchman's log, marks 16.9 feet apart.

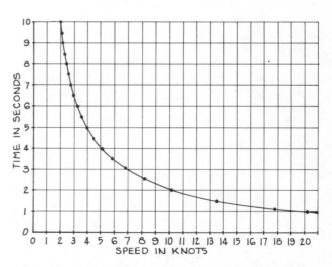

Figure 9-8. Time-speed curve for the Dutchman's log, marks 33.8 feet apart.

your boat is making 7.1 knots. Because of this ease in reading, graphs are much better than tables.

If your boat has no marks on deck, and you have no way of laying out any such marks, the length of the boat can be used as the unit of measurement. This is the system I use often in *Li'l Tiger*, because we do not have our deck marked for the Dutchman's log. We used the length of the boat, with excellent results, in *Asperida II* during our transatlantic passage after a shark ate our last taffrail log rotor. To make this work, you must know the precise length of your boat. This is the horizontal distance between the stem and the stern. On boats with bowsprits, it may be a problem to locate exactly where the stem begins, but it should not be too difficult. To find the boat's speed, have someone throw a chip overboard ahead and to leeward. At the instant the chip is abeam at the stem sing out "mark" and start the stopwatch or the second count. At the instant the chip is abeam at the stern stop the stopwatch or count. Note the number of seconds it took the chip to pass from stem to stern. Divide these seconds into the length of the boat and multiply the dividend by .5921. The product is your speed in knots.

The figure .5921 is arrived at by the formula $\frac{S}{1} : \frac{3600}{6080}$. S is the speed of the vessel in knots, 1 is the speed of the vessel in feet per second, 3,600 is the number of seconds in an hour, and 6,080 is the number of feet in a mile. All this ratio says is that, if you are making one knot, you are also making one foot every 0.5921 seconds. Thus, if you are making two knots, you are making one foot each .5921 ÷ 2 seconds.

All this impressive arithmetic is for those of you who want to understand how these rules of thumb are derived. If you are like a lot of your fellows, who are mainly interested in getting the job done and leaving the "higher mathematics" to others, all you need do is find the speed of your boat in feet per second, and multiply this speed in feet per second by .5921 to get the speed in knots. Here is an example of how this works: My sloop *Li'l Tiger* is 22 feet, 3 inches overall. I estimate a point 3 inches abaft the leading edge of the stem so I can limit my figures to an even 22 feet. To get my speed, I have someone toss a chip off the bow. As the chip passes the bow he or she sings out "mark." I start my stopwatch. When the chip is abeam at the transom I stop my stopwatch. Assume the watch reads 2.5 seconds. I divide 2.5 seconds into 22 feet. *Li'l Tiger* is making 8.9 feet per second. I multiply 8.9 by .5921, and find *Li'l Tiger* is making 5.36 knots.

You could round off .5921 to .6, and you would not introduce serious error in a boat that is not moving too fast. But rules of thumb are only approximate at best, because the measurements of the bearings of the chip when abeam at the bow and when abeam at the stern are approximate. If you are not rushed, take the extra minute to work out the .5921 factor so as to at least make this part of the solution as accurate as possible. On the other hand, if you are busy as any ten guys should be feeling your way along at night in a fog, you might have to shorten your computations. Perhaps the bow lookout sings out: "Piling in the water on the port bow! Hold her steady, and she will pass close but clear." This is the time to tell him, "Give me a mark when that piling is abeam at the stem." Get the time it takes the length of the boat to pass the piling. Find her speed in feet per second. Multiply this by .6, and you will have a much better indication of her true speed than the best educated guess could give you.

10 AIDS TO NAVIGATION AND LANDMARKS

I mentioned buoys, beacons and lights in Chapter 1 as if they are very familiar things. To most of us who go to sea, or ply the inland waters and rivers, buoys, beacons, and lights are old friends. Yet it is nothing short of amazing how little many otherwise competent amateur and professional boatmen know about these lights, beacons, and buoys they take for granted.

Bowditch defines piloting as, "navigation involving frequent or continuous determination of position or a line of position relative to *geographical points*, to a high order of accuracy." The key words in this definition are *geographical points*. The italics are mine. In everyday language we call these geographical points *landmarks,* which can be anything from the silo next to somebody's barn to the pine snag at the mouth of 'Possum Creek. Landmarks may also be devices, objects, or structures placed or built in certain locations for the express purpose of assisting the navigator. It stands to reason that, if natural objects, such as the pine snag above, work so well, man-made objects placed or erected in the most advantageous places possible, for the prime purpose of aiding the navigator, should work even better. These man-made landmarks are called *aids to navigation.* Natural objects, used by the navigator to assist him in piloting his vessel, are *landmarks* in the mariner's vernacular.

Aids to navigation in the United States and U. S. territories are established and maintained by the United States Coast Guard. In addition the Commandant of the Coast Guard may give permission to individuals or groups to establish private aids to navigation. Such private aids must never be established without this prior approval of the Commandant of the Coast Guard. Once established, private aids must be maintained by the party who put them there, and they cannot be removed without permission of the Commandant. Such private aids

may vary in purpose from the race course markers put out by the local yacht club, fish haven markers put there by the state department of conservation, or the privately maintained channel markers into your friendly marina operator's place of business. (Fish havens, by the way, are artificial reefs.) When charted, any of these aids will carry the note on the chart "privately maintained."

Aids to navigation consist of such things as the major lights and lightships along our seacoasts; secondary lights, which sailors call beacons; lighted buoys; unlighted buoys; unlighted fixed aids, which sailors call daybeacons; river and harbor lights; and other lights as well as radiobeacons and loran stations. A special chapter on radio navigation will cover loran and radiobeacons. Except as necessary to avoid ambiguities, I will devote this chapter to talking about those aids to navigation that depend on visual or sound-producing features to give us at least part of the information they can supply. Many of the aids you will use may also have electronic aids associated with them.

The most familiar aids to navigation are the major lighthouses, lightships, and large navigation buoys. As you cruise along the Gulf Coast, you will see several lighthouses. You will also see almost every other aid to navigation available to the mariner. These aids are typical of the aids to navigation you will find in federal waters of the United States anywhere. So what I am going to tell you here applies equally well, in principle, to your own home waters, whether you live in Gulfport, Mississippi, Seattle, Washington, or Camden, Maine.

At the mouths of the several passes in from the Gulf of Mexico are buoys marking the entrances and outlining the channels that will take you to port. As you proceed into more sheltered waters, these buoys may be replaced by the lighted fixed structures, called by the mariner *beacons,* and these in turn give way to the unlighted buoys and daybeacons of the secondary channels. Somewhere along the way you are certain to cross or even cruise along the Intracoastal Waterway and use the aids to navigation marking this vital artery. Let's take a hard look at each of these aids. As a seaman and navigator they are your best friends. Learn to know them well. From the largest and most important lighthouse to the smallest, and yet very important, unlighted buoy or daybeacon, these aids may have distinctive colors, shapes, lights, numbers, or other markings to help you see them and know their purpose.

Coming from seaward or coasting along your passage to Gulfport in *War Hat*, the first aids you encounter will be the major lights at the entrances to harbors you seek, or those that mark prominent headlands or other major features of interest to the navigator. On the passage from Panama City to Gulfport, you will see Pensacola Light, Mobile Point Light, and Ship Island Light. Each of these aids are designated as primary seacoast aids.

LIGHTS

Every lighted aid will have a light that displays a special color and a special time sequence to make it identifiable among other lights in the vicinity. This combination of color and light timing is a light's *characteristic*. A complete description of the characteristic of any lighted aid can be found in the *Light List* volume covering the stretch of coast the light is established on. For the part of the Gulf Coast you are cruising in *War Hat*, you must use *Light List* Volume II, CG-160. Volume II of the *Light List* covers the Atlantic Coast from Little River, South Carolina to the south, and the Gulf Coast from the Straits of Florida to the Rio Grande, as well as the United States possessions in the West Indies. Before attempting any coastal passage you should have the current issue of the correct volume of the *Light List* on board, but having it on board will do you no good unless it is read and studied carefully. Especially study the general information section in the front of the volume. Then thumb through each additional section until you become familiar enough with its arrangement to look up any information you want without a lot of rustling and tearing of pages. Become familiar with this publication *before* you cast off. Midnight, off a sea-swept bar, in bad weather, is no place to become introduced to the *Light List*. You can get pretty frantic asking yourself if the light you see is the one you should steer for. Or does that light mark Boneyard Shoal?

Your chart will also give you the characteristics of all aids to navigation in the area the chart is intended to cover. The *Light List*, however, is your most comprehensive source of information concerning aids to navigation. The charts will give the characteristics of lighted aids, and the shape, color, and type of both lighted and unlighted aids, but for the most detailed description of any aid, whether lighted or unlighted, consult your *Light List*.

So you are standing off a bar on a dark and stormy night. You are trying to tell which light you should steer for. How can you tell which light is the one marking the shoal, and which light marks the entrance to the channel? Your landlubber companion describes them both as "blinking." But look at these two lights carefully. They are not blinking the same blink! Each of these lights has a different *characteristic*. To use the terms of your landsman friend, each light "blinks" at a different time interval, and during these intervals the times the light is on or dark during a given cycle of the sequence may vary. With this information, if you know precisely the characteristic of each of these lights, it is easy to tell which light you must avoid, and which light you must steer for.

Just what are these differences in characteristic a light may have? Of the two lights marking your imaginary shoal and entrance, one may have a steady flash, and the other may have a quick, interrupted flash. Then in on the headland there may be a light showing a light on for long periods followed by shorter periods of darkness. And here you are on a dark and stormy night trying to find your way in over the bar. It can be awfully confusing unless you know what all this means, and again, if you do know precisely what each of these different characteristics means, and how it is described, you can identify each of the lights.

In your *Light List* and on your charts you will find lights described as fixed, flashing, quick flashing, occulting, and such other descriptions as group flashing, group occulting, or equal interval. Each of these terms has a definite meaning. The Coast Guard published a booklet, *Marine Aids to Navigation, CG-193*, which is yours free for the asking. You can write off for it (see the list of addresses in Chapter 3), but better yet, visit your local Coast Guard unit. They are good folks for the sailor to know. CG-193 describes each of these light characteristics and gives a whole boat load of other good information about aids to navigation. But it is a good idea to see for ourselves, right here, what each of these terms means (see Figure 10-1).

Fixed lights are just that. A fixed light burns continually at an even stage of illumination.

Flashing lights flash at regular intervals. These

Illustration	Symbols and meaning		Phase description
	Lights which do not change color	Lights which show color variations	
	F.= Fixed...	Alt.= Alternating.	A continuous steady light.
	F.Fl.=Fixed and flashing	Alt. F.Fl.= Alternating fixed and flashing.	A fixed light varied at regular intervals by a flash of greater brilliance.
	F.Gp.Fl. = Fixed and group flashing.	Alt. F.Gp.Fl = Alternating fixed and group flashing.	A fixed light varied at regular intervals by groups of 2 or more flashes of greater brilliance.
SHOWS NOT MORE THAN 30 FLASHES PER MINUTE	Fl.=Flashing	Alt.Fl.= Alternating flashing.	Showing a single flash at regular intervals, the duration of light always being less than the duration of darkness.
	Gp. Fl. = Group flashing.	Alt.Gp.Fl.= Alternating group flashing.	Showing at regular intervals groups of 2 or more flashes
	Gp.Fl.(1+2) = Composite group flashing.	....	Light flashes are combined in alternate groups of different numbers.
	Mo.(A) = Morse Code.	....	Light in which flashes of different duration are grouped in such a manner as to produce a Morse character or characters.
	Qk. Fl. = Quick Flashing.	....	Shows not less than 60 flashes per minute.
	I.Qk. Fl. = Interrupted quick flashing.	....	Shows quick flashes for about 5 seconds, followed by a dark period of about 5 seconds.
	E.Int.= Equal interval. (Isophase)	....	Light with all durations of light and darkness equal.
	Occ.=Occulting.	Alt.Occ. = Alternating occulting.	A light totally eclipsed at regular intervals, the duration of light always greater than the duration of darkness
	Gp. Occ. = Group Occulting.	....	A light with a group of 2 or more eclipses at regular intervals
	Gp.Occ.(2+3) = Composite group occulting.	....	A light in which the occultations are combined in alternate groups of different numbers.

Light colors used and abbreviations: W = white, R = red, G = green.

Figure 10-1. Light phase characteristics.

intervals do not exceed thirty flashes a minute. The time during which the light is on, illuminated, is less than the time the light is off, dark. A flashing light may mark any aid except a fairway buoy or fairway beacon, junction buoy or junction beacon, or an obstruction buoy or obstruction beacon.

Quick flashing lights are lights that flash more than sixty times a minute. A quick flashing light means: "Look alive, Sailor!" because quick flashing lights mark sharp turns or sudden constrictions in a channel. Front range lights may also be quick flashing lights.

Interrupted quick flashing lights also flash at a rate of over sixty flashes a minute for about five seconds followed by a period of darkness of about five seconds. Interrupted quick flashing lights mark junctions in a channel. They may also mark wrecks or obstructions.

A light flashing the Morse code *dot dash*, the Morse code symbol for "A", marks the center of a channel or fairway.

Occulting lights can be described as just the opposite of flashing lights in that the period the light is on, illuminated, is longer than the period the light is off, dark, in a characteristic sequence. You may find occulting lights on primary seacoast aids, secondary lights, or the after lights of ranges.

The light phase of an *equal interval light* is just that. The period the light is on is equal to the period the light is off. Perhaps the time sequence of equal interval lights may be: on six seconds followed by off six seconds. This may vary as necessary to distinguish the light.

Composite lights combine two or more of the several types of illumination periods into a distinct characteristic for a particular light.

These are the main light phase characteristics of lights, though you may see others. In areas where many different lights can cause confusion, you will see all these characteristics displayed on the different lights, so each will have its distinctive identification characteristic. To identify a given light, you must time the light's characteristic with a stopwatch, unless you have mastered the art of counting seconds. Even then a stopwatch is better. Thus order is brought out of chaos. It is a real thrill and sense of accomplishment to be able to conduct your vessel through a crowded, complicated waterway of many channels, with complete confidence, because you know how to use your *Light List* and can identify those lights that show you your route.

Look back at Figure 8-3, which is a cut-out of Chart No. 1267. This chart shows the Pascagoula ship channel from the seabuoy to the harbor. Look

at it carefully. An abbreviated description of each aid in the area covered by this excerpt appears alongside the aid. For instance buoy number 1 of the Pascagoula ship channel is "FL G, 4 sec," which means that buoy number 1 flashes a green light every four seconds. You will find flashing lights, quick flashing lights, interrupted quick flashing lights, and equal interval lights. Each of these lights will have a specific time phase, as described above, and each light will also have a specific color phase.

THE COLOR OF LIGHTS

The color of lights on aids to navigation will be green, red, or white. Green lights will always be on black aids, or aids that are considered as black aids. Later in this chapter you will see that the colors of the aids themselves are important. Red lights are on aids having red as the significant color. White lights may be on either black or red aids, hence the color white has no significance. White lights may be found on black buoys or beacons or on red buoys or beacons. Lights of colors other than green, red, or white may be found on buoys or structures not associated with the system the Coast Guard uses to mark channels or obstructions.

PRIMARY SEACOAST AIDS

These are the major aids to navigation, represented predominantly by the familiar lighthouses. Lighthouses come in a variety of shapes and colors. The shape of a lighthouse is determined by the design requirements needed to make it stand the ravages of the sea and weather at its location. The color of a major lighthouse is chosen to make the lighthouse stand out from the background. The color of the light in a lighthouse is white, but the light may have a colored sector. This colored sector is visible to vessels approaching from the arc of the compass covered by the sector. An example of this is the red sector used to warn the navigator who can see it that he is standing into danger. The red sector of such a light will have the same time phase as the white sector.

Your *Light List* and your chart indicate the height of a light. This listed or charted height is the height above mean *high* water of the center of the *light source,* the light in the lighthouse, and not the top of the roof or other structural feature that may extend above the light itself. You will see the importance of this when you study the use of the sextant to compute distances off a lighthouse by vertical sextant angles.

Lightships and large navigation buoys serve the same purpose as lighthouses. These primary seacoast aids are placed in locations where the construction of a fixed structure is not feasible.

Figure 10-2. Two primary seacoast aids. Mobile Point Light at the entrance to Mobile Bay is on the left. Pensacola Light at the entrance to Pensacola Bay is on the right.

BUOYS

The simplest aid to navigation the average boatman will encounter is the small buoy marking a channel into some minor harbor. Such a buoy will most likely be unlighted, but it will have a very definite color and shape. It will have a reflector on it, which will reflect the beam of your searchlight, to help you spot the buoy at night. The color of the reflector will be the same color as a colored light on the buoy would be.

All buoys are not simple unlighted buoys. On the larger, more traveled waterways, buoys will be lighted, equipped with radar reflectors, and, in some cases, sound-producing devices. The lighted buoys will be of a specific color, and they will show a light of a particular color or a white light. There may be unlighted buoys even on the most important channels. The unlighted buoys will have a specific color or specific shape, and they will be equipped with colored reflectors as described.

What do all these shapes, colors of the buoys, colors of their lights, and reflectors mean? Why are these colors and shapes so important? Because buoys in the United States are established according to a system known as the *lateral system*. In the lateral system, channels, natural or man-made, are marked by a series of buoys or other aids along each side as necessary to guide the mariner. For the right-hand or starboard side of a channel, one shape and color is

used. For the left-hand or port side of the channel, another shape or color is used. For certain purposes, buoys or other aids may be of more than one color. To determine which side of the channel is to be considered the right or starboard side, or the port or left side, requires an arbitrary designation. After all, when you are heading to sea, one side of a channel is on your starboard hand, and when you are standing in, the opposite side of the channel is on your star-

Figure 10-3. Reefed down and standing out. Sand Island Light is ahead on the starboard bow.

Figure 10-4. The fairway or seabuoy at the entrance to Horn Island Pass, Pascagoula Ship Channel.

board hand. In the lateral system the sides of the channel are reckoned as to port or starboard side according to which side is on what hand *standing in from seaward.* Let's see how buoys are shaped, lighted, and colored in the lateral system.

The best way to understand buoys is to study them in place. We are going to move ahead in our passage along the coast for now, and assume our schooner *War Hat* is off Petit Bois Island, Chart No. 1267. You decide you want to make a call at Pascagoula, Mississippi. You set your course for the seabuoy.

The first buoy you see will be the seabuoy or fairway buoy. See Figure 8-3. This buoy is a black and white *vertically* striped buoy. It could be of any shape buoys come in, since, for fairway buoys, shape is not important. Fairway buoys may be nuns, cans, or towers; the seabuoy marking the entrance to Horn Island Pass is a tower buoy. The color of this buoy *is* important. The Pascagoula seabuoy or Horn Island Pass entrance buoy — call it by either name and anyone in those waters will know what you mean — is not numbered, but is marked with the letters HIP for Horn Island Pass. It is lighted, and flashes continuously with one short and one long flash, the Morse code symbol for "A". The Morse code letter "A" tells you right away the buoy is a fairway buoy. The color of this light is white; it is so marked on your chart. In all cases where the chart or the *Light List* do *not* give the color of a light described, the color of that light will be white. Notice how the chart

(Figure 8-3) describes this buoy: "Mo A, HIP, BW." These abbreviated notations tell you that the Horn Island Pass seabuoy is a fairway buoy.

Black and white buoys should always be passed close aboard. You may safely pass them on either side. Remember, though, all buoys are held in place by a chain or cable attached to their anchor on the bottom. Be sure to hold off enough to avoid fouling this chain or cable.

It is important to note that every entrance buoy is not a fairway buoy. The entrance buoys at Pensacola, Chart No. 1265; Mobile, Chart No. 1266; and Gulfport, Chart No. 1267 are not fairway buoys.

The Pascagoula ship channel (Figure 8-3) is a typical channel, marked according to the lateral system. You can see on the chart that, as you stand in, you will pass black buoys on your port hand, and you will pass red buoys on your starboard hand. In the lateral system, *red* buoys mark the right hand or *starboard* side of the channel *standing in.* These red buoys may be tower buoys, sometimes called structure buoys, or nun buoys.

Sailors tend to look first at buoys and aids to navigation according to their colors. So let's take a hard look at these red buoys.

Red nun buoys mark the starboard side of the channel when entering the channel from seaward. A nun buoy is one that looks like a truncated cone, floating tapered end up. A truncated cone is a cone with its point cut off. To an imaginative

Figure 10-5. A red nun buoy.

Figure 10-6. A red tower buoy. Even though this photograph is in black and white, you can tell the buoy is a red aid and marks the starboard side of the channel standing in because of the number "4".

sailor, the silhouette of such a buoy looks like a nun standing on the water. This special shape of a nun buoy indicates it is a buoy to be passed on your starboard hand. Pass this buoy on *its* port side. Figure 10-5 is a picture of a typical nun buoy.

As a marker of the starboard side of a channel, standing in, a nun buoy will be painted red. You can remember this by the three R's: Not 'reading, 'riting, and 'rithmatic, but *red right returning*. The reflector on a nun buoy will be red. Nun buoys are usually unlighted. This reflector aids you in seeing the buoy in the beam of your searchlight.

Lighted red buoys are tower structures on a float. At the top of the tower is a lantern. Tower buoys marking the starboard side of the channel are always painted red. Here the shape of the buoy is not significant. The light on the buoy will be red or white, and may be fixed, flashing, quick flashing, or occulting, depending on the exact purpose the buoy serves in marking the channel. The light will normally be a flashing light rather than a fixed light where the option is open, as flashing lights are easier to pick out if other lights are in the background. If this red buoy also marks a turn in the channel or a place where the channel is suddenly reduced in width, the light will be a quick flashing light. Figure 10-6 shows a red tower buoy.

In the lateral system, buoys are also numbered. The numbers begin at the seaward end of the channel and increase as you stand in. Buoys on the starboard side of the channel standing in (red buoys) are always evenly numbered. Thus, your red nun buoy or red tower buoy may be numbered 2, 4, 6, 8, 108, 208, or any other number divisible by two. The numbers are in sequence, but some numbers may be left out of the sequence. So if you pass buoy number 20 and then pass a string of buoys on the port side of the channel, with no red buoys opposite them, the next red buoy you pass may be number 26, 28, or higher, depending on the number of buoys in between to port.

Sometimes buoys will carry a number followed by the letter *A, B, C,* and so on. If you pass a red buoy numbered 22, and then pass another red buoy marked number 22A, this would mean buoy number 22A had been placed between buoys 22 and 24 to meet some need after buoys 22 and 24 had been established.

Black buoys are ones that mark the *port* side of the channel when returning from sea. Black buoys may be cans or towers.

Can buoys mark the left, or port, side of the channel when returning from sea. The can shape is significant, as a buoy so shaped must always be passed on your port hand to keep the channel. Can buoys look like their namesakes — big cans or drums, floating on end. When used to mark the port side of the

Figure 10-7. A black can buoy.

Figure 10-8. A lighted, black tower buoy.

channel, can buoys are painted black. They are usually unlighted but will carry a green reflector. No one has yet come up with a black reflector.

If lighted, a black buoy will be in the shape of a tower and will carry a green or white light. As in the case of red tower buoys, the light may be fixed, flashing, quick flashing, or occulting. If this buoy is one of many along the port side of a channel marking a reach, the light on the buoy will be fixed or flashing. If the buoy marks a turn in the channel or a sudden narrowing, the light will be quick flashing.

Black buoys marking the port side of the channel are *odd* numbered. The numbers begin at the seaward end of the channel as they do for red buoys. The first black buoy you encounter to port as you enter the Pascagoula ship channel, or any channel, will be buoy number 1. As you proceed into Mississippi Sound you will pass buoys numbered 3, 5, 7, 9, 11, and so on to the upper end of the channel. If there is a reach in the channel requiring more red buoys to starboard than black buoys to port, numbers may be omitted in the sequence. Thus, if between buoys number 37 and where buoy number 39 would normally be, there is a run of red buoys to starboard numbered 38, 40, 42, 44, 46, 48, and 50, with no opposite black buoys, the next black buoy you see may well be buoy number 49. If the number of buoys in a waterway is such as to cause the buoy numbers to become too large, the numbering will start over at some logical point. You may follow a series of buoys numbered up to a certain number, and then pick up

buoy number 1 to port and number 2 to starboard. This usually occurs at an intersection with another waterway or at some natural feature in the waterway. Thus, if you are coming up Mobile Bay, you would see buoy number 1 at the entrance from the Gulf of Mexico. If you continued up Mobile Bay and Mobile River to the mouth of the Alabama River, you would find the first aid to port to be number 1 and the first aid to starboard to be number 2 proceeding up the Alabama River.

As in the case of red buoys, you may also find in a channel black buoys numbered 21A, 21B, or 21C, and so on. This means buoys 21A or 21B or 21C were placed after buoys 21 and 23 were established. You will find buoys marked in this manner, with a number and a letter, in places where shifting bars and shoals make it necessary to place and then remove buoys frequently.

Red and black *horizontally* striped buoys mark junctions in a channel. They are also used to mark wrecks or other obstructions, either in a channel or in open water. Sailors speak of these buoys as "wreck buoys" or "junction buoys" according to how they are used. Red and black horizontally striped buoys are integrated into the lateral system. If unlighted, a

Figure 10-9. A red and black can buoy. Though the buoy retains the shape of a can, it has a radar-reflecting device on the top portion. The top band of color is black; if this buoy were a nun, the top band would be red. This buoy is unlighted, but the green light-reflecting squares on the radar reflector let the pilot know that it is to be kept to port, in the main channel, standing in.

Figure 10-10. A red and black tower buoy. The absence of a number indicates this is a wreck or junction buoy.

red and black buoy may be a nun buoy or a can buoy, depending on which side the buoy should be passed to keep in the main channel if the buoy marks a junction, and to indicate where the best water lies if the buoy is a wreck buoy.

If a red and black buoy is lighted, it will be a tower buoy. The light on the buoy will be an interrupted quick flashing light.

A red and black nun buoy will have a red band as the top stripe. This red top stripe or band and the nun shape indicate that this buoy, as a junction buoy, is to be regarded as a red buoy in relation to the primary channel. If the buoy is a wreck or obstruction buoy, the nun shape and red topmost stripe indicate the buoy is best passed on your starboard hand.

If the buoy is a red and black can buoy, the topmost stripe will be black. Here, the buoy, as a junction buoy, should be considered a black can buoy as regards the primary channel. If the buoy marks an obstruction, the black band and can shape indicate the best water lies to starboard of the buoy.

If the buoy is a red and black tower buoy, a red stripe at the top will indicate the buoy should be passed on your starboard hand to follow the main channel, or to find the best water. If the red and black tower buoy has a black stripe as the topmost stripe, the buoy should be passed on your port hand to keep the main channel, or find the best water.

How do you determine "returning from seaward"

in cases such as this? Suppose the obstruction buoy lies out of any marked channel. The best action here is to consult your chart. You will find some consistency in the system in that, if the buoy is in the approaches to a marked channel, the markings of the buoy will tend to follow the rules governing port and starboard for that channel. Don't take any chances though. Look at your chart!

Red and black horizontally striped buoys are never numbered. They may or may not be lettered, depending on their proximity to other red and black buoys.

Any buoy should always be used in close consultation with your charts. This is particularly true of junction buoys and obstruction buoys.

Almost all buoys today are fitted with radar reflectors. Even can and nun buoys are so equipped in most cases. In addition, lighted tower buoys may be fitted with some type of sound-producing device. These devices may be actuated by the motion of the buoy in the seaway, or they may be electrically actuated. There are several types of these sound-producing buoys.

A whistle buoy works from air compressed in the whistle as the buoy rises and falls with the sea. The seabuoy off Mobile Bay is a whistle buoy. See Figure

Figure 10-11. The seabuoy off Mobile Bay Entrance. The large whistle, actuated by air compressed when the buoy rises and falls in the sea, can be seen clearly in the center of the tower structure. You can hear this whistle five miles away on a still night, if enough sea swell is running. Notice, too, the wake from the current at the waterline of the buoy. Currents at this point may exceed four or five knots under some conditions.

63

10-11. The sound this buoy makes is exactly the same as the noise made by a lovesick bull. You can hear this buoy for miles on still nights, or when a heavy sea is running off the bar. The oldtimers on Dauphin Island swear that in the great hurricane of 1906 the seabuoy whistled so loudly all the cows on Dauphin Island swam out to sea and drowned.* Years ago my friends and I used to cruise the waters near the mouth of Mobile Bay in my open catboat. Many nights we slept rolled up in a blanket on the south beach of Dauphin Island. Our greatest hazard was a visit from one of the wild bulls that ranged this island. Dauphin Island is a modern, civilized resort now, but in those days the south beach of Dauphin Island was a wild and woolly place, where prudence was always the better part of valor. When one of these wild boy cows came bellowing down the beach in the middle of the night, we made a hurried retreat by swimming out to the boat. The sharks that came into the Bay after dark were much less to be feared. This doggone whistle buoy was often the cause of a cold night swim. When a wind shift caused the sound of this buoy to be carried in to us, we would awake with a start and scramble for the anchored boat, thinking we were about to have company.

Bell buoys have large bells which are rung by the motion of the buoy in the sea. Some bell buoys have electrically operated hammers to strike the bell. In addition to whistle buoys and bell buoys, there are gong buoys, horn buoys, and other types of sound-producing buoys.

All sound buoys are designed to help the navigator find them, and identify them in periods of low visibility. When navigating in periods of low visibility, remember that no buoy makes enough noise to be heard through the ports and bulkheads of a tightly closed wheelhouse, or over the roar of a hooked up engine. At such times you should be running dead slow or stopped. And, if you can't muster the courage to go out on a cold, wet deck, at least open a port and listen carefully. After all, swimming is likely to be wetter and colder than standing on any deck.

A word of caution about all buoys is in order here. No matter how confident you may be, never rely on one single buoy for the safety of your ship. If fixed landmarks are available, always use these fixed landmarks to find your vessel's position. Buoys lead a hard life. To begin with, they are often put in places where the ravages of wind and weather make the placing of fixed structures unfeasible. Storms

*This legend was passed on to me by Julian Lee Rayford, in my opinion one of the nation's and South Alabama's great chroniclers.

blow buoys off station. They get rammed, sunk, and dragged around by the very boats and ships they are put there to serve. Never pass any buoy too close aboard. Often a buoy may be anchored on the shelf or shoal it marks, because the good water nearby is too deep for its sinker and chain. Buoys and fixed aids may be set many feet from the banks of a channel. Consult your chart for actual channel widths. Measure the distance between the aids, across the channel, and compare the difference. In the middle reach of the Mobile ship channel, the channel is 400 feet wide. The distance across the channel between the beacons and buoys is 600 feet.

SPECIAL-PURPOSE BUOYS
Special-purpose buoys are not part of the lateral system of buoyage. Special-purpose buoys are used to mark quarantine areas, anchorages, fish net areas, or any other location in which traffic must be restricted, controlled, or even prohibited. These buoys are marked according to the particular purpose they serve.

Anchorage buoys mark approved anchorage areas and are white. Quarantine buoys mark quarantine anchorages and are yellow. Fish net buoys mark fish net areas and are black and white with *horizontal* stripes. Please don't mistake these buoys for the vertically striped, black and white fairway buoys. A mistake like this could make you the owner of a torn up fish net you did not want, it could ruin your cruise, and it could also make the owner of the net remember you in his prayers. He will ask the Good Lord to please keep you on the beach from now on.

White buoys with a green top mark areas where dredging or surveying is being done. Orange and white *horizontally* striped buoys are special-purpose buoys used to mark areas set aside for uses not designated above, such as fish haven buoys.

Orange and white *vertically* striped buoys mark areas set aside for seaplane use. Please don't mistake these buoys for the horizontally striped buoys which may be marking your favorite artificial reef. If you are fishing in a marked area and some guy is buzzing you in a float plane, check which way the stripes run, up and down or crossways. And don't think seaplanes are out of date. They are used every day in great numbers, along any coast with an offshore oil or fishing industry.

BUOYS IN THE INTRACOASTAL WATERWAY
All aids in the Intracoastal Waterway will have some part of their color scheme in yellow. If you are cruising along and you see a buoy, or any other aid to navigation, that has the color yellow on it along with

Figure 10-12. A red nun buoy in the Intracoastal Waterway. Except for the yellow band just above the number 74A, this buoy is shaped, colored, and numbered as any other buoy in the lateral system.

its other more familiar colors, you will know right away that this aid marks a part of the ICW. Buoys will have a yellow band on them, unless they are dual-purpose buoys, which are buoys used to mark two separate channels or waterways. Figure 10-12 shows a typical buoy in the Intracoastal Waterway; this buoy is *not* a dual-purpose buoy. This buoy does not serve to mark two different channels that happen to run in coincidence along the reach the buoy is in. So this buoy must be kept to starboard as any other red nun buoy would be while standing in.

As the lateral system requires red buoys to be kept to starboard and black buoys to be kept to port when returning from sea, it is necessary to designate which direction of travel in the Intracoastal Waterway shall be considered as returning from sea, or "standing in" as the sailors say. The Intracoastal Waterway starts and ends in protected waters. You are never really returning from the open sea. The Intracoastal Waterway begins at Manasquan Inlet in New Jersey and ends at the Mexican border at Brownsville, Texas. For the purpose of determining "entering from seaward" or " standing in," any course in the Intracoastal Waterway that will take your vessel farther away from Manasquan Inlet and closer to Brownsville, Texas, is considered to be returning from sea. Thus, if you are steering a course that will ultimately take you south along the Atlantic Coast and west along the Gulf Coast, red buoys with a yellow band must be kept on your starboard hand, and black buoys with a yellow band must be kept to port. If

you happen to make a hairpin turn along the way down the Atlantic Coast and find yourself heading in a northerly direction for awhile, the rule still applies because your ultimate course made good would carry you south and away from Manasquan Inlet. The same applies along the west coast of Florida. Along the west coast of Florida, the Intracoastal Waterway runs in a northerly direction, but boats heading north in this stretch of the ICW get closer to Brownsville. Their ultimate direction will be westerly.

DUAL-PURPOSE BUOYS IN THE INTRACOASTAL WATERWAY

Let's go back to Chapter 1. When you were making your departure from Panama City, you passed several buoys in the upper reaches of the main ship channel which were dual-purpose buoys. These buoys marked the starboard side of the main ship channel for vessels standing in from the Gulf of Mexico to call at Panama City. These same buoys marked the *port* side of the Intracoastal Waterway for vessels "standing in" in the ICW. Yet each of these buoys is in absolute accord with the plan of the lateral system. This is quite a feat, isn't it? How in the world is it done? I explained briefly how this was accomplished in Chapter 1. A closer look now would be in order.

If you study Chart No. 1263 with the St. Andrews

Figure 10-13. A dual-purpose buoy in the main ship channel at Panama City, Florida. This is a black buoy, but the yellow square to the left of the 9, partially obscured by things that sometimes obscure marks on aids to navigation, tells the mariner this buoy is also an aid to navigation in the ICW and must be considered a black buoy in the ICW.

Figure 10-14. A black can buoy in the main ship channel at Panama City, Florida. The number 21 indicates that the buoy is a black aid in the main channel, but, if you look very closely, you will see, just above the number 21, a small yellow triangle, which indicates the buoy is also a mark in the ICW. That the yellow object is a triangle indicates this buoy must be taken as a "red" buoy by vessels transiting the ICW. Coincidentally, this buoy also shows the ravages of its service, which gives credence to what has been said earlier about buoys leading hard lives.

Across the same reach of the channel is *red* buoy number 20. Our westbound boat in the Intracoastal Waterway is keeping this buoy on her *port* hand. Her pilot knows he must do this because this red buoy is marked with a yellow square, which indicates that this buoy should be considered a black buoy by vessels following the Intracoastal Waterway.

This dual system of marking holds even in cases where the direction of travel, returning from sea, in the Intracoastal Waterway and the main channel does not conflict. Look at Figure 7-8 again. Had your boat turned left after clearing the bar above Courtney Point while coming in from the Gulf, she would pass buoy number 5 on her port hand and buoy number 6 on her starboard hand. Our westbound boat in the Intracoastal Waterway would do exactly the same. Here the ICW and the main ship channel run in the same direction as far as entering from the sea is concerned. But the dual marking system is still followed. Red buoy number 6 will also have a yellow triangle on it; black buoy number 5 will have a yellow square on it. This way the pilot of the westbound boat can be absolutely sure he is passing these buoys correctly.

Bay area in mind, you will find that buoys numbered 15 through 25 are dual-purpose buoys. Look back at Figure 7-8. These buoys mark the channel from the Gulf into Panama City, and they also mark the Intracoastal Waterway. The color, shape, and numbers on these buoys will conform to the needs of the main ship channel under the lateral system. A ship coming in from the Gulf in the main ship channel must keep these black buoys, numbered 15 through 25, and any other black buoys in the channel, on her port side. Her course will be in an easterly direction. There is no problem here.

The conflict comes when a boat is westbound in the Intracoastal Waterway; this boat must keep these *black* buoys to *starboard!* Yet, as a westbound boat in the Intracoastal Waterway, she is considered to be entering from the sea. How does her pilot know what to do?

The answer is one that serves any sailor well: "Look alive!" Give these black buoys on your starboard hand a close look. Each one of these black buoys will have a yellow triangle on it. This yellow *triangle* indicates these black buoys should be considered as *red* buoys by boats following the Intracoastal Waterway. Figure 10-14 shows buoy number 21 at Panama City.

Figure 10-15. A black tower buoy in the main ship channel at Panama City. To the left of the number 15 is a small yellow triangle, indicating that the buoy also serves as an ICW marker. The yellow triangle tells pilots that this black buoy must be considered a red buoy by boats in the ICW.

66

BEACONS AND DAYBEACONS

The Coast Guard calls any aid to navigation that is built in place a fixed structure. This term is used to designate anything from a primary seacoast aid, such as Pensacola Light, to a board on a single piling marking the channel into the Bon Secour River (Chart No. 1266). In the jargon of the sailor, however, primary fixed structure aids are called lighthouses, and secondary structures are called beacons or daybeacons. As this work is for the everyday sailor, we will use the sailor's vernacular.

If a secondary structure has a light on it, sailors call it a beacon. Beacons serve the same purpose as lighted buoys. If the structure is unlighted, it is called a daybeacon. Daybeacons serve the same purpose as a can or nun buoy. A beacon may be an elaborate structure, distinguishable from a primary aid only by its smaller size and candlepower, or it can be anything in between down to a single piling with a battery-powered lantern on it. Beacons and daybeacons are used in places where conditions make the use of a fixed structure more feasible than the use of a buoy. The colors of beacons and the characteristics of their lights have exactly the same meaning as the colors of buoys and the characteristics of their lights. The colors of reflectors on daybeacons follow the same rules as those on unlighted buoys.

For daytime use, beacons and daybeacons have daymarks. The colors of these daymarks conform to the lateral system. A beacon or daybeacon with a black daymark indicates the port side of the channel returning from sea. One with a red daymark indicates the starboard side of the channel standing in. A daymark with red and black horizontal stripes serves precisely the same purpose as a buoy marked with red and black horizontal stripes. You may even find beacons and daybeacons with black and white vertically striped daymarks used in lieu of fairway buoys.

The shapes of daymarks on beacons and daybeacons tend to parallel the shapes of buoys in those places where the shapes of buoys are significant. The red daymark of a beacon or daybeacon marking the starboard side of a channel will be triangular in shape. The silhouette of a nun buoy suggests a triangle. The black* daymark of a beacon or daybeacon marking the port side of a channel will be square, suggesting the rectangular shape of a can buoy's silhouette. (The daymark of a "black" beacon may

*On newly established aids, or on beacons on which the daymark has been replaced, the Coast Guard is now using green daymarks in lieu of the black (or white) daymark.

Figure 10-16. The USCGC *Salvia* hard at work on a Sunday morning, placing a buoy in the ship channel at Panama City. The buoy had been blown off station by a recent violent storm, and the Coast Guard, one of the best friends the mariner has, was on the job getting displaced aids back on station, even if it would take 24 hours a day, seven days a week.

be white with a green border in cases where a black daymark would not be readily visible due to background or other causes.) The red horizontally striped daymarks tag right along in the same pattern. If the top band is red, the daymark will be triangular in shape. If the top band is black, the daymark will be rectangular in shape. Black and white vertically striped daymarks will be of a shape not easily confused with the shape of the daymarks on red or black beacons.

Whether on a lighted or unlighted structure, daymarks will have a reflective border. On square day-

Figure 10-17. A red daymark on a lighted beacon.

Figure 10-18. A black daymark on a lighted beacon.

marks, marking the port side of a channel, the color of the reflective border will be green. On a triangular daymark, marking the starboard side of a channel, the reflective border will be red.

POINTERS

Daybeacons marking small craft channels may carry only a pointed board or "pointer" as a daymark. If the daybeacon marks the starboard side of the channel standing in, the pointer will be red and the pointed end will carry a red reflector. The pointed end of the red daymark will point to port to indicate the channel lies to port of the daybeacon, and the daybeacon should be passed on your starboard hand on entering. If the daybeacon marks the port side of the channel, the pointer will be black with a green reflector on the pointed end, and the pointer will point to starboard.

All beacons and daybeacons used as channel markers in the lateral system are numbered. Beacons and daybeacons marking the starboard side of the channel are even numbered. Beacons and daybeacons marking the port side of the channel are odd numbered. Beacons and daybeacons with red and black horizontal stripes, and those with vertical

Figure 10-19. A red daymark on an unlighted beacon.

Figure 10-20. A black daymark on an unlighted beacon.

68

Figure 10-21. A red and black junction beacon in the ICW, which marks the junction of the Intracoastal Waterway and the channel into Bayou Aloe on Dauphin Island, west of Dauphin Island Bridge. As the beacon must be passed on the port hand by westbound vessels, returning from seaward in the Gulf ICW, the top band of the daymark is black.

black and white stripes, are never numbered. This is the same system of numbering used on buoys.

BEACONS AND DAYBEACONS IN THE INTRACOASTAL WATERWAY

Beacons and daybeacons in the Intracoastal Waterway parallel the function of buoys in the Intracoastal Waterway. The daymarks on beacons and daybeacons in the Intracoastal Waterway will have a yellow strip immediately under the number or letter on the daymark. For dual-purpose beacons and daybeacons, the yellow squares and yellow triangles, this time on the daymarks, will again guide the pilot of a vessel traversing the Intracoastal Waterway.

Beacons and daybeacons lead lives almost as hazardous as buoys. Of course, they do not get dragged hundreds of yards off station and remain afloat to flash the wrong information, as a buoy off station will do. Beacons and daybeacons do get run down by ships, boats, or barges with alarming frequency. Storms can blow them away too. The lights on beacons may go out. So be prepared to find the beacon or daybeacon you need most to be missing.

Despite the warnings I have given you about lost and off-station buoys, beacons, and daybeacons, the United States Coast Guard does a fantastically good job of keeping our aids to navigation where they belong and working properly. You can help. First write the commander of your Coast Guard District and ask him to send you the *Local Notices to Mariners,* which will keep you apprised of changes. Then any time you see an aid to navigation destroyed, off station, or in any other way out of order, notify the Coast Guard. As for yourself: Never moor to or make fast to any aid to navigation; to do so is against Federal law. If you ever damage an aid to navigation, or see an aid to navigation that is damaged or off station, report the matter to the nearest Coast Guard unit as soon as possible; by radio, if you have one.

RANGES

I introduced you to ranges in the chapter on the compass. Ranges consist of two structures. These structures are situated so as to be aligned with the centerline of the reach of the channel the range defines. The after structure is much taller than the forward structure. You use the range to tell when you are in the center of the channel by getting the structures precisely in line. Ranges are never in the channel, and often ranges may be quite removed from the channel. In Figure 8-3 both structures of Range C of the Pascagoula ship channel are on the land. So are those of Range B of the Bayou Cassotte channel. To use a range properly you must consult your chart and your sailing directions or coast pilot. The chart will show you the reach of the channel the range covers. At some point you must turn, if the channel turns, and the chart will tell you at which buoy, beacon, or daybeacon to make this turn. From your sailing directions or coast pilot, you get the same information verbally. You can get the approach heading of the range by measuring it on your chart. All navigators know that the precision you get with plotting instruments, under some conditions, leaves something to be desired. Your coast pilot or sailing directions will give you the exact approach heading of the range. If your course is to follow the channel away from the range, calculate your departure heading by subtracting 180° from the approach heading of the range. Remember, both of these headings are true headings. Be sure to uncorrect your compass to know the compass course to steer.

As you approach a range or depart from a range, you may find you cannot hold the compass course you must steer to stay on the range. This is true even if you know your compass error very accurately. Why? Because set and drift, or leeway, may be setting you off the range. A good navigator will soon determine the amount of course change from his computed compass course required to stay on the range. From this he can calculate his set and drift or his leeway.

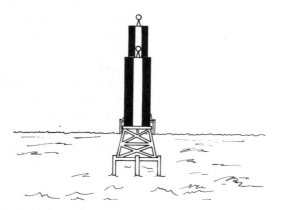

Figure 10-22. The daymarks of two range structures showing how they would appear when a vessel is on the range.

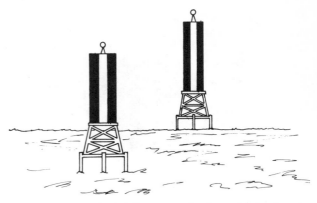

Figure 10-23. The same range as in Figure 10-22, but the vessel is off the range. The vessel is too far to the right. At night, the lights, rather than the daymarks, would identify the range.

We will see more of set and drift and leeway in a later chapter.

Ranges may be lighted or unlighted. On a lighted range, the light on the forward structure is often a quick flashing light. Study Figure 8-3 carefully. There are several ranges on this part of Chart No. 1267, and the characteristic of each of the lights on each range is given.

UNIFORM STATE WATERWAY MARKING SYSTEM

Although this work is about coastal navigation, a coastal passage can end up at a destination well inland. The gunkhole you seek may be way up some inland river or bay. If so, you may find the channel into your secret haven marked in accordance with the Uniform State Waterway Marking System. This system is designed to achieve two purposes. By the use of buoys and markers, the Uniform State Waterway Marking System aids the navigator by marking the limits of channels in much the same way the Federal system does. In addition, the Uniform State Waterway Marking System uses a cardinal system of markers to mark hazards. It also provides for regulatory markers to warn boatmen of dangers, restricted areas, such as swimming areas, directions to places of interest, speed control areas, as well as other purposes. Channel markers in the Uniform State Waterway Marking System follow the lateral system very closely with very important exceptions. In the Uniform State Marking System you may see *red can* buoys! For more information on this buoyage system, see *Marine Aids to Navigation,* CG-193, available from your nearest Coast Guard unit.

FOREIGN BUOYAGE SYSTEMS

This chapter has been limited so far to aids to navigation in the United States and her territories. A foreign cruise is the dream of every yachtsman, and a near certainty for those who make their living on salt water. In many parts of the world, the aids to navigation systems will be the same as the lateral system used in the United States. In other countries the systems used may be quite different. If you are going to call at a port in a country where the aids to navigation are different from the ones we are used to in our home waters, it is essential you be aware of this difference in time to keep your vessel out of danger.

An example of just how confusing this can be is

Figure 10-24. A typical range structure.

70

realized when you find in many European countries *red* buoys mark the *port* side of the channel, and *black* buoys mark the *starboard* side of the channel. You may also find buoys of shapes and colors you never dreamed of. The sailing directions will tell you the system of buoyage used in a particular port. Appendix J of the 1962 edition of *Bowditch* explains many of the buoyage systems found throughout the world.

LANDMARKS

In navigation any fixed object used by the navigator as a reference point for fixing his vessel's position is called a *landmark*. The navigator does not include established aids to navigation in the term landmark, although such aids strictly speaking are landmarks. The navigator reserves the term landmark for man-made objects not intended as aids to navigation, and to natural features that will aid him. Landmarks may be used in conjunction with regular aids to navigation. If no established aids are available, landmarks are often the only means a navigator may have for getting a fix.

The sailor in home waters only needs to know the location and significance of any landmark to use it to guide him in safe navigation. I am speaking here of the fellow who can run into some uncharted and unmarked inlet on a dark night by lining up his course with something on the beach. The something

may be two trees lined up as a range. This is local knowledge. The coastal pilot in unfamiliar waters must rely on charts and the landmarks charted on these charts to navigate his boat. Landmarks must be accurately located on the charts. Occasionally some object may be of value to the pilot even though its exact location is not determined. Such objects will be indicated on the chart by a very small circle as a symbol. If the object is accurately located, the symbol on the chart is a small circle with a dot in the middle. *Chart Number 1*, available from the National Ocean Survey, illustrates these symbols. To use any object as a landmark to get a fix, the object must be accurately charted. See *Bowditch*, 1962 edition, Appendix K, for excerpts from Chart Number 1.

Landmarks may be man-made things, such as silos, water tanks, church steeples, or anything that stands out from its surroundings well enough to be easily seen and identified. The shape of such an object should provide an obvious point to take a bearing on. You would take a bearing on the steeple and not the church; the silo and not the barn.

Natural landmarks can be equally useful to the navigator. Natural landmarks can be rocky spires, mountain peaks, sheer cliff faces (for tangent bearings), defined stands of trees, or any other natural object that is permanent enough in nature. As we continue in our study of coastal navigation, you will see how these natural features are used by the pilot.

11 HOW TO COMPUTE THE VISIBILITY OF LIGHTS

The *Light List* gives the visibility of a light in two columns, one for the nominal range and the other for the geographic range. The *nominal range* of a light is the maximum range a light may be seen in clear weather as a result of its candlepower. Clear weather is defined as weather with at least 10 nautical miles of visibility. The *geographic range* of a light depends on the height of the light above the surface of the earth. Sometimes a light on a high headland will not have the candlepower to reach out to the light's geographic range. In this case, the charted visibility of the light will be the nominal range of the light. On the other hand, a very bright light may have a nominal range in excess of the geographic range of the light. In this case, the charted visibility of the light will be the geographic range of the light.

Nominal range is not the same as luminous range*. The *luminous range* of a light depends on the combined effect of the light's nominal range and the weather conditions existing at the time. It is extremely important for a navigator coasting or making a landfall from sea to know when he may expect to see a light. If the navigator fails to see a light within a reasonable period around the time he calculated he should, as a prudent navigator, he should exercise extreme caution and begin checking his reckoning and his position by all means available. Knowing how to use the *Light List* and knowing how to calculate when a certain light should be visible from the deck or bridge of your boat are two of the most important skills a navigator must master. How would you, as navigator, calculate the visible range of a light on a stormy night when visibility is reduced to five miles?

Bowditch, 1962 edition, article 916, page 263, gives a definition of luminous range that agrees more closely with the definition for nominal range as given in the *Light List*. The student should be very careful to keep this discrepancy in mind when studying *Bowditch* and the *Light List* at the same time.

Let's work this problem out step by step. As navigator in *War Hat* you are making a landfall on Pensacola, Florida. The reported visibility at the entrance to Pensacola Bay is five miles. When would you advise your skipper he should see Pensacola Light? Before you can answer this question, a closer look at the *Light List* is in order.

Open your *Light List,* Volume II, CG-160, in this case, to the seacoast section. According to the table of contents on page v, the seacoast section is the first section following the general section. The Florida Gulf Coast part of the seacoast section begins with light list number 97. The table of contents for this section and all subsequent sections of the *Light List* is indexed by light list number, and *not* by page number. The Alabama Gulf Coast begins with light list number 153. Pensacola Light must have a light list number lying between 97 and 153. You can go to the index in the back of the *Light List* and see Pensacola Light has a light list number of 149. Pensacola Light is number 149 in the sequence of aids to navigation listed in the seacoast section of the Light List. If you are familiar enough with this part of the Gulf Coast, it may not be necessary to look up Pensacola Light in the index. You can flip open the seacoast section of the *Light List*, find the Florida Gulf Coast pages, and thumb forward or backward until you find the page of the Florida Gulf Coast that Pensacola Light is on. You will find Pensacola Light listed opposite number 149. Had you been looking for the light by light list number, you would have opened the book to the page with number 149 on it.

What is the number 1652 just after number 149 opposite Pensacola Light in the index? This number 1652 is in the same type face, and it is separated from the number 149 only by a comma. It also is listed right under 149 in the first column of the seacoast section of the *Light List*. It is the light list number of Pensacola Light in the Bays, Rivers, and Harbors section of the *Light List*, since Pensacola Light also functions as a harbor aid. See Figure 11-1 and note how each column is headed and the particular

72

(1) No.	(2) Name Characteristic	(3) Location Lat. N. Long. W.	(4) Nominal Range Intensity	(5) Geographic Range	(6) Structure Ht. above ground Ht. above water	(7) Remarks Year

FLORIDA, ALABAMA AND MISSISSIPPI   EIGHT DISTRICT

GULF COAST [1]
(Chart 1265)

(1) No.	(2) Name Characteristic	(3) Location Lat. N. Long. W.	(4) Nominal Range Intensity	(5) Geographic Range	(6) Structure Ht. above ground Ht. above water	(7) Remarks Year
149 1652 J3394	PENSACOLA LIGHT .... Fl. W., 20s	On north side of west end of bay. 30 20.7 87 18.5	27 1,500,000	20	Conical brick tower, lower third white, upper two-thirds black. 191 171	White light visible from 222° to 090°. Aircraft warning light shows F. R. from 090° to 222°. 1825–1858
150 1649	Pensacola Bay Entrance Whistle Buoy 1. Fl. W., 6s(1sfl)	In 54 feet, west of Caucus Channel. Range line. 30 16.3 87 17.5	 300	....	Black	Ra ref.
150.50 1693.50	Perdide Pass Entrance Lighted Buoy P. Mo. (A) W. (For Pensacola Bay, see No. 1649) (Chart 1266)	In 30 feet............ 30 15.6 87 33.5	 130	....	Black and white vertical stripes.	Ra ref.
153 J3436	SAND ISLAND LIGHT........... Gp. Fl. W., 10s 0.5sfl., 2sec. 0.5sfl., 7sec. 2 flashes.	On west side of main entrance to Mobile Bay. 30 11.3 88 03.0	12 4,500	17	Black conical tower........... 131	1838–1873
154 1698 J3438.1	MOBILE POINT LIGHT .... Fl. W., 10s Resident Personnel.	Near Fort Morgan 30 13.7 88 01.5	27 1,700,000	17	Red rectangular daymark on skeleton tower. On same structure and 55 feet above Mobile Point Range Rear Light. 125	Aircraft warning light shows F. R. RADIOBEACON: Antenna 345 feet 157° from light tower. See p. XVIII for method of operation. Special Radio Direction Finder Calibration Service, See p. XX. Storm warning signal displayed during daytime southwest of light. 1822–1966
155 1695	Mobile Entrance Lighted Whistle Buoy 1. Fl. W., 4s (For Mobile Bay, see No. 1695) (Chart 1267)	In 58 feet 30 08.1 88 03.9	 400	....	Black	Ra ref.
155.50 1800.50	Petit Bois Pass Lighted Bell Buoy 1. Fl. W., 2.5s	In 28 feet........... 30 12.7 88 18.5	 350	....	Black.....................	Ra ref.

Figure 11-1. An excerpt from the seacoast section of the *Light List,* Vol. II.

information *each column* contains. Under "Nominal Range," column 4 of the *Light List* extract, the nominal range of the light is listed — 27 miles.

Now let's proceed with the step by step solution of our problem.

STEP 1
Open the seacoast section of the *Light List* and find Pensacola Light. Under column 4 extract the nominal range of Pensacola Light, 27 miles.

STEP 2
You must now compute the luminous range of Pensacola Light on this particular night when the visibility is five miles. Turn back to the general section of the *Light List*. On page x you will see a diagram headed "Luminous Range Diagram." Carefully study the directions for using this diagram. In a nutshell these directions tell you the remaining steps to solve your problem. See Figure 11-2, which is taken directly from the *Light List*.

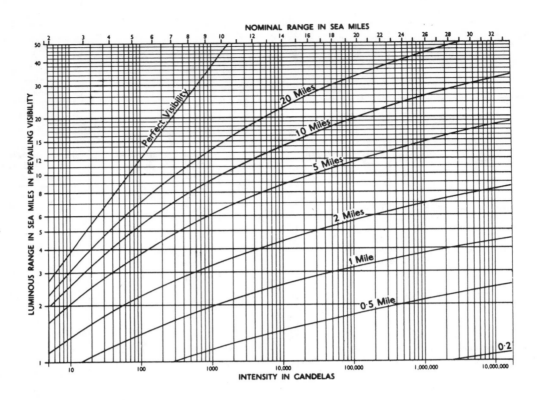

Figure 11-2. Luminous range diagram from the *Light List,* Vol. II.

STEP 3

To find the luminous range of a light under a specific limit of visibility, read across the top of the diagram until you come to the nominal range of Pensacola Light. From Step 1 you know this to be 27 miles, which is represented by a mark between numbers 26 and 28.

STEP 4

You may use a pair of dividers for this step if you want to, but eyeball accuracy is quite sufficient. Imagine another vertical line under the 27 mark, parallel to the vertical line extending down under 26. Go down this imaginary line until it intersects the five-mile visibility curve.

At this intersection of the imaginary vertical line and the five mile visibility curve, a horizontal line cuts both lines. Follow this horizontal line across the diagram to the left, and at the intersection of this horizontal line and the vertical scale on the left side of the diagram, read the luminous range of Pensacola Light — 15 miles under the prevailing visibility of five miles.

STEP 5

Determine your present DR position. Figure the time

at which your DR will be 15 miles off Pensacola Light. You determine the position of your DR 15 miles off by striking an arc of 15 miles radius with Pensacola Light as the center. The intersection of your course with this arc is the DR position at which you will be 15 miles off Pensacola Light. With your dividers measure the distance between this future DR and your present DR. Compute the time it will take your boat to run this distance. Add this time to the time of your present DR. The sum will be the time at which you should see Pensacola Light. But one more factor must be considered.

You can expect to see Pensacola Light when you are 15 miles off when the visibility is five miles, because you checked to be sure the *geographic range* of Pensacola Light was at least 15 miles for *your* height of eye. How did you do this? From the *Light List,* column 6, you found that Pensacola Light is 191 feet above mean high water. Tides along the Gulf Coast are not of sufficient range to require any adjustment to this tabulated height for the stage of the tide. You opened *Bowditch* to Table 8 and found any object 190 feet high would be visible for 15.8 miles, even if your height of eye is zero. Figure 11-3 is a reprint of this table. Aboard *War Hat* your height of eye will be at least eight feet. You

74

know the geographic range of Pensacola Light from *War Hat* will exceed the luminous range.

You must always confirm the geographic range of a light from *your* boat, because if the luminous range of a light under the prevailing conditions exceeds the geographic range of the light from your boat, you will not see the light until you are within this geographic range. You may see a loom of the light, which is the reflection of the light in the sky, and this can be very helpful, but you will not see the light itself.

I emphasize from *your* boat because the charted visibility and the geographic range of a light listed in the *Light List* are for a height of eye that is 15 feet above the sea. You must make an adjustment to this listed geographic range if your height of eye is not 15 feet. If your bridge is higher, you will see the light sooner, and if your conning station is lower, you will not see the light as soon. The curvature of the earth makes the distance at which things are visible above the horizon dependent on the height of the object and the height of the eye of the observer.

TABLE 8

Distance of the Horizon

Height feet	Nautical miles	Statute miles	Height feet	Nautical miles	Statute miles	Height feet	Nautical miles	Statute miles
1	1.1	1.3	120	12.5	14.4	940	35.1	40.4
2	1.6	1.9	125	12.8	14.7	960	35.4	40.8
3	2.0	2.3	130	13.0	15.0	980	35.8	41.2
4	2.3	2.6	135	13.3	15.3	1,000	36.2	41.6
5	2.6	2.9	140	13.5	15.6	1,100	37.9	43.7
6	2.8	3.2	145	13.8	15.9	1,200	39.6	45.6
7	3.0	3.5	150	14.0	16.1	1,300	41.2	47.5
8	3.2	3.7	160	14.5	16.7	1,400	42.8	49.3
9	3.4	4.0	170	14.9	17.2	1,500	44.3	51.0
10	3.6	4.2	180	15.3	17.7	1,600	45.8	52.7
11	3.8	4.4	190	15.8	18.2	1,700	47.2	54.3
12	4.0	4.6	200	16.2	18.6	1,800	48.5	55.9
13	4.1	4.7	210	16.6	19.1	1,900	49.9	57.4
14	4.3	4.9	220	17.0	19.5	2,000	51.2	58.9
15	4.4	5.1	230	17.3	20.0	2,100	52.4	60.4
16	4.6	5.3	240	17.7	20.4	2,200	53.7	61.8
17	4.7	5.4	250	18.1	20.8	2,300	54.9	63.2
18	4.9	5.6	260	18.4	21.2	2,400	56.0	64.5
19	5.0	5.7	270	18.8	21.6	2,500	57.2	65.8
20	5.1	5.9	280	19.1	22.0	2,600	58.3	67.2
21	5.2	6.0	290	19.5	22.4	2,700	59.4	68.4
22	5.4	6.2	300	19.8	22.8	2,800	60.5	69.7
23	5.5	6.3	310	20.1	23.2	2,900	61.6	70.9
24	5.6	6.5	320	20.5	23.6	3,000	62.7	72.1
25	5.7	6.6	330	20.8	23.9	3,100	63.7	73.3
26	5.8	6.7	340	21.1	24.3	3,200	64.7	74.5
27	5.9	6.8	350	21.4	24.6	3,300	65.7	75.7
28	6.1	7.0	360	21.7	25.0	3,400	66.7	76.8
29	6.2	7.1	370	22.0	25.3	3,500	67.7	77.9
30	6.3	7.2	380	22.3	25.7	3,600	68.6	79.0
31	6.4	7.3	390	22.6	26.0	3,700	69.6	80.1
32	6.5	7.5	400	22.9	26.3	3,800	70.5	81.2
33	6.6	7.6	410	23.2	26.7	3,900	71.4	82.2
34	6.7	7.7	420	23.4	27.0	4,000	72.4	83.3
35	6.8	7.8	430	23.7	27.3	4,100	73.3	84.3
36	6.9	7.9	440	24.0	27.6	4,200	74.1	85.4
37	7.0	8.0	450	24.3	27.9	4,300	75.0	86.4
38	7.1	8.1	460	24.5	28.2	4,400	75.9	87.4
39	7.1	8.2	470	24.8	28.6	4,500	76.7	88.3
40	7.2	8.3	480	25.1	28.9	4,600	77.6	89.3
41	7.3	8.4	490	25.3	29.2	4,700	78.4	90.3
42	7.4	8.5	500	25.6	29.4	4,800	79.3	91.2
43	7.5	8.6	520	26.1	30.0	4,900	80.1	92.2
44	7.6	8.7	540	26.6	30.6	5,000	80.9	93.1
45	7.7	8.8	560	27.1	31.2	6,000	88.6	102.0
46	7.8	8.9	580	27.6	31.7	7,000	95.7	110.2
47	7.8	9.0	600	28.0	32.3	8,000	102.3	117.8
48	7.9	9.1	620	28.5	32.8	9,000	108.5	124.9
49	8.0	9.2	640	28.9	33.3	10,000	114.4	131.7
50	8.1	9.3	660	29.4	33.8	15,000	140.1	161.3
55	8.5	9.8	680	29.8	34.3	20,000	161.8	186.3
60	8.9	10.2	700	30.3	34.8	25,000	180.9	208.2
65	9.2	10.6	720	30.7	35.3	30,000	198.1	228.1
70	9.6	11.0	740	31.1	35.8	35,000	214.0	246.4
75	9.9	11.4	760	31.5	36.3	40,000	228.8	263.4
80	10.2	11.8	780	31.9	36.8	45,000	242.7	279.4
85	10.5	12.1	800	32.4	37.3	50,000	255.8	294.5
90	10.9	12.5	820	32.8	37.7	60,000	280.2	322.6
95	11.2	12.8	840	33.2	38.2	70,000	302.7	348.4
100	11.4	13.2	860	33.5	38.6	80,000	323.6	372.5
105	11.7	13.5	880	33.9	39.1	90,000	343.2	395.1
110	12.0	13.8	900	34.3	39.5	100,000	361.8	416.5
115	12.3	14.1	920	34.7	39.9	200,000	511.6	589.0

Figure 11-3. A reprint of Table 8 from *Bowditch*.

Now, how do you make this adjustment for your own height of eye to the geographic range of a light? Let's take it step by step with another example:

STEP 1
It is a clear night with visibility better than 10 miles. Your vessel is standing in for Mobile. As navigator, you want to know when to expect to pick up Mobile Point Light. Your first step is to look up Mobile Point Light in the *Light List* (Figure 11-1). You find the nominal range is 27 miles, and the geographic range is 17 miles. From column 6 you see Mobile Point Light is 125 feet above water.

STEP 2
Your height of eye on *War Hat* is 8 feet. Open *Bowditch* to Table 8 (see Figure 11-3). For a height of eye of 8 feet, the distance to the visible horizon is 3.2 miles. Be sure to use the nautical mile column in Table 8. Mobile Point Light is 125 feet high, and from Table 8 you see that the distance to the visible horizon from a height of 125 feet is 12.8 miles. Add these two distances:

For height of eye of 8 feet	3.2
For height of light of 125 feet	12.8
Geographic range from your boat	16.0 miles

You should see Mobile Point Light when you are 16 miles off.

STEP 3
Compute the time at which your DR will be 16 miles off Mobile Point Light. This is the time when you should see Mobile Point Light.

Suppose you are the navigator of a steamer which has a bridge 50 feet above the water. You are making a landfall at Mobile on a clear, dark night. How far off should you expect to see Mobile Point Light?

STEP 1
From the *Light List* you find Mobile Point Light is 125 feet above the water. This light has a nominal range of 27 miles and a geographic range of 17 miles. Refer back to Figure 11-1.

STEP 2
From Table 8 of *Bowditch*, Figure 11-3, you find the distance to the horizon at a height of 50 feet is 8.1 miles. For a height of 125 feet, the distance to the horizon is 12.8 miles. Thus:

$$8.2$$
$$+\ 12.8\ \text{miles}$$
$$21.0\ \text{miles}$$

You can expect to see Mobile Point Light when your steamer is 21 miles off the light, because the nominal range of this light is 27 miles even though its geographic range is only 17 miles. The geographic range of Mobile Point Light from *your* steamer is 21 miles.

At sea you will usually first see any light when your boat is on the crest of a wave. This is true not only because the horizon may be obscured while your boat is in the trough of the sea, but also because the crest raises your boat above sea level, and your height of eye is increased with a corresponding momentary increase of the geographic range of the light from your boat.

Another example of this is "bobbing a light." To bob a light, the navigator will look at a light from a standing position when he first sees it. When he is sure he sees the light he will crouch. This small lessening of the navigator's height of eye as he crouches will cause the light to disappear below the horizon. If the navigator can see the light when he stands, and cannot see it when he crouches, he knows he must be very near the maximum distance off at which he could expect to see the light from his vessel, and very near the distance off at which he computed he would see the light. From this trick the navigator can tell approximately how far off the light he is.

On a small vessel such as *War Hat*, where the geographic range of a light from aboard the boat is always less than the listed geographic range, the navigator computes a constant to deduct from the listed geographic range of any light he is working with. From Table 8 of *Bowditch*, you find the difference in distance to the horizon for heights of eye of 8 feet and 15 feet to be 1.2 miles. So if you deduct 1.2 miles from the charted or listed geographical range of Mobile Point Light, which is 17 miles, you will find that Mobile Point Light should be visible 15.8 miles off from your boat. This is close enough to the 16 miles you computed in the example above to cause no difficulty. This constant would work for any light from any boat on which the navigator had a height of eye of eight feet.

As navigator of the steamer referred to earlier, you would find the difference in distance to the visible horizon for heights of 15 feet and 50 feet. This difference is 3.7 miles. You would *add* 3.7 miles to the geographic range of the light. From the bridge of the steamer you would expect to see Mobile Point Light 20.7 miles off.

When you use a constant that is added to the geographic range of a light, be sure that the nominal range of the light is sufficient to make the light visible at this greater distance.

If you do not have a copy of *Bowditch*, there is a short table on page vi of the *Light List*. This table furnishes the same information as Table 8, but due to its abbreviated nature, interpolation is required for very precise results.

It is essential to know when you can reasonably expect to see the lights you will encounter on making a passage. As navigator, it is your job to compute these times, not only for yourself, but for the others on their watches. You should pass this information on by writing your instructions in your night orders. On a coastal passage, you would compute the time the watch could expect to pick up each light as your boat proceeds along the coast. If, during your watch below, a light fails to come into view within a few minutes of the time you calculated it should, the watch must call you, and, if necessary, the skipper should also be rousted out.

How do you know the light you see is Pensacola Light or Mobile Point Light or whatever light you are looking for? You recognize the light you are looking for by its characteristic. When you see the light, take your stopwatch and time the sequence of the light's characteristic. If you don't have a stopwatch, count the seconds. If you are standing in for Caucus Cut into Pensacola Bay, and you see a white light flashing every 20 seconds, by count or stopwatch, you know this must be Pensacola Light.

The *Light List* is your best friend when it comes to working with any aid to navigation. If you are not familiar with a coast, you can have trouble locating some aids on a chart. Column 3 of the *Light List* gives the latitude and longitude of the major aids or a brief physical description of the aid's location. Often both the coordinates and a physical description of the aid's location is given.

If you are making an approach to an aid by day, and you want to know the type of structure a light is on, and its color, check column 6 of the *Light List*, which gives a short description of every aid in the *Light List*. Refer to Figure 11-1 again. From column 6 you see Pensacola Light is a conical brick tower, painted black and white. Mobile Point Light is a red rectangular day mark on a skeleton tower. Perdido Pass South Fish Haven Buoy is an orange and white buoy with horizontal bands.

Column 7 of the *Light List* tabulates the characteristics of any sound-producing devices associated with an aid to navigation. Radio and other electronic devices associated with an aid are listed in column 7. Study Figure 11-1 for an idea of the information found in each column of the *Light List*, or better yet, buy a *Light List* covering the waters you will operate your boat in and familiarize yourself with it. At the same time, you will become more familiar with your own waters.

A few practice problems will help you remember what we have been discussing in this chapter. Work these problems carefully, because computing the time at which you can expect to pick up a light is one of the most important things a navigator must do when making a landfall on that light during darkness. The problems I am giving you here are essentially the same as those you will need to solve as a navigator at sea.

PRACTICE PROBLEMS

1. You are navigator on an ocean tug making a landfall at Gulfport, Mississippi. The height of eye from the bridge of your tug is 26 feet. It is a clear night. The *Light List* gives the nominal range of Ship Island Light as 10 miles and the geographic range of this light as 16 miles. The height of the light at Ship Island Light is 84 feet. At what distance off would you expect to sight Ship Island Light?

2. You are the navigator of a small sloop closing with the land to make a night landfall on Mobile Point Light. In order to see the light sooner, you go aloft and, from your perch on the spreaders, your height of eye is 21 feet. At what distance off would you expect to see Mobile Point Light?

3. Before you can make your landfall on Mobile Point Light, problem 2, weather makes up, and the marine advisory informs you that visibility at the mouth of Mobile Bay is four miles. At what range would you expect to see Mobile Point Light?

4. You are second mate, navigator, of a steamer steering 000°T for Pensacola Entrance. The height of eye from the bridge of your steamer is 31 feet. At what distance off would you expect to see Pensacola Light?

ANSWERS

1. 10 miles. See *Light List* definition of nominal range.

2. Ht. of eye 21 feet   5.2 miles
   Ht. of light 125 ft.   <u>12.8 miles</u>
                                18.0 miles

3. 11 miles.

4. Ht. of eye 31 feet   6.4 miles
   Ht. of light 191 ft.   <u>15.8 miles</u>
                                22.2 miles

12   BEARINGS: COMPASS, TRUE, AND RELATIVE

In Chapter 2 I defined a bearing as the direction in which an object lies from you. A bearing is the line of sight along which you must look to see an object. If you see something, and you wish to head for the object, the bearing of the object is the direction you must go to get there. You can measure this direction by measuring the angle this direction makes, in a clockwise direction, with the meridian from true north. If you measure the direction an object lies from you to be 047⁰, you would say the object bears 047⁰. The bearing of anything is the course you must steer to go to that thing.

Here, we are talking about the use of bearings in piloting. Thus we are interested in bearings of stationary objects, such as landmarks or aids to navigation that help you, the navigator, fix your vessel's position. When you study seamanship and maneuvering, you will study the use of bearings of moving things, but this is not part of the scope of this work.

Navigation is a precise science. For bearings to be of use to the navigator, these bearings must be measured with the best possible accuracy. The basic instrument for measuring the bearing of an object from your boat is the compass on your boat. Even though you want the best possible accuracy, it is not always possible to be too precise from the deck of a small boat, and if you are not in confined or dangerous waters, extreme accuracy may not be as important as timeliness. Running down a coast, keeping your position by rule of thumb methods, a glance over your compass card may be sufficiently accurate, if done with a little care. After you have practiced a bit, you may be surprised at just how accurate you can be with this simple method. An even better system is to use the shadow pin of your compass as a rear sight, and by lining the shadow pin up with the object you are observing, you can read the compass bearing of the object with a considerable degree of accuracy. Neither of these methods, however, is sufficiently accurate for the type of

navigation needed to take a boat of any size and draft into confined waters. Yet on a small boat in a running sea, this eyeballing across the compass card or shadow pin may be the best you can do. For more accuracy your compass should be fitted with a bearing circle, or you should have some other means of taking a bearing.

A bearing circle consists of a brass or bronze ring, or any other suitable non-magnetic material, fashioned to fit snugly to the rim of your compass bowl. The use of a bearing circle, or *azimuth circle* as it is sometimes called, requires a compass manufactured with this purpose in mind. The rim of the compass bowl must accommodate the bearing circle in such a manner that the circle fits snugly and evenly, but is free to move with a slight pressure. The circle is equipped with two diametrically opposed sights that can be raised for observation and closed flat for stowage. The front sight consists of an open frame with a vertical wire in the middle. The rear sight is a rectangular piece of flat metal with a vertical slit in it. The line of sight through the two sights passes across the center of the compass card. Thus if you fit your compass with a bearing circle, and look through the rear sight at a lighthouse or any aid or landmark, with the wire of the front sight on the object you are observing, the wire will be directly over the compass card at the point of the compass bearing of the object. Sometimes it requires considerable skill, as well as double-jointed eyeballs, to keep the sight lined up on your target and to read the compass card at the same time. To help you see the object you are observing and the compass card at the same time, without such ocular gymnastics, most bearing circles are equipped with a prism or mirror. Figures 12-1 and 12-2 show a bearing circle.

Bearings taken with your magnetic compass are compass bearings. In the chapters on the compass and compass error, you learned that compass courses must always be corrected to determine true courses

Figure 12-1. A bearing circle.

so you can plot your DR track. Similarly, a compass bearing must be corrected to a true bearing before the bearing can be plotted. Correcting a compass bearing to a true bearing is no more difficult than correcting a compass course to a true course. You use the same rules and procedures. One thing you must remember, unless you want to make the most common error many navigators make, is that deviation always depends on your vessel's *course*. The bearing of any object from you is *not* your course. You must enter your boat's deviation table with the *compass course* you are steering to get the proper deviation correction. Let's correct and plot two bearings to show you what I mean.

Figure 12-2. A bearing circle mounted on a compass.

You are on a course of 240ºC. You observe the light on Choctawhatchee Bay Entrance jetty to bear 047ºC, and the tower on the beach, about 2.3 miles to the west, to bear 332ºC. See Chart No. 1264. What is the true bearing of the light on the Choctawhatchee Bay Entrance jetty? What is the true bearing of the tower on the beach? You correct these two bearings this way:

STEP 1 (For the light on the jetty).
Write down the memory aid C D M V T in a vertical sequence.

STEP 2
Fill in the values you already know.

C 047º   (The compass bearing of the light.)
D   8ºW   (From the deviation table in Figure
             6-4 for a compass *course* of 240º.)
M 039º
V   3ºE   (From the compass rose nearest your
             DR on Chart No. 1264.)
T 042º

The true bearing of the light on the Choctawhatchee Bay Entrance jetty is 042º. What is the true bearing of the tower? You correct your compass bearing of the tower in the same way.

C 332º
D   8ºW   (You are still on course 240ºC.)
M 324º
V   3ºE
T 327º

There was nothing hard about that, was there? You still must add easterly error and subtract westerly error as you did in correcting compass courses. Just do not confuse the bearing with your course when entering the deviation table. If you change course between one bearing and then take another bearing, you must use the deviation for the new course. An example of what happens when you change course between bearings can be illustrated by restating the problem you just worked to provide a course change between the two bearings. Assume you observe the jetty light and the tower from the same position. The problem is now stated like this:

You are steering a course of 240ºC. You observe the light on the east jetty at Choctawhatchee Bay Entrance to bear 047ºC. You change course to 030ºC, and observe the tower two miles down the beach to the westward to bear 317ºC. What is the true bearing of the jetty light? What is the true bearing of the tower?

Here is how you solve this problem. First correct the compass bearing of the jetty light to a True bearing as you did before.

C 047°
D 8°W
M 039°
V 3°E
T 042°   (The same true bearing as before.)

This is precisely the same solution as the solution in the first example. You found your deviation to be 8°W by entering the deviation table with a compass course of 240°. Let's see what happens, though, when you correct your second bearing, the one on the tower.

C 317°
D 7°E   (Your deviation is now 7°E because your *course* is now 030°C.)
M 324°
V 3°E
T 327°

What is the difference here? The true bearing of the tower is the same as it turned out to be in the first example, and it should be, as your vessel is in the same position. The compass bearing was not the same, however. Why? Because when you changed course from 240°C to 030°C, your deviation changed from 8°W to 7°E. As long as your boat remains in the same position, the true bearing of a stationary object will not change.

These examples should show you the importance of using the proper deviation correction to correct a compass bearing. This follows the same old axiom you learned in Chapters 4 and 5: *Deviation varies with the heading of your vessel.*

It is important to know how to uncorrect true bearings as well as to know how to correct compass bearings to get true bearings. This may never have entered your mind, but think a minute. When picking up a light, or getting the first glimpse of the distant shore when making a landfall, the sharp-eyed navigator is likely to see what he is looking for much sooner if he knows exactly where to look. Again an example will illustrate what I mean.

Suppose you are making a landfall on the seabuoy at Mobile Bay Entrance. You compute the visible range of Mobile Point Light to be 15 miles from the deck of your boat. By plotting, you determine the true bearing of Mobile Point Light should be 025°T when the light first comes into sight, that is, providing your vessel is at the DR position you forecast she would be when you first see the light. If your boat is on a course of 047°C, what should the compass bearing of Mobile Point Light be when it first becomes visible? The solution:

T 025°
V 4°E
M 021°
D 5°E
C 016°

The compass bearing of Mobile Point Light should be 016° when the light is first sighted.

Picking up a light, or making any landfall, on a bearing reasonably close to the bearing you calculated the light or landfall should bear is as important, if not more important, as picking up the light or landfall at the *time* you figured you should. In Chapter 11 I emphasized the seriousness of failing to see a light at a time reasonably close to the time you figured you should see it. If the time is wrong, your dead reckoning is seriously in error, or your entire navigation is most likely in serious error. If the light or landfall appears at a bearing quite different from the one expected, this, too, can indicate a serious error in your navigation.

Suppose you are approaching the seabuoy at the entrance to Mobile Bay from the south southwest. It is night. If your course is truly north northeast, the light or buoy should bear 022°T when you first see it, if you are heading right for the buoy. But you will see Mobile Point Light long before you will see the seabuoy at the entrance to Mobile Bay. By computing the visible range of Mobile Point Light from your boat, under existing weather conditions, you determine the bearing of Mobile Point Light should be 025°C when you first sight it. In order to know where to look you must also know the compass bearing to seek the light on. But more important, you must know the compass bearing on which the light should first appear to indicate if you are, or are not, on course. Now suppose Mobile Point Light comes into view on a bearing of 049°T. What does this mean? It means you are well north of your course. You could be getting too near the shoals off Sand Island! By the same token, if Mobile Point Light first comes into view at a bearing of 006°C, it would mean your vessel is well south of her course, and she could run right by the seabuoy at the entrance to Mobile Bay without anyone ever seeing it.

In truth, the time you pick up a light or landfall and the bearing on which you first see your objective are interrelated. Only when you are on course will the computed and actual bearings on which you see an object agree; but then it is possible that the time of the sighting will be off. In most cases if your DR is off enough to affect seriously the bearing at first sighting, the time will be off too. As navigator, any such differences in times or bearings should tell you your navigation is in serious error. This information should ring an alarm bell in your mind! You must do something without delay. Fix your vessel's position if you can. If you cannot fix her position, at least do something that will take her out of danger. If in doubt as to any better choice, you can always head her out to sea.

Please excuse the above digression. I think the message was worth the time it took to convey. Now let's get back to our study of bearings. Let's talk about relative bearings.

Steering compasses and even standard compasses, on boats big enough to have standard compasses, are often located in areas that make the use of a bearing circle difficult. Then, too, bearing circles are devices reserved for the larger compasses found on the larger vessels. Most boats the size we are dealing with may have only the steering compass, located to best serve the helmsman. Often this makes the compass a very unhandy instrument for taking bearings. Thus another instrument is used in conjunction with the boat's compass to take bearings. This instrument is the *pelorus*.

The pelorus consists of a "dumb compass," which is a compass card etched or engraved on a brass plate. (In the mid-twentieth century, this plate may be almost any metal or plastic. But we are talking about the pelorus as it is still made in its best quality.) This brass compass card, or "dumb compass," is mounted on another plate, slightly larger in diameter, which is set in gimbals and ballasted to keep the whole affair somewhat near level while the

Figure 12-3. A pelorus mounted in gimbals and a yoke, which can be mounted on a standard on the wing of the bridge. A pelorus can also be mounted in a box for portability.

boat does her thing in a boisterous sea. Like many man-made attempts to keep things level at sea, this gimbal and ballast arrangement leaves much to be desired, especially on smaller vessels. Yet this arrangement is the best we can do as far as peloruses are concerned. A bar with sight vanes, much like those on the bearing circle, is centered across the compass rose of the pelorus. Two concentric clamp nuts lock the compass rose of the dumb compass into position on the mounting plate when set, and hold the sight bar in position when an observation is taken. This assembly is then mounted in a box to make the pelorus portable, or fixed in a yoke on a stand on the wing of the bridge of a larger vessel where portability is not needed.

The pelorus can be used in two ways. The clamp screw locking the dumb compass card can be loosened, and the brass card can be turned to match the compass course your boat is steering. The clamp nut is again tightened to lock the card into place. To take a bearing after aligning the card of the dumb compass of the pelorus with your steering compass, all you need to do is observe the object you wish to take a bearing on through the sight vanes, and you can read the compass bearing of the object right off the pelorus; provided, of course, that the boat is exactly on course. Steering the boat and taking the bearing usually require two persons. The navigator sights his landmark or aid through the sight vanes of the pelorus. He then must hold the object he is observing dead in the sights as the boat swings from side to side of its course as all boats do. At the instant the compass lines up the lubber's line with the compass course the helmsman is trying to steer, the helmsman sings out "Mark!" At this instant the navigator notes the bearing. This way the navigator knows the boat is on course and the pelorus and the magnetic compass are in alignment when the bearing is taken. Thus, in this case, the pelorus bearing is the same as the compass bearing of the object observed.

For reasons that become apparent with practice, most of us who use the pelorus extensively in navigation prefer to take *relative bearings*. Relative bearings are bearings taken relative to the boat's course, or more specifically relative to her heading. The bow is the 000° position or relative "north". Both the method of using the pelorus I described in the previous paragraph and the relative-bearing technique are used interchangeably by most navigators, but relative bearings have obvious advantages that carry over into other aspects of the seaman's trade as well as navigation. So as a seaman as well as a navigator, you must understand relative bearings.

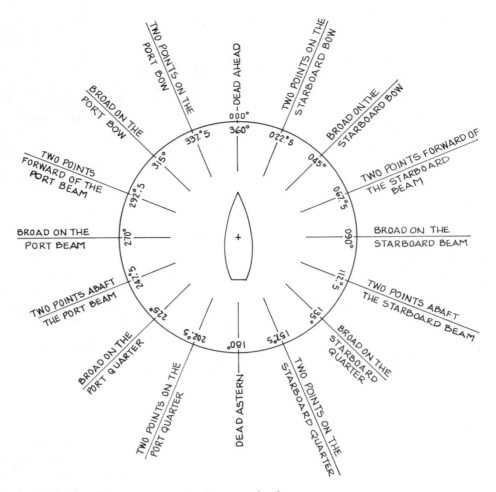

Figure 12-4. Relative bearings by degrees and points.

Lookouts and watchstanders call out relative, rather than compass, bearings. A lookout sees something on the bow, he sings out: "Sail two points on the port bow." This is the old system related to the compass used in the age of sail, where the courses as well as the bearings were designated in points and quarter points. A lookout's measurement is almost always made by seaman's eye. The lookout does not use a bearing circle or any other bearing finder, although the watch officer might. Seamen use judgment to estimate the bearing. The lookout in the chains of *War Hat* would sing out "sail dead ahead." Or "sail broad on the starboard bow." What do these terms mean? This question is best answered by first looking at the division of the compass card.

There are 32 points to the mariner's compass. Each point is 11¼°. Thus there are eight points to a quadrant. Those of you who have only known courses and bearings in degrees might be surprised by a system

like this, but if you have ever tried to hold a yawing boat on course, on the night watch, running in the trades, you will understand why the point and quarter point system of compass courses was used, and why it has been so acceptable. The reason is simply that the nearest anyone can steer a small boat in a seaway is within a quarter of a point of the correct course.

Now let's define some of those terms; see Figure 12-4. An object directly in front of you is said to be "dead ahead." An object 022½° on the bow is said to be "two points on the starboard bow." An object bearing 090° to your course is "broad on the starboard beam" or "abeam." An object bearing 135° from your bow, or course, is "broad on the starboard quarter." If you see your competition in an offshore race 180° from your course, she is "dead astern."

The terms "two points on the starboard bow" or "broad on the starboard beam" as well as the intermediate points and fractional points can be reduced to very specific angular measurement, but the only place you see such terms as "two points on the starboard bow" used in navigation today is in some older texts and on Coast Guard license examinations. For this reason alone it is important for you to understand these terms, but also, these terms are in everyday use by seamen in other applications, as I explained previously. The modern navigator, however, finds it more feasible to measure relative bearings in degrees. Figure 12-5 is an illustration of the relative compass graduated in degrees.

Dead ahead is 000⁰ or 360⁰. Thus an object dead ahead is said to bear 000⁰ *relative* or 360⁰ *relative*. As always, directions are reckoned clockwise through 360⁰ around the ship. Thus a light bearing broad on the starboard bow bears 045⁰ relative. And to continue around with our relative compass, a light bearing 225⁰ relative bears broad on the *port* quarter. If the light bears 270⁰R, it is broad on the port beam, and, if the bearing is 315⁰R, the light is broad on the port bow.

To observe relative bearings, the dumb compass of the pelorus is set to align the 000⁰ of the card with dead ahead. This makes the dead astern point 180⁰R. Thus the 000⁰/180⁰ axis of the dumb compass rose is parallel to the keel of your boat. To take a bearing on a light or other landmark, the navigator sights the thing he is observing through the sight vanes of the pelorus, and the *navigator,* not the helmsman, sings out "Mark!" The helmsman notes the compass *heading* at the instant the navigator sings out mark. The navigator reads the pelorus bearing of the light, or other object he is taking a bearing on, by simply reading the bearing on the card of the dumb compass. Thus if the bearing of Pensacola Light was observed to be 225⁰, the bearing would be said to be "broad on the port quarter," if seen by your lookout, but "225⁰ relative" if taken by you, the navigator, through your pelorus.

What is the advantage of using relative bearings in taking bearings with a pelorus? Why not set your pelorus so the dumb compass of the pelorus corresponds to your course? The best answer to these queries is another question. Have you ever tried to hold the sights of a pelorus on target in any kind of a sea, while the quartermaster fought to bring the boat on course so a compass bearing could be observed? It can be aggravating. As navigator, you know when your sights are on target, and, if you are observing relative bearings, *you* sing out; the helmsman notes the *heading*, which may be several degrees off course, and you read the relative bearing from the pelorus. Herein lies the big advantage of relative

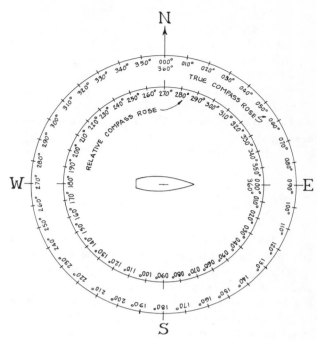

Figure 12-5. Relative bearings as measured in degrees from the bow of the boat. The boat is on a course of 090⁰T. The outer rose is the true compass rose; the inner rose is the relative compass rose. Thus, an object bearing 000⁰R will bear 090⁰T. An object bearing 090⁰R will bear 180⁰T.

bearings; as navigator, you run the show.

Relative bearings must be converted to true bearings before they are useful to the navigator. You can only plot true bearings. For no fathomable reason, converting relative bearings to true bearings is another one of those bogies that frighten fledging navigators. There is no reason why this should be so. We have a simple formula for converting relative bearings to true bearings. The formula is: True course plus relative bearing equals true bearing. (Actually, true heading plus relative bearing equals true bearing may be more accurate as the boat may be on a heading a few degrees off course when the bearing is taken.) That is all there is to it. Again, a few sample problems will illustrate what I mean:

Assume your vessel is on a course of 264⁰C. You observe that the light on the east jetty at the entrance to Choctawhatchee Bay bears 133⁰ relative (133⁰R). Deviation for this heading is 8⁰W; the variation at your DR position is 3⁰E. What is the true bearing of the jetty light?

STEP 1

Correct your compass course of 264⁰ to the true course.

C 264⁰
D   8⁰W
M 256⁰
V   3⁰E
T 259⁰

STEP 2
Add the true course of 259⁰ to the observed relative bearing of 133⁰.

$$259°T$$
$$133°$$
$$\overline{392°}$$
$$-360°$$
$$\overline{032°T}$$

As 392⁰ exceeds 360⁰ it is necessary to subtract 360⁰ from the sum to get the true bearing of 032⁰.

Let's try another problem: Your boat is on a course of 049⁰C. You take a bearing on a light bearing 046⁰R. You also observe another light to bear 290⁰R. Deviation for this heading is 4⁰E, and your chart shows the variation at your DR position to be 3⁰E. Convert these two relative bearings to true bearings.

STEP 1
Correct your compass course of 049⁰ to a true course.

C 049⁰
D   5⁰E
M 054⁰
V   3⁰E
T 057⁰

STEP 2
Add the observed relative bearings to your true course.

First bearing:	046⁰R	Second bearing:	290⁰R
	057⁰T		057⁰T
True bearings	103⁰		347⁰

Some navigators will add relative bearings to the compass course, and then they will correct each compass bearing. (Relative bearing plus compass course equals compass bearing.) This just makes extra work because each compass bearing must then be corrected to a true bearing. If you first correct your boat's course to a true course, and then add relative bearings observed to the true course, each bearing derived will be a true bearing. Thus you save repetitious effort. The time saved can be essential in pilot waters.

Bearing circles on a magnetic compass and a pelorus to take relative bearings or compass bearings are the classical instruments the navigator uses to take bearings on vessels not equipped with gyros and gyro repeaters. A gyro repeater is a remote indicator that repeats the indication of the master gyro. Gyro repeaters are necessary because the master gyro compass is usually tucked away down in the body of the vessel where it is less affected by the motion of the vessel in a seaway. But as the boats get smaller these instruments begin to show some severe limitations. For those of us trying to use real navigation techniques on our very small cruising boats, there are other instruments well worth mentioning. Needless to say, these same instruments work quite well on large vessels too. The hand-held bearing compass is one of the most popular instruments for this purpose used on small craft. This instrument combines a magnetic compass with sights to enable a navigator to hold the compass in his hand while taking bearings. See Figure 12-6.

On a small vessel where certain quadrants of the boat's compass may be obscured, the advantages of a hand-held bearing compass are obvious. The main disadvantage of the hand-held bearing compass is the problem of determining deviation. As you walk around the deck of your boat, you move around in the boat's magnetic field. Your deviation changes each time you change position. On some wooden boats and on some fiberglass boats, however, the vessel's magnetism can be so negligible as to cause little deviation. This is something you must determine, though. Remember you can change or induce deviation in a boat without otherwise significant magnetic qualities by putting aboard canned stores or other gear and tackle. When you do have

Figure 12-6. Using a hand-held bearing compass.

deviation on your boat, try to find areas far enough away from the location of any magnetic materials so the magnetic influence is reduced. If this is not feasible, you can get an idea of the deviation in your hand-held bearing compass in much the same way you found the deviation in your steering compass. Find one spot on deck, if possible, from which you can take bearings in any quadrant. Then run a range or swing ship. All in all, if you keep in mind these limitations, the hand-held bearing compass is the best tool for the small craft navigator to use in taking compass bearings.

Vessels equipped with gyro repeaters use an alidade for taking bearings. An alidade is best described as a bearing circle with a telescopic sight. (Strictly speaking, an alidade is any sighting device, even the open sight vanes on the pelorus. But the sailor means only the telescopic alidade when he uses the word.) The telescope's sharp target image plus the gyro's accuracy combine to give very accurate bearings when corrected for gyro error. Gyro error is named east or west just as is magnetic compass error. Gyros, however, have only one error, and if the gyro is properly adjusted and maintained, this error is both very small and constant. Thus the accuracy and dependability of the gyro compass exceeds that of the magnetic compass. For this reason, despite their relatively higher cost, gyro compasses are found today on fairly small commercial vessels. If the owner can afford one, and the boat's service warrants one, a gyro compass is well worth the cost. Let's take a quick look at an example of applying gyro error:

You are steering a course of 278° PGC (per gyro compass). Your gyro error is 1°E. What is your true course? The answer:

GC 278°
GE   1°E
_____
279°T

Your course is 279° True. You still add easterly error, as always, when correcting, but you only have one small error to contend with.

Again practice should help you fix in your mind the way to correct compass bearings and convert relative bearings to true bearings. Work the following problems.

PRACTICE PROBLEMS

1. Your boat is on a course of 178°C. You take a bearing on a light bearing 236°C. The variation at your DR position is 6°W. What is the true bearing of the light? (Remember to use the deviation table in Figure 6-4).

2. Your boat is on a course of 033°C. You calculate you should see Sand Island Light bearing 021°T at 1530 ship's time. Variation in the area is 4°E. On what compass bearing would you expect to see Sand Island Light?

3. Your boat is on a course of 327°C. You have aligned your pelorus to agree with your boat's compass course. You see a water tank bearing 249°C. If the variation in your area is 9°W, what is the true bearing of the water tank?

4. Your boat is on a course of 141°C. You take a bearing on a church steeple bearing 317°R. The variation at your DR is 4°E. What is the true bearing of the church steeple?

ANSWERS
1. 226°T   2. 010°C
3. 243°T   4. 101°T

13   LINES OF POSITION

Certainly no question is harder to answer than the question of which came first, the chicken or the egg, unless it is the question every teacher of navigation has to answer: should bearings or lines of position be explained first? Bearings and lines of position, which we will often call LOP's, go together like cake and icing. But just as you can have cake with icing, you can also have cake without icing, and likewise you can have lines of position with or from bearings, and you can have lines of position without bearings. This is an essential concept, because the beginning navigator so often gets his fixes exclusively from LOP's resulting from bearings that he never realizes the other ways lines of position may be obtained.

All positions derived from the modern navigation techniques you are likely to use depend on lines of position. Even modern celestial navigation depends almost exclusively on LOP's. Understanding lines of position can well be the most important concept you must learn if you truly want to be a navigator. A line of position can be defined as the location of all the points your vessel may be on under a given set of conditions. This line may be a straight line, such as an LOP resulting from a bearing; it may be a circle or a segment of a circle; or it may plot as some other mathematical curve.

Anybody who sets foot in a boat uses lines of position without realizing it. For instance: Two fellows were in a skiff fishing. They had been having fabulous luck, but it was time to go in. As they were in a new spot, they wanted to be sure they could find this place again. One of these fellows had a pocket compass. He sighted over his compass to a tall tree on the bank. He said to his companion, "We can come back here to where that big cypress tree bears 125° on my pocket compass." Our friend in his skiff had obtained a line of position by taking a bearing.

If a lighthouse, church steeple, or any other aid to navigation or landmark is observed to bear a certain direction from you, all you have to do is plot this bearing on your chart to pass through the object you observed, and you know your boat must be somewhere on this "line of bearing." Your boat is somewhere on this line drawn on your chart. So a true bearing, plotted on a Mercator chart, is a line of position. Furthermore this bearing is a straight line of position. See Figure 13-1.

To plot the LOP shown in Figure 13-1, the navigator first lines up his parallel rulers with the direction of the bearing on the compass rose of his chart. He then steps the rulers over to the point where one edge

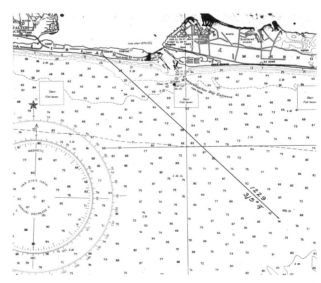

Figure 13-1. A bearing of 315°T plotted on the tower on the beach just west of the entrance to Choctawhatchee Bay, Florida, Chart No. 1264. From the labeling of the plotted bearing, anyone, including the navigator who took the bearing, can later determine the time the bearing was taken and the direction of the bearing. As navigator, you know your boat must be somewhere on this line of position.

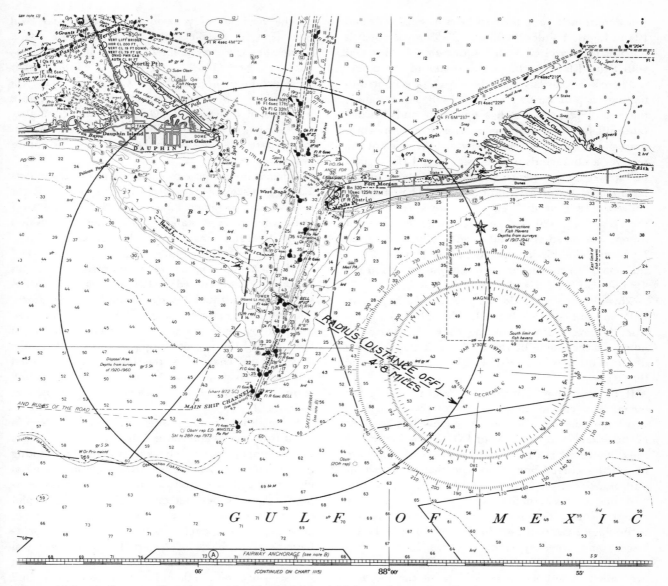

Figure 13-2. A distance-off circle plotted with Sand Island Light as the center. The boat must lie somewhere on this circle whose radius is 4.8 miles.

of the rulers passes precisely through the charted position of the landmark or aid he took the bearing on. The line of position is then drawn in the opposite direction, the reciprocal direction, from the bearing, as this is the direction your boat lies *from the object*. Thus, if a lighthouse bears 315°T from your boat, your boat bears 135°T from the lighthouse. The line of position runs in a direction, or is oriented on an axis, of 315°/135°T. When you plot your LOP resulting from this bearing, it is essential you label it as in Figure 13-1. To label an LOP resulting from a bearing, you write the time the bearing was taken above the LOP and the true direction of the bearing under the LOP.

Circular lines of position are even simpler in concept. Your high school geometry course defined a circle as the locus of all points equidistant from a fixed point called the center. Direction is not mentioned. Using this definition for navigation, you see that if you can find the distance your vessel is off an aid to navigation or landmark, all you need do is draw a circle, with this distance off as the radius of the circle, and the aid or landmark as the center of the circle. You know your vessel must lie somewhere on this circle. To illustrate this let's look at Figure 13-2, which is a cutout from Chart No. 1266, Mobile Bay, showing Sand Island Light. Assume that by vertical sextant angle, range finder, or other means you determined your boat to be 4.8 miles off Sand Island Light. To plot the line of position your boat is on, just draw a circle with a radius of 4.8 miles and with Sand Island Light as the center of the circle.

There are occasions when the navigator is limited to finding his position by a circular LOP. For instance, there is the case in which a navigator finds his distance off from an aid to navigation, in fog, by comparing the time interval between the instant he receives a characteristic radio signal and the instant he receives a characteristic sound signal, both signals having been broadcast simultaneously. The navigator converts this time difference into distance by using the factor of 1,120 feet per second as the speed of sound. The speed of the radio signal is instantaneous. I will explain this in more detail in Chapter 21 of this book. For now suffice it to say you know you are 4.8 miles off Sand Island Light.

This distance-off circle is a line of position. As an LOP it must also be labeled. The labeling in this case, however, consists of the time of observation noted on the inside of the circle, and the time the distance off was observed noted on the outside of the circle.

If by soundings, approximate bearings, or other means, you can deduce the part of the circle your vessel must be on, you need plot only this segment of the distance-off circle. Your LOP is this segment of the distance-off circle. Thus by distance off you have obtained a curved line of position that is a circle or part of a circle.

A line of position may also be part of a more complex curve. The most common LOP of this type is the line of position used to fix a position by loran, Decca, and other hyperbolic systems used in electronic navigation. These electronic navigation systems are called hyperbolic systems because the locus of the possible points your boat may be, as determined by the read-out of your loran or other gear, will plot as a hyperbolic curve on a Mercator chart. Remember the curved lines, printed in pastel inks, on Chart No. 1115? I told you in Chapter 3 that these are loran lines and that Chart No. 1115 is a loran chart. These lines are curved because they are segments of a hyperbola. Only by studying smaller scale charts, or examining lines near the base line on loran charts, is it possible to see the hyperbolic nature of these curves.

It is not my purpose to explain loran at this point. Loran is discussed extensively in Chapter 21. Right now you are studying lines of position, and what I want you to understand is that lines of position on a Mercator chart may plot as staight lines, circles or segments of a circle, or other types of curves.

One other concept I want to introduce in this chapter is how curved LOP's may be plotted as straight lines without any significant loss of accuracy. This situation exists when the scale of the chart you are plotting on is not too small, and the radius of the curved LOP is quite large. In this situation, the scale of the chart plus the large radius involved cause the navigator to work only with a very small segment of a curved LOP, which essentially plots as a straight line.

So much for lines of position. The ideas to keep in mind from this chapter are: Lines of position are the basic components of position finding by piloting (terrestrial observations), celestial navigation (celestial observations), and electronic navigation (radio bearings and hyperbolic systems); these LOP's may plot on your Mercator chart, depending on their type, as straight lines, circles or parts of a circle, or as hyperbolas or parts of hyperbolas. Now that you know all there is to know about lines of position let's see what you use them for. Perhaps you may find yourself in a fix.

14 THE FIX AND THE RUNNING FIX

In the preceding chapters I have implied that, if you uncorrect your compass and then steer your course carefully, you cannot help but proceed in the direction you intend to go. Now if you also know your exact speed and the time you were underway on this course, you will know precisely how far your vessel has gone. Thus, if you know your point of departure, your course steered, and your distance run, you should know exactly where you are at the end of this run. Theoretically your DR position will be your actual position.

Oh, only were this so! How often does a navigator set what appears to be a safe course only to have his vessel end up in serious danger or even disaster. Why? These navigators all figured their courses and speeds accurately enough in the beginning. How can such things happen? The answer to this question is apparent when you consider that even though your course and speed *through the water* may be accurate, the water itself may be moving and your boat may also be affected by the wind blowing her in a certain direction. Steering errors are always a factor, too, even with automatic pilots. So we see how you, our confident navigator, who has laid down a carefully plotted course, can cruise on to perdition.

The insidious motion of the water, force of the wind, or errors in steering, individually or combined, cause your boat to diverge from her DR track. How do you tell you are being affected by these forces? You can tell by accurately fixing the position of your vessel at frequent enough intervals to alert you to any divergence from your intended course in time to take corrective action.

In Chapter 1, I told you that on a large, deep-draft vessel operating close to the beach, this fixing of your vessel's position can be a continuous evolution of bearings, plots, sextant angles, or other observations. On a smaller boat, such as a yacht or fishing vessel, it may be satisfactory to get a fix only at set intervals.

All fixes are obtained by plotting two or more lines of position. This is the only way to get a fix with LOP's. Let's take another look at our two friends from Chapter 13 who wanted to know how to get back to their lucky fishing spot. When the first fellow said they could come back to where the big cypress tree bears 125° on his pocket compass, his companion thought a moment, and said: "That won't tell us if we are over our fishing hole. Why don't you sight on that tree over there, too?" The bearing of that tree made a large angle when it intersected the bearing of the first tree.

The first man replied: "Good! That tree bears 020° on my pocket compass."

Our fishing friends now had two lines of position. If you have ever done any serious fishing, you have used this means of locating your favorite fishing spots. It is only common sense, and much of navigation is only common sense.

These two fellows knew they were on both of these lines they had observed. If they had a chart, and if they were able to pinpoint on it the location of the trees they took their bearings on, they could draw these bearings on their chart. The lines would cross, if the bearings were taken accurately. The point of intersection, the cross, of these two lines of position is the only place they could be on both these lines at the same time. Thus the intersection of two or more lines of position will give you a *fix*. Had our friends taken more bearings so as to have three or more LOP's that crossed at the same point, they would have had an even more reliable fix, because an error in any one bearing would have caused it to plot away from the resulting fix.

For the fix to be accurate, these LOP's must result from simultaneous observations. Simultaneous strictly means at the exact same time, but in navigation the word simultaneous is used to mean at near enough the same time so that no significant error occurs. You can take two or three bearings, one after the other, and consider them simultaneous, but you must move with speed and precision. Even if you are only making eight knots, your boat will move a quarter of a mile in two minutes. If you can get two accurate bearings in two minutes on a small boat in a seaway, you are a pretty good navigator. On a ship of any size, you should be able to grab a "cut" (bearing) in just a few seconds. Yet, unless you are working in very confined waters and on a very large scale chart, the time element involved in a round of bearings may not introduce dangerous error for a small boat. On a large vessel in such confined waters, you had better be making considerably less than eight knots. You should *slow down, stop, even anchor* if in doubt, in close quarters, and if it is feasible to do so. On a large ship, too, you would actually be observing strictly simultaneous bearings. As a navigator of a destroyer, you would have two or more quartermasters on each alidade taking simultaneous bearings and coordinating their observations by

calling "Stand by!" and "Mark!" when on target. As navigator, your job would be to correct the bearings and plot the LOP's. It is a thrill and an inspiration to see a skilled bridge team safely navigate a large ship up a narrow channel without local knowledge, but relying only on the charts and sailing directions.

On a merchantman or small vessel, it is usually all up to you when just coasting. As navigator of *War Hat*, let's see how you would take your bearings and plot your fix. You are coasting from Panama City to Gulfport. Let's return to where you were in Chapter 7 to continue our imaginary voyage.

In the practice problems of Chapter 7, you departed your 1700 DR to go to the assistance of a boat in distress. Your 1734 DR was Latitude 30° 07.'1 N, Longitude 86° 08.'9 W. From this 1734 DR you come to course 347°T to return to your planned track at point *B*. As navigator it is up to you to put *War Hat* right on position at point *B*. Plot the course 347°T

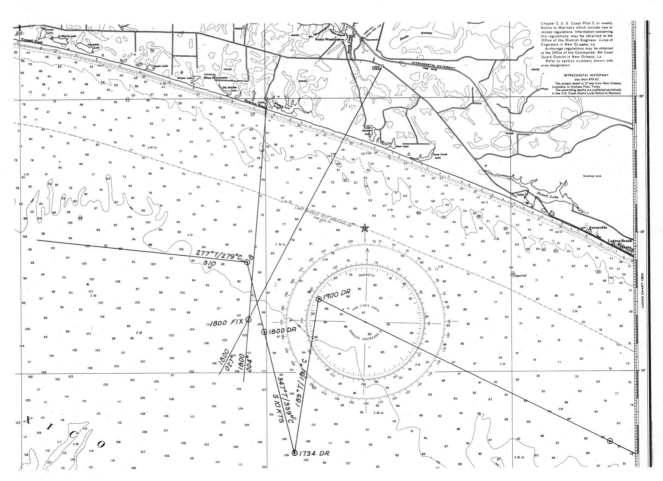

Figure 14-1. A fix from two bearings.

90

on the chart and then you can proceed steering 339°C.

As you approach the coast, certain landmarks come into sight. You identify these objects and locate them on the chart. Now you should take a round of bearings on each of these landmarks to get a fix so you can see if you are making good your intended course. A quick look at the chart, Chart No. 1264, shows only the tank at Grayton Beach as a possible landmark. You cannot get a fix from a bearing on this tank alone, but there is another landmark quite a distance inland. This second landmark is the lookout tower NNE of point *B*, about three miles inland. Sunset is about 1714 and darkness follows soon. With your dividers, you measure the distance from your 1734 DR to point *B* to be 7.1 miles. At 10 knots, *War Hat* should make the run from her 1734 DR to point *B* in 42 minutes. By dead reckoning she should be at point *B* at 1812. But dead reckoning isn't exact enough. You want to *fix* your position at point *B*.

Tanks such as the one at Grayton Beach and towers such as the lookout tower are required to be lighted as a safety measure to air navigation. This serves you, the marine navigator, well, too, because in the descending darkness you can identify both these landmarks from the deck of *War Hat*. Now I will admit it would require excellent visibility to see these landmarks from your DR position, but, for the sake of illustration, let's assume the visibility is that good.

At 1800 you observe the lookout tower to bear 025°C. You make your observation with a hand-held bearing compass. As soon as you note the bearing of the lookout tower you take a bearing on the tank at Grayton Beach. This tank bears 002° by hand-held bearing compass. How do you plot your fix?

Your first step is to correct your compass bearings to true bearings. As you are using a hand-held bearing compass, you cannot use the deviation table you constructed in Chapter 6 (Figure 6-4). This table was devised for your steering compass. Assume, though, that you know the deviation for your hand-held bearing compass *for the place you are on deck* and *the course you are steering* to be 1°W. You proceed as before (in Chapters 12 and 13.)

STEP 1
Write your correction formula in a vertical column — actually two vertical columns, as you must head up a column for each landmark you took a bearing on.

STEP 2
Fill in the information you have.

Lookout tower	Tank at Grayton Beach
C 025°	C 002°
D 1°W	D 1°W
M	M
V 3°E (from your chart)	V 3°E (from your chart)
T	T

STEP 3
Solve first for the magnetic bearings at each object, then solve for the true bearings.

Lookout tower	Tank at Grayton Beach
C 025°	C 002°
D 1°W	D 1°W
M 024°	M 001°
V 3°E	V 3°E
T 027°	T 004°

STEP 4
Plot the two *true* bearings by setting your parallel rulers on the compass rose so as to align the edge nearest your DR position in such a manner as to pass through the center of the compass rose and cross precisely over the 027° point of the outer, or true, rose for the lookout tower. Be precise in this alignment. In plotting you should always work as precisely and as accurately as possible. Now carefully "walk" your parallel rulers over so the aligned edge passes directly through the position of the lookout tower, and draw a line from the lookout tower along the edge of the parallel ruler, out into the Gulf. *Do not* draw through the symbol for the tower itself. Sooner or later you will erase this line, and if you draw the line through the symbol, you may erase the symbol too. Extend this line, which is your line of bearing and your plotted LOP, a mile or so beyond your DR. Label this LOP with the time and true direction of your bearing. Repeat this procedure, using the bearing of 004°T, for the tank at Grayton Beach, and label this LOP, too, with the time and true direction.

Lo and behold, these two LOP's cross! You know your boat is on both of the LOP's. The only spot at which your boat can be on both of these two LOP's at the same instant is the point at which they cross. Consequently the intersection of two or more lines of position, observed at the same time, gives you your vessel's position. Navigators call this a *fix*.

As navigator of *War Hat* you should draw a small circle around the intersection of the two LOP's you just plotted, and label this "1800 fix." Figure 14-1 is a cut-out of Chart No. 1264 illustrating the lines of position and your resulting 1800 fix.

Your 1800 fix shows *War Hat* well ahead of her 1800 DR. She is also slightly west of the rhumb line from her 1734 DR to point *B*. A course change is in order. With your parallel rulers you find your new course to be 357°T. This uncorrects to a compass course of 346°. The distance to go to point *B* is 2.1 miles, which at 10 knots means a run of 12 minutes plus. You order the course changed to 346°C, and at 1812 you again change course to 277°T/279°C. By DR you are at point *B*. Another pair of bearings on the tank at Grayton Beach and the lookout tower could confirm this, but since you are in open water, dead reckoning is accurate enough.

At 1912 you are under sail alone with a light nor'easter sending you reaching down the coast. You check your speed, and find it now to be six knots. A thorough review of Chart Nos. 1115, 1264, 1265, 1266, and 1267 shows no hazards along the beach. All you need to do is maintain your distance off the beach and stay far enough out to avoid the restricted and prohibited areas just east of the midway point down Santa Rosa Island. Otherwise you could safely come almost within hailing distance. But to take advantage of the westerly set of the current and to avoid getting too close to the land, you decide to maintain your planned rhumb line course. You stand down the coast fixing your position from

time to time, and further confirming your distance off by a method I am going to discuss in the next chapter.

But before I go on, a few additional comments are in order regarding fixes from lines of position obtained by bearings. Three or more lines of position may not always cross at a precise point. Often, due to the limits of accuracy obtainable in your observations, the most carefully observed bearings will plot as a small triangle. This can happen on any size vessel, but is most likely to happen on a small boat bouncing around in the open sea.

Figure 14-2 is an actual plot of bearings from my sloop *Li'l Tiger*. There are two fixes plotted in Figure 14-2, but it is the 1047 fix I want you to look at. We actually made this passage, the passage you are making in *War Hat*, in *Li'l Tiger* in April of 1973 just to assure ourselves we weren't spoofing you about what you can and cannot see in the way of landmarks and aids along this stretch of coast. We did fudge a little by setting a course of 270°T from buoy number 1 instead of running out to the seabuoy. Anyhow, the 1047 fix in Figure 14-2 does plot as a small triangle, less than a mile on any side, and only 0.2 miles on

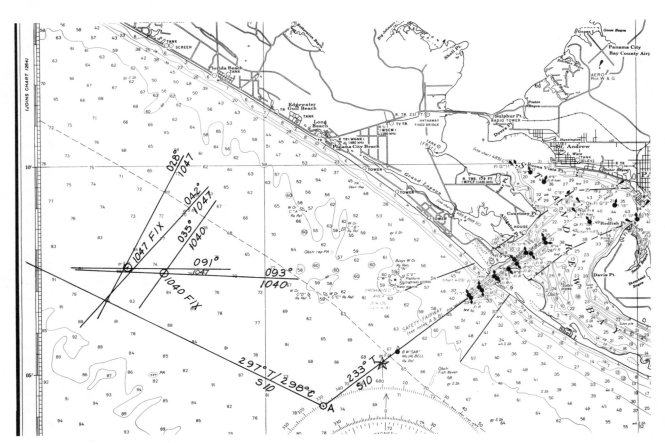

Figure 14-2. A fix from three or more bearings more often than not plots as a small triangle.

the shortest side. This requires the navigator to apply a little judgement in determining where he really is. The fix is plotted from three bearings: the Florida Beach tank at 028°T; the tower at Edgewater Gulf Beach bearing 042°T, and the platform bearing 091°T.

The first and most obvious thing to note is that the angular difference between the bearings on the tank and the tower is only 14°. This difference in angle is not great enough for accurate fixes because an error of 1° will cause considerable change in the point where these two bearings cross. Sometimes, however, as here, due to haze on the beach, this difference between bearings may be the best you can get. For example, if I observed a bearing on the tower to be 043°T, my three LOP's would have crossed at a point right on my fix! Bearings should have as much angular difference as possible with a cross of 90° being the very best. The bearing of the platform is 091°T. This gives an excellent spread with either or both of the first two bearings. Between the points this third LOP, the bearing on the platform, crosses each of the other LOP's is the base of our small triangle. These points are only 0.2 miles apart. From this it is obvious that our most likely position lies on this last LOP halfway between the first two LOP's.

Sometimes, even with a good angular difference, bearings between three or more LOP's will not cross at a precise point. Usually your triangle, or other shape depending on the number of LOP's, will be nearly equal on each side. Unless you know that one of the three LOP's is less reliable for some reason, the center of the triangle would be considered your fix.

From this you can see that, no matter how precise we try to be, we can never eliminate judgement as a factor in safe navigation. Navigation will always be an art as well as a science. Skill and judgement, in any art, come from experience and practice.

Let's go on now and talk about circular LOP's. At daylight on the morning of the 22nd you are coasting along the Alabama shore. At 0630 you see Sand Island Light on your starboard bow, and with your sextant you find your distance off to be 4.8 miles. (The actual method for determining distances off by vertical sextant angles is covered in Chapter 16.) Mobile Point Light structure is also visible in the clear morning air about two points forward of your starboard beam. You take a vertical sextant angle on Mobile Point Light and find you are 5.4 miles off. Look back at Figure 13-2. If you draw a circle from Mobile Point Light as the center with a radius of 5.4 miles, this circle will cross the distance-off circle from Sand Island Light about two miles north of your rhumb line. (See Figure 14-3). But this same circle

also intersects the Sand Island Light circle at another place! This second intersection is just south of Dauphin Island at the entrance to Pelican Pass. How do you know you aren't at this point? Where are you?

The answer to these questions comes from common sense again. You know you couldn't be at this second point and have Sand Island Light on your starboard bow and Mobile Point Light nearly abeam if you are steering 261°T. If you are in doubt, your seaman's eye should tell you that you are well over a mile off the beach. And if you are still in doubt, your fathometer or lead line will show that you are in 48 feet of water and not 24.

Any time you have two position circles you will have two points at which these circles cross. The second cross will almost always be far enough removed from your true position to be obvious unless the distance between the centers of the two circles approaches twice the distance off. Then the distance-off circles may cross at two points quite close together. Thus, as you try to find bearings with a wide angular difference, you should also try to work distance-off problems from objects that will cause your position circles to cross with two intersections well removed from each other.

From the very beginning I have insisted that you must have two or more LOP's to get a fix. Sooner or later some wag is going to bet you he can get a fix from one LOP. Go on and take his bet. This guy will jump back at you and say: "A bearing and a distance off will give you a fix! Pay me!" Then it is your turn. Explain to this would-be wise guy that a distance off, in effect, is an LOP also. Make him pay you! For example: Suppose when you saw Sand Island Light that you found its bearing to be 298°T. Had you plotted this bearing, you would have fixed your position at exactly the same place your distance-off circle from Mobile Point Light put you. Again see Figure 14-3. In this case your distance off Mobile Point Light would be a third LOP. So if you are the betting kind, bet someone you can get a fix by two simultaneous observations of the same aid or landmark. You should have plenty of takers. But be sure the aid or landmark you select is one you can get your distance off from and one which you can get a bearing on at the same time, too.

This brings us to another concept — the *running fix*. There are many times when you cannot get simultaneous observations on two objects, but must take your cut on the first object and then wait until another suitable object comes into view, or wait until the bearing of the first object changes enough to give a wide angle between the first and second bear-

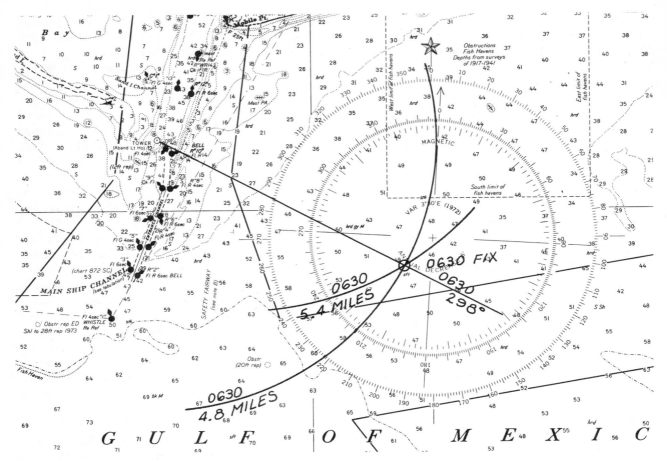

Figure 14-3. A fix by a bearing and distance off, as well as two distance-off circles.

ings. But you get a fix by knowing that your boat is on two lines of position at the same time. You must equate these two bearings to a common time. How do you do this?

Let's go back where *War Hat* was at 1812 the evening before. When you reached point *B*, by dead reckoning, you came left to course 277°T. At 1912 you secured your engine and continued under sail. Your log showed you were making six knots. At this time, 2012, you took a bearing, with your hand-bearing compass, on a quick-flashing light bearing 357°C. You corrected this bearing to 359°T. You identified this quick-flashing light as the light at Choctawhatchee Bay Entrance. As this LOP crosses your rhumb line course at nearly 90° (actually 82°), this one bearing tells you a lot. It crosses your rhumb line about one mile ahead of your DR. The most obvious thing this one LOP tells you is that you are making around seven knots and not the six your log shows! Yet this one LOP does *not* give you a fix. (See Figure 14-4.)

At your distance offshore this quick-flashing light is the only identifiable light you can see. Conse-

quently, you can get only one LOP — a bearing on the Choctawhatchee Bay Entrance Light. There is nothing else in sight. At your apparent distance offshore, you are outside the nominal range of this light, but the *Light List* shows you are well within the geographic range of the jetty light. In the clear, fall air, the light is easily seen from aloft.

One of the nice things about a hand-bearing compass is that you can even carry it aloft, if necessary, to raise your height of eye enough to see a light. So, with one hand for yourself and one for the ship, lay aloft and get your bearings.

You plot your bearing of 359°T. It crosses your rhumb line about one mile ahead of your 2012 DR. You must now wait long enough for the bearing on the Choctawhatchee Bay Entrance Light to change enough to make the second LOP cross the first bearing at a wide enough angle. At 2042, thirty minutes later, you take another bearing on this same light. This second bearing corrects to 038°T.

You now have two lines of position, and you should be able to get a fix; except these two LOP's were taken at different times! How can you get a fix in a

94

situation like this? You must advance your 2012 LOP to equate it in time with your 2042 LOP. How do you do this? Here it is, step by step:

STEP 1

Determine your most accurate speed. First consider your 2012 LOP. You are obviously making seven knots.

STEP 2

If you take the point at which this 2012 LOP crosses your course, and with dividers step off from this point to the west 3.5 miles, the distance you would run in 30 minutes at seven knots, and then draw a line parallel to your 2012 LOP through this point, you have in effect moved your LOP along with your DR. Your 2012 LOP will maintain the same relationship to your 2042 DR as it did to your original 2012 DR. Your 2012 LOP, from the bearing on the jetty light, plotted one mile ahead of your 2012 DR. Your advanced 2012 to 2042 LOP should plot one mile ahead of your 2042 DR. You should label this LOP "2012/2042" over and "359°" under.

This is how you advance an LOP from a bearing and this is all there is to it. Don't look for any mystery. There is none. This specific situation illustrates how you advance a line of position when plotting a running fix. It makes no difference where you get your later LOP. You may observe another bearing on something else. Regardless, there are just two things to remember in advancing a line of position:

1. The advanced LOP will always bear the same relative position to the advanced DR and the DR at the time of observation. Thus, if the LOP plotted one mile ahead of the DR at the time the bearing was

taken, the advanced LOP will plot one mile ahead of the DR at the time to which the LOP was advanced, even if your boat changed course.

2. Advanced LOP's are always parallel to the original LOP, again, even if you change course. If your original bearing was 359°T, your advanced LOP plots in the same direction — 359°T.

Even though I am being redundant, I am going to reiterate, in more general terms, what I have just said, interspersing some special situations. To advance an LOP, begin with the point where the LOP crosses your course line. If the LOP does not cross your course line because it is nearly parallel to your course, you must lay another line exactly parallel to your course in such a position that this parallel line will cross the LOP. A case such as this occurs when you take bearings on objects nearly dead ahead or nearly dead astern. You then advance this point where your LOP crosses your course, or the line parallel to your course, exactly as you would your DR. If you are making seven knots, your point of crossing makes seven knots. If the LOP crosses one mile ahead of your DR, the LOP will remain one mile ahead of the DR when advanced whether you steer a straight course, change course, go astern, or steam in circles.

How do you advance an LOP that is exactly parallel to your course? Your bearing on the platform in Figure 14-2 was almost dead astern. How would you have advanced this LOP had it been exactly parallel to your course? The answer is: you wouldn't have needed to advance this LOP. It is also your true course line.

You can also advance lines of position resulting from distance-off circles. How? Very easily. All you

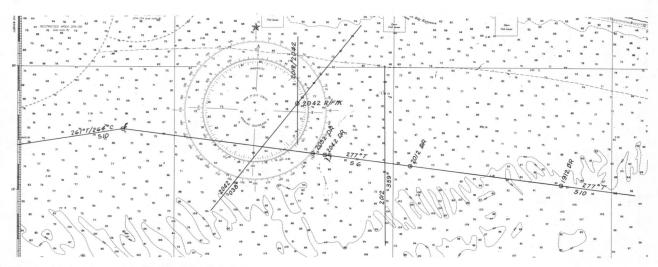

Figure 14-4. A running fix from two bearings.

need to do is draw a line parallel to your course through the center of the circle. You then advance the center of your distance-off circle along this line parallel to your course line for the distance run, and, with the advanced point as the center, draw another circle or arc of the circle with a radius equal to the distance off. This second circle or arc will be your advanced LOP. See Figure 14-5, which shows an imaginary island. You will recall in the very beginning of this book that I warned you I might take you far off to another corner of the world to illustrate a point. So suppose you are now coasting along some tropical island. Your course is 318°T; speed 10 knots.

There are two peaks on the island too far apart to be seen at the same time. The unpopulated coast offers no other landmarks. You have no instrument with which to take a bearing, except by sighting over your compass. You want more accuracy than this, however. But you don't need to take a bearing. Your sextant is all you need.

Follow the plot in Figure 14-5. At 0830 you find you are 20 miles off the peak at the southeast end of the island. At 1030 the haze clears and you can see the peak at the northwest end of the island. Your sextant reveals that you are 26 miles off from this second peak. Advance the center of the distance

circle from the first peak 20 miles (the distance you would run at 10 knots in two hours) along a line parallel to your course. From this second point strike an arc 20 miles in radius, your original distance off. This arc is your advanced circular LOP. Label it "0830/1030 — 20 mi." as shown in Figure 14-5. Now draw another arc 26 miles in radius with the second peak as a center. Where this arc crosses your 0830/1030 LOP is your running fix. That is all there is to it.

Why would a navigator want a fix such as that in Figure 14-5? The answer is obvious. He is taking his departure. It is assumed that prior to 0830 he made his landfall and carried his vessel safely by her closest point of approach to the land by proper pilotage. The land now falls away and as the boat pulls to sea, the navigator grabs the best fix at the last moment for his departure.

You can advance any distance-off circle in this manner. In confined waters you may be working with distances off of only a few miles or less. You would advance the resulting LOP's in exactly the same way. Chapters 16 and 17 go into greater detail on the sextant and distance-off circles as tools for the coastwise navigator. Meanwhile, let's return to *War Hat* and continue along the south coast of Florida.

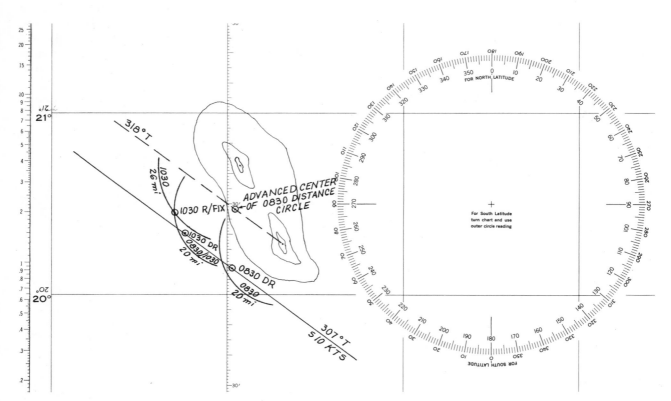

Figure 14-5. Advancing a circular LOP.

15   DISTANCE OFF BY ANGLES ON THE BOW

At 2042 your running fix showed *War Hat* almost two miles north of the rhumb line. The skipper ordered a course change to 261°T/264°C to put her right on course for point *C* and announced, "I'm hitting the sack. Keep her off the beach, mate," and disappeared below.

You are alone on deck, at night, with a great big handful of schooner, reaching along a low-lying coast, and the skipper says, "Keep her off the beach." You can't argue with the fact that this is a good idea, but *how*? You don't have radar. You can hardly let the helm go long enough to take a bearing much less plot a position. Yet this low-lying beach is so hard to see. The tree line may be a mile back from the water's edge; you could be right on the sand before you realize you are in trouble. Of course, if things get really sticky, you can call the watch below, and someone else could steer while you get a fix. (It wouldn't help to roust the boys corking off in the forward end of the cockpit.) Or you could head out to sea on a course you know will get you into good water. Neither one of these solutions is the best, however, because the guy below needs his forty winks when he can get it, and running way south of your rhumb line just to keep offshore is a waste of time. If you are capable of standing a night wheel watch, or a wheel watch at any time, in a situation such as you now find yourself in, you should be able to keep a sufficiently accurate estimate of your distance off the beach. But *how*?

Remember what I said in the chapter before this one? A careful study of your chart shows there are no real hazards even fairly close in. All you must avoid is the restricted area off Santa Rosa Island. Your rhumb line passes a mile south of this restricted area and 6½ miles off the beach. If you stay on the rhumb line, you stay out of trouble. As one old salt said: "You don't got to know where you are. You got to know where you ain't!" If you know you "ain't"

closer than 6½ miles to the beach, you know you are safe.

To help you keep 6½ miles off the beach, we have several rules of thumb. Each involves taking two bearings with a run between. Each assumes you do not change course between the first and second bearing. The accuracy of the results you get from using these rules will depend on how accurately you observe the bearings involved and on how accurately you know your course and speed. The techniques I am going to show you are very useful, and, in running this coast in *Li'l Tiger*, we use them all the time.

BOW AND BEAM BEARINGS

The first and easiest method of calculating distance off is to use bow and beam bearings. To find your distance by bow and beam bearings, you take a bearing on an object when it bears 45° on the bow, either 045°R or 315°R, and then run until the object is abeam, bearing either 090°R or 270°R. The distance run between the time you took the first bearing and the time you took the second bearing is the distance at which you will pass the object abeam. As you are abeam at the time you took the second bearing, this is the distance off at the time of the second bearing.

For example, no sooner does the skipper disappear below than you notice the aircraft warning light on the overhead power cable tower just west of Fort Walton Beach, on Santa Rosa Island, bearing 309°C. It is 2042. At 2135 the aircraft warning light bears 354°C. As your course is 264°C the first bearing is on your starboard bow or 045°R (264° + 045° = 309°). The second bearing is broad on you starboard beam or 090°R. Here is where your hand-held bearing compass comes in handy. With one hand on the wheel, it is no trick at all to take these bearings. And, since you are looking only for changes in bearing due to distance run, you do not need to correct these two bearings.

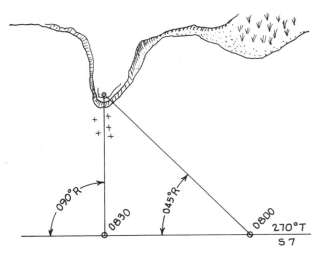

Figure 15-1. A typical use of a bow and beam bearing. At 0800 a vessel making seven knots takes a bearing on a light bearing 045°R, and at 0830 she takes another bearing on the same light bearing 090°R. How far is she off the light? Since she has run 3.5 miles in the 30 minutes between 0800 and 0830, she must be 3.5 miles off the light.

You have sailed for 53 minutes between the two bearings. At 7 knots you will have sailed 6.2 miles in 53 minutes. Thus at 2135, *War Hat* is 6.2 miles off the tower.

If you took your bearings accurately, you now have a running fix, if you care to plot it, because you took your bearings on a charted object. You have a bearing and a distance off. Your most likely source of error is in your dead reckoning. On the other hand, the beauty of this method is that you know you are 6.2 miles off the tower. If you know how close the tower is to the beach, you know how far off the beach you are. *War Hat* is *not* 6.2 miles offshore. The tower is 0.4 miles back from the beach. Thus *War Hat* is *5.8* miles off the beach. *You do not need a fix to know* War Hat *is 5.8 miles off the beach*. Figure 15-1 illustrates the use of bow and beam bearings.

In using these rules you must remember that the distance you obtain is the distance off the *object*. You must know the exact location of the object if you wish to plot a running fix from it. On the other hand, if you know positively that an object is on the water's edge, you need not know anything else about where it is, if you want only to find your distance off the beach. An example of what I mean is best illustrated in the explanation of our next rule of thumb concerning angles on the bow.

War Hat stands west along the coast. The nor'-easter has freshened and kicked up a wet chop, so you want to ease up under the lee of the land. At 2212 you come to course of 296°T to get closer into the beach. This course will clear the restricted area nicely. At 2330 your DR puts you 2.5 miles off the beach; you come back to your course of 261°T to parallel your rhumb line. You are pretty close in now, so you must look alive. But there are no charted aids along this stretch of beach! As you change course, you do notice a light, and with your glasses you find the light is in the yard of a beach cottage. A glance over the hand-held bearing compass shows the bearing of the light to be slightly over 283°C or between 022°R and 023°R. If you don't own a hand-held bearing compass, just sight across the card of your steering compass. If they don't turn that darn light out too soon, you have it made. With a first bearing of 22°/23°R you are set up to apply both of two rules involving angles on the bow. The rules are *doubling the angle* and the *seven-tenths rule*.

DOUBLING THE ANGLE

This rule simply states that if you observe an object on your bow at a certain angle, and then run until the object bears at an angle on the bow equal to twice the first angle, the distance your vessel runs between the bearings is the distance she is off the object at the time of the second bearing. So, you are still boiling along at seven knots because you shortened sail in the freshening nor'easter; the boy did wake up and cast a Dutchman's log for you. At 2353 the light in the yard bears 306°C or 045°R. Without taking your hands off the wheel you run through your mental calculation: 7 knots is 700 feet a minute, 700 times 23 is 16,100. This divided by 6,000 is 2 4/6 or 2.66 miles. You are 2.6 miles off the light. As the light is now broad on your bow, you know this is a safe distance off.

THE SEVEN-TENTHS RULE

At this time, however, it is useful to know how far off you should expect to pass the light abeam. Another rule tells us that if we observe an object to bear 22½° on our bow, and then run until we have the object bearing 45° on our bow, the distance we will pass the object abeam is seven-tenths of the distance run. Now eye-balling a bearing over a compass provides useful accuracy, but not accuracy to one-half a degree or even one degree. So, if you don't have a hand-held bearing compass you can consider your 022°R/023°R as 022½°R, and with your 045°R have all the accuracy you need. Thus 7/10 of 2.6 is 1.8. You will pass the light 1.8 miles off. Figure 15-2 illustrates both doubling the angle and the seven-tenths rule.

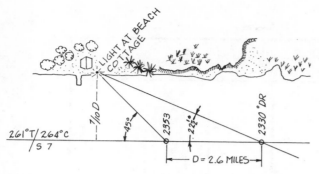

261°T/264°C
/S 7

Figure 15-2. Doubling the angle, and the seven-tenths rule.

You should continue to time your run from the 045°R bearing, because, at the time the light is abeam, you can calculate your distance off by figuring the distance you have run and thus check the predicted distance off you just computed by the seventenths rule.

THE 26½° — 45° RULE

If you missed the 022°R bearing on this otherwise unimportant yard light, you could have used still another rule to find your distance off. And, whether you missed the 22½° bearing or not, you should always use the next means available to check your calculations. The 26½° — 45° rule states that, if you observe an object 26½° on your bow (026.°5R or 333.°5R) and then after a run between, observe the same object bearing 45° on the bow (045°R or 315°R), then the distance your boat ran between the bearings is the distance you will be off the object when it is abeam.

Suppose as you continue down the beach another light appears. This time it is nothing but a big bonfire some happy youngsters are burning on the beach. This time your young watchmate has fetched your sextant. (How you use the sextant to take bearings is described in Chapter 17). You accurately observe the bonfire to bear 26½ degrees on your starboard bow. The time is 0036. At 0053 the bonfire bears 45° on your bow. You have run 17 minutes at 7 knots for a distance of 11,900 feet or two miles. You know you will pass the bonfire two miles off. Figure 15-3 illustrates this rule.

In my first three examples of angles on the bow to determine distance off, I have used bearings taken with a hand-held bearing compass or by sighting over the steering compass. I did this because when you are alone on watch, stuck on the helm, this may be the best you can do. Yet, if you have a good seaman's eye, you will be surprised how accurate you can be just by sighting over your boat's steering compass. As I said, I use these techniques along with the speed,

time, distance solutions of Chapter 8 whenever I am running coastwise outside. This way, with my handheld bearing compass or seaman's eye over the steering compass and mental solutions to my distance-run problems, I know accurately enough how far off the beach I am. And I never have to leave the wheel to plot a bearing! On *Li'l Tiger,* a 22-foot deep-water sloop, there isn't room for much sophisticated gear.

In my last example above I mentioned the sextant for observing these angles. I did this because, if eyeball accuracy is the best you can do, under some conditions, you should not forget that, when circumstances permit, these distance-off techniques can be extremely accurate. The hand-held bearing compass will give you all the accuracy you normally need, but if you require more precision or don't own a handheld bearing compass, your sextant will give you even more accurate results. I am always inspired by the competent navigator who, with sextant in hand, can carry a vessel on a safe passage through confined waters. This man has done his homework.

DISTANCE OFF BY TWO BEARINGS

If the above rules of thumb are not enough, Dr. Bowditch and his disciples have provided us with an even more comprehensive means of finding both distance off and distance to pass abeam of a landmark by two bearings and a run between. In the 1962 edition of *Bowditch,* this information is found in Table 7 (see Figure 15-4, which reproduces part of the table). Of course, you must have *Bowditch* handy to refer to Table 7, and handling a book the size of *Bowditch* is not something you can do easily and steer at the same time. Nevertheless, Table 7 is a very handy table and you should know how to use it. After all, you will not always be so confined to the

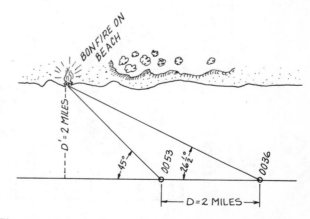

Figure 15-3. The 26½°/45° rule for angles on the bow.

TABLE 7

Distance of an Object by Two Bearings

Difference between the course and second bearing	20°		22°		24°		26°		28°		30°		32°	
30	1.97	0.98												
32	1.64	0.87	2.16	1.14										
34	1.41	0.79	1.80	1.01	2.34	1.31								
36	1.24	0.73	1.55	0.91	1.96	1.15	2.52	1.48						
38	1.11	0.68	1.36	0.84	1.68	1.04	2.11	1.30	2.70	1.66				
40	1.00	0.64	1.21	0.78	1.48	0.95	1.81	1.16	2.26	1.45	2.88	1.85		
42	0.91	0.61	1.10	0.73	1.32	0.88	1.59	1.06	1.94	1.30	2.40	1.61	3.05	2.04
44	0.84	0.58	1.00	0.69	1.19	0.83	1.42	0.98	1.70	1.18	2.07	1.44	2.55	1.77
46	0.78	0.56	0.92	0.66	1.09	0.78	1.28	0.92	1.52	1.09	1.81	1.30	2.19	1.58
48	0.73	0.54	0.85	0.64	1.00	0.74	1.17	0.87	1.37	1.02	1.62	1.20	1.92	1.43
50	0.68	0.52	0.80	0.61	0.93	0.71	1.08	0.83	1.25	0.96	1.46	1.12	1.71	1.31
52	0.65	0.51	0.75	0.59	0.87	0.68	1.00	0.79	1.15	0.91	1.33	1.05	1.55	1.22
54	0.61	0.49	0.71	0.57	0.81	0.66	0.93	0.76	1.07	0.87	1.23	0.99	1.41	1.14
56	0.58	0.48	0.67	0.56	0.77	0.64	0.88	0.73	1.00	0.83	1.14	0.95	1.30	1.08
58	0.56	0.47	0.64	0.54	0.73	0.62	0.83	0.70	0.94	0.80	1.07	0.90	1.21	1.03
60	0.53	0.46	0.61	0.53	0.69	0.60	0.78	0.68	0.89	0.77	1.00	0.87	1.13	0.98
62	0.51	0.45	0.58	0.51	0.66	0.58	0.75	0.66	0.84	0.74	0.94	0.83	1.06	0.94
64	0.49	0.44	0.56	0.50	0.63	0.57	0.71	0.64	0.80	0.72	0.89	0.80	1.00	0.90
66	0.48	0.43	0.54	0.49	0.61	0.56	0.68	0.62	0.76	0.70	0.85	0.78	0.95	0.87
68	0.46	0.43	0.52	0.48	0.59	0.54	0.66	0.61	0.73	0.68	0.81	0.75	0.90	0.84
70	0.45	0.42	0.50	0.47	0.57	0.53	0.63	0.59	0.70	0.66	0.78	0.73	0.86	0.81
72	0.43	0.41	0.49	0.47	0.55	0.52	0.61	0.58	0.68	0.64	0.75	0.71	0.82	0.78
74	0.42	0.41	0.48	0.46	0.53	0.51	0.59	0.57	0.65	0.63	0.72	0.69	0.79	0.76
76	0.41	0.40	0.46	0.45	0.52	0.50	0.57	0.56	0.63	0.61	0.70	0.67	0.76	0.74
78	0.40	0.39	0.45	0.44	0.50	0.49	0.56	0.54	0.61	0.60	0.67	0.66	0.74	0.72
80	0.39	0.39	0.44	0.44	0.49	0.48	0.54	0.53	0.60	0.59	0.65	0.64	0.71	0.70
82	0.39	0.38	0.43	0.43	0.48	0.47	0.53	0.52	0.58	0.57	0.63	0.63	0.69	0.69
84	0.38	0.38	0.42	0.42	0.47	0.47	0.52	0.51	0.57	0.56	0.62	0.61	0.67	0.67
86	0.37	0.37	0.42	0.42	0.46	0.46	0.51	0.51	0.55	0.55	0.60	0.60	0.66	0.65
88	0.37	0.37	0.41	0.41	0.45	0.45	0.50	0.50	0.54	0.54	0.59	0.59	0.64	0.64
90	0.36	0.36	0.40	0.40	0.45	0.45	0.49	0.49	0.53	0.53	0.58	0.58	0.62	0.62
92	0.36	0.36	0.40	0.40	0.44	0.44	0.48	0.48	0.52	0.52	0.57	0.57	0.61	0.61
94	0.36	0.35	0.39	0.39	0.43	0.43	0.47	0.47	0.51	0.51	0.56	0.55	0.60	0.60
96	0.35	0.35	0.39	0.39	0.43	0.43	0.47	0.46	0.51	0.50	0.55	0.54	0.59	0.59
98	0.35	0.35	0.39	0.38	0.42	0.42	0.46	0.46	0.50	0.50	0.54	0.53	0.58	0.57
100	0.35	0.34	0.38	0.38	0.42	0.41	0.46	0.45	0.49	0.49	0.53	0.52	0.57	0.56
102	0.35	0.34	0.38	0.37	0.42	0.41	0.45	0.44	0.49	0.48	0.53	0.51	0.56	0.55
104	0.34	0.33	0.38	0.37	0.41	0.40	0.45	0.43	0.48	0.47	0.52	0.50	0.56	0.54
106	0.34	0.33	0.38	0.36	0.41	0.39	0.45	0.43	0.48	0.46	0.52	0.50	0.55	0.53
108	0.34	0.32	0.38	0.36	0.41	0.39	0.44	0.42	0.48	0.45	0.51	0.49	0.55	0.52
110	0.34	0.32	0.37	0.35	0.41	0.38	0.44	0.41	0.47	0.44	0.51	0.48	0.54	0.51
112	0.34	0.32	0.37	0.35	0.41	0.38	0.44	0.41	0.47	0.44	0.50	0.47	0.54	0.50
114	0.34	0.31	0.37	0.34	0.41	0.37	0.44	0.40	0.47	0.43	0.50	0.46	0.54	0.49
116	0.34	0.31	0.38	0.34	0.41	0.37	0.44	0.39	0.47	0.42	0.50	0.45	0.53	0.48
118	0.35	0.31	0.38	0.33	0.41	0.36	0.44	0.39	0.47	0.41	0.50	0.44	0.53	0.47
120	0.35	0.30	0.38	0.33	0.41	0.36	0.44	0.38	0.47	0.41	0.50	0.43	0.53	0.46
122	0.35	0.30	0.38	0.32	0.41	0.35	0.44	0.37	0.47	0.40	0.50	0.42	0.53	0.45
124	0.35	0.29	0.38	0.32	0.41	0.34	0.44	0.37	0.47	0.39	0.50	0.42	0.53	0.44
126	0.36	0.29	0.39	0.31	0.42	0.34	0.45	0.36	0.47	0.38	0.50	0.41	0.53	0.43
128	0.36	0.28	0.39	0.31	0.42	0.33	0.45	0.35	0.48	0.38	0.50	0.40	0.53	0.42
130	0.36	0.28	0.39	0.30	0.42	0.32	0.45	0.35	0.48	0.37	0.51	0.39	0.54	0.41
132	0.37	0.27	0.40	0.30	0.43	0.32	0.46	0.34	0.48	0.36	0.51	0.38	0.54	0.40
134	0.37	0.27	0.40	0.29	0.43	0.31	0.46	0.33	0.49	0.35	0.52	0.37	0.54	0.39
136	0.38	0.26	0.41	0.28	0.44	0.30	0.47	0.32	0.49	0.34	0.52	0.36	0.55	0.38
138	0.39	0.26	0.42	0.28	0.45	0.30	0.47	0.32	0.50	0.33	0.53	0.35	0.55	0.37
140	0.39	0.25	0.42	0.27	0.45	0.29	0.48	0.31	0.51	0.33	0.53	0.34	0.56	0.36
142	0.40	0.25	0.43	0.27	0.46	0.28	0.49	0.30	0.51	0.32	0.54	0.33	0.56	0.35
144	0.41	0.24	0.44	0.26	0.47	0.28	0.50	0.29	0.52	0.31	0.55	0.32	0.57	0.34
146	0.42	0.24	0.45	0.25	0.48	0.27	0.51	0.28	0.53	0.30	0.56	0.31	0.58	0.32
148	0.43	0.23	0.46	0.25	0.49	0.26	0.52	0.27	0.54	0.29	0.57	0.30	0.59	0.31
150	0.45	0.22	0.48	0.24	0.50	0.25	0.53	0.26	0.55	0.28	0.58	0.29	0.61	0.30
152	0.46	0.22	0.49	0.23	0.52	0.24	0.54	0.25	0.57	0.27	0.59	0.28	0.62	0.29
154	0.48	0.21	0.50	0.22	0.53	0.23	0.56	0.24	0.58	0.25	0.60	0.26	0.62	0.27
156	0.49	0.20	0.52	0.21	0.55	0.22	0.57	0.23	0.60	0.24	0.62	0.25	0.64	0.26
158	0.51	0.19	0.54	0.20	0.57	0.21	0.59	0.22	0.61	0.23	0.63	0.24	0.66	0.25
160	0.53	0.18	0.56	0.19	0.59	0.20	0.61	0.21	0.63	0.22	0.65	0.22	0.67	0.23

Figure 15-4. An excerpt from Table 7 from *Bowditch.*

wheel that you can't be relieved long enough to take a bearing, or you may even be able to steer and turn pages too, if sea conditions permit. One big advantage of Table 7 lies in not needing to wait until your bearings reach any certain number of degrees relative to your course before they are useable for computing distance off and distance abeam. As long as the bearings are tabulated in Table 7, in such a manner as to orient both bearings into the same column, the bearings can be used.

From Figure 15-4 you can see that Table 7 consists of a series of columns, beginning with 20° heading the first column, and each column increasing in increments of 2°. Thus you have columns headed 20°, 22°, on up to 160°. There are six pages to Table 7. These degree headings of the columns in Table 7 are the angles the first bearing of any object observed makes with your vessel's course. The legend above the column headings tells you these degree headings are the angular difference between your boat's course and the first bearing. If you have an object to starboard bearing 038°R as the first bearing, the 38° column is the column you must enter. If you have an object on your port bow bearing 322°R, you still must use the 38° column, but to determine this, it is necessary to subtract 322° from 360°, as 360° is the relative course, and 360° minus 322° equals 38°. Thus the bearing of the object to port also makes an angle of 38° with your boat's course.

At the extreme left-hand side of Table 7 is a series of columns headed "Difference between the course and second bearing." The first number in these columns is 30°, the second is 32°, with each number increasing in increments of 2°, until at the bottom of the column is 160°. From this, it is obvious you must have a minimum difference of 10° between bearings to use the table.

Suppose your boat is making 9 knots. At 1000 you observe a lighthouse bearing 032°R. At 1030 you observe the same lighthouse bearing 054°R. You maintained your course and speed between the two bearings. How far off the light are you at the time of the second bearing? How far off the light will you pass the light abeam? Solution:

STEP 1
Find the column headed 32°, as 032°R is the angle your first bearing made with your course.

STEP 2
In the left-hand column headed "Difference between the course and second bearing" go down to the 54° line. 054° is the angle the second bearing makes with your course.

STEP 3
Follow this 54° line across the table to the 32° column. Now you must face something you probably noticed before. Each column is divided into two sub-columns. The left-hand sub-column lists the factor by which you must multiply your distance run to get your distance off at the time of the second bearing. For the 32° column and 54° line, this factor is 1.41. The right-hand sub-column lists the factor by which you must multiply the distance your boat ran between bearings to get the distance you will pass the object abeam. For the 32° column and 54° line this factor is 1.14.

STEP 4
(a). At 9 knots you will run 4.5 miles in 30 minutes. Multiply 1.41 by 4.5 miles and get 6.34. You are 6.3 miles off the lighthouse at the time of the second bearing. (On a chart of the scale of the coastal charts we have been using in this work you could actually plot or measure this distance at 6.34.)

(b). Multiply 1.14 by 4.5 miles and get 5.13. You will be 5.1 miles off when the lighthouse is abeam. As the lighthouse is a charted object, you have, in effect, a running fix. But Table 7 will give you your distance off an object whether you know the charted position of the object or not. Here again, safe navigation is possible since this method tells how far off you are and how far you will pass abeam, without actually fixing your position. You can navigate safely by determining, for example, that there are no hazards greater than three miles off, and then maintain four or more miles, as you think best, to give a sufficient margin of safety.

Let's look at another example using two bearings, this time on an object to port. Your boat is making 7.5 knots. At 2140 you observe a light bearing 336°R. At 2205 you observe the same light bearing 312°R. How far off the light are you at 2205? How far off will you be when the light is abeam?

STEP 1
Determine the angle the first bearing of the light makes with your course. To do this, subtract 336° from 360°, as your landmark or aid is to port. The difference is 24°. You must use the vertical column in Table 7 headed 24°.

STEP 2
Now find the line you must select in the vertical column on the left-hand side of the table for the angle between the course and second bearing. To do this subtract 312° from 360°. The angle between your course and the second bearing is 48°.

STEP 3

Go down the left-hand column of the table to the 48° line. Move across this line to the 24° column, and from the left-hand sub-column extract 1.00, your distance-off factor at the time of the second bearing. From the right-hand sub-column extract 0.74, the factor for distance off at the time you will be abeam. (You have a coincidence here, in that you doubled the angle. Thus the distance run is the distance off at the time of second bearing. Yet Table 7 is still useful to find the distance off abeam. And look, it is nearly three-quarters of the distance run. Many navigators browse through Table 7 to add rules such as this to their bag of tricks.)

STEP 4

The time between 2140 and 2205 is 25 minutes. From Table 19 of *Bowditch* you find your boat will go 3.1 miles in 25 minutes at 7.5 knots. Multiply 3.1 by 1.00; your distance off at the time of the second bearing is 3.1 miles.

Multiply 3.1 by 0.74 to find your distance off abeam. You will pass abeam 2.29 or 2.3 miles off the light.

A set of rules for finding the angle a bearing is making with your course is apparent. The rules are:

1. To determine the angle a bearing on an object to starboard makes with your course, subtract the *course* from the bearing. In the first example above of relative bearings, 000°, your course, was subtracted from 032°R to give 32°.

2. To determine the angle a bearing on an object to port makes with your course, subtract the *bearing* from your course. In the second example a bearing of 336°R was subtracted from a course of 360°, your relative course, to find the 24° column heading for your first bearing.

These rules also apply with compass courses and compass bearings. Let's see how. This time, as you proceed along the coast on a course of 260°C, you spot a tall tree-top at the water's edge bearing 286°C. The time is 0956. You are making 6.5 knots. At 1029 the tree bears 328°C. How far off the tree are you? How far will you be off when the tree is abeam?

STEP 1

The tree is to starboard; subtract *course* from bearing when the object is to starboard. Your course of 260° subtracted from 286° gives an angle of 26° with your course for the first bearing.

STEP 2

Subtract 260° from 328°. The second bearing makes an angle of 68° with your course.

STEP 3

The intersection of the 26° column and the 68° line gives factors of 0.66 in the left-hand sub-column and 0.61 in the right-hand sub-column.

STEP 4

You have run for 33 minutes between bearings. Your distance run is 3.6 miles. 3.6 × 0.66 = 2.37. You are 2.4 miles off at the time of the second bearing. 3.6 × 0.61 = 2.19. You will be 2.2 miles off when the tree is abeam.

Suppose you are still on a course of 260°C. At 1141 you see a pier-head bearing 238°. At 1206 the pier-head bears 210°. How far off are you at 1206? How far off will you pass the pier abeam?

STEP 1

The pier-head is to port; subtract *bearings* from the course when the object is to port.

STEP 2

Subtract 210° from 260°.

STEPS 3 AND 4

As before.

To keep you from getting confused later, I am going to provide you with two more examples of how to find the angle a bearing on an object makes with your course.

The first of these examples: You are on a course of 352°C. You sight an object bearing 028°C. How do you subtract 352° from 028°? The object is to starboard, so you must subtract your course from the bearing. To do this add 360° to the bearing of 028°. The sum is 388°. Subtract 352° from 388°. The angle the bearing makes with your course is 36°.

The next example: You are on a course of 028°C and an object bears 352°C. The object is to port. You add 360° to your 028°C course and subtract 352° from your course. Why do I bother to tell you something so obvious? Because my experience tells me that very obvious things, like this, give navigators, especially beginners, the most trouble.

You can use Table 7 for angles astern, or an angle forward of the beam and an angle abaft the beam. You are not limited to angles on the bow. This alone makes Table 7 a very useful tool for the pilot. Study the table. Practice using it in different situations.

DANGER BEARINGS

Another application of angles on the bow is found in the use of danger bearings. Often, when making a landfall, or picking up the next aid to navigation along a coast, there is no immediate way for a navi-

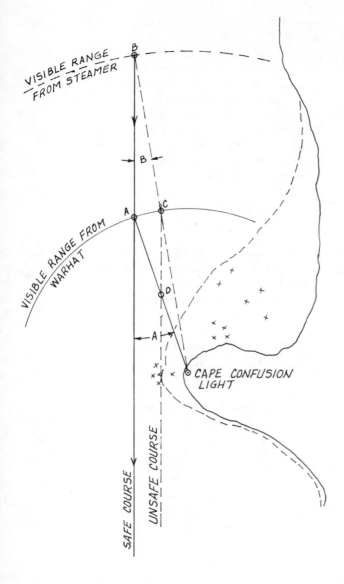

VISIBLE RANGE FROM STEAMER

VISIBLE RANGE FROM WARHAT

CAPE CONFUSION LIGHT

SAFE COURSE

UNSAFE COURSE

Figure 15-5.   Danger bearings.

cause of the distance, the bearing does not yet indicate danger. To illustrate:

In Figure 15-5 *War Hat* and a steamer are on the same course. This course will carry them safely by the rocks and shoals around Cape Confusion. As the navigator in *War Hat*, you compute the visible range of the light on the cape. In the daytime you would compute the range at which you should see the light structure. In either case you would refer to Table 8 of *Bowditch* and the *Light List*. The problem is the same. The solid arc in the figure represents the visible range of the light structure on the cape from *War Hat*. Point *A* is the position at which the light or light tower will first be seen by you, the navigator, in *War Hat*. Angle *A* is the danger bearing from point *A*. If the angle of Cape Confusion Light equals *A* when the light is first sighted, *War Hat* is on course, *provided* the light is first sighted at the *time* you predict your DR position to be at point *A*. Then, if you hold your course and angle *A* increases, you should pass safely by the cape.

What happens if you see the light some time after you predicted you should? If the light is much later coming into view, possibly because of reduced visibility, but the first bearing you observe gives an angle on the bow equal to *A*, do you sigh with relief? No, and by no means no! Under these conditions, you could be at *D*, or even closer in and well on your way to making the maritime news under the headline "Lost at Sea."

Suppose you pick up the light at about the *time* predicted, but the angle on the bow equals angle *B* in Figure 15-5. Your time is correct, but now the angle on the bow is less than the minimum danger angle you computed. You may be on your way to making headlines again. This time you could very well be at point *C*. The important thing I am illustrating here is that you must see the light or object at the *time* and *angle* predicted to use danger bearings properly.

The mate on watch on the steamer predicts he will see the light when the steamer reaches point *B*, and the angle on her port bow will equal angle *B*. If, at the time predicted, he does see the light bearing at an angle on his bow equal to *B*, he has an indication his steamer is on her safe course. Yet angle *B* was the angle you would have observed from *War Hat* if you first spotted the light at point *C*. From this it should be obvious that computing and using danger bearings are individual problems for each boat under each set of circumstances. In any navigating situation, you should never rely on any one technique to keep you out of trouble. A vessel passing a cape, such as the one in Figure 15-5, would use her depth-finder and, when close enough, verti-

gator to fix his vessel's position. A danger bearing will indicate to him if he is standing into danger or proceeding safely.

Using danger bearings is not quite as simple as some of the allegedly more profound texts would have you believe, however. The proper use of a danger bearing depends on the skilled combination of several of the techniques you have already learned. (See Figure 15-5). The first thing you must do is compute the range of visibility of the aid or landmark you intend to take your danger bearing on. This is the visible range of the object from your boat. From Figure 15-5 you can see that beyond this range the object can bear within the danger limits, but, becal sextant angles, as well as any other means available to check her navigation.

PRACTICE PROBLEMS

1. You observe a buoy bearing 045° relative. Your boat is making 10 knots. Twenty-four minutes later the buoy bears 090°R. How far off the buoy are you?

2. You are running down the coast in your outboard at 25 knots on a course of 092°C. At 0620 you see a beach cottage on your port bow bearing 069°C to 070°C. You are bouncing around a bit. At 0632 the cottage bears 047°C. How far off the beach are you? How far off will you be when the cottage is abeam?

3. You are shrimping along the coast of the Gulf of Mexico east of Destin, Florida. Your course is 335°C. At 0754 you see a high rise apartment building on the beach bearing between 001° and 002°. Your boat is making 3 knots. At 0910 the same building bears 020°C. How far off will you be off when the building bears 065°C?

4. You are standing down the coast under sail on a course of 256°C. At 2106 you see a light bearing 028°R. Your log shows your speed to be 5.5 knots. At 2204 the same light bears 068°R. How far off the light are you? How far off will you pass the light abeam?

5. Your vessel is in the clear, but a fog bank hides the coast. Your course is 137°C. Your speed is 12 knots. At 1018 a rift appears in the fog and you see a rock on the edge of a cliff with the surf pounding the cliff's base. The rock bears 113°C. The fog closes back in, but at 1108 another rift in the fog appears and the rock is visible again bearing 007°C. How far off the cliff are you? How far off will you be when the rock is abeam?

6. If you gave up on the second part of question 5, how far off *were* you when the rock was abeam?

Answers

1. 4.0 miles. You took a bow and beam bearing.

2. (a) 5 miles off. Use doubling the angle method.

    (b) 3.5 miles abeam. Use 7/10 rule.

3. 3.8 miles. Use the 26½/45° rule.

4. (a) 3.9 miles.

    (b) 3.7 miles. Use Table 7.

5. (a) 4.2 miles off.

    (b) You have already passed abeam! Use Table 7.

6. You were 3.2 miles off when abeam.

16   HOW TO USE VERTICAL SEXTANT ANGLES

Whenever I teach navigation, I cannot hide my eagerness to encourage my students to equip themselves with a good mariner's sextant. Their invariable response is: "I would buy a good sextant, but I will never go offshore far enough to use it." How wrong can they be?

Admittedly a sextant is an absolute essential to safe offshore navigation, but, in the hands of a competent pilot, the mariner's sextant is the most accurate instrument available for inshore navigation. And, if he uses it properly, the coastal pilot will make many more observations with his sextant than the celestial navigator in the course of a given period. In my opinion, the two best position-finding instruments for the small boat navigator in visual conditions are the hand-held bearing compass and the sextant. Of the two the mariner's sextant is far more precise, but does require a little more skill to use.

For some reason the sextant has been neglected by modern navigators as a piloting instrument. The old navigators used the sextant continuously. You only have to read your marine history books to see how much. Perhaps it is because we passed through a period where big ships, stable enough for accurate pelorus or alidade bearings, made most of the long voyages, and only a few daring, hardy souls went far to sea in small boats. The boating boom has brought us again to a time when many very small vessels are being built that are quite safe to make offshore passages, if sailed by a competent crew, whether commercial fishermen or amateur yachtsmen. And our wonderful American boatmen are sailing forth. These little ships, some, like my *Li'l Tiger*, even under five tons, do *not* make steady platforms for pelorus bearings. The skipper of such a little boat needs something else to navigate his boat safely in pilot waters. This something else is the sextant.

The sextant is a precision instrument used to measure angles. With a sextant you can measure the horizontal angle between two objects with your position as the vertex, or you can measure the vertical angle that the tip of a mountain peak, the light of a lighthouse, or a celestial body makes with the horizon.

As in the case of any precision instrument, some skill is required to get the best from a sextant. You develop this skill the same way a golfer develops his skill at putting. The golfer selects a putter that he feels is best for him, and then practices with this putter every chance he gets. You should select a sextant that you feel best suits your needs, and practice with it every chance you get. Even at home, in your den or living room, take your sextant out of its box and familiarize yourself with it. You can measure vertical and horizontal angles between things in the room. Then when you get afloat you will be that much farther ahead. This practice is important because, at first, things are hard to see in the limited field of the sextant's telescope. To start with, you may think you will never get the hang of it, but don't get discouraged. Keep trying, and soon you will be making observations like an old salt.

I am going to give you a few pointers about selecting and using a sextant; for more information read *Bowditch*, 1962 edition, Articles 1501 through 1510, which describes the sextant very well.

Selecting a suitable sextant can be a problem. A good mariner's sextant is expensive, yet the price of a good sextant is seldom as much as the price of some of the electronic gear small craft operators buy. A loran set may cost four or five times as much as a good sextant, is only good for limited ranges, and requires periodic maintenance. A sextant is usable anywhere in the world, and will last several lifetimes with just a little tender loving care. I own a very old sextant that is still perfectly usable.

On a very small boat, a standard-size sextant may present a stowage problem. Even the smaller standard-size instruments are kept in boxes about 12" ×

Figure 16-1. A mariner's sextant.

$12'' \times 6''$. If you cannot spare this much room, or your budget can't stand the cost of a standard-size sextant, one of the small-craft sextants may be just what you need. Francis Barker and Son Limited, England, makes a very good instrument they call their Small Craft Precision Sextant (see Figure 16-2). It takes up about as much room as your camera, and it probably costs less, too, if you have a good camera.

There is one drawback to these smaller instruments; they usually have telescopes of low magnification. This makes them good only for limited ranges when used in piloting, although the useful range of these instruments is enough in most cases. They are quite good for sun sights and other celestial observations. On my personal sextant, a large Tamaya sextant, I have a 7×50 prismatic telescope.

Figure 16-2. A small craft sextant (from Francis Barker & Son Ltd., Kent, England).

I can see a lighthouse tower such as Pensacola Light, or Sand Island Light, twelve miles off ! I may have to climb the rigging to see the tower, but I can see it.

Climbing the rigging brings up another point. A sextant is a precision instrument, and good navigators are cranky old maids about their sextants. A minor bump can damage one seriously. Drop it, and you may need to figure out how to make a very nautical looking lamp out of it. Most likely that is all it will be good for. At best a dropped sextant must be sent to a properly equipped shop to detect any damage, particularly such a thing as a bent frame.

Your sextant belongs in one of two places, secured in its box or carefully held in your hand. *Never* lay it on the chart table. The slightest roll of your boat will send it galloping off the table and crashing to the deck.

In handling your sextant you should grasp it either by the handle to use it, or, if necessary, by the frame to lift it from its box. *Never* lift a sextant in such a manner that any strain is exerted on the index arm, sun shades, telescope, or especially the mirrors.

How do you use a sextant? A short description of how a sextant is made will help answer this. (See Figure 16-3.) The main component of a good sextant is the arc, which is cast and etched into the frame. At the center of this arc is a pivoted mirror. This is the index mirror. At the edge of the frame away from the observer is another mirror, the horizon mirror. The horizon mirror consists of a piece of glass mirrored on the half next to the frame and clear glass on the other half. The horizon mirror is centered so the junction of the mirrored and the clear portions of the glass vertically bisects the field of the telescope. Both the index mirror and the horizon mirror must be perpendicular to the plane of the sextant's arc. Attached to the index mirror, and pivoted concentrically with it, is an arm extending from the mirror to the arc. This arm is lockable in any place on the arc, and then it can be moved precisely by means of a tangent screw. To measure an angle between two objects, the navigator looks at one object through the telescope, and moves the index arm until the index mirror reflects the second object into the horizon mirror. A pointer on the index arm is calibrated to read the degrees measured at the point the index arm stops. Measurements to the nearest tenth of a minute of arc appear on the vernier or micrometer drum, depending on the type of sextant.

To take a vertical angle observation of a mountain peak of known height, a lighthouse, or any suitable object, for example, the navigator moves the index arm until the very tip of the object touches the hori-

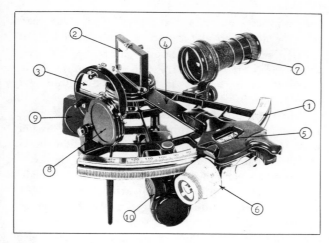

Figure 16-3. The parts of a sextant are (1) the arc, (2) index mirror, (3) horizon mirror, (4) index arm, (5) pointer, (6) micrometer drum, (7) telescope, (8) horizon shades, (9) index shades, and (10) handle.

zon. (See Figure 16-4.) When the navigator has the tip of the peak exactly on the horizon, or the base of the mountain, he "swings" or twists the sextant around the axis of his sight several degrees in either direction. The tip of the peak should rise above the horizon as the telescope is so twisted and will coincide with the horizon only when the plane of the arc of the sextant is exactly vertical. Navigators call this "swinging the arc." The sextant must be vertical to get a true vertical angle. The angle is read, in degrees, minutes, and tenths of a minute from a pointer on the index arm and the vernier scale. This angle is the sextant altitude, designated H_s, and must be corrected to get the true or observed altitude, which is designated H_o.

A vertical sextant angle must be corrected for two errors when vertical angles made by terrestrial objects are observed. The sextant itself may be out of adjustment, and read incorrectly. This error is usually due to maladjustment of the mirrors and is known as *index error*, IE. The correction for index error is the *index correction*. Seasoned navigators will take the index error out of a sextant, but if you do not know how to adjust a sextant to remove index error, you can still use your sextant with confidence, provided you determine the index error in the instrument. To find your index error, move the index arm until the pointer reads zero. Be sure the micrometer drum or vernier is zeroed at this time also, otherwise your sextant may really be set to read a few tenths of minutes from zero. When the sextant is zeroed, look through the telescope at the horizon. The true horizon and its reflected image should be in coincidence,

and they should stay together when the arc is swung. If the true horizon and the reflected image are not in coincidence, the index arm should be moved until the visible horizon and the reflected image are in coincidence. Then read your sextant. The difference between the reading and the zero is the index error.

If the index error points to the right of the zero mark, it is pointing below the zero mark. It is, in the mariner's vernacular, "off the arc." The sextant

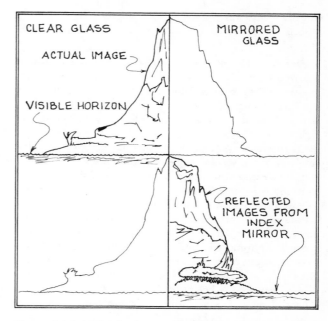

Figure 16-4. The horizon mirror of a sextant in use. The left half of the mirror is clear glass, so the observer can look through the eyepiece of the sextant at the visible horizon. The right half of the glass is mirrored. The navigator moves the index arm of the sextant to bring the reflected image of the object or body he is observing into the required coincidence with the horizon. When the image is adjusted to the precise position, a good sextant will provide an angular measurement to at least the nearest tenth of a minute of arc. Here, the navigator is measuring the vertical angle the summit of a mountain of known height makes with his visible horizon. To do this the navigator "split" the mountain in two at the highest point of the summit with the vertical intersection of the clear glass and the mirrored glass. He then moved the index arm of the sextant until the reflected half of the mountain top aligned precisely with the visible horizon. The illustration shows the right half of the actual image imposed lightly on the mirrored half of the glass, and the left half of the reflected image imposed lightly on the clear glass. This is really how the mountain and its reflected image would look to the navigator. An optical illusion permits you to see two images of the same mountain at the same time. Just be absolutely sure the reflected image is the lower one!

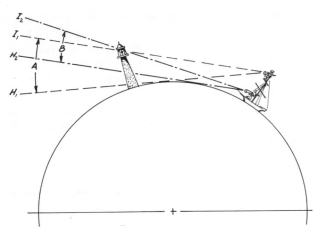

Figure 16-5. Height of eye error. The semicircle represents an arc of a great circle of the earth passing through the position of the boat and the lighthouse. Two men are on the boat. One man is aloft, the other is on the deck. They are both taking vertical sextant angle observations on the lighthouse. The lower dotted line from the man aloft to H_1 is the visible horizon of the man in the crosstrees. The angle A is the sextant angle, H_s, the man aloft observes. The upper dotted line from I_1 is the line of sight from the light to the man aloft, and is the line reflected by the index mirror. The dashed line from the man on deck to H_2 is the visible horizon of the man on deck. The angle B is the sextant altitude, H_s, the man on deck observes. The upper dashed line from I_2 is the line of sight from the light to the man on deck. Note that both lines I_1 and I_2 pass through the center of the light and not across the roof of the lighthouse, because the heights of lights are listed in the *Light List* and on charts according to the height of the light source.

The angles in this figure are greatly exaggerated for the sake of illustration. The man aloft can see a much wider horizon because of his height. Angle A is much greater than B because of this difference in height of eye of the observers. Both men are obtaining a greater angle than would be observed if their eyes were at sea level. Thus, a dip correction must always be applied if the observer's eye is above sea level, and this dip correction is always subtracted from sextant altitude.

measures between $0°$ to at least $120°$, and a measurement below zero is outside this range. In this case the sextant will measure too low. Most sextants, however, do have arcs graduated to several degrees below the zero mark, and can thus measure angles less than zero. This reading below the zero mark must be added to any sextant altitude to get the observed altitude H_o. So, if the index pointer points to a value on the arc to the right of the zero, it is reading below

zero and said to be "off the arc." The value read must be added to any sextant altitude, that is "put on" the sextant altitude. So navigators say, if the index error is off the arc, the *index correction,* designated IC, must be put on the sextant altitude. Or simply, "if it is off, it is on."

When the pointer points to the left of the zero, it means the sextant will measure angles to be higher than they really are. As the pointer is inside the $0°$ to $120°$ range, the error is said to be "on the arc." Because this error makes the sextant read too high, the value read must be subtracted, taken "off," from the sextant altitude to get a correct observed altitude. If the index error is "on" the arc, the index correction is "off" the sextant altitude, and vice versa. Therefore navigators remember these rules by: "if it is on, it is off," and "if it is off, it is on."

One important consideration must be borne in mind when reading the index error "off" the arc or less than zero. In this case, the reading of the micrometer drum or vernier must be subtracted from $60°$ to get the correct minutes and tenths of a minute of the index correction.

When using vertical sextant altitudes in *piloting*, you have only one other correction to apply to your sextant altitude. This is the error known as *dip*, and the correction for *dip* is based on your height of eye. Inspection of Table 8 of *Bowditch* (Figure 11-3) will show you that the higher you are above the surface of the sea, the farther away the visible horizon is from you. As the visible horizon is the locus of the points where your line of sight is tangent to the earth's surface, the higher you are above the surface of the earth, the greater the angle an elevated object, whether terrestrial or celestial, will make with your horizon. Figure 16-5 illustrates this correction and shows how it varies for different heights of eye.

There are basically two situations when determining distance off by vertical sextant angles. The first and simplest situation is an observation of an object of known height whose base or waterline is beyond your visible horizon. The second situation is an observation of an object of known height whose base is closer to you than your visible horizon. This second situation is probably the most involved and difficult observation to reduce and plot of any of the techniques used in piloting. Yet even this is not that difficult once you have mastered the method.

The earlier editions of *Bowditch* claimed the navigator was concerned with two cases in using vertical sextant angles. One case was the use of vertical sextant angles to find distance off from objects over five miles away. The other case was the use of vertical sextant angles of objects less than five miles off. As I see it

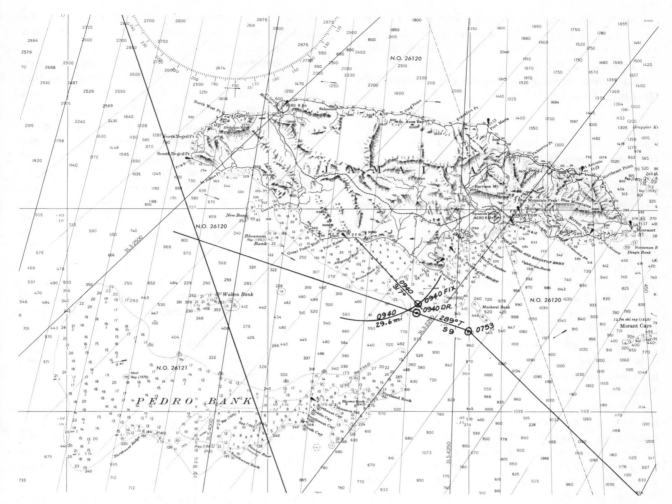

Figure 16-6. Coasting along the coast of Jamaica.

there are really three cases, and, when I work an example for you, to show how each case applies, I believe you will agree with me. I also believe you will become a convinced user of vertical sextant angles.

The first case is the use of vertical sextant angles on objects whose distance from you exceeds five miles, and, since we are talking about small craft, when your height of eye is less than 25 feet. You will see the purpose of this second requirement as we continue.

Case 1

In Figure 14-5, I illustrated the way you advance a circular LOP. I told you the navigator had obtained the distances off to plot these circular LOP's by observing vertical angles on mountain peaks with his sextant. Vessels bound for the Yucatan Channel when coming up from South America use these angles. The "caravan route" to make this passage takes you right by the south side of Jamaica. The

course to Jamaica from Maracaibo, Venezuela, is about 315°T to make a landfall on Portland Head bearing a point or so on the starboard bow. When about 22½ miles off Portland Head, the course is changed to 289°T to pass five miles southwest of Blossom Bank, because the chart shows a depth of less than five fathoms on the bank. We always avoid these banks because of the possibility of uncharted knolls and coral heads. Figure 16-6 is reproduced from Chart No. 26120 of the Defense Mapping Agency Hydrographic Center, and it shows the island of Jamaica.

You make your landfall on Portland Head at 0753 and change course to 289°T. *War Hat* is moving along at a nice 9 knots. Your course carries you too far offshore to see any established aids to navigation. You know strong currents in the area can ruin your dead reckoning. At 0940 you take a vertical sextant angle observation on a mountain top about five miles

109

east of Port Kaiser. The chart shows this peak to be 2,090 feet in height. The sextant angle, Hs, is 0° 29.'1. The mountain bears 318°T. What is *War Hat*'s position at 0940?

You have a bearing. You need your distance off. Here is how you get it:

STEP 1

Plot your 0940 DR. In 1 hour and 47 minutes *War Hat* should cover 16 miles.

STEP 2

Record your sight and correct your sextant altitude. You have an index error of 1.'1 off the arc. You must add 1.'1 to your Hs. Your height of eye is 8 feet. To find the dip correction, *Bowditch* refers you to Table 22, which begins on page 1278 of the 1962 edition of *Bowditch*. But Table 22 tabulates dip for height of eye in five-foot increments! You can interpolate, and this is easy enough. It is even easier, however, to use the dip corrections on the inside cover of the *Nautical Almanac,* which is a government publication designed primarily to give data concerning heavenly bodies for celestial navigation. Yet the *Nautical Almanac* does have a lot of useful general information, such as these dip tables. And if you do not have a *Nautical Almanac* this same table is reprinted in Appendix V, page 1136, of *Bowditch* as an extract from the *Nautical Almanac*. We will use the *Nautical Almanac* table when we can (see Figure 16-7). On the right-hand side is a small table headed "Dip." Go down the height of eye column of this table until you come to 8 feet. Between 8 feet and 8.6 feet, extract the correction –2.8 and subtract this from your Hs.

Hs	0° 29.'1
I.C.	+ 1. 1
Dip	– 2. 8
Ho	0° 27.'4

STEP 3

Open *Bowditch* to Table 9, Distance by Vertical Angle (see Figure 16-8). The table consists of five pages. On each page are twelve central columns headed with the difference in feet between the height of eye and the height of the observer, and beneath this, each column is subheaded "miles." Height differences range from 50 feet to 12,000 feet. There are columns on the left and right side of the table headed "angle." The angles listed are observed angles, Ho. Of course, it is not feasible to list every possible vertical angle you may observe. Angles tabulated begin with 0°10' and increase in 1' increments

for the first five minutes of increase in arc. As the angles increase, the increments between tabulated angles become larger.

You are ready to enter the table. Thumb through several pages until you find the column heading nearest to, but less than, 2,090 feet. Or really less than 2,082 feet, since your height of eye is 8 feet. This is the "2000" column on page 1257. Now go to the nearest "angle" column, and run down this column until you find the angle nearest to, but *less* than 0° 27.'4. This angle is 0° 25'. Go across the 0° 25' line to the 2,000-feet column. This is easy because the 2,000-feet column is the first column on the left and is adjacent to the angle column. Read 30.0 miles. If the mountain had been 2,008 feet tall and your observed angle had been 0° 25', you would have been 30 miles off the peak. Sadly, things seldom work out this way. You must interpolate for difference in sextant angle. So while on the 0° 25' line, move over to the 2,200-feet column and extract 32.'2. Set up a little form like the one in Figure 16-9 and enter your information from the table. The form is not printed but one you set up yourself in your navigator's notebook.

STEP 4

Please don't let the word "interpolate" scare you. Interpolation isn't all that difficult. Your next move is to the angle nearest to 0° 27.'4, but *greater than* 0° 27.'4. The angle is 0° 30'. On the 0° 30' line under 2,000 feet, extract 27.'2. Move one column to the right and extract 29.'3. Add this to your form (Figure 16-9). Remember, 29.'3 in the table means 29.3 miles.

STEP 5

Subtract the lesser angle from the greater angle, then subtract the lesser distance from the greater distance for 2,000 feet of height and the lesser distance from the greater for 2,200 feet of height. For a difference in sextant angle of 5 minutes, the distance off varies 2.8 miles on an object whose difference in height is 2,000 feet at these angles, and 2.9 miles for an object whose difference is 2,200 feet. But your actual Ho was 0° 27.'4, so subtract 0° 25' from 0° 27.'4. You get 2.'4. Multiply $\frac{2.'4}{5}$ by 2.'8 and get 1.34 miles. This is the difference in distance you would have been off with an Ho of 0° 27.'1 had the mountain been 2,008 feet high.

Multiply $\frac{2.'4}{5}$ by 2.'9 and get 1.'39, the difference, for a height of 2,208.

APPENDIX V

EXTRACTS FROM *NAUTICAL ALMANAC*

ALTITUDE CORRECTION TABLES 10°–90°—SUN, STARS, PLANETS

SUN (OCT.–MAR. / APR.–SEPT.)

App. Alt.	Lower Limb	Upper Limb	App. Alt.	Lower Limb	Upper Limb
9 34	+10·8	−22·7	9 39	+10·6	−22·4
9 45	+10·9	−22·6	9 51	+10·7	−22·3
9 56	+11·0	−22·5	10 03	+10·8	−22·2
10 08	+11·1	−22·4	10 15	+10·9	−22·1
10 21	+11·2	−22·3	10 27	+11·0	−22·0
10 34	+11·3	−22·2	10 40	+11·1	−21·9
10 47	+11·4	−22·1	10 54	+11·2	−21·8
11 01	+11·5	−22·0	11 08	+11·3	−21·7
11 15	+11·6	−21·9	11 23	+11·4	−21·6
11 30	+11·7	−21·8	11 38	+11·5	−21·5
11 46	+11·8	−21·7	11 54	+11·6	−21·4
12 02	+11·9	−21·6	12 10	+11·7	−21·3
12 19	+12·0	−21·5	12 28	+11·8	−21·2
12 37	+12·1	−21·4	12 46	+11·9	−21·1
12 55	+12·2	−21·3	13 05	+12·0	−21·0
13 14	+12·3	−21·2	13 24	+12·1	−20·9
13 35	+12·4	−21·1	13 45	+12·2	−20·8
13 56	+12·5	−21·0	14 07	+12·3	−20·7
14 18	+12·6	−20·9	14 30	+12·4	−20·6
14 42	+12·7	−20·8	14 54	+12·5	−20·5
15 06	+12·8	−20·7	15 19	+12·6	−20·4
15 32	+12·9	−20·6	15 46	+12·7	−20·3
15 59	+13·0	−20·5	16 14	+12·8	−20·2
16 28	+13·1	−20·4	16 44	+12·9	−20·1
16 59	+13·2	−20·3	17 15	+13·0	−20·0
17 32	+13·3	−20·2	17 48	+13·1	−19·9
18 06	+13·4	−20·1	18 24	+13·2	−19·8
18 42	+13·5	−20·0	19 01	+13·3	−19·7
19 21	+13·6	−19·9	19 42	+13·4	−19·6
20 03	+13·7	−19·8	20 25	+13·5	−19·5
20 48	+13·8	−19·7	21 11	+13·6	−19·4
21 35	+13·9	−19·6	22 00	+13·7	−19·3
22 26	+14·0	−19·5	22 54	+13·8	−19·2
23 22	+14·1	−19·4	23 51	+13·9	−19·1
24 21	+14·2	−19·3	24 53	+14·0	−19·0
25 26	+14·3	−19·2	26 00	+14·1	−18·9
26 36	+14·4	−19·1	27 13	+14·2	−18·8
27 52	+14·5	−19·0	28 33	+14·3	−18·7
29 15	+14·6	−18·9	30 00	+14·4	−18·6
30 46	+14·7	−18·8	31 35	+14·5	−18·5
32 26	+14·8	−18·7	33 20	+14·6	−18·4
34 17	+14·9	−18·6	35 17	+14·7	−18·3
36 20	+15·0	−18·5	37 26	+14·8	−18·2
38 36	+15·1	−18·4	39 50	+14·9	−18·1
41 08	+15·2	−18·3	42 31	+15·0	−18·0
43 59	+15·3	−18·2	45 31	+15·1	−17·9
47 10	+15·4	−18·1	48 55	+15·2	−17·8
50 46	+15·5	−18·0	52 44	+15·3	−17·7
54 49	+15·6	−17·9	57 02	+15·4	−17·6
59 23	+15·7	−17·8	61 51	+15·5	−17·5
64 30	+15·8	−17·7	67 17	+15·6	−17·4
70 12	+15·9	−17·6	73 16	+15·7	−17·3
76 26	+16·0	−17·5	79 43	+15·8	−17·2
83 05	+16·1	−17·4	86 32	+15·9	−17·1
90 00			90 00		

STARS AND PLANETS

App. Alt.	Corrⁿ
9 56	−5·3
10 08	−5·2
10 20	−5·1
10 33	−5·0
10 46	−4·9
11 00	−4·8
11 14	−4·7
11 29	−4·6
11 45	−4·5
12 01	−4·4
12 18	−4·3
12 35	−4·2
12 54	−4·1
13 13	−4·0
13 33	−3·9
13 54	−3·8
14 16	−3·7
14 40	−3·6
15 04	−3·5
15 30	−3·4
15 57	−3·3
16 26	−3·2
16 56	−3·1
17 28	−3·0
18 02	−2·9
18 38	−2·8
19 17	−2·7
19 58	−2·6
20 42	−2·5
21 28	−2·4
22 19	−2·3
23 13	−2·2
24 11	−2·1
25 14	−2·0
26 22	−1·9
27 36	−1·8
28 56	−1·7
30 24	−1·6
32 00	−1·5
33 45	−1·4
35 40	−1·3
37 48	−1·2
40 08	−1·1
42 44	−1·0
45 36	−0·9
48 47	−0·8
52 18	−0·7
56 11	−0·6
60 28	−0·5
65 08	−0·4
70 11	−0·3
75 34	−0·2
81 13	−0·1
87 03	−0·1
90 00	0·0

Additional Corrⁿ — 1958

VENUS

Jan. 1–Jan. 10

App. Alt.	Additional Corrⁿ
6	+0·5
20	+0·6
31	+0·7

Jan. 11–Feb. 14

4	+0·6
12	+0·7
22	+0·8

Feb. 15–Feb. 21

6	+0·5
20	+0·6
31	+0·7

Feb. 22–Mar. 9

11	+0·4
41	+0·5

Mar. 10–Apr. 4

46	+0·3

Apr. 5–May 19

47	+0·2

May 20–Dec. 31

42	+0·1

MARS

Jan. 1–Sept. 3

60	+0·1

Sept. 4–Dec. 31

34	+0·3
60	+0·2
80	+0·1

DIP

Ht. of Eye (ft.)	Corrⁿ	Ht. of Eye (ft.)	Corrⁿ
1·1	−1·1	44	−6·5
1·4	−1·2	45	−6·6
1·6	−1·3	47	−6·7
1·9	−1·4	48	−6·8
2·2	−1·5	49	−6·9
2·5	−1·6	51	−7·0
2·8	−1·7	52	−7·1
3·2	−1·8	54	−7·2
3·6	−1·9	55	−7·3
4·0	−2·0	57	−7·4
4·4	−2·1	58	−7·5
4·9	−2·2	60	−7·6
5·3	−2·3	62	−7·7
5·8	−2·4	63	−7·8
6·3	−2·5	65	−7·9
6·9	−2·6	67	−8·0
7·4	−2·7	68	−8·1
8·0	−2·8	70	−8·2
8·6	−2·9	72	−8·3
9·2	−3·0	74	−8·4
9·8	−3·1	75	−8·5
10·5	−3·2	77	−8·6
11·2	−3·3	79	−8·7
11·9	−3·4	81	−8·8
12·6	−3·5	83	−8·9
13·3	−3·6	85	−9·0
14·1	−3·7	87	−9·1
14·9	−3·8	88	−9·2
15·7	−3·9	90	−9·3
16·5	−4·0	92	−9·4
17·4	−4·1	94	−9·5
18·3	−4·2	96	−9·6
19·1	−4·3	98	−9·7
20·1	−4·4	101	−9·8
21·0	−4·5	103	−9·9
22·0	−4·6	105	−10·0
22·9	−4·7	107	−10·1
23·9	−4·8	109	−10·2
24·9	−4·9	111	−10·3
26·0	−5·0	113	−10·4
27·1	−5·1	116	−10·5
28·1	−5·2	118	−10·6
29·2	−5·3	120	−10·7
30·4	−5·4	122	−10·8
31·5	−5·5	125	−10·9
32·7	−5·6	127	−11·0
33·9	−5·7	129	−11·1
35·1	−5·8	132	−11·2
36·3	−5·9	134	−11·3
37·6	−6·0	136	−11·4
38·9	−6·1	139	−11·5
40·1	−6·2	141	−11·6
41·5	−6·3	144	−11·7
42·8	−6·4	146	−11·8
44·2		149	

App. Alt. = Apparent altitude = Sextant altitude corrected for index error and dip.

Figure 16-7. Extract from the *Nautical Almanac* showing the dip correction table.

TABLE 9

Distance by Vertical Angle

Angle	Height of object, in feet												Angle
	2,000	2,200	2,400	2,600	2,800	3,000	3,200	3,400	3,600	3,800	4,000	4,200	
° ′	Miles	Miles	Miles	Miles	Miles	Miles	Miles	Miles	Miles	Miles	Miles	Miles	° ′
0 10	41. 2	43. 7	46. 1	48. 3	50. 5	52. 6	54. 7	56. 6	58. 6	60. 5	62. 3	64. 1	0 10
0 11	40. 3	42. 8	45. 1	47. 4	49. 6	51. 7	53. 7	55. 7	57. 6	59. 5	61. 3	63. 1	0 11
0 12	39. 5	41. 9	44. 2	46. 5	48. 6	50. 7	52. 8	54. 7	56. 7	58. 5	60. 3	62. 1	0 12
0 13	38. 6	41. 0	43. 3	45. 6	47. 7	49. 8	51. 8	53. 8	55. 7	57. 6	59. 4	61. 2	0 13
0 14	37. 8	40. 2	42. 5	44. 7	46. 9	48. 9	50. 9	52. 9	54. 8	56. 7	58. 5	60. 2	0 14
0 15	37. 0	39. 3	41. 6	43. 9	46. 0	48. 1	50. 1	52. 0	53. 9	55. 7	57. 5	59. 3	0 15
0 20	33. 2	35. 5	37. 8	39. 9	42. 0	44. 0	45. 9	47. 8	49. 7	51. 5	53. 2	55. 0	0 20
0 25	30. 0	32. 2	34. 4	36. 4	38. 4	40. 4	42. 2	44. 1	45. 9	47. 6	49. 3	51. 0	0 25
0 30	27. 2	29. 3	31. 4	33. 3	35. 3	37. 1	39. 0	40. 7	42. 5	44. 2	45. 8	47. 5	0 30
0 35	24. 9	26. 8	28. 8	30. 7	32. 5	34. 3	36. 0	37. 7	39. 4	41. 1	42. 7	44. 2	0 35
0 40	22. 8	24. 7	26. 5	28. 3	30. 1	31. 8	33. 4	35. 1	36. 7	38. 3	39. 8	41. 3	0 40
0 45	21. 0	22. 8	24. 5	26. 2	27. 9	29. 5	31. 1	32. 7	34. 2	35. 8	37. 2	38. 7	0 45
0 50	19. 4	21. 1	22. 8	24. 4	26. 0	27. 5	29. 1	30. 6	32. 0	33. 5	34. 9	36. 3	0 50
0 55	18. 1	19. 7	21. 2	22. 8	24. 3	25. 8	27. 2	28. 7	30. 1	31. 5	32. 8	34. 2	0 55
1 00	16. 9	18. 4	19. 8	21. 3	22. 7	24. 2	25. 6	26. 9	28. 3	29. 6	31. 0	32. 3	1 00
1 10	14. 8	16. 2	17. 5	18. 9	20. 2	21. 5	22. 7	24. 0	25. 2	26. 5	27. 7	28. 9	1 10
1 20	13. 2	14. 5	15. 7	16. 9	18. 1	19. 3	20. 4	21. 6	22. 7	23. 9	25. 0	26. 1	1 20
1 30	11. 9	13. 0	14. 1	15. 2	16. 3	17. 4	18. 5	19. 6	20. 6	21. 7	22. 7	23. 7	1 30
1 40	10. 8	11. 9	12. 9	13. 9	14. 9	15. 9	16. 9	17. 9	18. 9	19. 8	20. 8	21. 8	1 40
1 50	9. 9	10. 9	11. 8	12. 7	13. 7	14. 6	15. 5	16. 4	17. 4	18. 3	19. 2	20. 1	1 50
2 00	9. 1	10. 0	10. 9	11. 8	12. 6	13. 5	14. 4	15. 2	16. 1	16. 9	17. 7	18. 6	2 00
2 15	8. 2	9. 0	9. 8	10. 5	11. 3	12. 1	12. 9	13. 7	14. 4	15. 2	16. 0	16. 7	2 15
2 30	7. 4	8. 1	8. 8	9. 5	10. 3	11. 0	11. 7	12. 4	13. 1	13. 8	14. 5	15. 2	2 30
2 45	6. 7	7. 4	8. 1	8. 7	9. 4	10. 0	10. 7	11. 3	12. 0	12. 6	13. 3	13. 9	2 45
3 00	6. 2	6. 8	7. 4	8. 0	8. 6	9. 2	9. 8	10. 4	11. 0	11. 6	12. 2	12. 8	3 00
3 20	5. 6	6. 1	6. 7	7. 2	7. 8	8. 3	8. 9	9. 4	10. 0	10. 5	11. 0	11. 6	3 20
3 40	5. 1	5. 6	6. 1	6. 6	7. 1	7. 6	8. 1	8. 6	9. 1	9. 6	10. 1	10. 6	3 40
4 00	4. 7	5. 1	5. 6	6. 1	6. 5	7. 0	7. 4	7. 9	8. 3	8. 8	9. 3	9. 7	4 00
4 20	4. 3	4. 7	5. 2	5. 6	6. 0	6. 5	6. 9	7. 3	7. 7	8. 1	8. 6	9. 0	4 20
4 40	4. 0	4. 4	4. 8	5. 2	5. 6	6. 0	6. 4	6. 8	7. 2	7. 6	8. 0	8. 4	4 40
5 00	3. 7	4. 1	4. 5	4. 9	5. 2	5. 6	6. 0	6. 3	6. 7	7. 1	7. 4	7. 8	5 00
5 20	3. 5	3. 9	4. 2	4. 6	4. 9	5. 3	5. 6	5. 9	6. 3	6. 6	7. 0	7. 3	5 20
5 40	3. 3	3. 6	4. 0	4. 3	4. 6	4. 9	5. 3	5. 6	5. 9	6. 3	6. 6	6. 9	5 40
6 00	3. 1	3. 4	3. 7	4. 1	4. 4	4. 7	5. 0	5. 3	5. 6	5. 9	6. 2	6. 5	6 00
6 20	3. 0	3. 2	3. 5	3. 8	4. 1	4. 4	4. 7	5. 0	5. 3	5. 6	5. 9	6. 2	6 20
6 40	2. 8	3. 1	3. 4	3. 6	3. 9	4. 2	4. 5	4. 8	5. 0	5. 3	5. 6	5. 9	6 40
7 00	2. 7	2. 9	3. 2	3. 5	3. 7	4. 0	4. 3	4. 5	4. 8	5. 1	5. 3	5. 6	7 00
7 20	2. 6	2. 8	3. 1	3. 3	3. 6	3. 8	4. 1	4. 3	4. 6	4. 8	5. 1	5. 3	7 20
7 40	2. 4	2. 7	2. 9	3. 2	3. 4	3. 7	3. 9	4. 1	4. 4	4. 6	4. 9	5. 1	7 40
8 00	2. 3	2. 6	2. 8	3. 0	3. 3	3. 5	3. 7	4. 0	4. 2	4. 4	4. 7	4. 9	8 00
8 20	2. 2	2. 5	2. 7	2. 9	3. 1	3. 4	3. 6	3. 8	4. 0	4. 3	4. 5	4. 7	8 20
8 40	2. 2	2. 4	2. 6	2. 8	3. 0	3. 2	3. 4	3. 7	3. 9	4. 1	4. 3	4. 5	8 40
9 00	2. 1	2. 3	2. 5	2. 7	2. 9	3. 1	3. 3	3. 5	3. 7	3. 9	4. 1	4. 4	9 00
9 30	2. 0	2. 2	2. 4	2. 6	2. 8	2. 9	3. 1	3. 3	3. 5	3. 7	3. 9	4. 1	9 30
10 00	1. 9	2. 0	2. 2	2. 4	2. 6	2. 8	3. 0	3. 2	3. 4	3. 5	3. 7	3. 9	10 00
10 30	1. 8	2. 0	2. 1	2. 3	2. 5	2. 7	2. 8	3. 0	3. 2	3. 4	3. 5	3. 7	10 30
11 00	1. 7	1. 9	2. 0	2. 2	2. 4	2. 5	2. 7	2. 9	3. 0	3. 2	3. 4	3. 5	11 00
11 30	1. 6	1. 8	1. 9	2. 1	2. 3	2. 4	2. 6	2. 7	2. 9	3. 1	3. 2	3. 4	11 30
12 00	1. 5	1. 7	1. 9	2. 0	2. 2	2. 3	2. 5	2. 6	2. 8	2. 9	3. 1	3. 2	12 00
12 30	1. 5	1. 6	1. 8	1. 9	2. 1	2. 2	2. 4	2. 5	2. 7	2. 8	3. 0	3. 1	12 30
13 00	1. 4	1. 6	1. 7	1. 8	2. 0	2. 1	2. 3	2. 4	2. 6	2. 7	2. 9	3. 0	13 00
13 30	1. 4	1. 5	1. 6	1. 8	1. 9	2. 0	2. 2	2. 3	2. 5	2. 6	2. 7	2. 9	13 30
14 00	1. 3	1. 4	1. 6	1. 7	1. 8	2. 0	2. 1	2. 2	2. 4	2. 5	2. 6	2. 8	14 00
14 30	1. 3	1. 4	1. 5	1. 7	1. 8	1. 9	2. 0	2. 2	2. 3	2. 4	2. 5	2. 7	14 30
15 00	1. 2	1. 4	1. 5	1. 6	1. 7	1. 8	2. 0	2. 1	2. 2	2. 3	2. 5	2. 6	15 00
16 00	1. 1	1. 3	1. 4	1. 5	1. 6	1. 7	1. 8	1. 9	2. 1	2. 2	2. 3	2. 4	16 00
17 00	1. 1	1. 2	1. 3	1. 4	1. 5	1. 6	1. 7	1. 8	1. 9	2. 0	2. 2	2. 3	17 00
18 00	1. 0	1. 1	1. 2	1. 3	1. 4	1. 5	1. 6	1. 7	1. 8	1. 9	2. 0	2. 1	18 00
19 00	1. 0	1. 0	1. 1	1. 2	1. 3	1. 4	1. 5	1. 6	1. 7	1. 8	1. 9	2. 0	19 00
20 00	0. 9	1. 0	1. 1	1. 2	1. 3	1. 4	1. 4	1. 5	1. 6	1. 7	1. 8	1. 9	20 00

Figure 16-8.   Extract of Table 9 from *Bowditch*.

TABLE 9

Distance by Vertical Angle

Angle	Height of object, in feet												Angle
	50	60	70	80	90	100	110	120	130	140	160	180	
° ′	Miles	Miles	Miles	Miles	Miles	Miles	Miles	Miles	Miles	Miles	Miles	Miles	° ′
0 10	2. 55	3. 01	3. 45	3. 89	4. 31	4. 72	5. 11	5. 51	5. 89	6. 26	6. 99	7. 68	0 10
0 11	2. 36	2. 79	3. 20	3. 61	4. 01	4. 40	4. 78	5. 15	5. 51	5. 87	6. 57	7. 24	0 11
0 12	2. 19	2. 59	2. 99	3. 37	3. 75	4. 12	4. 48	4. 83	5. 18	5. 53	6. 19	6. 84	0 12
0 13	2. 04	2. 42	2. 80	3. 16	3. 52	3. 87	4. 21	4. 55	4. 89	5. 21	5. 85	6. 48	0 13
0 14	1. 91	2. 27	2. 62	2. 97	3. 31	3. 64	3. 97	4. 30	4. 61	4. 93	5. 54	6. 14	0 14
0 15	1. 79	2. 13	2. 46	2. 79	3. 12	3. 43	3. 75	4. 06	4. 36	4. 66	5. 25	5. 83	0 15
0 20	1. 37	1. 64	1. 90	2. 16	2. 42	2. 68	2. 93	3. 18	3. 43	3. 68	4. 16	4. 64	0 20
0 25	1. 11	1. 33	1. 54	1. 76	1. 97	2. 18	2. 39	2. 60	2. 81	3. 02	3. 42	3. 83	0 25
0 30	0. 93	1. 11	1. 29	1. 47	1. 65	1. 83	2. 01	2. 19	2. 37	2. 54	2. 89	3. 24	0 30
0 35	0. 80	0. 96	1. 11	1. 27	1. 43	1. 58	1. 74	1. 89	2. 05	2. 20	2. 51	2. 81	0 35
0 40	0. 70	0. 84	0. 98	1. 12	1. 26	1. 39	1. 53	1. 67	1. 81	1. 94	2. 21	2. 48	0 40
0 45	0. 62	0. 74	0. 87	0. 99	1. 12	1. 24	1. 36	1. 48	1. 61	1. 73	1. 97	2. 21	0 45
0 50	0. 56	0. 67	0. 78	0. 89	1. 01	1. 12	1. 23	1. 34	1. 45	1. 56	1. 78	2. 00	0 50
0 55	0. 51	0. 61	0. 72	0. 82	0. 92	1. 02	1. 12	1. 22	1. 32	1. 43	1. 63	1. 83	0 55
1 00	0. 47	0. 56	0. 65	0. 75	0. 84	0. 93	1. 02	1. 12	1. 21	1. 30	1. 49	1. 67	1 00
1 10	0. 40	0. 48	0. 56	0. 64	0. 72	0. 80	0. 88	0. 96	1. 04	1. 12	1. 28	1. 44	1 10
1 20	0. 35	0. 42	0. 49	0. 56	0. 63	0. 70	0. 77	0. 84	0. 91	0. 98	1. 12	1. 26	1 20
1 30	0. 31	0. 38	0. 44	0. 50	0. 56	0. 63	0. 69	0. 75	0. 81	0. 87	1. 00	1. 12	1 30
1 40	0. 28	0. 34	0. 39	0. 45	0. 51	0. 57	0. 62	0. 67	0. 73	0. 79	0. 90	1. 02	1 40
1 50	0. 26	0. 31	0. 36	0. 42	0. 47	0. 52	0. 56	0. 61	0. 66	0. 72	0. 82	0. 92	1 50
2 00	0. 24	0. 28	0. 33	0. 38	0. 43	0. 47	0. 53	0. 57	0. 62	0. 65	0. 77	0. 85	2 00
2 15	0. 21	0. 26	0. 30	0. 34	0. 38	0. 42	0. 46	0. 50	0. 54	0. 57	0. 65	0. 73	2 15
2 30	0. 19	0. 23	0. 26	0. 30	0. 34	0. 38	0. 41	0. 45	0. 49	0. 53	0. 60	0. 68	2 30
2 45	0. 17	0. 21	0. 24	0. 27	0. 31	0. 34	0. 37	0. 41	0. 44	0. 48	0. 55	0. 62	2 45
3 00	0. 16	0. 19	0. 22	0. 25	0. 28	0. 31	0. 35	0. 38	0. 41	0. 44	0. 50	0. 56	3 00
3 20	0. 14	0. 17	0. 20	0. 22	0. 25	0. 28	0. 31	0. 34	0. 37	0. 39	0. 45	0. 51	3 20
3 40	0. 13	0. 15	0. 18	0. 21	0. 23	0. 26	0. 28	0. 31	0. 33	0. 36	0. 41	0. 46	3 40
4 00	0. 12	0. 14	0. 16	0. 19	0. 21	0. 24	0. 26	0. 28	0. 31	0. 33	0. 38	0. 42	4 00
4 20	0. 11	0. 13	0. 15	0. 17	0. 19	0. 22	0. 24	0. 26	0. 28	0. 30	0. 35	0. 39	4 20
4 40	0. 10	0. 12	0. 14	0. 16	0. 18	0. 20	0. 22	0. 24	0. 26	0. 28	0. 32	0. 36	4 40
5 00		0. 11	0. 13	0. 15	0. 17	0. 19	0. 21	0. 22	0. 25	0. 26	0. 30	0. 34	5 00
5 20		0. 11	0. 12	0. 14	0. 16	0. 17	0. 19	0. 21	0. 23	0. 25	0. 28	0. 32	5 20
5 40		0. 10	0. 12	0. 13	0. 15	0. 17	0. 18	0. 20	0. 21	0. 23	0. 27	0. 30	5 40
6 00			0. 11	0. 12	0. 14	0. 15	0. 17	0. 19	0. 20	0. 22	0. 25	0. 28	6 00
6 20			0. 10	0. 12	0. 13	0. 15	0. 16	0. 18	0. 19	0. 21	0. 23	0. 27	6 20
6 40			0. 10	0. 11	0. 12	0. 14	0. 15	0. 17	0. 18	0. 19	0. 22	0. 25	6 40
7 00				0. 10	0. 12	0. 13	0. 14	0. 16	0. 17	0. 18	0. 21	0. 24	7 00
7 20				0. 10	0. 12	0. 13	0. 14	0. 15	0. 17	0. 18	0. 20	0. 23	7 20
7 40				0. 10	0. 11	0. 12	0. 13	0. 15	0. 16	0. 17	0. 19	0. 22	7 40
8 00					0. 10	0. 11	0. 13	0. 14	0. 15	0. 16	0. 19	0. 21	8 00
8 20					0. 10	0. 11	0. 13	0. 13	0. 14	0. 15	0. 18	0. 20	8 20
8 40						0. 11	0. 12	0. 13	0. 14	0. 15	0. 17	0. 19	8 40
9 00						0. 10	0. 12	0. 12	0. 14	0. 14	0. 17	0. 19	9 00
9 30						0. 10	0. 11	0. 12	0. 13	0. 14	0. 16	0. 18	9 30
10 00							0. 10	0. 11	0. 12	0. 13	0. 15	0. 17	10 00
10 30							0. 10	0. 11	0. 11	0. 12	0. 14	0. 16	10 30
11 00								0. 10	0. 11	0. 12	0. 13	0. 15	11 00
11 30								0. 10	0. 11	0. 12	0. 13	0. 14	11 30
12 00									0. 10	0. 11	0. 12	0. 14	12 00
12 30									0. 10	0. 11	0. 12	0. 14	12 30
13 00										0. 10	0. 11	0. 12	13 00
13 30										0. 10	0. 11	0. 12	13 30
14 00											0. 10	0. 12	14 00
14 30											0. 10	0. 12	14 30
15 00												0. 11	15 00
16 00												0. 10	16 00
17 00													17 00
18 00													18 00
19 00													19 00
20 00													20 00

STEP 2: Hs 0° 29.'1
     I.C. +1.'1
     DIP −2.'8

     Ho 0° 27.'4

	SEXTANT ANGLE	HEIGHT 2000'	HEIGHT 2200'
STEP 3:	0° 25'	30.'0	32.'2
STEP 4:	0° 30'	27.'2	29.'3
STEP 5:	05'	2.'8	2.'9

STEP 5: 2.4/5 × 2.'8 = 1.34

STEP 5: 2.4/5 × 2.'9 = 1.39

STEP 6:		28.66	30.81
STEP 6:	2008	2000	30.81
	2090	2200	28.66
	82	200	2.15

.41 × 2.15 = .903 + 28.66 = 29.56 MILES OFF

Figure 16-9. A simple table for working a Case 1 vertical sextant angle observation in the navigator's notebook.

STEP 6

Subtract 1.34 from 30.'0 for a distance off of 28.66 miles for a 2,008-foot mountain.

Subtract 1.39 from 32.'2 for a distance off of 30.81 miles for a 2,208-foot mountain.

But the mountain you observed was 2,090 feet. You must interpolate for the difference in height for the actual height of the mountain and the tabulated height differences in the table. The tabulated height differences were 2,000 feet and 2,200 feet. Subtract 2,008 from 2,090 and get 82 feet. Subtract 2,000 from 2,200 and get 200 feet. Subtract 28.'66 from 30.'81 and get 2.'15.

The difference in heights of 82 and 200 makes a fraction of 82/200. Multiply 2.'15 by '.41. (You reduced 82/200 to its lowest terms.) You get .8815. Call this .90 and add it to 28.66 for a total of 29.54. You are 29.5 miles off the mountain peak at 0940.

STEP 7

Plot your circular LOP with the mountain peak as the center and the radius as 29.6 miles. You are 2.6 miles north of your rhumb line, and on the bank. You would change course to the left and try to get off the 100-fathom curve again.

At this point a few comments are in order. You

may think this a long and tedious procedure, but it really is not. A competent navigator can work out a solution like this in a very short time. I took you through each step in exact precision to show you in detail how this is done, and also, despite the distances involved, the proximity of the bank made precise accuracy important. If you read your sextant correctly, your calculations would be accurate. On the other hand, if you did not interpolate at all, your maximum error would not have exceeded three miles. This is well within the accuracy accepted for celestial navigation, and most times when coasting well off a mountainous coast, this is all the accuracy required. Yet, in this situation, visual interpolation, which is easy with practice, will give you an order of accuracy as close as you can plot on a sailing chart. And, if a close situation requires a complete solution, you can work this out in only a few minutes—if you have practiced.

Once again, practice is the key. With practice comes the speed and accuracy required for safe navigation. Practice navigation every chance you get. Practice in home waters, where you can check your results against your local knowledge and develop the skill and experience to sail a strange coast with confidence.

Case 2

Case 2 involves determining distance off by vertical sextant angles of objects, usually closer than five miles, whose bases or waterlines are *beyond* the observer's visible horizon. At first blush this is exactly the same situation as Case 1 except that in Case 2 you must *determine* the visible horizon is closer to you than the base of the object. Otherwise, you may have a Case 3 solution. Refer back to Figure 13-2. The navigator found his distance off Sand Island Light to be 4.8 miles by vertical sextant angle. Here is how it was done.

STEP 1

Plot your dead reckoning up to the time of the sight.

STEP 2

Record your sight and correct your sextant altitude. Your Hs is 0° 14.'0. You have no index error. Your height of eye is 8 feet. Or is it? The chart and the *Light List* tell you that Sand Island Light is 121 feet above mean high water. The column in Table 9 has headings for 110 feet and 120 feet. If you step out of the cockpit onto the deck and raise your height three feet, your height of eye becomes 11 feet. What is important is that the difference between your height of eye and the height of the object, Sand Island Light,

114

is now 110 feet. By stepping up, you have eliminated the need for interpolating between the actual difference in the height of the object and the height of your eye and the tabulated difference.

And this is what makes Case 2 different from the others. You first consult Table 9 for an approximation of your distance off. You use the dip correction from page 1136 (Figure 16-7) — the *Nautical Almanac* extract in *Bowditch* — or from the *Nautical Almanac* itself, to get an entering angle. The correction for 11 feet lies between 10.5 feet and 11.2 feet in the dip table, and is -3.2. With a tentative H_o of $0° 10.'8$, you now enter Table 9. By inspection in the 110-foot height-of-eye column and the $0° 11'$ line in the angle column, you see that you are somewhere five miles off Sand Island Light, provided you have used the proper dip correction. But is this the proper dip correction? To answer this question you *must* consult Table 22 of *Bowditch*, which begins on page 1278 of the 1962 edition (Figure 16-10). Table

TABLE 22
Dip of the Sea Short of the Horizon

| Distance | Height of eye above the sea, in feet | | | | | | | | | | Distance |
	5	10	15	20	25	30	35	40	45	50	
Miles	'	'	'	'	'	'	'	'	'	'	*Miles*
0.1	28.3	56.6	84.9	113.2	141.5	169.8	198.0	226.3	254.6	282.9	0.1
0.2	14.2	28.4	42.5	56.7	70.8	84.9	99.1	113.2	127.4	141.5	0.2
0.3	9.6	19.0	28.4	37.8	47.3	56.7	66.1	75.6	85.0	94.4	0.3
0.4	7.2	14.3	21.4	28.5	35.5	42.6	49.7	56.7	63.8	70.9	0.4
0.5	5.9	11.5	17.2	22.8	28.5	34.2	39.8	45.5	51.1	56.8	0.5
0.6	5.0	9.7	14.4	19.1	23.8	28.5	33.3	38.0	42.7	47.4	0.6
0.7	4.3	8.4	12.4	16.5	20.5	24.5	28.6	32.6	36.7	40.7	0.7
0.8	3.9	7.4	10.9	14.5	18.0	21.5	25.1	28.6	32.2	35.7	0.8
0.9	3.5	6.7	9.8	12.9	16.1	19.2	22.4	25.5	28.7	31.8	0.9
1.0	3.2	6.1	8.9	11.7	14.6	17.4	20.2	23.0	25.9	28.7	1.0
1.1	3.0	5.6	8.2	10.7	13.3	15.9	18.5	21.0	23.6	26.2	1.1
1.2	2.9	5.2	7.6	9.9	12.3	14.6	17.0	19.4	21.7	24.1	1.2
1.3	2.7	4.9	7.1	9.2	11.4	13.6	15.8	17.9	20.1	22.3	1.3
1.4	2.6	4.6	6.6	8.7	10.7	12.7	14.7	16.7	18.8	20.8	1.4
1.5	2.5	4.4	6.3	8.2	10.0	11.9	13.8	15.7	17.6	19.5	1.5
1.6	2.4	4.2	6.0	7.7	9.5	11.3	13.0	14.8	16.6	18.3	1.6
1.7	2.4	4.0	5.7	7.4	9.0	10.7	12.4	14.0	15.7	17.3	1.7
1.8	2.3	3.9	5.5	7.0	8.6	10.2	11.7	13.3	14.9	16.5	1.8
1.9	2.3	3.8	5.3	6.7	8.2	9.7	11.2	12.7	14.2	15.7	1.9
2.0	2.2	3.7	5.1	6.5	7.9	9.3	10.7	12.1	13.6	15.0	2.0
2.1	2.2	3.6	4.9	6.3	7.6	9.0	10.3	11.6	13.0	14.3	2.1
2.2	2.2	3.5	4.8	6.1	7.3	8.6	9.9	11.2	12.5	13.8	2.2
2.3	2.2	3.4	4.6	5.9	7.1	8.3	9.6	10.8	12.0	13.3	2.3
2.4	2.2	3.4	4.5	5.7	6.9	8.1	9.2	10.4	11.6	12.8	2.4
2.5	2.2	3.3	4.4	5.6	6.7	7.8	9.0	10.1	11.2	12.4	2.5
2.6	2.2	3.3	4.3	5.4	6.5	7.6	8.7	9.8	10.9	12.0	2.6
2.7	2.2	3.2	4.3	5.3	6.4	7.4	8.4	9.5	10.6	11.6	2.7
2.8	2.2	3.2	4.2	5.2	6.2	7.2	8.2	9.2	10.3	11.3	2.8
2.9	2.2	3.2	4.1	5.1	6.1	7.1	8.0	9.0	10.0	11.0	2.9
3.0	2.2	3.1	4.1	5.0	6.0	6.9	7.8	8.8	9.7	10.7	3.0
3.1	2.2	3.1	4.0	4.9	5.9	6.8	7.7	8.6	9.5	10.4	3.1
3.2	2.2	3.1	4.0	4.9	5.7	6.6	7.5	8.4	9.3	10.2	3.2
3.3	2.2	3.1	3.9	4.8	5.7	6.5	7.4	8.2	9.1	9.9	3.3
3.4	2.2	3.1	3.9	4.7	5.6	6.4	7.2	8.1	8.9	9.7	3.4
3.5	2.2	3.1	3.9	4.7	5.5	6.3	7.1	7.9	8.7	9.5	3.5
3.6	2.2	3.1	3.8	4.6	5.4	6.2	7.0	7.8	8.6	9.4	3.6
3.7	2.2	3.1	3.8	4.6	5.4	6.1	6.9	7.7	8.4	9.2	3.7
3.8	2.2	3.1	3.8	4.6	5.3	6.0	6.8	7.5	8.3	9.0	3.8
3.9	2.2	3.1	3.8	4.5	5.2	6.0	6.7	7.4	8.1	8.9	3.9
4.0	2.2	3.1	3.8	4.5	5.2	5.9	6.6	7.3	8.0	8.7	4.0
4.1	2.2	3.1	3.8	4.5	5.1	5.8	6.5	7.2	7.9	8.6	4.1
4.2	2.2	3.1	3.8	4.4	5.1	5.8	6.5	7.1	7.8	8.5	4.2
4.3	2.2	3.1	3.8	4.4	5.1	5.7	6.4	7.0	7.7	8.4	4.3
4.4	2.2	3.1	3.8	4.4	5.0	5.7	6.3	7.0	7.6	8.3	4.4
4.5	2.2	3.1	3.8	4.4	5.0	5.6	6.3	6.9	7.5	8.2	4.5
4.6	2.2	3.1	3.8	4.4	5.0	5.6	6.2	6.8	7.4	8.1	4.6
4.7	2.2	3.1	3.8	4.4	5.0	5.6	6.2	6.8	7.4	8.0	4.7
4.8	2.2	3.1	3.8	4.4	4.9	5.5	6.1	6.7	7.3	7.9	4.8
4.9	2.2	3.1	3.8	4.3	4.9	5.5	6.1	6.7	7.2	7.8	4.9
5.0	2.2	3.1	3.8	4.3	4.9	5.5	6.0	6.6	7.2	7.7	5.0
5.5	2.2	3.1	3.8	4.3	4.9	5.4	5.9	6.4	6.9	7.4	5.5
6.0	2.2	3.1	3.8	4.3	4.9	5.3	5.8	6.3	6.7	7.2	6.0
6.5	2.2	3.1	3.8	4.3	4.9	5.3	5.7	6.2	6.6	7.1	6.5
7.0	2.2	3.1	3.8	4.3	4.9	5.3	5.7	6.1	6.5	6.9	7.0
7.5	2.2	3.1	3.8	4.3	4.9	5.3	5.7	6.1	6.5	6.9	7.5
8.0	2.2	3.1	3.8	4.3	4.9	5.3	5.7	6.1	6.5	6.9	8.0
8.5	2.2	3.1	3.8	4.3	4.9	5.3	5.7	6.1	6.5	6.9	8.5
9.0	2.2	3.1	3.8	4.3	4.9	5.3	5.7	6.1	6.5	6.9	9.0
9.5	2.2	3.1	3.8	4.3	4.9	5.3	5.7	6.1	6.5	6.9	9.5
10.0	2.2	3.1	3.8	4.3	4.9	5.3	5.7	6.1	6.5	6.9	10.0

Figure 16-10. Extract of Table 22 from *Bowditch*.

STEP 2: H_s 0° 14.'0

DIP — 3.'2

H_o 0° 10.'8

STEP 3:

SEXTANT ANGLE	HEIGHT DIFFERENCE	DISTANCE OFF
0° 10.'0	110'	5.'11
0° 11.'0	110'	4.'78
		0.'33

STEP 4: 0.8 X 0.33 = 0.264

5.11 − 0.26 = 4.85

Figure 16-11. A simple table for working a Case 2 vertical sextant angle observation in the navigator's notebook.

22 is designed primarily to give you the dip correction for heights of eye on objects between you and the sea (visible) horizon.

On each margin of the table is a distance column, and between these are columns for height of eye above sea level. The height-of-eye columns are tabulated in five-foot intervals. Pick the height of eye nearest to, but *greater* than, your height of eye of 11 feet. This is the 15-foot column. Go down the 15-foot column until you come to the line corresponding to a distance off nearest to, but *less* than, five miles. This distance is 4.9 miles, and the correction is well below a heavy black line zig-zagging across the table. This line divides distances short of the horizon from distances beyond the horizon. Since 4.9 miles lies below the line, you may now disregard Table 22 and use the correction you extracted from Figure 16-7. But it is essential that you assure yourself that your sea horizon is between you and Sand Island Light. Your correct H_o is 0° 10.'8, as previously approximated.

STEP 3

By stepping up three feet, you confined yourself to the 110-foot column of Table 9. Because of this, you need only interpolate for difference in angle. Set up a form as in Figure 16-11. For an angle of 0°10' and a height difference of 110 feet, your distance off is 5.11 miles. Enter these values in your form. For a sextant angle of 0° 11' your distance off is 4.78 miles. Enter these values in the form.

STEP 4

Subtract the distance 4.78 miles from 5.11 miles. The remainder is 0.33 miles. The difference in tabu-

lated angles is 1'. The difference between the H_o 0° 10.'8 and the tabulated angle of 0° 10' is 0.'8. Thus 0.'8 is your factor. Multiply 0.'8 by 0.'33 and get 0.'264. Round this off to .26 and subtract it from 5.11 miles. You are 4.85 miles off Sand Island Light. It is realistic to round this off to 4.9 miles, although you could plot the 4.85 distance on a chart of the scale involved here.

Now that wasn't very difficult was it? Case 2 is the simplest and handiest use of vertical angles, because you can eliminate interpolation for height by selecting your place of observation on board your boat. (You couldn't go up or down 100 feet in Case 1 to make your mountain top fall into one column.) I am not trying to fool you. I know you must usually make an educated guess as to your height of eye, but good navigators are purists. The more accurate you are, the better the results.

Case 3

Case 3 involves determining distance off by a vertical sextant angle of an object between you and the sea horizon; this may involve considerable interpolation. Yet, if one gray, foggy day a lighthouse looms through a rift in the fog, this distance off and a bearing may provide your only fix to let you set a safe course.

An example of Case 3 would work out like this: At 0741 you are anchored off Sand Island Light after creeping into an area of suitable depth in the fog. It is one of those mornings where marching fog banks expose and then obscure the navigator's landmarks. A rift in the fog exposes the light tower long enough for you to observe a vertical sextant angle of

Figure 16-12. The author taking a vertical sextant angle. The position of the index arm indicates that a small angle is being measured, which is to be expected, since most vertical sextant angles used in piloting are small.

0° 38.'6. At the same time, your mate grabbed a bearing on the light of 323°T. Determine your distance off Sand Island Light and plot your position.

STEP 1

I hope you haven't been running in a fog without keeping an up-to-the-minute DR, but, if you haven't, bring your DR up to the time you anchored at your position.

STEP 2

Record your sight. Set up a form for yourself as shown in Figure 16-13. Your seaman's eye tells you the distance off the light is not very great. A quick inspection of Table 9, *Bowditch*, tells you that this distance most likely is around a mile and a half or a mile and three-quarters. You turn to Table 22 (Figure 16-10). Use a height of eye of 10 feet. Again, position yourself where this is the best estimate of height of eye. The dip correction is $-4.'4$ for 1.5 miles, and $-3.'9$ for 1.8 miles. Both of these distances tell you that the base or waterline of Sand Island Light is much closer to you than the true horizon. Which distance do you use? Use 1.8 miles as the normal dip correction; from Figure 16-7, it is -3.1. Subtract 3.1 from your H_s of 0°38.'6 and get a tentative H_o of 0°35.'5. This is much nearer the 0°35' tabulated in the angle column of Table 9, and you find your distance off is about 1.74. But Table 22 tells you that your dip correction is $-4.'0$ for a distance of 1.7 miles. You must reject the H_o 0° 35.'5 and correct your H_s using a dip of $-4.'0$. Your H_o is now 0° 34.'6. You are lucky; 0° 34.'6 is again nearest 0° 35.'0, a tabulated angle. So when you refer back to Table 9, you again use the distance of 1.7 miles, and you get the same dip correction.

If Table 9 had provided you with another distance off, and visual interpolation is required for this, you would have had to return again to Table 22 for still another dip correction. Several references back and forth between Table 9 and Table 22 are sometimes required with Case 3 vertical angle computations before you get the same distance twice.

Correcting for dip short of the sea horizon can be involved. But you are anchored in a fog. You know the water is shoaling. Isn't it well worth your while to be able to get a good fix, even if it takes a little time?

STEP 3

From Table 9 you extract the distance off, under the 110-foot column for an angle of 0° 30.' It is 2.01 miles. In the same column extract a distance of 1.74 miles for an angle of 0° 35.' Put these values in the form (Figure 16-13).

STEP 4

You must interpolate again. Subtract 0° 34.'6 from 0° 35.'0 and get 0.'4. Multiply 0.'4 by 0.'27 and get .108 or .11. Add .11 to 1.74 and you find you are 1.85 miles off Sand Island Light.

No interpolation is made to correct for the one-foot height differential (Sand Island Light is 121 feet high), because your observation could not actually detect this difference.

No attempt has been made to correct for the stage of the tide. The maximum tidal range seldom exceeds two feet along the Gulf Coast. In some parts of the world tide must be reckoned with. If you are in an area having a considerable range of tide, you would compute the height of the tide at the time of the observation. How you make this computation is explained in Chapter 18, page 135. In the first explanation, the skipper wants to know the height of the tide above datum to see if he can get his boat into the fuel dock. Here, you want to know the height of the tide so you will know the actual height of the light you are observing. Remember, too, that the charted and listed heights of lights are heights above mean *high* water. The special considerations involved

STEP 2 : H_s 0° 38.'6
  DIP $-3.'1$

  0° 35.'5

STEP 2 : (FIRST REPETITION) H_s 0°38.'6
  DIP $-4.'0$

  H_o 0° 34.'6

STEP 3:	SEXTANT ANGLE	HEIGHT DIFFERENCE	DISTANCE OFF
	0° 30.'0	110'	2.'01
	0° 35.'0	110'	1.'74
	5.'0		.'27

STEP 4:   0° 35.'0
   $-$ 0° 34.'6

   0.'4   0.'4 × 0.'27 = .108

   .11
 $+$ 1.74

   1.85

Figure 16-13. A simple table for working a Case 3 vertical sextant angle observation in the navigator's notebook.

in finding the actual height of a light in such cases are also explained on page 137. Let me emphasize that the need to make this computation is reserved solely for areas having extreme tidal ranges, and for Case 3 vertical sextant angle observations where extremely precise calculations are necessary because of the short distances involved.

Case 3 is the most involved of all vertical angle solutions. If at all possible you should avoid the type in favor of Case 2 observations. You can often do this by taking your sight from a low enough position to put the sea horizon between you and the object. In taking any vertical angle of terrestial objects, the *lower* your height of eye, the more accurate your results are likely to be. This is just the opposite of sextant observations of celestial bodies, because the rough seas offshore make the distant horizon from a higher height of eye more satisfactory.

VERTICAL DANGER ANGLES

There is another use of vertical sextant angles that is very valuable to the navigator. Suppose your course required you to pass a headland or cape at a distance of at least two miles off to avoid a danger. There is a lighthouse on the cape. By the use of Tables 9 and 22 of *Bowditch*, you would compute the sextant angle that your sextant should read when you are two miles off the cape. You must even "uncorrect" your tabulated H_o by applying dip in reverse to get the required H_s. As you pass the cape you change course as necessary to keep your observed sextant angle from *exceeding* this computed sextant angle. As long as you observe a sextant angle *less* than the maximum computed angle, you are outside of your two-mile danger circle. Your computed sextant angle is a *maximum danger angle*.

An outlying bank or other hazard may also cause you to limit the maximum distance you pass this headland. You determine you can pass safely between these hazards if you stay inside a distance of four miles off. Again using Tables 9 and 22, or the other dip table, you calculate the sextant angle, H_s, at which your boat would be four miles off the cape. Then you steer your vessel to keep her inside the four-mile danger circle, too. As long as you keep this sextant angle *greater* than this computed *minimum danger angle*, you will be safely inside the four-mile circle.

Perhaps you have seen a navigator, with sextant in hand, standing on the deck as his boat traverses a channel off a cape. He doesn't consult a chart — he did that much earlier — but from time to time he orders a small course change to the left and a little later to the right. What is he doing? As his sextant

observations approach the maximum danger angle, he changes course to carry his boat away from the cape. Later, if he finds his sextant observations approach the minimum danger angle, he changes course to carry his boat nearer the cape. This way he carries her safely between two dangers with only his sextant and compass.

I may have at least convinced you that I believe in vertical sextant angles, and I assure you I do. Vertical sextant angles are a regular item in my bag of tricks. But I would be remiss if I did not warn you of two pitfalls that may trap you when using them.

First, remember you are always dealing with rather small angles. A slight error in sextant observation or interpolation will change your results. Be careful, and be aware of this possibility of error. You may interpolate for a difference in height of one foot. Don't kid yourself that you can really see this difference in the center of a lighthouse when you are just a mile off. You surely can't see such a difference when you are farther away. But, on the other hand, any refinement you can put into the solution will reduce cumulative error.

The second and, probably the most important, source of error in vertical sextant angles is refraction. By the very nature of your observations, especially Case 2 and Case 3 observations, the subject observed is near the horizon, where refraction is greatest. Always try to have some means of checking your results when using vertical angles. Of course, checking yourself is essential, no matter what means of fixing your position you use.

And one more thing, if any of you are pirates, racing skippers, or individuals outrunning your mothers-in-law, you can tell if you are gaining or losing, overtaking or being overhauled, by the change in sextant angle. You don't even have to know your quarry's masthead height. Observe a vertical angle. Wait a few minutes, and observe it again. If you are gaining, the angle will increase as you get closer to your quarry. If it is your competition chasing you, the sextant vertical angle will decrease as you pull away, or increase if you are being overhauled.

PRACTICE PROBLEMS

1. On a passage from Puerto Vallarta, Mexico, bound for Cabo San Lucas, Baja, California, you observe the Islas Tres Marias to starboard. Overcast skies preclude observation of the sun, and previous heavy weather makes a position urgent. With your sextant you observe a vertical angle on the 2,100-foot central peak of Isla Maria Madre to be 1° 06.'3. A vertical angle observation on the 1,500-foot central peak of Isla de Maria Magdelena reads 0° 58.'3.

Your height of eye is seven feet. Your sextant has an index error of 1.′3 on the arc. What is your distance off each peak?

2. Approaching the Gulfport Ship Channel in daylight, you observe Chandeleur Light on your port bow. Passing squalls obscure all other aids. You observe a vertical sextant angle on the light to be 0° 14.′1. The *Light List* gives the height of Chandeleur Light as 99 feet. You position yourself for a height of eye of nine feet. Your sextant has no index error. How far off the light are you?

ANSWERS
1. 17.2 miles off Isla Maria Madre
   14.30 miles off Isla de Maria Magdelena
2. 3.96 miles off

17   HOW TO USE HORIZONTAL SEXTANT ANGLES

Vertical sextant angles give results that are accurate enough for most situations. Horizontal sextant angles give positions accurate enough to satisfy even the most demanding cartographer (and I sure hope they all *are* demanding). They are the simplest of all sextant observations to take, providing you have mastered the skill of using your sextant. By using them, you can return to a sunken wreck miles offshore, pin-point a mooring, or determine your position with enough accuracy to pilot your boat in extremely close quarters. Of course, there will always be places you should never attempt to traverse without local knowledge and a marked channel.

To take a horizontal sextant angle, the navigator holds the sextant so the plane of the arc is horizontal (see Figure 17-1), and the mirrors and telescope are on the top side of the arc.

Suppose in your passage from Panama City to Gulfport in *War Hat* you anchor south of Sand Island to bottom fish. You stay there several hours because the fishing is unusually good. One of the crew dons his scuba gear — the water is only about fifty feet deep — and he dives down to see what is on the bottom. He comes up to report that *War Hat* is anchored over a half-buried wreck. The wreck is not old enough to harbor pieces of eight, but is an excellent secret fish haven. You want to pin-point this spot so you can return. How can you do it?

Look over toward Dauphin Island. You see the water tank in the center of the Island, the radar dome at the east end of the island, and, across the mouth of Mobile Bay, Mobile Point Light tower is clearly visible. If you measure the angle between the water tank, your position, and the domes with your sextant; and then measure the angle between the domes, your position, and Mobile Point Light, you will have a pair of horizontal sextant angles measured to the nearest minute and tenth of a minute of arc. You could never take a bearing this precisely.

120

Figure 17-2 illustrates what you see, and how each pair of objects looks when taking these horizontal angles. You must always look at the left-hand object first, which in this case is the water tank, and, by moving the index arm, bring the reflected image of the middle object, the radar dome, under the water tank, which you see directly through the clear half of the horizon glass. When you have the reflected image of the dome directly under the water tank, read your sextant and record the angle measured. For our exercise call that angle 19° 12.'7.

Figure 17-1. Taking a horizontal sextant angle. The navigator holds the sextant so the plane of the arc is parallel to the plane of the horizon, and the mirrors are on the top of the arc. Angles are then measured between objects by reflecting the object to the right into the horizon glass and under the object to the left. The left-hand object is viewed through the telescope and the clear part of the horizon glass.

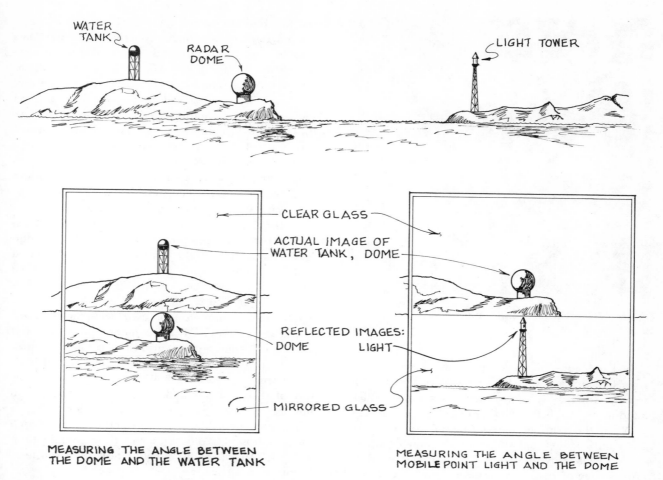

WATER TANK

RADAR DOME

LIGHT TOWER

CLEAR GLASS

ACTUAL IMAGE OF
WATER TANK, DOME

REFLECTED IMAGES:
DOME   LIGHT

MIRRORED GLASS

MEASURING THE ANGLE BETWEEN
THE DOME AND THE WATER TANK

MEASURING THE ANGLE BETWEEN
MOBILE POINT LIGHT AND THE DOME

Figure 17-2. Taking horizontal sextant angles. The upper part of the illustration is a sketch of what you see from *War Hat*'s position looking toward Dauphin Island. The left-hand drawing of the horizon glass shows how the reflected image of the dome is brought under the water tank by moving the index arm of the sextant. The right-hand drawing of the horizon glass shows how the reflected image of the light tower is brought under the true image of the dome to measure the second angle.

You are now ready to measure the second angle. Look at the radar dome, the center object of the three, through the clear half of your horizon mirror, and move the index arm until the reflected image of the light is precisely under the water tank. Read and record this second angle. We'll call it 28° 09.'7.

If you were a chart maker and wanted to plot this wreck's exact position on the chart, you would probably use a three-armed protractor, such as the one shown in Figure 17-3. The protractor, or station pointer as the British call this thing, illustrated is an extremely fine instrument. The movable arms are fitted with a vernier to enable the user to set the same angle on the arms of the protractor down to minutes of arc, with almost the same degree of resolution he obtained with his sextant.

The three-armed protractor is indeed a remarkable instrument, and what I am going to say applies basically to all three-armed protractors. The center arm of the protractor is fixed. The left-hand arm is movable so the first horizontal sextant angle can be set on the scale. The right-hand arm is also movable in like manner so the second horizontal sextant angle can be set in. As each arm is positioned to the precise arc and vernier reading corresponding to each observed sextant angle, a clamp screw is tightened to assure that the arms do not move off the settings.

A three-armed protractor may be a "right-hand" or a "left-hand" protractor, depending on which edge of the center arm is zeroed. If the instrument must be set with the left edge of the center arm at zero, it is a left-hand protractor. If settings are read with the

Figure 17-3. The three-armed protractor.

right-hand edge of the center arm at zero, it is a right-hand protractor. It is imperative that you determine whether your protractor is a right- or left-hand protractor before you try to use it.

When the arms of the protractor are set to the observed sextant angles, lay the protractor on the chart. Then move the protractor around until the proper edge of each arm passes through the charted position of each aid or landmark you observed. Until you get the hang of it, this may take a little time. But once you catch on it is not difficult. You will be surprised how little movement it takes to put the arms out of alignment, and conversely how one point and only one point on the chart will let each of the three arms pass precisely through their respective landmarks. The precision with which the protractor must be aligned is an index of the accuracy involved. When each arm passes exactly through its particular aid, put a mark in the center of the protractor, through the hole provided, on the chart. This mark is your position.

Unless you are a chartmaker, navigator on a heavy cruiser, or a marine consultant called on to position a dredge or establish a mooring, you are not going to need an instrument as precise as that shown in Figure 17-3. For ordinary plotting, an instrument such as the Weems Position Finder will give you all the resolution you need to plot (see Figure 17-4). In addition the Weems Position Finder has an index mirror on each arm. With this feature, you can actually take the horizontal angle observations, and, when each angle is found and the clamp screws are set, you can

lay the position finder on the chart and move it around until each arm is properly oriented to pass through the objects observed. The center of the protractor will be exactly over your position. The Weems Position Finder combines the principles of the sextant and the three-armed protractor. It is a good instrument, and relatively inexpensive compared to the cost of a sextant and a first-rate three-armed protractor. It is an intermediate or close-range instrument in my opinion, however, because there is no magnifying telescope to make distant objects stand out. But it is an excellent three-armed protractor quite suitable for ordinary navigational needs.

At the time of this writing, you can buy good navigational three-armed protractors for under ten dollars. You can also find them for ninety or a hundred dollars. These instruments are of plastic, and even the less expensive ones are usually equipped with a vernier for the best resolution.

The most common tool used for plotting horizontal sextant angles is the standard protractor and a piece of tissue paper. An ordinary dime store protractor such as the one your kids use in school is all you need (see Figure 17-5). Buy, beg, or borrow several sheets of onion skin paper, and you are in business. If you want to be sophisticated, buy a dollar protractor like the draftsmen use and a small sheet of frosted mylar. Either of these combinations will give you all the accuracy or resolution you need for ordinary navigation.

Here is how to use a protractor and tissue paper: The center line is the right leg of the first angle and the left leg of the second angle. When the angles are drawn, lay the tissue on the chart and move it around

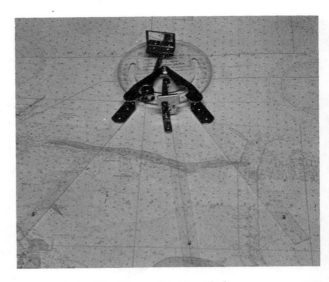

Figure 17-4. The Weems Position Finder.

until each of the three lines passes precisely through the aid or landmark you observed in measuring the angle. The common vertex of the two angles is your position.

When I described the techniques of observing horizontal sextant angles, I told you to record the observed angles to the nearest tenth of a minute, although I also told you that you would almost never attempt to plot an angle so closely, at least not in the course of ordinary navigation. Why record these angles so exactly if you can't use them? You cannot plot these angles with your protractor and tissue paper much closer than a half of a degree, but you can use them. How? You might want to return to the wreck you just found at a later date. One way to do it is by using *precise* horizontal sextant angles set to the nearest degree, minute, and tenth.

Before you weighed anchor it would have been wise to take a bearing on the Dauphin Island water tank. You took a bearing, which was 013.5°T. When you want to return to the wreck, stand out beyond the place you believe she is located. Turn to the bearing you observed, 013.5°T, and steer this as a course, heading right for the tank. You should proceed slowly and have the anchor ready to let go. As you approach the tank, take continuous horizontal angles between the dome and the water tank. The angles observed should be less than the angle you previously recorded, but they should increase as you approach the wreck. At the same time, if you have a mate, have your mate take horizontal angles with his or her sextant on the dome and Mobile Point Light. If you do not have a mate, you can catch a shot yourself from time to time. Your main interest at this time, however, is the angle between the water tank and the dome.

As the horizontal angle between the dome and the water tank approaches the required angle of 19°12.′7, your boat should have minimum way on. When you get this close you should preset your sextant. At the instant you read the angle you are looking for, stop your boat. If necessary, let go the hook; but keep it hove short. Now check yourself. If the first angle is still okay, observe the dome and the light. If the angle between the dome and the light is too large, move away from the light, but be careful to maintain the angle between the water tank and the dome. If the angle between the dome and the light is too small, move in a direction more toward the light, and again be careful to maintain the required angle between the tank and the dome.

This method is not as involved as it sounds. It is used by our fishermen in picking up their fishing gear and by the Coast Guard in placing buoys. Most successful party-boat skippers are very good at using

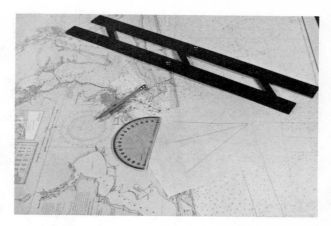

Figure 17-5. A standard protractor and piece of tissue paper used to plot horizontal sextant angles.

horizontal sextant angles, and each skipper will have his own secret list of those pairs of sextant angles that will put him over the choice spots he has discovered. The secret to holding the first angle, the angle between the water tank and the domes, is to steer a course toward or away from the light that would be a chord of a circle passing through your position, the water tank, and the dome. For those who have trouble visualizing the geometry of this method, Figure 17-6 lays it out in full.

War Hat is on a circle that passes through her position, the position of the water tank, and that of the dome on the east end of Dauphin Island. As long as she remains on this circle, the horizontal angle between the water tank and the dome will remain at 19° 12.′7. But only if she is over the wreck, will the angle between the dome and Mobile Point Light be exactly 28° 09.′7. If *War Hat* finds herself at position *A*, the angle between the dome and Mobile Point Light will be 23° 34.′0. This is less than 28° 09.′7. She must steer to try to remain on the circle, and move toward Mobile Point Light.

If *War Hat* finds herself at position *B*, the angle between the dome and Mobile Point Light will be 32° 45.′0. This is a larger angle than you are looking for. The course you must steer to move away from *A* to the wreck or from *B* to the wreck is a chord of the position circle. If you conned *War Hat* onto the circle with the water tank bearing 013.5°T, you would hardly end up as far away as position *A* or position *B*. I spread these positions apart on the circle so you could see more clearly the basic principles.

There is one situation you must watch for when using horizontal sextant angles. Be sure your position and the position of the three objects you are observing cannot be found on the circumference of the same circle. If the position circle passed through

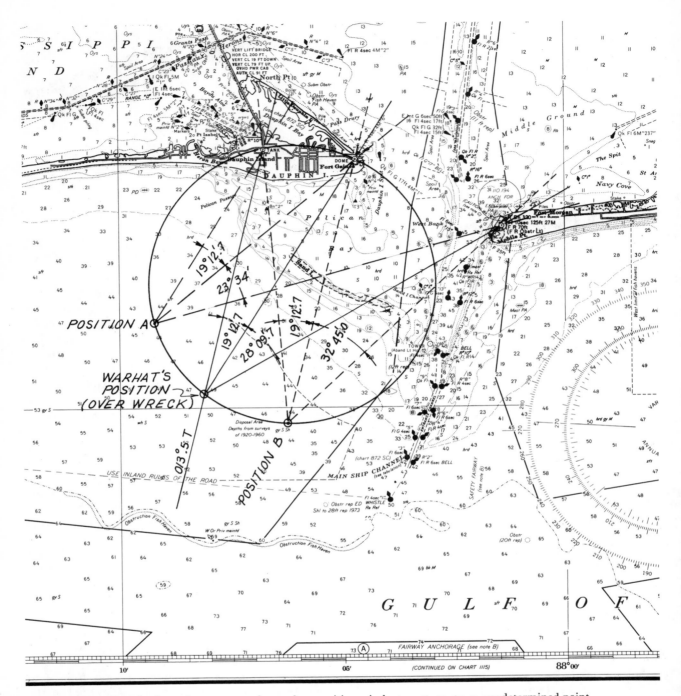

Figure 17-6. Using horizontal sextant angles and a position circle to return to a predetermined point.

War Hat's position, the water tank's, the dome's, *and* Mobile Point Light's, both horizontal angles would remain the same as long as *War Hat* remained on the circle. Her position would have plotted anywhere on the circle. Navigators call a pair of sextant angles that produce a circle passing through the three objects and the vessel's position a "revolver." You can really go round and round on a thing like this! To avoid revolvers, *always* try to pick your three objects so that they align in as nearly a straight line as possible. If three such objects are not available, check your plot to be absolutely sure you cannot draw a circle to pass through the position of your boat and the three objects you measured your angles on.

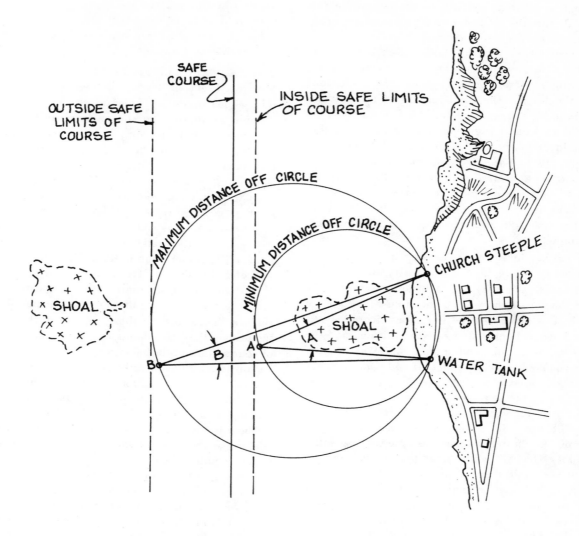

Figure 17-7. Horizontal danger angles. The navigator must steer his vessel so that she will remain between the inside and outside safe limits indicated by the circles. To do this he directs her course away from the land if the observed sextant angle approaches or becomes *greater* than angle A. He directs her course toward the land if the observed sextant angle approaches or becomes *lesser* than angle B.

HORIZONTAL DANGER ANGLES

Another application of the position circle in Figure 17-6 is possible. In Figure 17-7 you are standing along a coast. On the beach are a water tank and a church steeple. Between the points where these two landmarks would be abeam is a rocky shoal lying about one and a half miles offshore. You decide to pass this shoal with a half-mile margin of error. You want to remain two miles off the beach and a half mile off the shoal. Here is one way to do it:

Measure a point one-half mile outside the rock-bound shoal you want to avoid. Now, with your pro-

tractor, measure the angle made by a line from the point one-half mile outside the shoal to the water tank and another line from this point to the church steeple. Your third point one-half mile outside of the shoal is the vertex of the angle you are measuring. Let's call this point *A*, your *minimum* safe distance off, and let's call the angle, angle *A*, the *maximum* sextant angle allowable to keep the *minimum* safe distance off.

Draw a circle that passes through the water tank, church steeple, and the point one-half mile outside the shoal. As long as you maintain an angle equal to

125

the angle measured, you will be somewhere on this circle. Be sure the circle does not pass over any other hazard you are likely to encounter.

Use your sextant. If, after sailing a while, the angle you observe is greater than the angle of your position circle, you are inside of the position circle, and consequently closer to the shoal you are trying to avoid. You are inside your danger limits! You must stand off until the horizontal angle you observe with your sextant reduces to the angle you measured, angle *A*, in Figure 17-7. The angle you measured with your protractor is a *maximum* horizontal danger angle, because this angle represents the maximum horizontal sextant angle you can observe on the water tank and church steeple and stay *outside* the two-mile-off limit you set.

For passing between an outlying hazard and the beach or, as Figure 17-7 illustrates, passing between two hazards, you may use a minimum horizontal danger angle along with a maximum one. Note that there is another reef lying about five miles offshore. A deep channel runs between this reef and the shoal that is a mile and a half off. You decided earlier you could stay two miles off and pass the inner reef safely outside. After carefully studying your chart, you decide you can also stay inside a four and a half mile limit and safely avoid the reef lying farther offshore. So, by using the same water tank, the same church steeple, and this time the four-mile-off point, which is point *B*, as the vertex, you determine the angle these points make. This is angle *B* in Figure 17-7. To remain inside the four-mile-off limit, you must hold a course close enough to the beach to keep this second angle *greater* than the angle determined for angle *B*. Angle *B*, the minimum angle you determined you could observe with your sextant and remain safely inside four miles off, is your *minimum horizontal danger angle*.

If you want to limit your distance off to a distance no *less* than a predetermined minimum, you determine a *maximum* danger angle. If you want to limit your distance off to a distance no *greater* than a predetermined maximum, you determine a *minimum* danger angle.

If you stay outside of the maximum danger angle and inside the minimum danger angle, you have it made. Well, maybe, *but only as long as your position is between the two danger circles.* To use danger angles — and this applies equally as well to the vertical danger angles explained in Chapter 16 — you must have some means of coming up on the danger circles safely. You must have some means of fixing your position as you approach the points

where you can use the danger angles. You should have at least worked out minimum and maximum danger bearings to bring you safely onto or between the distance-off position circles (see Chapter 15).

THE SEXTANT AS A PELORUS

You can use your sextant in lieu of a pelorus for taking bearings, as I mentioned in Chapter 15. Assume you have a beacon on your starboard bow. The aid or landmark may be anywhere forward of your starboard beam. You want to take a bearing on this fixed aid to navigation to get a line of position. You have no other instrument for getting this bearing. Your steering compass is not in a position to sight over. You can still get your bearing, however, if there is some way you can get a line of sight along the deck exactly parallel with your keel. This line of sight will parallel your heading. Line up the head stay and the jib stay if you can see them. Or plan ahead and select or mark two prominent points, facing forward, on deck that are in a line parallel with the keel. Then, for the object on your starboard bow, sight along these two points, and move the index arm of your sextant until the object you are taking a bearing on is reflected directly under the line of objects or points paralleling your keel. At this moment yell "mark!" and read your sextant. The sextant reading is the relative bearing of the object on your starboard bow; add this relative bearing to your heading at the moment you sang out mark. The sum is your compass bearing, which should be corrected to a true bearing and plotted as your LOP.

Assume the next aid you want to take a bearing on is on your starboard quarter. You now need to align two points on deck that you can see with your sextant, that are in a line parallel to your vessel's keel, and that are visible to you facing aft. This time look at the aid through your sextant telescope, and move the index arm to bring your line on deck under the aid. Again sing out "mark," when the aid is over the reflection of the line on deck. Read your sextant, and *subtract* your sextant reading from 180⁰ to get the relative bearing of the aid. Convert this relative bearing to a true bearing and plot your LOP.

If the aid or landmark you observed were on your port quarter, you would sight aft along the deck with your sextant telescope and bring the aid under. To get your relative bearing, you would *add* the sextant reading to 180⁰. Then you would convert the relative bearing to a compass bearing, correct the compass bearing to true, and plot your LOP.

If you take a bearing on an object on your port bow, look at the object and bring the line on deck, facing forward, under the object. Read your sextant and subtract the sextant angle from 360° to get your relative bearing. Again convert the relative bearing to a compass bearing, correct the compass bearing to true, and plot your LOP.

You will find your sextant an excellent tool for taking bearings as described above, as long as you bear in mind two things: If the line parallel to your keel is accurately determined and well defined through the telescope, your sextant bearings (angles) will be accurate. The other consideration involves a matter of optics. Focusing a high-powered telescope, such as the 7 × 50 monocular prismatic monster I have on my Tamaya sextant, brings the distant object in beautifully, but puts objects on the deck of a small boat, such as your lined-up stays, out of focus. For this kind of work, a sextant of a lower power, such as the small craft types, is much better, and, if you can see your landmark in the distance, an open sight tube may be even better.

Get yourself a good sextant. From this and the previous chapter, you see how much you can use it. As I said in the beginning, if you never get out of sight of land, you can and should use your sextant as much, if not more, than the deepwater man making an offshore passage. Then, when you do go on to celestial navigation, you will know your instrument, and you will have developed the skill to use it.

18 HOW TO USE TIDE AND CURRENT TABLES

Knowledge of tides and tidal currents is extremely important for mariners. The navigator must know how the tides affect the depth of the water in which he navigates his vessel, and what effects he may find because of tidal currents. He needs to know whether these currents can help him on his way, impede him by slowing down his vessel's speed over the ground, or set him onto some danger. To assist the navigator, the National Ocean Survey publishes four volumes of tide tables and four volumes of current tables for each calendar year. These volumes cover the main portions of the entire world. Our purpose in this chapter is to learn how to glean the most information from these tables, and, with the application of good judgement, use this information correctly.

The first and most important thing to do, before attempting to use any publication, is to read it from cover to cover. For our work we are going to use the *Tide Tables, East Coast of North and South America (Including Greenland),* 1972 edition, and *Tidal Current Tables, Atlantic Coast of North America,* 1972 edition. A new edition of each set of the tide tables and a new edition of each set of the current tables are published each calendar year. From here on we will just call these two volumes the *Tide Tables* and the *Current Tables*. The format of these volumes is the same as all the other volumes in the series. If you learn to use these tables, you should be able to use any of the other tide and current tables available. Incidentally, you buy tide tables and current tables from the same Hydrographic Agent you buy your charts from.

TIDE TABLES

Tide is the vertical motion, rise and fall, of the water surface due to the gravitational attraction primarily of the moon and then the sun, and to a very small degree the attraction of other heavenly bodies. Tide tables *predict* the height of the tide above *datum.*

The datum used for reckoning the predicted heights of the tide is the same as the datum for soundings on the charts of the locality. With the use of these predicted heights of the tide and an up-to-date chart of an area, a navigator can predict the probable depth of the waters he intends to navigate at the time he expects his vessel to be in those waters.

In using the predictions in the *Tide Tables*, you, as navigator, must be aware of those things that can possibly alter the actual height of the tide from the predicted height. In an area such as the Gulf Coast, where the range of the tide is small, seldom over two feet between highest high water and lowest low water, the direction of the wind and the barometric pressure may completely overwhelm the tidal motion, so much so that when the tide tables predict a spring height of two feet above datum, a hard nor'wester and a rising barometer may produce an actual condition of height of tide two feet *below* datum. In a case like this the actual depth of the water is *four feet* less than predicted. This is a very common occurrence on the Gulf Coast and in many other parts of the world. Unless you reckon with the effects of the wind and barometric pressure, it is obvious you can get in serious trouble. Local knowledge is always the preferred source of this type of information, but frequently local knowledge is not available. Your *Coast Pilot* or *Sailing Directions* are a source of information concerning what effects wind and the atmospheric pressure have on the tides in an area.

If no local knowledge or other specific information is available, it will help you to know how wind and barometric pressure have a marked effect on the height of the tide at any time and any place. A high barometer tends to lower the height of the tide by lowering the height of sea level in the area of high barometric pressure. The weight of the air simply "squeezes" the water out of the high pressure area. An offshore wind tends to lower the height of the tide

128

by pushing the water out to sea. Together, these two forces tend to reinforce each other. Conversely, a low barometer tends to raise the height of the tide by raising sea level; an onshore breeze tends to raise the height of the tide. As navigator you must be always alert to possible variations in the predicted heights of the tide due to these influences.

Before I continue I want to implant clearly in your mind several definitions of terms sailors kick around, sometimes with abandon, when speaking about tides:

SPRING TIDES
Probably the most misunderstood words used in tidal terminology are the words *neap* and *spring tides*. A spring tide has no reference to the season, but is a tide experienced when the sun and the moon are in line, or nearly so. Astronomers call this phenomenon conjunction or opposition, depending on whether the moon is between the earth and sun, or the earth is between the sun and moon. You get spring tides when the sun and moon are in, or nearly in, conjunction, as with a new moon, or when the sun and moon are in, or nearly in, opposition, as with a full moon. In each of these cases the sun's and moon's gravities reinforce each other. You therefore get the greatest range of tide with spring tides.

NEAP TIDES
Neap tides occur when the moon is at or near its first and last quarter. The sun and moon are not in line at these times, but at quadrature. The gravitational forces of these two bodies tend to cancel each other. You get the least range of tide during a neap tide. There are further variations in tidal range due to the moon's declination, and whether the moon is at apogee or perigee. The position of the earth in orbit around the sun is also a factor in the range of the tide. But these things affect the basic spring or neap tides.

RANGE OF TIDE
The range of tide is the maximum difference between the highest high water and the lowest low water in a tidal day. A tidal day, or lunar day, averages 24 hours and 50 minutes.

TIME OF TIDE
Times of tide are tabulated to the *zone* meridian. Zone meridians are the meridians marking time changes of one hour as you go around the world from east to west, or vice versa. As fifteen degrees of longitude equals one hour of time, the zone meridians are those meridians divisible by 15, east or west of Greenwich, England (see Chapter 1); the zero meridian of

Greenwich itself is also a zone meridian. Thus, if the time is noon at Greenwich, at the meridian 15 degrees west of Greenwich the local time will be 1100, and at 30 degrees west of Greenwich the local time will be 1000. Conversely, at 15 degrees east of Greenwich the local time will be 1300, and at 30 degrees east of Greenwich the local time will be 1400. The time zone of a specific zone meridian extends seven and one-half degrees on either side of the zone meridian. Landlubbers keep standard time. Standard time is usually zone time modified to accommodate geographic and political requirements. For the coastal navigator, zone time almost always will be standard time also. But be sure to check. Time is never given in daylight saving or summer time. A footnote at the bottom of each page of the *Tide Tables* tells you the time meridian each time is based on.

You will hear sailors speak of the tide neaping or changing as well as the tide turning. A tide neaps, in the waterman's parlance, when it changes from a neap to a spring tide or from a spring tide to a neap tide. The tide neaps or changes about every seven days.

Do not confuse a changing tide with a turning tide. The tide turns twice or four times every lunar day depending on whether the tide is diurnal, semi-diurnal, or mixed. And here, when the sailor says the tide turns, he really means the tidal current turns. Remember that tide is the *vertical* motion of the water, and current is the *horizontal* motion of the water. I will say this again later on. The time of the turning of the direction of flow of a tidal current does *not* usually correspond with the times of high and low water, but may differ by several minutes to several hours.

Tides may be diurnal, semi-diurnal, or mixed. A diurnal tide is a tide that provides only one high tide and one low tide at a location each lunar day. The northern coast of the Gulf of Mexico — southern coast of the United States — has tides that are mostly diurnal.

A location has semi-diurnal tides when there are two pronounced high tides and two pronounced low tides each lunar day. The tides along the Atlantic Coast of the United States are mainly semi-diurnal.

Tides are said to be mixed when the semi-diurnal nature of the tides produces a considerable variation between the heights of the high waters and the heights of the low waters in a lunar day. With mixed tides a location experiences a high water, a high high water, a low water and a low low water (or lower low) water. The datum of West Coast charts is lower low water, since the Pacific coast of the United States experiences mainly mixed tides.

You will enjoy studying the chapter in *Bowditch* on tides. Much excellent information on the technical aspects of tides and tidal currents is given there in a manner that is very useful to any mariner. For you, though, it is time to get back to the *Tide Tables*.

The tide tables are divided into three tables. Table 1 lists 48 *reference stations* for which the predicted time and height of tide for any day of the year is tabulated. The use of Table 1 is quite simple. For example:

As navigator of *War Hat*, you find yourself inside Pelican Bay, south of Dauphin Island. It is early afternoon, Monday, 23 October, 1972. You are anchored, but you are thinking about getting underway. The skipper asks you the time of the next high tide. To answer his question you consult Table 1 of

the *Atlantic Coast Tide Table.* From your earlier reading of the *Tide Tables,* you know reference stations are listed in geographic order. In most cases, you would be familiar enough with the coast to know that Mobile is the next station after Pensacola, Florida. You could open the tables and flip to the right page. On a strange coast, however, you might need an index of reference stations to guide you. If you are not familiar with the Gulf Coast, you would open the *Tide Tables* to page 6, which tells you that the Mobile, Alabama, tidal data begins on page 138. You open the *Tide Tables* to page 138, where you see the tabulated tidal data for the first three months of 1972. Turn through pages 139 and 140 to page 141. On page 141 the first month is October, 1972 (see Figure 18-1).

MOBILE, ALABAMA, 1972

TIMES AND HEIGHTS OF HIGH AND LOW WATERS

		OCTOBER					NOVEMBER						DECEMBER				
DAY	TIME H.M.	HT. FT.	DAY	TIME H.M.	HT. FT.	DAY	TIME H.M.	HT. FT.	DAY	TIME H.M.	HT. FT.	DAY	TIME H.M.	HT. FT.	DAY	TIME H.M.	HT. FT.
1 SU	0612 1836	1.7 0.1	16 M	0512 1731	1.4 0.2	1 W	0538 1100 1524 2221	0.6 0.7 0.7 0.9	16 TH	0657 2124	0.5 1.0	1 F	0737 2104	-0.1 1.3	16 SA	0725 2026	-0.4 1.5
2 M	0748 1918	1.5 0.3	17 TU	0618 1806	1.2 0.4	2 TH	0650 2203	0.4 1.1	17 F	0706 2117	0.1 1.3	2 SA	0815 2125	-0.3 1.4	17 SU	0808 2106	-0.7 1.7
3 TU	1006 1940	1.3 0.5	18 W	0913 1815	1.1 0.6	3 F	0738 2212	0.2 1.3	18 SA	0754 2137	-0.2 1.6	3 SU	0850 2153	-0.4 1.5	18 M	0858 2156	-0.9 1.9
4 W	1149 1936	1.2 0.8	19 TH	0030 0516 1216 1723 2244	0.8 0.7 0.9 0.8 1.0	4 SA	0827 2233	0.0 1.5	19 SU	0836 2215	-0.5 1.8	4 M	0930 2237	-0.5 1.5	19 TU	0946 2250	-1.0 1.9
5 TH	0018 0614 1351 1824 2325	0.9 0.6 1.1 0.9 1.1	20 F	0651 2225	0.4 1.2	5 SU	0903 2302	-0.1 1.6	20 M	0932 2301	-0.7 2.0	5 TU	1010 2314	-0.5 1.5	20 W	1042 2345	-1.0 1.8
6 F	0731 2326	0.5 1.3	21 SA	0754 2254	0.1 1.6	6 M	0945 2331	-0.2 1.6	21 TU	1028 2346	-0.8 2.0	6 W	1055 2354	-0.5 1.5	21 TH	1128	-1.0
7 SA	0826 2341	0.3 1.4	22 SU	0857 2321	-0.1 1.8	7 TU	1033	-0.2	22 W	1128	-0.8	7 TH	1136	-0.5	22 F	0040 1209	1.7 -0.8
8 SU	0923	0.2	23 M	1004	-0.3	8 W	0006 1128	1.6 -0.3	23 TH	0038 1231	2.0 -0.8	8 F	0037 1211	1.5 -0.5	23 SA	0134 1243	1.5 -0.6
9 M	0002 1006	1.6 0.1	24 TU	0001 1115	2.0 -0.4	9 TH	0041 1225	1.6 -0.2	24 F	0132 1317	1.9 -0.6	9 SA	0114 1240	1.4 -0.5	24 SU	0215 1259	1.2 -0.3
10 TU	0037 1108	1.6 0.1	25 W	0053 1223	2.1 -0.5	10 F	0123 1319	1.6 -0.2	25 SA	0221 1405	1.6 -0.4	10 SU	0149 1306	1.3 -0.3	25 M	0258 1240	0.9 0.0
11 W	0106 1211	1.7 0.1	26 TH	0142 1337	2.1 -0.4	11 SA	0203 1400	1.5 -0.2	26 SU	0310 1430	1.4 -0.2	11 M	0224 1316	1.1 -0.2	26 TU	0300 1148 1943	0.6 0.1 0.6

Figure 18-1. Extract from Table 1 of the *Atlantic Coast Tide Tables.*

130

Under the month of October are two columns, and each of these two columns is composed of three sub-columns. The first sub-column is headed "Day". The day column lists the days of the month. The dates are indicated by a number corresponding to the dates, and the day of the week is indicated immediately beneath the number by a one- or two-letter abbreviation. To find the data for Monday, 23 October, you scan down the day column until you reach the number "23", and right beneath this number is the abbreviation "M".

The next sub-column is headed "Time H.M." for hours and minutes, and the third sub-column is headed "Ht. Ft." for height in feet. Opposite the 23rd, to your right, you read a time of 1004. Continuing to the third column you see the height of the tide at 1004 is -0.3 feet. No other times or heights are listed for Monday the 23rd. And since -0.3 is below datum, as indicated by the minus sign, it is apparent there will be only one tide, a low tide, on the 23rd, and since it is afternoon, it is after 1004. When will the next high tide be?

Drop down one day to Tuesday, the 24th, and opposite 24 read a time of 0001. Opposite this time read a height of tide of 2.0 feet. The next tide at Mobile, reckoned from the afternoon of Monday the 23rd, will be one minute after midnight the morning of Tuesday, October the 24th.

The tide table does not tell you this tide at 0001 is high tide, but if you glance below to the "TU" line, you see a time of 1115 and a height of -0.4. These numbers are the height of the tide above datum. Minus 0.4 is actually *below* datum, so the tide must be high at 0001 because then the tide is two feet *above* datum. High tide at Mobile will be at 0001 the 24th of October. Using the *Tide Tables* to find the time of high or low water at a reference station requires the same amount of skill it takes to look up your sailing buddy's telephone number.

What do you do with this information now that you have it? The whole idea is to find out how deep the water will be at, in this case, high tide at Mobile, Alabama. To do this you add the tabulated height of tide from the tide table to the depths on the chart. Look at the bottom of Figure 18-1. A footnote tells you that, "heights are reckoned from the datum of soundings on charts of the locality which is mean low water." If you want to sneak *War Hat* with her six-foot draft into Dog River, a river about five miles south of Mobile, you could do it around midnight of the 23rd-24th if it isn't too rough. Remember what wind and barometric pressure do to the height of the tide. Dog River has a bar with only five feet of water on it at mean low water. Five feet plus two

feet gives you a depth of seven feet. You have to remain in Dog River until the next high tide, however, unless you turn around and come out.

But you are anchored in Pelican Bay. You want to continue on your passage to Gulfport. Rather than go out the main ship channel at Mobile Bay Entrance, you consider saving distance by going out through Pelican Passage. *Coast Pilot 5* tells you a vessel drawing six feet can use Pelican Pass, but only with local knowledge. A friendly shrimper volunteers to provide this local knowledge. The chart shows a narrow but deep channel with shoals of four feet in depth at mean low water. You decide you can safely negotiate Pelican Passage at high tide. What time can you expect high tide at Pelican Passage?

To answer the above question you must turn to Table 2, "Tidal Differences and Other Constants," which begins with an explanation on page 202, and continues through a list of each subordinate station, listed in geographical order, for the places covered. Each subordinate station has a number, and the numbers are in sequence. If you know the name of a listed subordinate station, you can look it up in the index to Table 2 of the *Tide Tables* and get this number. As the numerical sequence follows the geographical sequence, the listings can aid you in locating an obscure subordinate station on your chart. Since you know that Alabama is next to Florida in geographic sequence, it is an easy matter to thumb through Table 2 to find Alabama on page 239 of the 1972 *Atlantic Coast Tide Tables* (see Figure 18-2).

There is no subordinate station listed for Pelican Passage, but a study of Chart No. 1266 shows Fort Gaines at Mobile Bay Entrance is only a mile or two from Pelican Passage (see that portion of Chart No. 1266 reproduced in Figure 17-6). It is reasonable to assume that the time of high tide at Fort Gaines will be about the same time as the time of high tide at Pelican Passage. Fort Gaines is listed as a subordinate station in Table 2.

Examine this portion of Table 2 (Figure 18-2) closely. The table begins with "Florida" in bold print under "Place" at the top. About ten lines or so down is "Alabama," and on the same line with "Alabama" is "on Mobile, p. 138." This means all the data for the subordinate stations on the Alabama Gulf Coast, except Bayou La Batre, must be applied to the time of tides at Mobile, which is the *reference station*. It pays to double-check your reference station. Bayou La Batre is on the Alabama Gulf Coast too, but the reference station for Bayou La Batre is Pensacola, Florida! And Pensacola pops up here *out* of sequence. It wouldn't be hard to overlook this, if you get in too big a hurry, and try to find the

TABLE 2.—TIDAL DIFFERENCES AND OTHER CONSTANTS

No.	PLACE	POSITION		DIFFERENCES				RANGES		Mean Tide Level
				Time		Height				
		Lat.	Long.	High water	Low water	High water	Low water	Mean	Di-urnal	
		° ′ N.	° ′ W.	h. m.	h. m.	feet	feet	feet	feet	feet
	FLORIDA, Gulf Coast—Continued			on PENSACOLA, p.134 Time meridian, 90°W.						
	Choctawhatchee Bay ‡									
3171	East Pass (Destin)---------------	30 24	86 31	-0 27	+1 20	*0.46	*0.46	-----	0.6	0.3
3173	Harris, The Narrows†-------------	30 24	86 44	+1 37	+2 51	+0.1	0.0	-----	1.4	0.7
3175	Fishing Bend, Santa Rosa Sound†-----	30 20	87 08	+0 41	+0 51	+0.1	0.0	-----	1.4	0.7
	Pensacola Bay									
3177	Entrance†-----------------------	30 20	87 19	-1 23	-0 34	-0.2	0.0	-----	1.1	0.5
3179	Warrington, 2 miles south of†---	30 21	87 16	-0 27	-0 30	0.0	0.0	-----	1.3	0.6
3181	PENSACOLA†	30 24	87 13	Daily predictions				-----	1.3	0.6
3183	Lora Point, Escambia Bay†------	30 31	87 10	+0 36	+1 03	+0.2	0.0	-----	1.5	0.7
3185	East Bay†-----------------------	30 27	86 55	+0 44	+1 17	+0.3	0.0	-----	1.6	0.8
3187	Bay Point, Blackwater River†----	30 34	87 00	+1 23	+1 27	+0.3	0.0	-----	1.6	0.8
3189	Milton, Blackwater River†-------	30 37	87 02	+1 40	+1 47	+0.3	0.0	-----	1.6	0.8
	ALABAMA			on MOBILE, p.138						
3191	Perdido Bay‡--------------------	-----	-----	-----	-----	-----	-----	----	----	----
3193	Mobile Point (Fort Morgan)†---------	30 14	88 01	-1 46	-1 32	-0.3	0.0	-----	1.2	0.6
3194	Fort Gaines, Mobile Bay Entrance†---	30 15	88 04	-1 51	-1 49	-0.2	0.0	-----	1.3	0.6
3195	Bon Secour, Bon Secour River-------	30 18	87 44	-1 13	-1 17	+0.1	0.0	-----	1.6	0.8
3196	Fowl River, Mobile Bay Entrance†-----	30 26	88 07	-0 19	-0 09	0.0	0.0	-----	1.5	0.8
3197	Great Point Clear, Mobile Bay†------	30 29	87 56	-1 03	-0 57	-0.1	0.0	-----	1.4	0.7
3198	MOBILE, Mobile River†---------------	30 41	88 02	Daily predictions				-----	1.5	0.8
3199	Lower Hall Landing, Tensaw River†---	30 49	87 55	+2 16	+3 05	-0.2	0.0	-----	1.3	0.6
				on PENSACOLA, p.134						
3200	Bayou La Batre, Mississippi Sound†--	30 22	88 16	-1 17	-1 04	+0.2	0.0	-----	1.5	0.8
	MISSISSIPPI									
3201	Horn Island Pass†--------------------	30 13	88 29	-0 31	-0 53	+0.4	0.0	-----	1.7	0.8
3202	Pascagoula, Mississippi Sound†-------	30 20	88 32	-0 40	-0 46	+0.2	0.0	-----	1.5	0.8
3203	Pascagoula River entrance†----------	30 21	88 34	0 00	-0 42	+0.3	0.0	-----	1.6	0.8
3205	Biloxi, Biloxi Bay†-----------------	30 24	88 51	-0 32	-0 20	+0.5	0.0	-----	1.8	0.9
3207	Ship Island Pass†-------------------	30 13	88 59	-0 42	-0 30	+0.4	0.0	-----	1.7	0.8
3209	Cat Island (West Point)†------------	30 14	89 10	-0 44	+0 07	+0.4	0.0	-----	1.7	0.8
3211	Bay St. Louis†----------------------	30 19	89 18	+0 53	+1 26	+0.3	0.0	-----	1.6	0.8
	LOUISIANA									
3213	Long Point, Lake Borgne†------------	30 09	89 36	+1 29	+1 42	-0.3	0.0	-----	1.0	0.5
3215	Shell Beach, Lake Borgne†-----------	29 52	89 41	+3 22	+4 11	0.0	0.0	-----	1.3	0.6
3217	Chandeleur Light†-------------------	30 03	88 52	-0 39	-0 21	-0.1	0.0	-----	1.2	0.6
3218	Gardner Island, Breton Sound†-------	29 41	89 23	-0 19	+0 18	+0.2	0.0	-----	1.5	0.8
3219	Breton Islands‡---------------------	29 30	89 10	-0 21	-0 15	0.0	0.0	-----	1.3	0.7
3221	Jack Bay†---------------------------	29 22	89 21	+0 12	+0 30	-0.1	0.0	-----	1.2	0.6
3222	Lonesome Bayou (Thomasin)†----------	29 14	89 03	-2 35	-2 47	-0.2	0.0	-----	1.1	0.5
	Mississippi River									
3223	Pass a Loutre entrance†---------	29 12	89 02	-1 48	-1 00	-0.1	0.0	-----	1.2	0.6
3224	Southeast Pass†-----------------	29 07	89 03	-2 32	-2 46	-0.1	0.0	-----	1.2	0.6
3225	Port Eads, South Pass†----------	29 01	89 10	-2 13	-2 35	-0.2	0.0	-----	1.1	0.5
3226	Joseph Bayou†-------------------	29 04	89 16	-2 32	-2 35	+0.1	0.0	-----	1.4	0.7
3227	Southwest Pass†-----------------	28 56	89 26	-2 34	-2 31	0.0	0.0	-----	1.3	0.6
3229	Head of Passes†-----------------	29 09	89 15	-1 47	-0 29	-0.4	0.0	-----	0.9	0.4
3230	New Orleans†--------------------	29 55	90 04	-----	-----	-----	-----	-----	(ᵃ)	----
3231	Paris Road Bridge†------------------	30 00	89 56	+4 09	+5 09	-0.2	0.0	-----	1.1	0.6
3232	Empire Jetty†-----------------------	29 15	89 36	-2 47	-2 34	0.0	0.0	-----	1.3	0.7
3233	Bastian Island†--------------------	29 17	89 40	-1 03	-0 37	-0.1	0.0	-----	1.2	0.6
3235	Quatre Bayous Pass†----------------	29 18	89 51	+0 34	-0 32	0.0	0.0	-----	1.3	0.6
3237	Barataria Pass†--------------------	29 16	89 57	-0 44	-0 59	-0.1	0.0	-----	1.2	0.6

‡In Choctawhatchee and Perdido Bays the periodic tide has a mean range less than one-half foot.
†Tide is chiefly diurnal.
ᵃAt New Orleans the diurnal range of the tide during low river stages averages 0.8 foot. There is no periodic tide at high river stages.

Figure 18-2. Extract from Table 2 of the *Atlantic Coast Tide Tables*.

time of tide at Bayou La Batre by using Mobile as a reference station. Be careful, a mistake like this can cause a lot of grief.

You want to know the time and height of high tide at Fort Gaines. As Mobile is the reference station for Fort Gaines, you must first find the time of high water at Mobile. You have already done this, but let's set up a form, as in Figure 18-3, and work out the solution step by step. You should use a form such as this in your navigator's notebook when working tide problems.

STEP 1

Extract the necessary tidal data from Table 1 for the reference station—Mobile, Alabama, in this case—and enter it in the form. As the next tide after 1500 ZT of the 23rd is at 0001 on the 24th, I have indicated this by putting the date in parentheses just after the time.

STEP 2

Open the *Tide Tables* to Table 2, and locate the Alabama section. Under "Alabama" run down the list to Fort Gaines. Fort Gaines is the third subordinate station listed. The data provided in Table 2 is divided into three major headings: Position, Difference, and Range.

The position column lists the position of the subordinate station to the nearest minute of latitude and longitude. At the moment, this information is not vital, as you have located Fort Gaines on your chart.

The differences columns provide the information you are looking for. Under the sub-heading "Time" are two columns. One column is headed "High water H.M." The second column is headed "Low water H.M." These two columns give the difference between the times of high water at the reference station and high water at the subordinate station, and the difference between time of low water at the reference station and the time of low water at the subordinate station. The "H.M." stands for hours and minutes. If you follow the line Fort Gaines is listed on across to the "Time, High Water" column you will see the figure -1 51. Extract -1^h 51^m and put it under "Time" and opposite Fort Gaines in the form in Figure 18-3. As the sign is minus, subtract 1^h 50^m from 00^h 01^m, the time of high water at Mobile. If the subtraction gives you trouble, think of 00^h 01^m as 24^h 01^m, and 24^h 01^m as 23^h 61^m. You find high tide at Fort Gaines is at 22^h 10^m. The date has reverted back to the 23rd. This is indicated by the date, in parenthesis, just after the time. If you wanted the time of the next low water at Fort Gaines, you could have stepped one column over and extracted

1^h 49^m, and taken this from the time of the next low water at Mobile.

STEP 3

Since you will be going over the bar with the maximum draft advisable according to the *Coast Pilot*, you want to know how much additional water you can expect over the charted depths. The next two columns under the difference heading are sub-headed "Height." The first "Height" column is headed "High water feet." This column gives the difference between the height of high water at the reference station and the height of high water at the subordinate station. On the Fort Gaines line of the high water column, extract 0.2 feet, and put this in the form under "Height H.W." Subtract 0.2 feet from 2.0 feet. The height of tide above datum is 1.8 feet at Fort Gaines. Add 1.8 feet to the four feet the chart shows on the shoals around Pelican Passage, and you see you can expect 5.8 feet of water on these shoals. This is not much if even a little sea and swell are running.

You are strictly confined to the channel. Maybe you better use the main ship channel. From the column headed "Low Water", you see that the difference in the height of tide at low water between the reference station and the subordinate station is zero. For the height of tide at low water at Fort Gaines, you use the height of the tide at low water for Mobile.

At some subordinate stations, the differences in height of tide are not given in feet for the addition to or subtraction from the height at the reference station. The corrections may be given as two figures, in parentheses, in the height columns. The first figure is a ratio that must be multiplied by the height of tide at the reference station. The second figure is a correction that must be added or subtracted from

DATE : 23 OCTOBER, 1972   ZT 1500   POSITION : PELICAN BAY

STEP 1 :

REFERENCE STATION	TIME	HT. H.W.	HT. L.W.
MOBILE, ALA.	0001 (24/10/72)	2.'0	

STEP 2 :   STEP 3 :

SUBORDINATE STATION		
FORT GAINES	-1^h 51^m	-0.'2
TIME OF TIDE @ FORT GAINES	22^h 10^m (23/10/72)	1.'8 HT. OF TIDE

Figure 18-3. A simple form for figuring the time of tide in the navigator's notebook.

TIMES AND HEIGHTS OF HIGH AND LOW WATERS

OCTOBER

DAY	TIME H.M.	HT. FT.	DAY	TIME H.M.	HT. FT.
1 SU	0303	4.4	16 M	0208	4.1
	0909	0.7		0808	1.2
	1538	5.2		1439	4.7
	2201	0.8		2100	1.2
2 M	0410	4.6	17 TU	0309	4.3
	1015	0.7		0915	1.0
	1642	5.2		1536	4.8
	2257	0.6		2153	0.9
3 TU	0509	4.9	18 W	0406	4.7
	1114	0.5		1013	0.8
	1735	5.2		1632	5.0
	2344	0.5		2242	0.6
4 W	0601	5.1	19 TH	0501	5.1
	1201	0.4		1108	0.5
	1824	5.3		1724	5.2
				2330	0.2
5 TH	0025	0.4	20 F	0555	5.5
	0647	5.3		1201	0.2
	1246	0.4		1815	5.3
	1907	5.2			
6 F	0103	0.4	21 SA	0015	-0.1
	0729	5.4		0643	5.9
	1326	0.4		1250	0.0
	1948	5.1		1903	5.4
7 SA	0139	0.3	22 SU	0102	-0.3
	0806	5.5		0734	6.2
	1405	0.5		1340	-0.1
	2023	5.0		1954	5.4
8 SU	0212	0.4	23 M	0149	-0.4
	0845	5.5		0825	6.3
	1442	0.6		1431	-0.1
	2100	4.9		2044	5.4
9 M	0244	0.5	24 TU	0238	-0.4
	0920	5.4		0916	6.3
	1516	0.7		1522	0.0
	2135	4.7		2135	5.2
10 TU	0319	0.6	25 W	0328	-0.2
	0956	5.3		1009	6.2
	1553	0.9		1617	0.2
	2208	4.5		2230	5.0
11 W	0352	0.7	26 TH	0423	0.0
	1033	5.1		1105	6.0
	1630	1.1		1718	0.4
	2247	4.3		2331	4.8
12 TH	0431	0.9	27 F	0521	0.3
	1112	5.0		1203	5.7
	1715	1.2		1821	0.6
	2328	4.1			
13 F	0515	1.1	28 SA	0032	4.6
	1200	4.8		0629	0.6
	1806	1.4		1307	5.4
				1930	0.8
14 SA	0015	4.0	29 SU	0137	4.6
	0604	1.2		0742	0.8
	1245	4.7		1411	5.2
	1900	1.4		2038	0.8
15 SU	0108	4.0	30 M	0246	4.6
	0703	1.3		0853	0.9
	1342	4.7		1514	5.0
	1959	1.4		2133	0.7
			31 TU	0350	4.8
				1000	0.8
				1613	4.9
				2228	0.6

NOVEMBER

DAY	TIME H.M.	HT. FT.	DAY	TIME H.M.	HT. FT.
1 W	0447	4.9	16 TH	0331	4.8
	1054	0.7		0940	0.6
	1708	4.9		1551	4.7
	2313	0.5		2202	0.2
2 TH	0536	5.1	17 F	0427	5.2
	1141	0.6		1039	0.4
	1756	4.9		1648	4.8
	2356	0.5		2255	-0.1
3 F	0621	5.3	18 SA	0526	5.5
	1224	0.6		1135	0.1
	1841	4.8		1743	4.9
				2346	-0.4
4 SA	0033	0.4	19 SU	0618	5.9
	0702	5.4		1230	-0.1
	1305	0.5		1839	5.0
	1919	4.7			
5 SU	0108	0.4	20 M	0037	-0.6
	0743	5.4		0713	6.1
	1344	0.6		1323	-0.2
	1958	4.7		1932	5.0
6 M	0141	0.4	21 TU	0127	-0.6
	0818	5.4		0807	6.2
	1419	0.6		1414	-0.3
	2033	4.5		2027	5.0
7 TU	0216	0.4	22 W	0220	-0.6
	0856	5.3		0859	6.2
	1455	0.7		1509	-0.2
	2110	4.4		2122	4.9
8 W	0249	0.5	23 TH	0311	-0.4
	0932	5.2		0952	6.0
	1530	0.8		1604	-0.1
	2145	4.3		2217	4.8
9 TH	0326	0.6	24 F	0407	-0.2
	1007	5.1		1048	5.8
	1611	0.9		1659	0.1
	2224	4.2		2316	4.7
10 F	0405	0.7	25 SA	0507	0.1
	1046	5.0		1144	5.4
	1649	1.0		1758	0.3
	2305	4.1			
11 SA	0446	0.9	26 SU	0013	4.6
	1129	4.8		0610	0.6
	1734	1.0		1243	5.1
	2347	4.1		1902	0.4
12 SU	0535	0.9	27 M	0116	4.5
	1214	4.7		0721	0.6
	1823	1.0		1342	4.8
				2001	0.5
13 M	0040	4.1	28 TU	0218	4.5
	0632	1.0		0826	0.7
	1303	4.6		1439	4.5
	1920	0.9		2058	0.5
14 TU	0133	4.2	29 W	0319	4.5
	0734	1.0		0930	0.7
	1357	4.6		1539	4.4
	2013	0.8		2149	0.5
15 W	0230	4.5	30 TH	0412	4.6
	0839	0.8		1025	0.7
	1454	4.6		1630	4.3
	2109	0.5		2238	0.4

DECEMBER

DAY	TIME H.M.	HT. FT.	DAY	TIME H.M.	HT. FT.
1 F	0507	4.8	16 SA	0400	4.9
	1116	0.6		1015	0.2
	1723	4.2		1616	4.2
	2320	0.3		2226	-0.4
2 SA	0553	4.9	17 SU	0500	5.2
	1201	0.5		1116	-0.1
	1812	4.2		1717	4.3
				2322	-0.6
3 SU	0001	0.3	18 M	0559	5.5
	0638	5.0		1212	-0.3
	1244	0.5		1818	4.4
	1853	4.2			
4 M	0038	0.2	19 TU	0017	-0.8
	0717	5.0		0657	5.7
	1322	0.4		1307	-0.4
	1932	4.1		1918	4.5
5 TU	0113	0.2	20 W	0112	-0.9
	0756	5.1		0752	5.8
	1359	0.4		1401	-0.5
	2011	4.1		2014	4.6
6 W	0151	0.2	21 TH	0204	-0.9
	0833	5.1		0845	5.7
	1436	0.4		1454	-0.6
	2049	4.1		2109	4.6
7 TH	0228	0.2	22 F	0257	-0.8
	0910	5.0		0937	5.6
	1512	0.4		1545	-0.5
	2127	4.0		2202	4.6
8 F	0303	0.2	23 SA	0353	-0.5
	0948	4.9		1028	5.3
	1549	0.4		1636	-0.4
	2204	4.0		2253	4.5
9 SA	0345	0.3	24 SU	0449	-0.3
	1024	4.8		1121	5.0
	1628	0.4		1728	-0.2
	2243	4.0		2349	4.4
10 SU	0427	0.4	25 M	0545	0.0
	1102	4.7		1210	4.6
	1709	0.4		1823	0.0
	2325	4.0			
11 M	0513	0.4	26 TU	0042	4.3
	1141	4.5		0644	0.3
	1752	0.4		1305	4.3
				1917	0.1
12 TU	0011	4.1	27 W	0139	4.2
	0606	0.5		0747	0.5
	1229	4.4		1356	4.0
	1841	0.3		2009	0.2
13 W	0102	4.2	28 TH	0236	4.1
	0703	0.5		0849	0.6
	1320	4.3		1452	3.7
	1933	0.2		2101	0.3
14 TH	0158	4.4	29 F	0333	4.1
	0808	0.5		0948	0.6
	1415	4.2		1551	3.6
	2030	0.0		2152	0.3
15 F	0259	4.7	30 SA	0429	4.2
	0912	0.3		1042	0.6
	1514	4.2		1642	3.5
	2127	-0.2		2241	0.2
			31 SU	0520	4.3
				1129	0.5
				1733	3.5
				2327	0.1

TIME MERIDIAN 75° W. 0000 IS MIDNIGHT. 1200 IS NOON.
HEIGHTS ARE RECKONED FROM THE DATUM OF SOUNDINGS ON CHARTS OF THE LOCALITY WHICH IS MEAN LOW WATER.

Figure 18-4. Extract from Table 1 of the *Atlantic Coast Tide Tables.*

the product of this multiplication. An example of a ratio *minus* a correction can be found at Godthaab, Greenland. An example of a ratio *plus* a correction can be found at Hare Bay, Newfoundland. Sometimes no correction need be applied to the ratio. Then the ratio is simply indicated by an asterisk. The differences for Little Penguin Island, Greenland, are an example of a simple ratio difference.

Tides along the upper coast of the Gulf of Mexico are diurnal. *Bowditch* and the *Coast Pilot* tell you this; if you look at both Tables 1 and 2, you can see this is so. Except when the tide is changing, Figure 18-1 shows only two tides each lunar day. Figure 18-4 is a reproduction of part of Table 1 showing October tidal data for Mayport, Florida, which is on the Atlantic Coast. The semidiurnal nature of the tides here is obvious.

The third major heading of Table 2 is "Range," and beneath this heading are two columns. The subheading of the left-hand column under "Range" is "Mean." This column gives the difference in height between mean high water and mean low water, at a location having semidiurnal or mixed tides. As the tides occurring at the substations appearing in Figure 18-4 are diurnal, there are no figures in this column.

The right-hand column under "Range" is the diurnal range of tide. This column gives the difference between the mean or average higher high water and the lower low water.

For some subordinate stations, not shown in Figure 18-4, the term "Spring" may be used to head the right-hand column under "Range." The range given, in this case, is the range occurring at spring tides. This average range will be larger than the mean range of semidiurnal or mixed tides.

Ranges of tides are important to the navigator because they indicate how much change in depth he may expect between high and low water. Admittedly, the foot or foot and one-half range of tide on the upper Gulf Coast is not much. But even a foot difference in depth can be critical.

The range of tide at Mobile is so small that we are seldom concerned with the water level between tides. At other locations where there is a considerable range of tide, the height of the tide above datum could be important to the navigator. Figure 18-4 shows that the range of the tide at Mayport, Florida, on October 24, 1972, between low water at 0238 and high water at 0916 is 6.7 feet. Suppose you are the skipper of a boat that draws six feet. You want to go alongside a fuel dock at Mayport on 24 October, but the chart shows a depth of four feet at mean low water. The time is 0630; you would be very interested in knowing

how high above datum the height of the tide is at 0630. It just might be high enough to let your boat get to the fuel dock. How much water do you have at the fuel dock at 0630? To answer this question you must refer to Table 3 — "Height of Tide at Any Time." Again a step-by-step solution in your navigator's notebook is advisable (see Figure 18-5).

STEP 1

By inspection, pick out the times bracketing 0630 at Mayport on 24 October. Enter these times and the heights for each in your form. The time and heights are 0238 and 0916, -0.4 feet and +6.3 feet. Put these values in your form.

STEP 2

Subtract the earlier time from the later to get the "duration of rise." The duration of rise at Mayport the 24th of October, 1972, is 6^h 38^m. If you were working from high water to low water, you would have gotten the "duration of fall." Table 3 is set up to accommodate either.

Subtract the height of tide at low water from the height of tide at high water. For this date and time interval at Mayport, the tide range is 6.7 feet. You subtracted a -0.4 feet from a +6.3 feet. To subtract a minus from a plus you add.

DATE : 24 OCTOBER , 1972

STEP 1:

TIME	HEIGHT
0238	-0.4
0916	6.3
	6.7

STEP 2:
6^h 48^m DURATION   6.7 RANGE

STEP 3:
09 16
06 30
2^h 46^m

STEP 4:
(BY INSPECTION OF UPPER BOX OF TABLE 3) 2^{h}40^m

STEP 5:

HEIGHT AT HIGH WATER	6.7 FEET
CORRECTION FOR 0630	2.2 FEET
HEIGHT OF TIDE @ 0630	4.5 FEET

Figure 18-5. Computing the height of the tide in the navigator's notebook.

TABLE 3.—HEIGHT OF TIDE AT ANY TIME

Duration of rise or fall, see footnote

| Time from the nearest high water or low water |||||||||||||||
h. m.	h. m.	h. m.	h. m.	h. m.	h. m.	h. m.	h. m.	h. m.	h. m.	h. m.	h. m.	h. m.	h. m.	h. m.	h. m.
4 00	0 08	0 16	0 24	0 32	0 40	0 48	0 56	1 04	1 12	1 20	1 28	1 36	1 44	1 52	2 00
4 20	0 09	0 17	0 26	0 35	0 43	0 52	1 01	1 09	1 18	1 27	1 35	1 44	1 53	2 01	2 10
4 40	0 09	0 19	0 28	0 37	0 47	0 56	1 05	1 15	1 24	1 33	1 43	1 52	2 01	2 11	2 20
5 00	0 10	0 20	0 30	0 40	0 50	1 00	1 10	1 20	1 30	1 40	1 50	2 00	2 10	2 20	2 30
5 20	0 11	0 21	0 32	0 43	0 53	1 04	1 15	1 25	1 36	1 47	1 57	2 08	2 19	2 29	2 40
5 40	0 11	0 23	0 34	0 45	0 57	1 08	1 19	1 31	1 42	1 53	2 05	2 16	2 27	2 39	2 50
6 00	0 12	0 24	0 36	0 48	1 00	1 12	1 24	1 36	1 48	2 00	2 12	2 24	2 36	2 48	3 00
6 20	0 13	0 25	0 38	0 51	1 03	1 16	1 29	1 41	1 54	2 07	2 19	2 32	2 45	2 57	3 10
6 40	0 13	0 27	0 40	0 53	1 07	1 20	1 33	1 47	2 00	2 13	2 27	2 40	2 53	3 07	3 20
7 00	0 14	0 28	0 42	0 56	1 10	1 24	1 38	1 52	2 06	2 20	2 34	2 48	3 02	3 16	3 30
7 20	0 15	0 29	0 44	0 59	1 13	1 28	1 43	1 57	2 12	2 27	2 41	2 56	3 11	3 25	3 40
7 40	0 15	0 31	0 46	1 01	1 17	1 32	1 47	2 03	2 18	2 33	2 49	3 04	3 19	3 35	3 50
8 00	0 16	0 32	0 48	1 04	1 20	1 36	1 52	2 08	2 24	2 40	2 56	3 12	3 28	3 44	4 00
8 20	0 17	0 33	0 50	1 07	1 23	1 40	1 57	2 13	2 30	2 47	3 03	3 20	3 37	3 53	4 10
8 40	0 17	0 35	0 52	1 09	1 27	1 44	2 01	2 19	2 36	2 53	3 11	3 28	3 45	4 03	4 20
9 00	0 18	0 36	0 54	1 12	1 30	1 48	2 06	2 24	2 42	3 00	3 18	3 36	3 54	4 12	4 30
9 20	0 19	0 37	0 56	1 15	1 33	1 52	2 11	2 29	2 48	3 07	3 25	3 44	4 03	4 21	4 40
9 40	0 19	0 39	0 58	1 17	1 37	1 56	2 15	2 35	2 54	3 13	3 33	3 52	4 11	4 31	4 50
10 00	0 20	0 40	1 00	1 20	1 40	2 00	2 20	2 40	3 00	3 20	3 40	4 00	4 20	4 40	5 00
10 20	0 21	0 41	1 02	1 23	1 43	2 04	2 25	2 45	3 06	3 27	3 47	4 08	4 29	4 49	5 10
10 40	0 21	0 43	1 04	1 25	1 47	2 08	2 29	2 51	3 12	3 33	3 55	4 16	4 37	4 59	5 20

Range of tide, see footnote

| Correction to height |||||||||||||||
Ft.	Ft.	Ft.	Ft.	Ft.	Ft.	Ft.	Ft.	Ft.	Ft.	Ft.	Ft.	Ft.	Ft.	Ft.	Ft.
0.5	0.0	0.0	0.0	0.0	0.0	0.0	0.1	0.1	0.1	0.1	0.1	0.2	0.2	0.2	0.2
1.0	0.0	0.0	0.0	0.0	0.1	0.1	0.1	0.2	0.2	0.2	0.3	0.3	0.4	0.4	0.5
1.5	0.0	0.0	0.0	0.1	0.1	0.1	0.2	0.2	0.3	0.4	0.4	0.5	0.6	0.7	0.8
2.0	0.0	0.0	0.0	0.1	0.1	0.2	0.3	0.3	0.4	0.5	0.6	0.7	0.8	0.9	1.0
2.5	0.0	0.0	0.1	0.1	0.2	0.2	0.3	0.4	0.5	0.6	0.7	0.9	1.0	1.1	1.2
3.0	0.0	0.0	0.1	0.1	0.2	0.3	0.4	0.5	0.6	0.8	0.9	1.0	1.2	1.3	1.5
3.5	0.0	0.0	0.1	0.2	0.2	0.3	0.4	0.6	0.7	0.9	1.0	1.2	1.4	1.6	1.8
4.0	0.0	0.0	0.1	0.2	0.3	0.4	0.5	0.7	0.8	1.0	1.2	1.4	1.6	1.8	2.0
4.5	0.0	0.0	0.1	0.2	0.3	0.4	0.6	0.7	0.9	1.1	1.3	1.6	1.8	2.0	2.2
5.0	0.0	0.1	0.1	0.2	0.3	0.5	0.6	0.8	1.0	1.2	1.5	1.7	2.0	2.2	2.5
5.5	0.0	0.1	0.1	0.2	0.4	0.5	0.7	0.9	1.1	1.4	1.6	1.9	2.2	2.5	2.8
6.0	0.0	0.1	0.1	0.3	0.4	0.6	0.8	1.0	1.2	1.5	1.8	2.1	2.4	2.7	3.0
6.5	0.0	0.1	0.2	0.3	0.4	0.6	0.8	1.1	1.3	1.6	1.9	2.2	2.6	2.9	3.2
7.0	0.0	0.1	0.2	0.3	0.5	0.7	0.9	1.2	1.4	1.8	2.1	2.4	2.8	3.1	3.5
7.5	0.0	0.1	0.2	0.3	0.5	0.7	1.0	1.2	1.5	1.9	2.2	2.6	3.0	3.4	3.8
8.0	0.0	0.1	0.2	0.3	0.5	0.8	1.0	1.3	1.6	2.0	2.4	2.8	3.2	3.6	4.0
8.5	0.0	0.1	0.2	0.4	0.6	0.8	1.1	1.4	1.8	2.1	2.5	2.9	3.4	3.8	4.2
9.0	0.0	0.1	0.2	0.4	0.6	0.9	1.2	1.5	1.9	2.2	2.7	3.1	3.6	4.0	4.5
9.5	0.0	0.1	0.2	0.4	0.6	0.9	1.2	1.6	2.0	2.4	2.8	3.3	3.8	4.3	4.8
10.0	0.0	0.1	0.2	0.4	0.7	1.0	1.3	1.7	2.1	2.5	3.0	3.5	4.0	4.5	5.0
10.5	0.0	0.1	0.3	0.5	0.7	1.0	1.3	1.7	2.2	2.6	3.1	3.6	4.2	4.7	5.2
11.0	0.0	0.1	0.3	0.5	0.7	1.1	1.4	1.8	2.3	2.8	3.3	3.8	4.4	4.9	5.5
11.5	0.0	0.1	0.3	0.5	0.8	1.1	1.5	1.9	2.4	2.9	3.4	4.0	4.6	5.1	5.8
12.0	0.0	0.1	0.3	0.5	0.8	1.1	1.5	2.0	2.5	3.0	3.6	4.1	4.8	5.4	6.0
12.5	0.0	0.1	0.3	0.5	0.8	1.2	1.6	2.1	2.6	3.1	3.7	4.3	5.0	5.6	6.2
13.0	0.0	0.1	0.3	0.6	0.9	1.2	1.7	2.2	2.7	3.2	3.9	4.5	5.1	5.8	6.5
13.5	0.0	0.1	0.3	0.6	0.9	1.3	1.7	2.2	2.8	3.4	4.0	4.7	5.3	6.0	6.8
14.0	0.0	0.2	0.3	0.6	0.9	1.3	1.8	2.3	2.9	3.5	4.2	4.8	5.5	6.3	7.0
14.5	0.0	0.2	0.4	0.6	1.0	1.4	1.9	2.4	3.0	3.6	4.3	5.0	5.7	6.5	7.2
15.0	0.0	0.2	0.4	0.6	1.0	1.4	1.9	2.5	3.1	3.8	4.4	5.2	5.9	6.7	7.5
15.5	0.0	0.2	0.4	0.7	1.0	1.5	2.0	2.6	3.2	3.9	4.6	5.4	6.1	6.9	7.8
16.0	0.0	0.2	0.4	0.7	1.1	1.5	2.1	2.6	3.3	4.0	4.7	5.5	6.3	7.2	8.0
16.5	0.0	0.2	0.4	0.7	1.1	1.6	2.1	2.7	3.4	4.1	4.9	5.7	6.5	7.4	8.2
17.0	0.0	0.2	0.4	0.7	1.1	1.6	2.2	2.8	3.5	4.2	5.0	5.9	6.7	7.6	8.5
17.5	0.0	0.2	0.4	0.8	1.2	1.7	2.2	2.9	3.6	4.4	5.2	6.0	6.9	7.8	8.8
18.0	0.0	0.2	0.4	0.8	1.2	1.7	2.3	3.0	3.7	4.5	5.3	6.2	7.1	8.1	9.0
18.5	0.1	0.2	0.5	0.8	1.2	1.8	2.4	3.1	3.8	4.6	5.5	6.4	7.3	8.3	9.2
19.0	0.1	0.2	0.5	0.8	1.3	1.8	2.4	3.1	3.9	4.8	5.6	6.6	7.5	8.5	9.5
19.5	0.1	0.2	0.5	0.8	1.3	1.9	2.5	3.2	4.0	4.9	5.8	6.7	7.7	8.7	9.8
20.0	0.1	0.2	0.5	0.9	1.3	1.9	2.6	3.3	4.1	5.0	5.9	6.9	7.9	9.0	10.0

Obtain from the predictions the high water and low water, one of which is before and the other after the time for which the height is required. The difference between the times of occurrence of these tides is the duration of rise or fall, and the difference between their heights is the range of tide for the above table. Find the difference between the nearest high or low water and the time for which the height is required.

Enter the table with the duration of rise or fall, printed in heavy-faced type, which most nearly agrees with the actual value, and on that horizontal line find the time from the nearest high or low water which agrees most nearly with the corresponding actual difference. The correction sought is in the column directly below, on the line with the range of tide.

When the nearest tide is high water, subtract the correction.

When the nearest tide is low water, add the correction.

Figure 18-6. Table 3 from the *Atlantic Coast Tide Tables.*

STEP 3

Find the time interval from the time of tide, 0630, to the nearest high or low water. As high water at 0916 is the nearest, subtract 0630 from 0916. The time from 0630 to high water is $2^h 46^m$. You are now ready to enter Table 3.

STEP 4

Table 3 is divided into two portions. You first enter the top part of the table. In this boxed-in upper part, the duration of rise or fall of tide is listed on the left-hand margin in a vertical column (see Figure 18-6). The possible durations of rise or fall are tabulated in intervals of 20 minutes beginning with 4 hours, and ending with 10 hours and 40 minutes. To enter the table, select the duration nearest the $6^h 38^m$ you computed in Figure 18-5. The nearest interval of duration is $6^h 40^m$. On the $6^h 40^m$ line, run across the table to your right until you find the time that most nearly agrees with the time until the next high (or in some cases low) water. This interval is $2^h 40^m$, and it appears in the right-hand column of the upper box, fourth from the right margin.

STEP 5

Run down this column, as found by Step 4, until you reach a line for a range that most nearly agrees with the range of tide you determined in Step 2. For your problem, the range is 6.7 feet. In the lower box of Table 3, ranges are tabulated in a vertical column on the far left. Look down this column to the 6.5 line, the range nearest to 6.7 feet. Run across the 6.5 line to the column on the right that you found in Step 4, and extract your correction of 2.2 feet. Since you are working to the nearest high water, subtract this correction from 6.´7. The remainder is the height of the tide for the time computed. At 0630 on the 24th of October, 1972, the height of the tide is 4.5 feet. Barring variations due to wind, barometer, or other conditions, you should have eight and a half feet of water at the fuel dock. No need to wait around. You can carry your six-foot draft into the slip safely.

Another time a navigator needs to know the height of the tide at a given time is when he is observing vertical sextant angles of objects close aboard (Case 3 type) and he is also in an area experiencing very great ranges of tide. The problem is complicated somewhat because the charts and the *Light List* give the heights of aids to navigation and topographical features reckoned above mean *high* water.

With Table 3 of the *Tide Tables* you find the height of the tide at a given time as the height above datum; but datum, in the *Tide Tables*, is reckoned as mean *low* water on the Atlantic and Gulf Coasts and low low water on the Pacific Coast. The use of the high water reference for heights of listed or charted aids and other objects must be reconciled with the use of low water datums if you are taking vertical sextant angles on an object. The range of the tide seriously affects the actual height of the object above the surface of the sea. Fortunately, this reconciliation is not often required, but it may be required at a most crucial moment. To illustrate how you solve this problem let's use a hypothetical situation:

You find your vessel in a body of water where the tidal ranges reach 55 feet. You observe a vertical sextant angle on a light; the charted height of the light at mean high water and your height of eye give a difference of 100 feet. At the time of your observation, the tide is somewhere between high and low water. What is the actual difference in height between your height of eye and the height of the light at the time of observation? You must have this information to enter Table 9 of *Bowditch*. The solution is as follows:

STEP 1

Find the height of tide at the time of the observation by use of Table 3, as explained in the example for the vessel going to the fuel dock at Mayport. As I have already adequately explained this procedure, let's assume you determine the height of the tide at the time of your observation to be 30 feet.

STEP 2

Find the height of mean *high* water above datum. You can look for this information in the *Tide Tables* until the cook stands a watch, but you will never find it there. This information is not readily available. Sometimes the height of mean high water may appear on a chart; the British Admiralty charts are good about this. You can often find the height of mean high water in the *Coast Pilot* or the *Sailing Directions,* if the tidal ranges in the area discussed are sufficient to make this information valuable. A check of the *Tide Tables* will always tell you if you even need to consider the height of the tide at the time of your observation. Some judgement is required on your part. Table 9 of *Bowditch* does indicate that a height difference of 10 feet can cause variations of as much as 0.7 miles on an object whose tabulated height difference is 180 feet. So you can see it is important to know the height difference you are observing. But let's get back to our problem. Assume you find on your chart a note which tells you that the height of mean high water at your vessel's position is 50 feet.

From the height of mean high water, 50 feet, subtract the height of the tide at the time of your observation.

Ht. of mean high water	50'
Ht. of tide	30'
Difference	20'

The level of the sea at the time you made your vertical sextant angle observation was 20 feet *below* the level used to chart the height of the light. You must add 20 feet to the listed and charted height of the light.

Ht. of light	100'
Ht. of tide below HW	20'
Ht. difference at time of observation	120'

You must enter Table 9 of *Bowditch* with a difference in height of 120 feet. If you did not bother to make this computation, and entered Table 9 with a height difference of 100 feet, your computations could be off as much as 0.7 miles! This is far too much variation to tolerate in areas where you would be taking Case 3 vertical sextant angle observations.

Tables 4, 5, and 6 of the *Tide Tables* give information regarding the rising and setting of the sun, local mean time, and the rising and setting of the moon at various places. To use these tables precisely requires some understanding of the relationship between longitude and time. On the other hand mere inspection can tell you if you can expect a moon to light things up for you at night. Hopefully, the sun will rise for you each day.

All in all, use of the *Tide Tables* is quite easy. The explanations in the tables may be brief, but they are excellent.

LUNAR INTERVALS

Sometimes you may find yourself in a part of the world where no tide data is tabulated. You may need to know the times of low water and the times of high water. In cases like these you can use lunar intervals. The moon is the greatest tide-producing force, and for this reason sailors say the tide follows the moon. The lunar interval is the interval between the time the moon crosses your meridian in upper transit and the next high tide. (Upper transit means to cross or transit the meridian you are actually on. A body is in upper transit when it is halfway across the sky at your longitude. At this time the body will bear due north, 000°T, or due south 180°T. A common example of a body in upper transit is the sun when it crosses the meridian of your position at noon.) The lunar interval for a port is usually given in the

Sailing Directions, and it may also be given on the charts. You should know how to use the lunar intervals to find the times of tide. This knowledge could come in handy if you ever make the foreign cruise of your dreams.

CURRENT TABLES

The rankest beginner knows the importance of having enough water to float his boat safely. For this reason the usefulness of *Tide Tables* soon becomes obvious. Of equal concern to the navigator is the currents he can expect to encounter on a passage. All currents are important to the navigator. The more or less permanent currents of the oceans are made known to the navigator by the pilot charts, *Sailing Directions*, and other publications. Along the coasts, in the estuaries and tidal streams, the navigator encounters currents that are generated by the rise and fall of the tides.* In this section you are going to study tidal currents.

Current is the *horizontal motion of the water.* Tidal current is horizontal motion of the water in response to the rise and fall of the tide. But the time of change in direction of flood and ebb does not necessarily conform to the times of high or low water. Nor does the time of maximum velocity of the ebb or flood correspond to the time of high or low water. These differences in time between these events may vary from a few minutes to several hours. Do not make the very common mistake so many sailors make of assuming that, since high tide is at a particular time, you can expect "an outgoing tide," meaning an ebbing tidal current any time after the time of high water. Quite to the contrary, the tidal current may continue to flood for a long time after high water.

Where is all that water going? It is just passing through. Take Mobile Bay. High water at Fort Morgan, at the mouth of the bay, is 1 hour and 32 minutes before high water at Mobile. So at high water at Fort Morgan the current is still booming in

---

*Tidal currents can also be experienced far at sea. Read the sailing directions for the Western Caribbean Sea for example. My own experience confirms this. In the fall of 1972 as navigator of an ocean tug proceeding W by N between Grand Cayman and the Yucatan I was fascinated to observe a northerly set of several hours followed by a southerly set of several hours. The duration of these sets approximated the duration of rise and the duration of fall of the tides. The *average* set did correspond to the pilot chart.

on its way to Mobile. At high water at Mobile the current will still continue to flood until it has filled every creek, bay, and bayou at the head of Mobile Bay all the way to the head of tidewater on the Tombigbee River at Coffeeville Lock, 116 miles upstream. Only when you reach the extreme geographical limit of flow may the time of high water and the time of slack flood approach coincidence.

Another important point to remember is that the range of the tide is not always an indication of the velocity of the tidal current. Tides in an area having a great range of tide may not generate as fast a tidal current as an area having a much smaller range of tide. Under some combined conditions of wind, tide, and weather, the current at Mobile Bay Entrance, mean range about 1.5 feet, may reach 8 or 10 knots. To predict the tidal currents you should expect to find at a given place and time, you have to use the *Tidal Current Tables*.

The *Tidal Current Tables* are published by the National Ocean Survey. They are published for the Atlantic coast of North America and for the Pacific coast of North America.

Before we open the *Tidal Current Tables*, a description of the types of tidal currents you may encounter is necessary. In bays, estuaries, sounds, and rivers the tidal currents are directional. The current flow is in one direction with the outflowing ebb, and in the more or less opposite direction with the inflowing flood. It is a reversing current. On the open sea and along the coasts, away from the directional effects of any inlets, tidal currents are rotational. The direction of flow changes steadily with the passing of the moon and sun. In a complete tidal cycle the direction of flow of a rotary tidal current will pass through every point of the compass. And just as the wind and weather may affect the rise and fall of the tides, so may these things also affect the flow of tidal currents. As I write this, the extremely severe floods in the Mississippi River Valley this spring have caused a complete disruption of all normal tidal and ocean currents along the upper coast of the Gulf of Mexico. Your *Coast Pilot* or *Sailing Directions* will often give you information concerning the effects of meteorological forces on the tidal currents in an area, and these publications will also tell if the currents are likely to be rotational or directional.

Get a current set of *Tidal Current Tables* (I couldn't resist the pun) and read them thoroughly. Figure 18-7 is a reproduction of the table of contents from *Tidal Current Tables, 1972, Atlantic Coast of North America*. We are going to concern ourselves primarily with Tables 1, 2, 3, and 4, and take a quick look at Table 5.

CONTENTS

Figure 18-7. Contents of the *Tidal Current Tables, Atlantic Coast of North America.*

MOBILE BAY ENTRANCE, ALA., 1972

F—FLOOD, DIR. 025° TRUE   E—EBB, DIR. 190° TRUE

SEPTEMBER

DAY	SLACK WATER TIME H.M.	MAXIMUM CURRENT TIME H.M.	VEL. KNOTS	DAY	SLACK WATER TIME H.M.	MAXIMUM CURRENT TIME H.M.	VEL. KNOTS
1 F	0509 1740	1122	2.4E	16 SA	0507 1718	1122 2336	1.8E 1.6F
2 SA	0622 1847	0003 1228	2.4F 2.5E	17 SU	0616 1819	1227	1.8E
3 SU	0732 1953	0117 1328	2.3F 2.4E	18 M	0720 1918	0041 1316	1.6F 1.8E
4 M	0840 2058	0233 1424	2.1F 2.1E	19 TU	0823 2019	0154 1414	1.5F 1.7E
5 TU	0943 2203	0343 1509	1.9F 1.8E	20 W	0927 2129	0312 1454	1.3F 1.4E
6 W	1045 2320	0506 1549	1.5F 1.3E	21 TH	1044 2338	0415 1557	1.0F 0.9E
7 TH	1151	0628 1630	1.1F 0.8E	22 F	1300	0710	0.7F
8 F	0148 1326	0811 1648 *2121	0.7F 0.3E (*)	23 SA	0544 2057	0044 1148	0.4F 0.5E
9 SA	0608	0156 1041 *1700 *1805	0.3E 0.4F (*) (*)	24 SU	0918 2247	0320 1700	0.9E 1.1F
10 SU	0930 2347	0409 1815	0.6E 0.6F	25 M	1110	0451 1808	1.5E 1.7F
11 M	1132	0532 1855	0.9E 0.9F	26 TU	0001 1232	0600 1912	2.0E 2.2F
12 TU	0048 1253	0640 1939	1.2E 1.2F	27 W	0110 1346	0716 2014	2.3E 2.4F
13 W	0146 1402	0757 2027	1.4E 1.4F	28 TH	0219 1456	0831 2117	2.5E 2.5F
14 TH	0248 1508	0906 2127	1.5E 1.5F	29 F	0331 1605	0941 2224	2.5E 2.4F
15 F	0356 1613	1015 2225	1.7E 1.6F	30 SA	0443 1712	1051 2336	2.4E 2.1F

OCTOBER

DAY	SLACK WATER TIME H.M.	MAXIMUM CURRENT TIME H.M.	VEL. KNOTS	DAY	SLACK WATER TIME H.M.	MAXIMUM CURRENT TIME H.M.	VEL. KNOTS
1 SU	0556 1817	1155	2.1E	16 M	0512 1717	1123 2319	1.7E 1.4F
2 M	0707 1919	0046 1243	1.8F 1.7E	17 TU	0615 1810	1212 2357	1.4E 1.0F
3 TU	0817 2024	0209 1327	1.3F 1.2E	18 W	0726 1908	1306	1.0E
4 W	0934 2308	0406 1407	0.9F 0.7E	19 TH	0924	0037 1355 *2051	0.5F 0.4E (*)
5 TH		0635 *1442 *1918	0.5F (*) (*)	20 F	1953	*0056 1018	(*) 0.3F
6 F	0545 2120	0129 1333	0.4E 0.3F	21 SA	0741 2102	0204 1508	0.9E 1.0F
7 SA	0814 2210	0300 1651	0.8E 0.7F	22 SU	0906 2201	0308 1605	1.6E 1.7F
8 SU	0936 2252	0341 1706	1.2E 1.1F	23 M	1016 2259	0402 1701	2.2E 2.3F
9 M	1036 2334	0437 1736	1.5E 1.4F	24 TU	1123	0505 1757	2.6E 2.7F
10 TU	1132	0526 1817	1.7E 1.6F	25 W	0000 1229	0602 1900	2.8E 2.9F
11 W	0020 1229	0615 1859	1.8E 1.7F	26 TH	0103 1334	0704 1959	2.9E 2.8F
12 TH	0111 1328	0722 1946	1.8E 1.8F	27 F	0207 1438	0809 2059	2.7E 2.6F
13 F	0208 1428	0823 2036	1.8E 1.8F	28 SA	0310 1538	0912 2154	2.4E 2.2F
14 SA	0309 1527	0927 2130	1.8E 1.7F	29 SU	0413 1632	1010 2250	2.0E 1.6F
15 SU	0411 1624	1028 2225	1.8E 1.6F	30 M	0512 1715	1056 2334	1.5E 1.0F
				31 TU	0609 1730	1130 2200	0.9E 0.4F

TIME MERIDIAN 90° W.   0000 IS MIDNIGHT.   1200 IS NOON.
*CURRENT WEAK AND VARIABLE.

Figure 18-8.   Extract from Table 1 of the *Tidal Current Tables.*

You decide it is better to be safe than sorry, and not to attempt Pelican Passage, but let *War Hat* remain at anchor in Pelican Bay the night of 23 October 1972. A fresh southerly breeze has the Gulf stirred up. As the Bahamians say, "There is a rage on the bar." Under these circumstances the tidal currents have a very strong effect on sea conditions on the bar. To plan your departure you are vitally interested in what the tidal currents will be doing on the morning of the 24th of October.

Open the *Current Tables* to Table 1. Read the explanation of Table 1 on pages 7 and 8. Then thumb through Table 1 until you come to the part of the table headed "Mobile Bay Entrance, Ala., 1972," and find the columns for October (see Figure 18-8). Beneath the heading is the notation "F - Flood, Dir. 025°True, E-Ebb, Dir. 190°True." A footnote at the bottom tells you that the time meridian is 90°W, 0000 is midnight and 1200 is noon. A second footnote, indicated by an asterisk, calls attention to currents that are weak and variable. You will see that, except for variations needed to tabulate the special information on current, Table 1 of the *Current Tables* resembles Table 1 of the *Tide Tables* and is as easy to use.

Run down the October day column to the date "24th." The next column is headed "Slack Water Time H.M." In this column there is one time, 1123, listed for 24 October. Slack water at Mobile Bay Entrance this date is at 1123. This is "Slack water — flood begins." (How do you know flood begins?) Slip over one more column to the right and you find a double column headed "Maximum Current" with the two sub-columns headed "Time" and "Vel." At 0505 on the 24th there is an entry 2.6E. This indicates a maximum ebb with a velocity of 2.6 knots. With slack water at 1123 following a maximum ebb at 0505, the reverse current must be a flood.

It would be nice to stand out early the morning of the 24th with over two knots of current on your stern, wouldn't it? Well only maybe! A current of 2.6 knots setting 190°T into a strong south wind can't help but kick up one mean sea in a narrow channel as you have at Mobile Bay Entrance. As the wind promises to get no worse, you decide to wait for slack water. Things should get better by then. Besides, the maximum current of 2.7 knots at flood will not occur until over 8 hours later.

The above use of the *Current Tables* shows a blend of good navigation and good seamanship. If your boat were strictly a sailing vessel, you would have had to use the maximum ebb to assist you in beating out of the channel against the fresh south wind.

You can use *Current Tables* to tell you when the most comfortable passage is likely and when the tidal current is most likely to make a passage possible or impossible. In the same manner you can use the *Tide Tables* to predict when the tide will be low enough for gathering scallops or soft shell crabs, or you can use them to predict when the rising tide will be high enough to gig flounders. And you can predict by the *Tide Tables* when you may have enough water over a bar or alongside a pier to carry your draft safely. *Tide Tables* and *Current Tables* are companion publications. You cannot get the full benefit of one without the other.

Table 2 of the *Current Tables* gives the differences in current data for subordinate stations coordinated with the reference stations listed in Table 1. Again, the format parallels the format of Table 2 of the *Tide Tables* (see Figure 18-9). Current variations from the norm are much more individualistic than tide predictions. In using Table 2, you will find footnote references rather than differences in many cases. In some areas the footnotes take more space on a page of Table 2 than do the listings for the subordinate stations. Otherwise, the use of the table comes in a few easy steps. For example, the navigator of a sloop standing down Mobile Bay on 24 October 1972, wants to know what currents to expect, and the time of slack water maximum ebb and maximum flood at a station six miles above Mobile Point in the ship channel. "Channel, 6 miles N of Mobile Point" is a subordinate station on Mobile Bay Entrance in Table 2.

STEP 1

Find Mobile Bay in Table 2 (Figure 18-9). At the top of the table a note tells you that the data of the subordinate stations is based on Mobile Bay Entrance, page 118. Extract the time of slack water; the time and velocity of maximum ebb; and the time and velocity of maximum flood for Mobile Bay Entrance from Table 1, as you just did as navigator of *War Hat*. Set up these figures in a form like the one in Figure 18-10. Note that the navigator went back and picked up the last slack water at 2259 the night of October 23rd.

STEP 2

Below the Mobile Bay Entrance entry in Table 2, find "Channel, 6 miles N of Mobile Point." You are not interested in the latitude and longitude unless you need to confirm that your position is nearer this reference station than any other. You are interested in the time differences. For slack water extract $+0^h 50^m$; and for maximum current extract $+1^h 00^m$. Put these values in the form, and apply these

TABLE 2.—CURRENT DIFFERENCES AND OTHER CONSTANTS

No.	PLACE	POSITION		TIME DIFFERENCES		VELOCITY RATIOS		MAXIMUM CURRENTS			
								Flood		Ebb	
		Lat.	Long.	Slack water	Maximum current	Maximum flood	Maximum ebb	Direction (true)	Diurnal velocity	Direction (true)	Diurnal velocity
		° ' N.	° ' W.	h. m.	h. m.			deg.	knots	deg.	knots
	PENSACOLA BAY			on MOBILE BAY ENT., p.118							
				Time meridian, 90°W.							
5965	Pensacola Bay entrance, midchannel----	30 20	87 18	-0 15	-0 55	1.1	1.2	75	1.6	255	1.8
	MOBILE BAY										
5970	Main Ship Channel entrance------------	30 09	88 03	-----	+0 50	0.5	0.7	345	0.7	180	1.0
5975	MOBILE BAY ENT. (off Mobile Point)----	30 14	88 02	Daily predictions				25	1.4	190	1.5
5980	Channel, 6 miles N. of Mobile Point---	30 20	88 02	+0 50	+1 00	0.4	0.3	30	0.6	210	0.5
5985	Great Point Clear, channel west of----	30 29	88 01	(1)	(1)	(1)	(1)	----	----	----	----
5990	Mobile River entrance-----------------	30 40	88 02	+4 10	a+4 55	0.2	0.5	335	0.3	150	0.7
5995	Tensaw River entrance (bridge)--------	30 41	88 01	+0 30	b+1 35	0.3	0.7	30	0.4	220	1.0
6000	Pass Aux Herons (ent. to Miss. Sound)*	30 17	88 08	+0 15	+0 10	0.9	0.9	70	1.3	245	1.3
	MISSISSIPPI SOUND										
6005	Pascagoula River highway bridge-------	30 22	88 34	(3)	(2)	0.9	0.8	15	1.2	200	1.2
	LOUISIANA COAST										
6010	Quatre Bayoux Pass, Barataria Bay-----	29 19	89 51	+1 10	+0 35	0.9	0.9	290	1.2	105	1.3
6015	Pass Abel, Barataria Bay--------------	29 18	89 54	+0 35	+0 30	0.6	1.1	315	0.9	145	1.6
6020	Barataria Pass, Barataria Bay---------	29 16	89 57	+1 45	+0 50	1.1	0.9	315	1.5	120	1.3
6025	Barataria Bay, 1.1mi. NE. of Manilla--	29 26	89 58	+3 55	+3 55	0.3	0.3	355	0.4	160	0.5
6030	Caminada Pass, Barataria Bay----------	29 12	90 03	+1 20	+0 20	1.1	1.0	295	1.5	120	1.5
6035	Seabrook Bridge, New Orleans----------	30 02	90 02	(3)	+7 45	0.9	0.6	350	1.2	170	0.9
				on GALVESTON BAY ENTRANCE, p.124							
6040	Cat Island Pass, Terrebonne Bay-------	29 05	90 34	-2 40	-2 30	0.6	0.6	15	1.1	195	1.5
6045	Wine Island Pass---------------------	29 04	90 38	-5 00	-4 45	1.0	0.8	325	1.7	160	1.9
6050	Caillou Boca, Caillou Bay-------------	29 04	90 48	c-0 45	-0 45	0.8	0.3	95	1.3	265	0.7
6055	Calcasieu Pass-----------------------	29 46	93 21	(4)	-0 45	1.0	1.0	20	1.7	205	2.3
6060	Calcasieu Pass, 35 miles south of-----	29 10	93 19	(5)	(5)	(5)	(5)	----	----	----	----
6065	Calcasieu Pass, 67 miles south of-----	28 40	93 20	(6)	(6)	(6)	(6)	----	----	----	----
	TEXAS										
	Sabine Pass										
6070	Texas Point, 1.7 miles SSE. of-----	29 39	93 50	-0 15	-0 25	0.6	0.7	335	1.1	145	1.6
6075	Sabine, channel east of-------------	29 43	93 52	-0 15	0 00	0.9	0.7	335	1.6	140	1.7
6080	Port Arthur Canal entrance---------	29 46	93 54	+0 55	+1 25	0.5	0.6	310	0.9	110	1.3
6085	Mesquite Pt., La. Causeway bridge--	29 46	93 54	-0 20	-0 30	0.9	1.0	330	1.6	150	2.2
	GALVESTON BAY										
6090	GALVESTON BAY ENT. (between jetties)--	29 21	94 42	Daily predictions				300	1.7	100	2.3
6095	Bolivar Roads, 0.5mi. N. of Ft. Point-	29 21	94 46	+0 50	+0 20	1.0	0.8	285	1.7	110	1.8
6100	Quarantine Station, 0.3 mile S. of----	29 20	94 47	(3)	-1 10	0.6	0.4	195	1.1	10	0.8
6105	Galveston Channel, west end----------	29 19	94 49	(3)	-0 10	1.0	0.6	270	1.7	105	1.5
6110	Galveston Causeway RR. bridge--------	29 18	94 53	d-0 25	-0 15	0.4	0.4	210	0.7	25	0.8
6115	Houston Channel, W. of Port Bolivar---	29 22	94 48	+0 50	+0 30	0.8	0.6	330	1.3	165	1.4
6120	Houston Ship Channel (Red Fish Bar)---	29 30	94 52	+1 40	+1 40	0.8	0.8	320	1.3	145	1.8
	TEXAS COAST										
6123	Matagorda Channel--------------------	28 25	96 19	-0 35	-0 50	1.2	0.8	315	2.0	140	1.9
6125	Aransas Pass-------------------------	27 50	97 03	+0 40	(7)	0.5	0.5	310	0.9	115	1.2
6130	Sabine Bank-------------------------	29 18	94 00	(8)	(8)	(8)	(8)	----	----	----	----
6135	Heald Bank, 28 miles SSE. of---------	28 40	94 00	(8)	(8)	(8)	(8)	----	----	----	----

[1] Current is weak, usually setting southward.
[2] Maximum flood, +0h 50m; maximum ebb, -1h 00m.
[3] Times of slack are variable.
[4] Flood begins, -0h 20m; ebb begins, +2h 10m.
[5] Current weak and variable.
[6] Current weak and variable. Current is somewhat rotary turning clockwise.
[7] Maximum flood, +1h 05m; maximum ebb, -0h 10m.
[8] Current is somewhat rotary, the velocity seldom exceeds 0.3 knot.
[a] Flood only, for ebb use +2h 45m.
[b] Flood only, for ebb use -0h 20m.
[c] Beginning of flood, for beginning of ebb use +1h 25m.
[d] Beginning of flood, slacks before ebb are erratic.
* Currents are materially affected by winds.

Figure 18-9. **Extract from Table 2 of the *Tidal Current Tables*.**

DATE : 24 OCTOBER , 1972

STEP 1:	SLACK WATER	MAX. EBB TIME VEL.	SLACK WATER	MAX. FLOOD TIME VEL.
MOBILE BAY ENT.	2259(10/23)	0505 2.6	1123	1757 2.7
STEP 2 :	+0ʰ50ᵐ	+1ʰ00ᵐ / 06ʰ05ᵐ	+0ʰ50ᵐ	+1ʰ00ᵐ / 18ʰ57ᵐ
CHANNEL 6 MILES N	23-49		12-13	
STEP 3:		X0.3		X0.4
CHANNEL 6 MILES N		0.8		1.1

Figure 18-10. A simple form for figuring tidal currents in the navigator's notebook.

differences in accordance with the sign. Here you must add. Slack water, ebb, begins at this subordinate station at 2349 the evening of the 23rd. Slack water, flood, begins at 1213 the 24th. The time of maximum velocity of the ebb current is 0605. The time of the maximum velocity of the flood is 1857.

STEP 3

Find the velocity of the currents this navigator may expect. Go to the columns under the heading "Velocity Ratio." From the column for maximum flood extract 0.4, and from the column for maximum ebb extract 0.3. Put these ratios in the form — the flood ratio under flood velocity and the ebb ratio under ebb velocity — and multiply the proper velocity by the proper ratio. The maximum velocity at ebb is 0.8 knots. The maximum velocity at flood is 1.1 knots.

Table 3 in the *Current Tables* provides the velocity of the tidal current at any time. For instance, if *War Hat* did not get underway until 1430 the afternoon of the 24th, and you see she will be proceeding down the main ship channel at 1510, the tidal current will be setting against you. You want to know the velocity or "strength," as sailors call it, of this current. Here is how you find this velocity:

STEP 1

Go to Table 1 for the daily predictions for 24 October 1972, extract the current data for the time immediately before and after 1510, and jot this data down in your navigator's notebook as in Figure 18-11.

STEP 2

Subtract the time of slack, flood (1123) from the time of maximum current, 1757, and get 6ʰ 34ᵐ. Subtract the time of slack water, 1123, from the time on board ship when you wish to know the current velocity, 1510, and get 3ʰ 47ᵐ.

STEP 3

This is an intermediate step used frequently with currents caused by diurnal tides. If the maximum interval you figure is 5ʰ 40ᵐ or less, this step is not necessary. But 5ʰ 40ᵐ is the maximum interval tabulated in Table 3, and the interval between slack water and maximum velocity is 6ʰ 34ᵐ (see Figure 18-12). You must divide both of the above intervals by 2. One half of 3ʰ 47ᵐ is 1ʰ 54ᵐ. One half of 6ʰ 34ᵐ is 3ʰ 17ᵐ.

STEP 4

Intervals between slack and maximum current are tabulated in vertical columns with heading increments of 20 minutes across the top of the table. With 3ʰ 17ᵐ as your first argument, enter Table A of Table 3 by going across the top of the table to the 3ʰ 20ᵐ interval column. The tabulated value nearest to 3ʰ 17ᵐ is 3ʰ 20ᵐ. Intervals between desired time and slack water are tabulated as lines in a vertical column on the left of Table A. Use 2ʰ 00ᵐ as your second entering argument to Table A, because 2ʰ 00ᵐ is the nearest tabulated value to 1ʰ 54ᵐ. At the junction of the 3ʰ 20ᵐ column and the 2ʰ 00ᵐ line extract the factor 0.8. Multiply the maximum velocity, 2.7, by 0.8 and get a predicted velocity of 2.2 knots. *War Hat* will be bucking a 2.2-knot current.

What is Table B of Table 3 used for? Read the footnote to the table in Figure 18-12.

Table 4 gives the duration of slack (see Figure 18-13). How long will it take for slack water at Mobile Bay Entrance to reach 0.5 knots on the 24th? By inspection go down the left-hand column of Table A of Table 4 to 2.0 knots and across to the *0.5 knots* column. Read 58 minutes. The next figure below on the 3.0-knot line of the 0.5-knots column is 38 minutes. Visual interpolation between 2.0 knots and 3.0 knots for a maximum current of 2.7 knots indicates a time of 44 minutes before the tidal current will reach 0.5 knots.

STEP 1:	TIME	MAXIMUM TIME	CURRENT VELOCITY
SLACK-FLOOD BEGINS	1123	1757	2.7
STEP 2 :			
SHIP'S TIME	1510		
TIME INTERVALS	3ʰ47ᵐ	6ʰ34ᵐ	
STEP 3 :	3ʰ47ᵐ ÷ 2 = 1ʰ55ᵐ	6ʰ34ᵐ ÷ 2 = 3ʰ17ᵐ	
STEP 4 :	2.7 × 0.8 = 2.16, OR 2.2		

Figure 18-11. Figuring the velocity of the tidal current.

TABLE 3.—VELOCITY OF CURRENT AT ANY TIME

TABLE A														

Interval between slack and maximum current

	h. m. 1 20	h. m. 1 40	h. m. 2 00	h. m. 2 20	h. m. 2 40	h. m. 3 00	h. m. 3 20	h. m. 3 40	h. m. 4 00	h. m. 4 20	h. m. 4 40	h. m. 5 00	h. m. 5 20	h. m. 5 40
h. m.	f.	f.	f.	f.	f.	f.	f.	f.	f.	f.	f.	f.	f.	f.
0 20	0.4	0.3	0.3	0.2	0.2	0.2	0.2	0.1	0.1	0.1	0.1	0.1	0.1	0.1
0 40	0.7	0.6	0.5	0.4	0.4	0.3	0.3	0.3	0.3	0.2	0.2	0.2	0.2	0.2
1 00	0.9	0.8	0.7	0.6	0.6	0.5	0.5	0.4	0.4	0.4	0.3	0.3	0.3	0.3
1 20	1.0	1.0	0.9	0.8	0.7	0.6	0.6	0.5	0.5	0.5	0.4	0.4	0.4	0.4
1 40	---	1.0	1.0	0.9	0.8	0.8	0.7	0.7	0.6	0.6	0.5	0.5	0.5	0.4
2 00	---	---	1.0	1.0	0.9	0.9	0.8	0.8	0.7	0.7	0.6	0.6	0.6	0.5
2 20	---	---	---	1.0	1.0	0.9	0.9	0.8	0.8	0.7	0.7	0.7	0.6	0.6
2 40	---	---	---	---	1.0	1.0	1.0	0.9	0.9	0.8	0.8	0.7	0.7	0.7
3 00	---	---	---	---	---	1.0	1.0	1.0	0.9	0.9	0.8	0.8	0.8	0.7
3 20	---	---	---	---	---	---	1.0	1.0	1.0	0.9	0.9	0.9	0.8	0.8
3 40	---	---	---	---	---	---	---	1.0	1.0	1.0	0.9	0.9	0.9	0.9
4 00	---	---	---	---	---	---	---	---	1.0	1.0	1.0	1.0	0.9	0.9
4 20	---	---	---	---	---	---	---	---	---	1.0	1.0	1.0	1.0	0.9
4 40	---	---	---	---	---	---	---	---	---	---	1.0	1.0	1.0	1.0
5 00	---	---	---	---	---	---	---	---	---	---	---	1.0	1.0	1.0
5 20	---	---	---	---	---	---	---	---	---	---	---	---	1.0	1.0
5 40	---	---	---	---	---	---	---	---	---	---	---	---	---	1.0

Interval between slack and desired time

TABLE B														

Interval between slack and maximum current

	h. m. 1 20	h. m. 1 40	h. m. 2 00	h. m. 2 20	h. m. 2 40	h. m. 3 00	h. m. 3 20	h. m. 3 40	h. m. 4 00	h. m. 4 20	h. m. 4 40	h. m. 5 00	h. m. 5 20	h. m. 5 40
h. m.	f.	f.	f.	f.	f.	f.	f.	f.	f.	f.	f.	f.	f.	f.
0 20	0.5	0.4	0.4	0.3	0.3	0.3	0.3	0.3	0.2	0.2	0.2	0.2	0.2	0.2
0 40	0.8	0.7	0.6	0.5	0.5	0.5	0.4	0.4	0.4	0.4	0.3	0.3	0.3	0.3
1 00	0.9	0.8	0.8	0.7	0.7	0.6	0.6	0.5	0.5	0.5	0.4	0.4	0.4	0.4
1 20	1.0	1.0	0.9	0.8	0.8	0.7	0.7	0.6	0.6	0.6	0.5	0.5	0.5	0.5
1 40	---	1.0	1.0	0.9	0.9	0.8	0.8	0.7	0.7	0.7	0.6	0.6	0.6	0.6
2 00	---	---	1.0	1.0	0.9	0.9	0.9	0.8	0.8	0.7	0.7	0.7	0.7	0.6
2 20	---	---	---	1.0	1.0	1.0	0.9	0.9	0.8	0.8	0.8	0.7	0.7	0.7
2 40	---	---	---	---	1.0	1.0	1.0	0.9	0.9	0.9	0.8	0.8	0.8	0.7
3 00	---	---	---	---	---	1.0	1.0	1.0	0.9	0.9	0.9	0.9	0.8	0.8
3 20	---	---	---	---	---	---	1.0	1.0	1.0	1.0	0.9	0.9	0.9	0.8
3 40	---	---	---	---	---	---	---	1.0	1.0	1.0	1.0	0.9	0.9	0.9
4 00	---	---	---	---	---	---	---	---	1.0	1.0	1.0	1.0	0.9	0.9
4 20	---	---	---	---	---	---	---	---	---	1.0	1.0	1.0	1.0	0.9
4 40	---	---	---	---	---	---	---	---	---	---	1.0	1.0	1.0	1.0
5 00	---	---	---	---	---	---	---	---	---	---	---	1.0	1.0	1.0
5 20	---	---	---	---	---	---	---	---	---	---	---	---	1.0	1.0
5 40	---	---	---	---	---	---	---	---	---	---	---	---	---	1.0

Interval between slack and desired time

Use Table A for all places except those listed below for Table B.
Use Table B for Cape Cod Canal, Hell Gate, Chesapeake and Delaware Canal and all stations in Table 2 which are referred to them.

1. From predictions find the time of slack water and the time and velocity of maximum current (flood or ebb), one of which is immediately before and the other after the time for which the velocity is desired.
2. Find the interval of time between the above slack and maximum current, and enter the top of Table A or B with the interval which most nearly agrees with this value.
3. Find the interval of time between the above slack and the time desired, and enter the side of Table A or B with the interval which most nearly agrees with this value.
4. Find, in the table, the factor corresponding to the above two intervals, and multiply the maximum velocity by this factor. The result will be the approximate velocity at the time desired.

Figure 18-12. Table 3 from the *Tidal Current Tables.*

To me the *Tidal Current Tables* are one of the most interesting publications a navigator can read. This publication is interesting because it is so full of useful information. The sections on the Gulf Stream, wind-driven currents, combination currents, current diagrams, and rotary tidal currents are all excellent sources of information to the navigator. Any navigator who does not use the information in Table 5 to solve his set and drift problems when passing one of the ship graveyards listed in the table would be remiss. As for set and drift and what to do about it, that is a whole new chapter.

The predicted times of slack water given in this publication indicate the instant of zero velocity, which is only momentary. There is a period each side of slack water, however, during which the current is so weak that for practical purposes it may be considered as negligible.

The following tables give, for various maximum currents, the approximate period of time during which weak currents not exceeding 0.1 to 0.5 knot will be encountered. This duration includes the last of the flood or ebb and the beginning of the following ebb or flood, that is, half of the duration will be before and half after the time of slack water.

Table A should be used for all places *except* those listed below for Table B.

Table B should be used for **Cape Cod Canal, Hell Gate, Chesapeake and Delaware Canal,** and all stations in Table 2 which are referred to them.

Duration of weak current near time of slack water

TABLE A

Maximum current	Period with a velocity not more than—				
	0.1 knot	0.2 knot	0.3 knot	0.4 knot	0.5 knot
Knots	*Minutes*	*Minutes*	*Minutes*	*Minutes*	*Minutes*
1.0	23	46	70	94	120
1.5	15	31	46	62	78
2.0	11	23	35	46	58
3.0	8	15	23	31	38
4.0	6	11	17	23	29
5.0	5	9	14	18	23
6.0	4	8	11	15	19
7.0	3	7	10	13	16
8.0	3	6	9	11	14
9.0	3	5	8	10	13
10.0	2	5	7	9	11

TABLE B

Maximum current	Period with a velocity not more than—				
	0.1 knot	0.2 knot	0.3 knot	0.4 knot	0.5 knot
Knots	*Minutes*	*Minutes*	*Minutes*	*Minutes*	*Minutes*
1.0	13	28	46	66	89
1.5	8	18	28	39	52
2.0	6	13	20	28	36
3.0	4	8	13	18	22
4.0	3	6	9	13	17
5.0	3	5	8	10	13

When there is a difference between the velocities of the maximum flood and ebb preceding and following the slack for which the duration is desired, it will be sufficiently accurate for practical purposes to find a separate duration for each maximum velocity and take the average of the two as the duration of the weak current.

Figure 18-13. Table 4 from the *Tidal Current Tables.*

19   LEEWAY, SET, AND DRIFT

Have you ever stood at the stern of a boat underway and watched her wake? Did you notice that frequently her wake made an angle to windward with a relative bearing dead astern? Obviously she was slipping off to leeward. She is not making her course good; she is making *leeway*. Leeway is the error introduced into the course of a vessel by the action of wind and waves. Leeway is the motion of a vessel *through the water* caused by these forces. As navigator, you will be vitally concerned with leeway when working up an estimated position, EP, in computing a course and distance run.

I almost used the term dead reckoning instead of estimated position, because, in the days of sail, leeway was a regular factor in computing a ship's dead reckoning. Today, on modern ships, dead reckoning considers only true course and distance by log. As we continue, though, exceptions to this definition creep in. A navigator who makes a speed of six knots by log, but observes his vessel is making seven knots according to a series of fixes, will certainly use seven knots to calculate his distance run to work up his DR. By the same token, a small craft navigator will use leeway in working up his DR. I learned to navigate under the tutelage of men who

made their living at sea under sail. Dead reckoning in those days was done by traverse tables and traverse sailing, which is a mathematical means of working up a vessel's dead reckoning without the use of charts and plotting. The navigator took into account the effects of all forces known or believed to be affecting the accuracy of his course and speed. When the navigator set up his traverse table, he treated *leeway* as a *compass error.* * Figures 19-1 and 19-2 illustrate how this was done. But I am not about to teach dead reckoning by traverse table, although this method of keeping a DR is as accurate and as easy, if not easier sometimes, as plotting. Even though traverse tables have fallen out of favor, leeway is still best treated as a compass error.

As navigator of *War Hat* you clear the seabuoy at Mobile Bay Entrance, secure the noise maker, set all plain sail, close hauled, and fair away on a compass course of 231º. When *War Hat* picks up way and reaches her speed, you stand up and look dead astern. You estimate her wake is angling off on her

*Of course leeway in no way affects the compass itself. Leeway does cause your boat to track on a course different from her compass course.

VESSEL: SCHOONER "WAR HAT"

BOUND : MOBILE

DATE : 24 OCTOBER ,1972

TO : YUCATAN CHANNEL

COMPASS STEERED	L'WAY	COMPASS	DEV.	MAG.	VAR.	T	DIST. MILES	DIFF. LAT. N	DIFF. LAT. S	DEPARTURE E	DEPARTURE W
231°	6° E	237°	8° W	229°	4° E	233°	61		36.7		48.7
162°	4° W	158°	3° W	155°	4° E	159°	48		44.8	17.2	

Figure 19-1. Traverse table. The column headings are mostly self-explanatory. Difference in latitude and departure are from Table III of *Bowditch*. Departure has an entirely different meaning from the one used previously in this book. The complete solution to this problem is given in 19-2.

VESSEL: SCHOONER "WAR HAT" DATE: 24 OCTOBER, 1972

OUT OF: MOBILE, ALA. U.S.A. BOUND: YUCATAN CHANNEL

COMPASS STEERED	L'WAY	COMP.	DEV.	MAG.	VAR.	TRUE	DIST. MILES	DIFF. LAT.		DEPARTURE	
								N	S	E	W
231°	6°E	237°	8°W	229°	4°E	233°	61		36.7		48.7
162°	4°W	158°	3°W	155°	4°E	159°	48		44.8	17.2	
							SUM		81.5 S	17.2	48.7
							DIFF LAT.		1°21.5 S		17.2
							DEPARTURE				31.5 W

DEPARTURE, MOBILE BUOY #1 @ L 30° 08.1 N
LON 88° 03.9 W

DEPARTURE 31.5 W
DIFF OF LONGITUDE   36.0 W
DEPARTURE LONG.   88° 03.9 W
DR LONGITUDE   88° 39.9 W

COURSE MADE GOOD 201°T, DISTANCE MADE GOOD 87 MILES.

Figure 19-2. The DR position solution by the traverse sailing method.

LAT. DEPARTURE 30° 08.1 N
DIFF LAT.   1° 21.5 S
DR LATITUDE   28° 47.6 N
              30° 08.1 N
SUM   58° 55.7
½ SUM   29° 27.9 MIDDLE LAT.

DR POSIT. LAT.   28° 47.6 N
         LONG.   88° 39.9 W

port quarter at about 6° (see Figure 19-3). You could actually measure this angle with your pelorus, but you trust your seaman's eye. As the wake is off *War Hat*'s port quarter, her course made good is to the right of her course steered. Thus her leeway is an easterly error to her course. Had her wake tended to starboard, her course made good would have been to the left of her heading and the error for leeway would have been westerly. You want to figure your course made good to plot your DR. You use the same system you learned in Chapter 5 to correct a compass course, but, instead of Compass, Deviation, Magnetic, Variation, True, you use Course Steered, Leeway, Compass, Deviation, Magnetic, Variation, True. To make the solution simple write the letters C$_s$, L, C, D, M, V, T in a vertical column:

C$_s$ Course Steered
L   Leeway
C   Compass
D   Deviation
M   Magnetic
V   Variation
T   True

To correct your course as you sail away from the seabuoy at Mobile Bay, you set up and work your solution like this:

C$_s$ 231°   Course you are steering
L   6°E
C   237°
D   8°W   From the deviation card
M   229°
V   4°E   From charts
T   233°

You are following the track of the ship in Figure 19-2, and this makes our examples consistent. After running 61 miles by log on the course 233°T, you come about and fair away full and by on course 162°C. But this is the compass course your helmsman is steering. *War Hat*'s wake is now making an angle of 4° on her starboard quarter, with a line dead astern. She is actually making good a course to the left of the course she is steering. The course error caused by leeway is westerly. Correcting the course to plot your DR looks like this:

C$_s$ 162°
L   4°W
C   158°
D   3°W
M   155°
V   4°E
T   159°

War Hat is making good a course of 159°T.

The above system is the best way to handle correc-

147

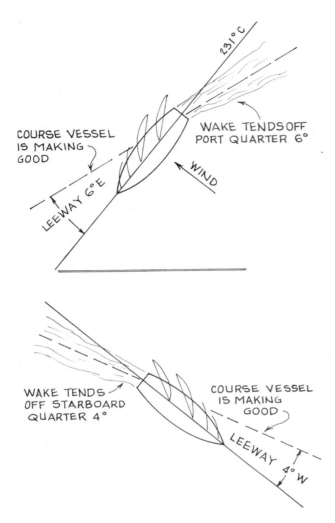

Figure 19-3. Determining leeway. In the upper part of the diagram, the boat is on the port tack. Her wake makes an angle with her course steered of 6° on her port quarter. The course she is actually making good is to the right of her course steered. The leeway error is easterly. In the lower diagram, the 4° angle is to starboard. She is making good a course to her left. The leeway is westerly. All angles are exaggerated.

tions for leeway. There are some purists who insist leeway should be handled exactly the same as a current set and drift problem, which I will cover next. This is a perfectly good method except that it is extremely difficult to estimate the set, which is the direction in which the forces causing errors are acting, and the drift, which is the speed at which the force is moving your vessel in this direction. You must know these components, set and drift, to set up accurately your vector diagram to solve for leeway this way. When you eyeball your wake or measure it with a pelorus, you are already dealing with the

resultant of this vector diagram. You can't estimate or measure the resultant forces to get your vessel's leeway with such accuracy. Treating leeway as a compass error is by far the best means of handling it.

CURRENT SAILING, DETERMINING EFFECTS OF SET AND DRIFT

Current sailing is a different matter. After you have used the *Tidal Current Tables*, consulted your pilot charts, or otherwise discovered what currents are affecting your course by any other means, you have to work a vector problem, unless the current is directly opposite to your course, or directly with your course, in which case you only add or subtract the drift from your speed to find out what the current is going to do to you. Current is the horizontal movement of the water itself. You could be set by a current, but, in the absence of leeway, your wake would trail dead astern. Consequently, there is no direct visual way to measure or estimate set and drift due to current as there is for leeway. Suppose after standing out from the Mobile Bay seabuoy for a while you pass one of

Figure 19-4. Current wake around buoys.

those special purpose buoys the State of Alabama's Department of Conservation and Natural Resources has put out in the Gulf to mark an artificial fishing reef. The way any buoy tends will indicate the set of the current, and an estimate of the velocity of the current wake around the buoy will indicate the drift (see Figure 19-4). By observing the way this buoy is tending and noting the current wake around the buoy, you estimate *War Hat* is experiencing a current setting of 160° at 2.5 knots. *War Hat* is logging 8 knots. Where is this set of 160° and drift of 2.5 knots going to put you?

To solve a set and drift problem such as this, I prefer to plot on the compass rose of a standard plotting sheet. You could use a blank piece of paper along with a scale and a protractor with almost as much ease. But a plotting sheet has a scale for measuring your speed and the drift, and a compass

rose for measuring your course and the current's set. You can use a plotting sheet with nothing more than your parallel rulers and your dividers. I am going to give you a good description of a plotting sheet in the next to the last chapter of this book, but for now all you need to know is that a plotting sheet is a Mercator projection with nothing on it but parallels of latitude, meridians of longitude, and a compass rose. Here is how to solve *War Hat*'s set and drift problem:

STEP 1

Break out a plotting sheet and lay it on your chart table so the compass rose is flat. The center of the compass rose is your departure. *War Hat*'s true course is 233°, so draw a line from the center of the compass rose through 233° (see Figure 19-5). The parallels of latitude are 1° apart on the plotting

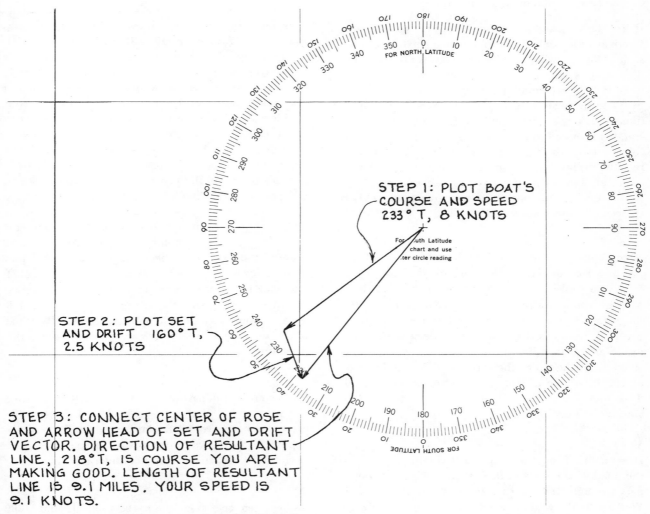

STEP 1: PLOT BOAT'S COURSE AND SPEED 233° T, 8 KNOTS

STEP 2: PLOT SET AND DRIFT 160° T, 2.5 KNOTS

STEP 3: CONNECT CENTER OF ROSE AND ARROW HEAD OF SET AND DRIFT VECTOR. DIRECTION OF RESULTANT LINE, 218° T, IS COURSE YOU ARE MAKING GOOD. LENGTH OF RESULTANT LINE IS 9.1 MILES. YOUR SPEED IS 9.1 KNOTS.

Figure 19-5. Determining course and speed made good.

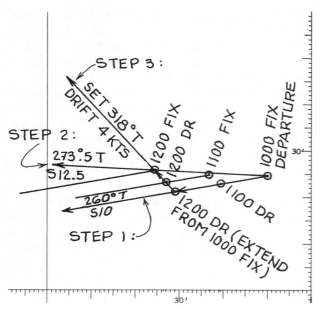

Figure 19-6. Determining set and drift.

sheet. This makes a minute of arc of latitude, one nautical mile, only 1/15 of an inch on the latitude scale. (The drawing reproduced here is not to scale.) The scale is four inches to a degree at the equator. This is a pretty small scale, but since you are not going to be measuring actual distances, but proportionate distances, you can let five minutes of arc equal one mile. Mark this line from the center of the compass rose through 233°; its length should be five times eight, or 40 minutes long. This will represent an hour's run at 8 knots on a course of 233°T. At the end of this line draw an arrowhead. This is your course and speed vector.

STEP 2

Align your parallel rulers with the center of the compass rose and the 160° mark on the rose. Carefully step your parallel rulers over to the arrowhead of your course-speed vector. As your scale for this diagram is five minutes of arc equals one mile, measure 12.5 minutes off the latitude scale you are working in and draw a line this length along your parallel rulers from the tip of the arrowhead *in* the direction of 160°T. At the end of this line put an arrowhead. This line 2.5 miles, scaled 12.5 minutes, 160°, is your set and drift vector.

STEP 3

Draw a line from the center of the compass rose to the head of the set and drift vector. This line would pass through 218° on the compass rose if extended. You are making good a course of 218°T. Measure this line with your dividers. The line is 46 minutes

of arc on the latitude scale. Forty-six divided by five is 9.2. You are making good a speed of 9.2 knots.

If you don't have a plotting sheet, you can work a problem like this on the compass rose of a chart. Use the true compass rose and draw your vectors in lightly, so you don't ruin your chart.

Let's analyze what you really did when you scaled out this graphic solution to *War Hat*'s set and drift problem. What you drew was a vector diagram. You plotted your DR position for *War Hat* as if she had run one hour at 8 knots on a course of 233°T. The center of the compass rose was her point of departure. Then you plotted another DR, as she also ran for one hour on a course of 160°T at 2.5 knots from this first DR. You did this because, while she was going 233°T at 8 knots, she was also going 160°T at 2.5 knots on account of the set of the current. A good example of what happens occurs when a man walks across a moving conveyor belt. If he walks straight across, he does not arrive at a point straight across the belt from where he left. The belt carries him along the distance it moved while he was walking across. This second DR is *War Hat*'s true position after this hour's run. I am assuming you accurately know your own course and speed, and accurately know the set and drift. A line from your point of departure at the center of the compass rose to your position at the head of the set and drift vector arrow is the course to this position, and since this is your position, it must be the course you made good. The length of this line is the distance *War Hat* ran from her departure at the center of the compass rose to this position. The line is 9.1 miles long, and you have run for one hour. You are making good 9.1 knots.

Any time you know two components of a vector triangle you can solve for the third. Now look at Figure 19-6. You have been keeping a careful plot along a coast. You are steering a course of 260°T and making turns on your tachometer for 10 knots. A current is apparently setting you off your DR because your fixes do not plot along the DR. What is the set and drift of this current? To answer this question:

STEP 1

From your first departure extend your DR to the time of your last fix. You must go back and do this, because you began your DR plot from each fix as a new departure during your run down the coast. You are obviously being set north at a considerable rate.

STEP 2

As is often the case, your 1000, 1100, and 1200 fixes do not plot exactly on a straight line because

150

of many factors — for instance eddies in the current, variations in set and drift, and slight errors in taking bearings. With your 1000 fix as a beginning, draw a straight line evenly between your series of fixes. The direction of this line, 273.5°T, is the course you are making good. Measure the length of this line. You have been running for two hours, and the line is 25 miles long. Your boat is making good a speed of 12.5 knots (25 divided by 2 = 12.5).

STEP 3

From your 1200 DR as extended from your 1000 fix, draw a line through your 1200 fix. The direction of this line is 318°T. The set of the current is 318°T. This line measures 8 miles in length. You have been set 318°T for a distance of 8 miles in two hours. Your set is 318°T, the drift is 4 knots.

You can figure the set and drift affecting your boat if you can get good fixes. You can determine the set and drift of the tidal current from the *Tidal Current Tables*. You can determine the probable set and drift of ocean currents from charts, pilot charts, and sailing directions. To navigate your boat safely you must always know what the set and drift of the current is doing to you. This is one reason navigators try to fix their position every few hours, even when they are hundreds of miles offshore. These fixes tell them rather quickly if they are experiencing any current.

An excellent example of the grief set and drift can cause if the navigator chooses to ignore it shows up in navigating vessels from the Gulf Coast of the United States to the Yucatan Channel. I have made this passage several times myself. The course from the seabuoy at Mobile Bay Entrance to a point 20 miles west of Cape San Antonio at the west end of Cuba is 164°T. A current out of the Yucatan Channel sets across the Gulf at around 065°T, drift about 1½ knots. (These figures are from my own navigator's notebook and do not necessarily conform to the averages given on the pilot chart or sailing directions. Wind and weather affect ocean currents too.) Vessels experience this current as much as 150 miles off Cape San Antonio going south. Failure to heed this current can put a boat dangerously close to the coast of Cuba or right on Arecife De Los Colorados. In a 10-knot ship your current diagram looks like Figure 19-7. As the set and drift of this current is constant over a considerable distance, the diagram is based on an eight-hour run.

The navigator plots the passage from Mobile to the position due west of Cape San Antonio, Cuba, on National Ocean Survey Chart No. 1007. It is a simple matter to plot the resulting vector triangle on Chart 1007 to determine the course you will make

good. It is also easy enough and better to work up the same vector triangle on a page of your navigator's notebook, especially if you don't have a plotting sheet. Save your chart. You need a scale, and it is essential that you use the same scale for each leg or vector of the triangle. As navigators seldom have rulers or scales handy, it is a simple matter to use the scale on the chart to draw the diagram in your notebook. To draw the vector diagram as shown in Figure 19-7, the navigator starts like this:

STEP 1

Draw a line exactly 80 miles long by the latitude scale of Chart No. 1007 on the page of your navigator's notebook. At one end of this line put an arrowhead. At the other end draw a small circle like the circle you put around a position on a chart. The line is your course-speed vector. The 80 miles is the distance you would run in eight hours at 10 knots.

You could scale this course-speed vector out on the basis of a one-hour run, but the scale would be too small on Chart No. 1007. The vector would be less than one-quarter of an inch long! Most textbooks tell you to use an hour's run to work your set and drift problems. They also tell you to use a ruler to scale the vectors. You could let one-half an inch equal a mile. You would have then drawn the above line five inches long. At 10 knots, scaled a half-inch to the mile, five inches is an hour's run. But most likely, if you are like many navigators, you would have to hunt high and low for a ruler. Why not use the scale of your chart, and select units large enough to make your vector diagram big enough to make your results accurate? Convinced?

STEP 2

Your course is 164°T. The set of the current is 065°T. Subtract 065°T from 164°T, and get 99°. You now need to subtract 99° from 180° because the angle 99° is the complement of this angle of the vector

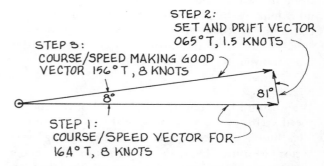

Figure 19-7. Determining set and drift with a protractor and scale.

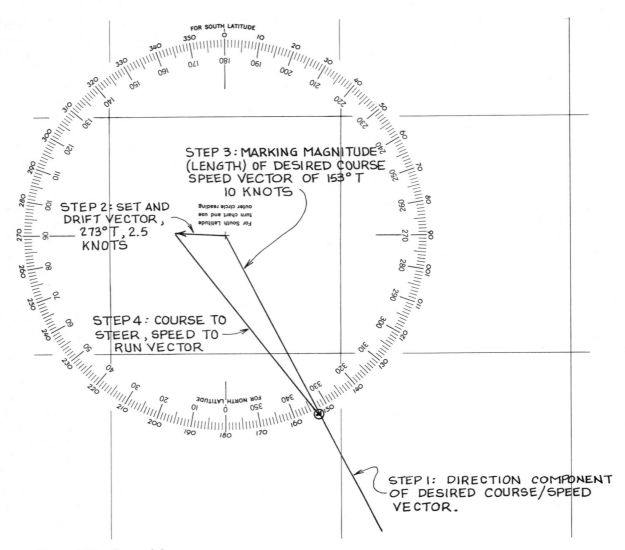

Figure 19-8. Determining course to steer.

triangle at the intersection of your course-speed leg (vector) and your set-drift leg. 180° – 99° = 81°. With your course-speed vector as the base, measure an angle of 81° with a protractor, and draw a line from the arrowhead of the course-speed vector 12 miles long by the same latitude scale you used for the course-speed vector. A drift of 1.5 knots for 8 hours equals 12 miles. Put an arrowhead at the end of this line; it is your set and drift vector.

STEP 3
Draw a third line from the circled end of the course-speed vector to the arrowhead of the set-drift vector. This line is the course-speed you are making good vector. Measure the angle the course-speed making good vector makes with the course-speed vector from Step 1. It is 8°. As the course you are making good is

to the left of the course you are steering, 164°, you must subtract 8° from 164°. Your vessel is making good a course of 156°T. With your dividers measure the length of this course-speed making good vector. It is 80 miles by the latitude scale of your chart. Your vessel is making good a speed of 10 knots (80 divided by 8 equals 10). The reason you are being set without any apparent effect on your speed is that the current is acting at almost a right angle (81°) to the course you are steering.

To see how important set and drift can be, assume you were on course at a position Lat. 24° 15.'0 N, Long. 86° 05.'0 W when you worked this problem. If you have Chart No. 1007, lay a course of 156°T from this position. This course puts you right on the west end of Arecife De Los Colorados. Running on reefs can make a lot of people unhappy.

CURRENT SAILING, COMPENSATING FOR SET AND DRIFT

I have given you two examples of how to tell what set and drift are doing to you, and one example of how to calculate the set and drift you are experiencing. The next question you might ask yourself is: "If I know how much set and drift I am experiencing, what can I do about it?" This can be approached in two ways. Here is the first method: The rhumb line course from your position to your destination is 153ºT and your cruising speed is ten knots, but a current setting 273ºT, drift 2.5 knots is affecting your ship. What course should you steer and what speed over the ground should you make good? The key factor in this approach is that you are not going to change speed. You are going to maintain 10 knots.

Break out a plotting sheet. Remember, you can use the compass rose on a chart; or you can use a plain piece of paper with a ruler, or dividers, or your chart scale and a protractor, just as you did to solve the problems involving the effects of set and drift. You could use a maneuvering board, too, because maneuvering boards are made to solve just this type of problem, but it is not likely a small vessel will have maneuvering boards aboard; the compass rose on a plotting sheet will do equally as well.

STEP 1

Lay out the plotting sheet as you did before. The center of the compass rose is your departure (see Figure 19-8). Draw a line from the center of the compass rose through 153º. At this point you do not need to measure any length or distance on this line, but be sure to make it long. This line is *not* yet a vector because it has only direction, and no size. To be a vector a line must have direction *and* size (magnitude), which in this case is the length of the line.

STEP 2

Draw your set and drift *vector* by drawing a line from the *center* of the compass rose through 273ºT. Make this line 2.5 miles long. To give an adequate scale, let five minutes of latitude between the center parallels, 22º and 23º in Figure 19-8, equal one mile. To be 2.5 miles long by this scale, the line must be 12.′5 of latitude long. Put an arrowhead at the outer end of this 273ºT, 2.5-mile set and drift vector.

STEP 3

Take a drawing compass and open it to a radius of 10 miles (50 minutes of latitude on the scale). With the tip of the arrowhead of the set and drift vector as the center, strike an arc 10 miles in radius across the desired course line you drew in Step 1. Draw a straight line to connect the arrow point of the set and drift vector with the point at which the arc crosses the desired course line. Take your parallel rulers and measure the direction of this line from the center of the compass rose. The direction is 140ºT, which means that you must steer 140ºT if you want to maintain 10 knots and make good a course of 153ºT.

What speed would you make good? Measure the distance from the center of the compass rose to the point where the 10-mile arc crosses the 153ºT desired course line. The distance is 42′ of latitude, and 42 divided by 5 equals 8.4. You will make good a speed of 8.4 knots. And, since your desired course line of 153ºT has a length of 8.4 miles, this line is now a vector. Let's call it your *desired course vector.*

The second way to approach compensating for set and drift is to adjust your speed and course to make good a predetermined speed (in this case, 10 knots). The conditions are the same as in the previous solution — the rhumb line course is 153ºT and there is a current setting 273ºT, drift 2.5 knots. Let's see how you solve this one.

STEP 1

Break out a plotting sheet and work from the compass rose (see Figure 19-9). From the center of the compass rose, draw a line through 153º. It is not necessary to measure length along this line at this time.

STEP 2

Draw the set and drift vector from the center of the compass rose, 273ºT, 2.5 miles long. As before, five minutes of latitude between 22º and 23º equal one mile. Don't forget to put your arrow point at the outboard end of this line.

STEP 3

With your dividers measure 50′ of latitude for 10 miles *along* the 153ºT desired course line you drew in Step 1. Put an arrowhead at this point and a small circle around it. You have your desired *course* and desired *speed* vector.

STEP 4

Draw a straight line from the arrow point of the set and drift vector to the arrow point of the desired course and speed vector. This line is your course to steer, speed to run vector. Measure the length of this line. It is 58′ of latitude in length, and 58 divided by 5 equals 11.6. You must make 11.6 knots. With your parallel rulers measure the direction of this line. The direction is 142ºT. You must make a speed of

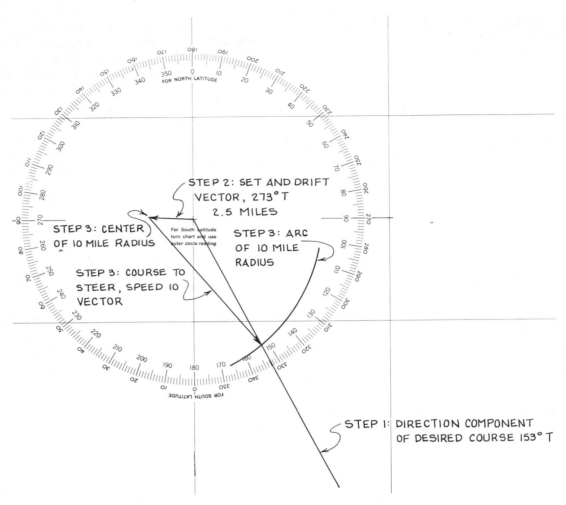

Figure 19-9. Determining course and speed to steer.

11.6 knots on a course of 142°T when contending with a set of 273°T and a drift of 2.5 knots, if you want to make good a course of 153°T and a speed of 10 knots.

It may help you to remember how to work current sailing problems by vector diagrams if you keep in mind the following comparison of the steps involved:

Effects of Set and Drift

For solving for effects of set and drift; finding course and speed made good:

1. Draw the course steered, speed run vector. Put an arrow point on the outboard end pointing in the direction of the course.

2. Draw the set and drift vector from the *arrow point* of the course steered, speed run vector and put an arrow point on the outboard end of this vector.

3. Draw a straight line from departure point or tail of course steered, speed run vector to the arrow point of the set and drift vector. Measure the direction of

this line. The direction is the course made good. Measure the length of the vector, and divide by the time run for the speed made good in knots.

Compensating for Set and Drift

For compensating for set and drift; finding course to steer, or course to steer/speed to run:

1. Draw the direction component of the desired course only.

2. Draw the set and drift vector from the *tail* (center of compass rose) of the desired component, and put an arrow point on the end.

3. Use the arrow point of the set and drift vector as the center, and strike an arc of a radius, equal in length to your speed in knots, to cross the desired course line. Draw a straight line from the arrow point of the set and drift vector to the intersection of the arc and the desired course. This line will be your course to steer.

4. If you desire to make good a course and speed,

154

draw a line the direction and length, to correspond to the speed, for your desired speed and desired course. At the outboard end of this line put an arrowhead. This line *is* a vector. Draw a straight line to connect the arrow point of the set and drift vector with the arrow point of this desired course-speed vector. This straight line is your course to steer, speed to run vector. Measure its direction for the course you must steer. Measure its length for the speed at which you must run.

Another interesting comparison is to consider the effects of a given set and drift on vessels at various speeds. Let's see what happens to a 30-knot destroyer, a 15-knot cargo vessel, a 10-knot fishing boat, and a 5-knot sailboat. Each of these vessels is on a course of 090°T with a current of 2 knots setting 180°T. Figure 19-10 illustrates the relative effect of the current on

each vessel. In a 30-mile run, the destroyer *A* is set 2 miles off her course, the cargo vessel *B* is set 4 miles off, the fishing vessel *C* is set 6 miles off, and the sailboat *D* is set 12 miles off. From this it is apparent that, for a given distance *or* a given time, the higher the relative velocity (that is, set and drift) of the current, the more effect set and drift will have on your course. Certainly you know this. We have all had the really alarming, if not frightening, experience of having a slow boat caught in a fast current. In case you missed it, however, the 30-knot destroyer experienced a significant error in her course, too. Even fast ships cannot afford to ignore set and drift.

All this adds up. The navigator must know how to keep a good dead reckoning. He must know how to fix his vessel's position; how to compare his fixes with his DR track to compute his set and drift; and how to figure a course, and sometimes a speed, to run to offset the effects of set and drift. Then, when he puts his boat on the course he computed, at the speed decided, he starts the whole cycle all over again. Good navigation is demanding. You can run all day and have your fixes plot right on your DR, but if you don't get and plot those fixes, you will not know if you are or are not being set off your DR.

When the master of a clipper ship computed his dead reckoning, he took into account all the known forces affecting his vessel. The modern navigator considers only speed and time, for distance; and the true course steered, for direction. Even if the speed is always the logged speed, the modern navigator would be foolish to ignore possible or actual other factors that would affect his position if he knew or even suspected they existed. How does he reconcile this strict definition of a DR track with fact when the sailing directions, current tables, pilot charts, or his own observations tell him his vessel is being set off course? As navigator of a modern ship, you would keep two plots when confronted with a situation such as this.

In Figure 19-11 you, the navigator, are in a boat steering a true course of 090°. You are logging 10 knots through the water. Visibility is restricted, and you are running on dead reckoning. You have reason to believe a current of 3 knots setting 160°T may be affecting your vessel. You first become aware of this set and drift at 0600. Your first step is:

STEP 1

Advance your 0600 DR to 0700. On a plotting sheet, construct a vector diagram to find the course you are making good. You may wish to draw the vector diagram on the chart as shown in Figure 19-11. Either way, you plot the course you believe you are making

A. DESTROYER , COURSE 090° T, SPEED 30.
COURSE MADE GOOD 094° T, SPEED MADE
GOOD 30.5 KNOTS.

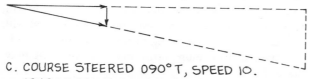

B. CARGO VESSEL , COURSE 090° T, SPEED 15.
COURSE MADE GOOD 098° T.

C. COURSE STEERED 090° T, SPEED 10.
COURSE MADE GOOD 101° T,

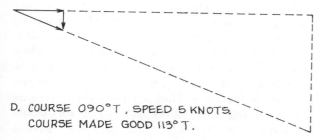

D. COURSE 090° T, SPEED 5 KNOTS.
COURSE MADE GOOD 113° T.

Figure 19-10. The relative effect of current on various vessels.

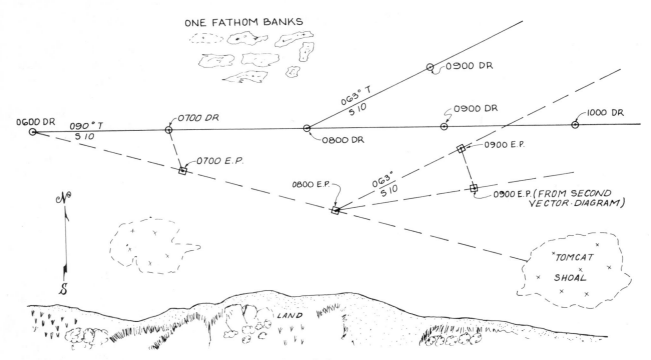

Figure 19-11. Comparing the DR plot and the estimated plot.

good from the 0600 DR and lay off the distance you believe you made good along this course. Draw a neat *square* around this point and label it 0700 EP, for *estimated position*.

STEP 2

Provided you have no new set and drift factors, or other information, you continue on course 090°T, and you maintain your DR plot. You also advance the course you may be making good. At 0800 you mark your 0800 DR *and* your 0800 EP.

STEP 3

By extending the estimated course made good, it is apparent that your ship is going to arrive on Tomcat Shoal before the hour is up. Whether your set and drift information is correct or not, a course change is in order. From your 0800 EP you come to a course of 063°T. Now, advance your DR to the new 0900 DR along course 063°T. Advance the estimated track from your 0800 EP along a course of 063°T at *10 knots* and mark this position as your 0900 EP. The 063°T course from either your 0800 DR or your 0800 EP will take your vessel well clear of Tomcat Shoal, and still not carry you too close to One Fathom Bank to the north.

The man at the wheel says, "We have it made, don't we?"

Have you? If you *are* being set 160° at 3 knots, your 0900 EP as above is not possibly correct. Plotting this 0900 EP is an intermediate step.

STEP 4

Construct another vector diagram as if the 0800 EP were your DR (departure) and as if your 0900 EP were your 0900 DR. This will tell you what will happen to your boat *if* your 0800 EP were truly your actual position and the 160° set, 3-knot drift is still with your vessel. The resulting course made good will also carry you three miles north of Tomcat Shoal. You have a little more assurance that you just may "have it made."

At the completion of Step 4, you have three possible positions plotted. These positions are your 0900 DR as plotted after the 0800 course change; the 0900 EP as plotted from the 0800 EP, without considering set and drift; and the 0900 EP as plotted from the 0800 EP by constructing a set and drift diagram. You don't really know which one of these positions is correct, but you based all this plotting on information that was, to some degree, valid. Yet you don't know *how valid*. Had you been absolutely sure of your set and drift, all the fancy chart work would not have been necessary. Odds are your vessel is somewhere between the vicinity of the 0900 DR and the second 0900 EP you plotted from the second

156

vector diagram. What is important is that the course 063° *would be a safe course from any of these possible positions.*

In a situation such as described above, any seaman worthy of the name would be using every means possible to check his results. He should get RDF bearings if possible (see Chapter 20). He should certainly take soundings, and slow down to heave the lead for a bottom sample, if the nature of the bottom changes enough to tell him something. From the sum of this information, the navigator would exercise his best judgement, and pick a *most probable position, MPP.* This MPP could be anywhere in the area of his DR and his two EPs.

Suppose the bottom is all white sand at 10 fathoms between One Fathom Bank and Tomcat Shoal. Not much help here. Suppose also that the RDF is back home on the kitchen table. But when you pass a crab trap buoy about 0745, your seaman's eye and a quick glance over the compass tells you that the 163° set and 3-knot drift the pilot chart promised is darn near right. At 0800 you would be prudent to take the 0800 EP as your MPP. By the same token, if the crab trap buoy had not indicated any current, you would have considered the DR as the MPP. If you observed a different set and drift, you would have constructed another current diagram.

PRACTICE PROBLEMS (use the deviation table in Chapter 6)

1. Your boat is steering a course of 298°C. She is making 3° easterly leeway. Variation at her position is 8°W. What is her true course?

2. Your boat is trawling. You notice the warps are tending 8° on your starboard quarter. You are steering 017°C. Variation from your chart is 2°E. What true course are you making good?

3. Your course is 118°T, speed 8 knots. From observing a buoy, you estimate you are being affected by a current of 355°T set, drift 1 knot. What course

are you making good? What speed are you making good?

4. You have been steering 309°T. A line faired through a series of fixes is along a course of 287°T. You have been running three hours at 12 knots. Your last fix is 31 miles from your departure. What is the set and drift of the current you are experiencing? What speed have you been making good? What course have you been making good?

5. Your vessel cruises at 12 knots. You want to make good a course of 076°T. The chart and sailing directions tell you to expect a current setting 147°T at a drift of 2.7 knots for the next 3 hours. What course must you steer to make good a course of 076°T? What speed will your boat make good?

6. Your relief is to be waiting at the seabuoy at 1500. Your DR puts you 50 miles away from the sea-buoy at 1000 on a bearing of 231°T from the buoy. A current setting at 176°T, drift 2.5 knots, will be on your port bow all the way in. At what speed must you run to make the seabuoy at 1500? What course must you steer?

7. You are sailing on a close reach and logging 7.5 knots on the port tack, steering a course of 161°. You estimate leeway, by the wake on your port quarter, to be 6°. Variation is 3°E. A check of the tidal current table indicates a current setting 347° with a drift of 2 knots. What course and speed are you making good?

ANSWERS

1. 289°T
2. 019°T
3. Course 112°T
   Speed 7.5 knots
4. Set 188°T
   Drift 4.5 knots
   Speed 10.0 knots
   Course 287°T
5. Course 064°T
   Speed 12.4 knots
6. Course 041°
   Speed 11.6 knots
7. Course 167°T
   Speed 5.5 knots

20 HOW TO USE SOUNDINGS IN NAVIGATION

Even some otherwise experienced navigators never consider checking the depth of the water their vessel is in except to find out if the water is deep enough to float her. No one is against knowing that you have enough water to carry your boat's draft. I will even concede this is the most important reason a navigator wants to know the depth of the water. My point is that there are other very valid uses of soundings in navigation.

But since it is important to know how to determine the depth of water under your keel, let's look at taking soundings. A navigator "takes a sounding" when he measures the vertical distance or "depth" of the water from the surface of the water to the sea bottom. In modern navigation, soundings are usually taken with electronic depth-finding devices, although one of the earliest of all devices, the lead line, is still very much with us.

There are many excellent electronic depth finders on the market. Sailors seem to call them all "fathometers," because this is the trade name of one of the first and best such machines made. Most fathometers work on an echo sounding and ranging principle. The machine times the period required for a sound signal to travel to the bottom and return. This time applied to the average speed of sound in water is a function of the water's depth.

The echo sounder consists primarily of an indicator and a transducer. The original signal and the return signal are received by the transducer. The time interval between the transmission and return of the signal is measured electronically. An indicator on the bridge or in the cockpit reads out the depth of the water as measured. The transducer is attached to the hull well below the waterline. On very small boats you can fit portable depth finders by mounting the transducer in a detachable mount on the transom. Vessels of any size can have a permanently installed transducer mounted on or near the bottom of the hull. Some boats have their transducers mounted in a box filled with water or another liquid. It is inside the hull sheathing below the waterline. This eliminates the need for a through-hull fitting, and prevents fouling of the transducer. This brings up one of the most important considerations in using a fathometer. If your boat draws six feet, and the transducer is mounted on her bottom at the point of her deepest draft, the echo sounder will measure a depth that is six feet less than the actual depth. I have seen otherwise sensible people scratch their heads in bewilderment because they knew their boat drew six feet, but the depth finder was showing only a depth of five feet. They couldn't figure how their six-foot-draft hull could even move in five feet of water! Besides the chart showed the depth to be 11 feet. Of course, these fellows *were* in 11 feet of water (five feet of indicated depth plus six feet of draft equals eleven feet). To read properly an echo-sounding depth finder, you must always *add* the depth the transducer is under the water to the depth indicated. On a commercial vessel where the draft at the transducer may vary with the vessel's load condition, the figure to be added to the indicated depth may vary.

The indicators found on small vessels — and on large vessels, too — may be either a flashing type or a combination beeper/flasher, which indicates the depth on a dial by a flash and accompanying sound signal. The number on the dial at which the signal flashes, or sounds and flashes, indicates the depth of the water. The latest models may have a digital read-out. The depth may be read in feet or fathoms depending on the scale selected by the navigator. The better depth finders measure depths over 100 feet, but you can buy good ones that will not measure in excess of 100 feet. My recommendation is to get the greatest depth-measuring capacity you can; it should be at least 100 feet. A very worthwhile addition to any depth-sounder is a warning signal that will sound off when a previously determined depth is reached as the vessel enters shallow water.

The recording depth finder records the measured depth of the water on a piece of chemically treated paper. Because of the special advantages of each, most boats of any size will carry both a flashing-type depth finder and a recording depth finder. The recording depth finders are normally more complicated and hence more expensive. Some depth finders incorporate the features of a visual dial, digital read-out, and a recorder. The big advantage, to me, of the recording type of echo-sounding depth finder is that the machine makes an automatic record of soundings over a given time/distance. In navigation this is a very convenient feature.

Despite the very excellent electronic depth-finding devices available today, the lead and lead line are still with us. Coast Guard regulations require a lead and lead line on most inspected vessels regardless of the other equipment carried. Sailors call this rig "the lead" or "hand lead." Common sense dictates that any vessel of any size should carry a hand lead. The hand lead costs very little and of course requires no installation. If you check the line for wear and stretch, it never needs calibrating, nor does it short circuit, blow fuses, or require any power supply other than the man in the chains "heaving the lead." And last but not least, the hand lead can tell you the type of bottom — whether it is mud, sand, clay, or gravel — as well as tell you the depth. About the best an electronic depth finder can do is tell you if the bottom is hard or soft. Conversely, an echo-sounder can locate fish for you. About the only way you could find fish with a hand lead would be to conk one on the noggin.

The hand lead consists of a lead that weighs between 5 and 15 pounds and a suitable length of line (see Figure 20-1). An eye is molded in the upper end of the lead for attaching the lead line. A hole is molded or bored in the bottom of the lead for *arming* it. The old texts exhorted the navigator to place a lump of beeswax or tallow in this hole, and thus *arm* the lead. Traces of mud, sand, ooze, shell, or whatever the bottom is composed of, stick to the wax or tallow, and the navigator can compare the sample brought up with the type of bottom indicated on the chart. Today, I doubt if any ship can rustle up much beeswax or tallow for arming the lead. A few years back, brown laundry soap made an excellent substitute for beeswax or tallow, but today detergents have run brown laundry soap into oblivion. Now we use butter or margarine to arm the lead.

In areas where little variation in depth occurs, a bottom sample can be crucial. My good friend,

Figure 20-1. A lead line.

Captain Alton Simms, of Simms Brothers Towing Company, has told me that tows running the flats of Mississippi Sound, when visibility is reduced, depend not on depth, but the change in the nature of the bottom to know when to change course. Regrettably, dredging and erosion have deposited a uniform layer of silt over the bottom in many places, so that bottom samples are not as dependable as they used to be. Yet there still are areas enough like the way the Good Lord made them to make a sample of the bottom very useful.

The standard lead line, for the hand lead, is 20 fathoms in length. On small vessels operating in shallow waters, the first two to four fathoms of the lead line should be marked in feet. No one has come up with any standard for marking the feet in these first four fathoms. A lot of navigators use a piece of yarn passed through the lay of the line at each foot. A knot in the yarn indicates one foot; two knots, two feet; and on up to one fathom, and then they start over. Often the first knot is placed at a length from the lead equal to the boat's minimum draft on the theory that if you carry six feet of draft into five feet of water, the fast passage is over, at least for awhile, and you won't be too concerned with the lesser depths for that reason.

The standard markings of the hand lead line begin at two fathoms and are marked as follows:

2 fathoms	2 strips of leather
3 fathoms	3 strips of leather
5 fathoms	a piece of white bunting
7 fathoms	a piece of red bunting
10 fathoms	a piece of leather with a hole in it
13 fathoms	a piece of blue bunting
15 fathoms	a piece of white bunting
17 fathoms	a piece of red bunting
20 fathoms	a strand with two knots in it

The hand lead is cast or "heaved" by a man in the chains. In very close waters, if it is necessary to keep going because you cannot anchor, it may be advisable to have a man in each bow with a lead line. The lead is swung in a vertical circle overhead and cast in front of the boat to windward. The ship shouldn't be making over four knots. As the vessel passes over the lead, the line is hove taut and the depth is read at the water's surface. At night, the depth is read by feeling the marks. Fractions of fathoms are estimated. It is essential that the leadsman know how far his hand is above the water's surface, and this distance must be deducted from the depth read to get the true depth when gauging by feel.

The leadsman's chant is a necessary, useful, and romantic part of the old seafaring tradition that still lives with us. By using his seaman's eye, a good leadsman calls depths to an accurate approximation of the nearest foot and a half. He calls depths by chanting "by the mark" to indicate whole fathom depths marked on the lead line. "By the deep" indicates whole fathom depths between the marks. If the depth exceeds the mark or deep by one half or quarter, the chant is "and a half six" or "and a quarter six" if, for instance, the lead shows six fathoms plus a half fathom or a quarter fathom. The term "less a quarter six" means the lead line indicates five and three quarter fathoms.

A good leadsman was a good chantyman too in days gone by. Between his loud calls of the soundings, he would intersperse his own ribald verse to keep the rhythm of heaving the lead and chanting the marks. An example of the chant of the leadsman, continuously sounding, in a ship coming up on and crossing the bar on a five-fathom shoal some dark and rainy night would sound like this:

By the mark seven!
By the mark seven
Less a quarter seven
Don't reckon the cap'n 'll ever get to heaven.
And a half six!
And a quarter six
And a quarter six
Reckon I'll have to row 'im cross the River Styx!
By the deep six!
By the deep six
Less a quarter six
Less a half six
T'aint no night to be on the water
And a quarter five
And a quarter five
Ought to be in bed with the captain's daughter
By the mark five!

By the mark five!
She's shoalin' fast; better look alive
And a quarter five
And a half five
Less a quarter six
*By the deep six!**

And she passes safely over the bar. The soundings are sung out loudly enough to be heard clearly on the bridge or poop. The interspersed verse is chanted in a lower voice for the benefit of the crew, or maybe just loud enough for the captain to wonder if he ought to brace the leadsman up . . . But the safety of the ship comes first, and you don't interfere with the leadsman.

Heavier leads called the deep-sea lead or "dips'y" lead (80 to 50 pounds) and coasting lead (30 to 50 pounds) were carried by vessels in days gone by. Even in 40 fathoms, a series of accurate depths can aid the navigator. Today, echo-sounders are used instead of deep-sea leads and coasting leads, but these leads are often carried on large vessels as back-up equipment.

You should carry an echo-sounder provided you can afford one and your boat can accommodate one. Echo-sounders are not very expensive. You should *always* carry a hand lead aboard, whether you have an echo-sounder or not. On a small cruising boat, a fifteen-foot cane pole, marked off in feet, may be the most useful device. Or just mark off the handle of the boat hook at one-foot intervals.

No book can cover all aspects of all the various devices using echo-sounding as a depth-finding principle. My purpose is to help you to use the information you obtain through soundings for better navigation. Yet a reasonable understanding of the principles involved is essential to the intelligent use of this equipment. To round out your knowledge you should read and study all available material you can find on the subject. An excellent book is *Navigating and Finding Fish with Electronics* by G. D. Dunlap, published by International Marine Publishing Company of Camden, Maine.

We are talking about draft relative to water depths. If your boat carries a certain draft, how shallow can the water be for her to navigate safely? Assume she draws six feet. Can she go where the chart indicates six feet of water? Can she go where the chart indicates seven feet? Can she navigate safely

*The chants of the leadsman given here are from my memory of the leadsman's chants as recited by my friend, Julian Lee Rayford of Mobile, and my own recollection of using the hand lead at sea.

160

in ten feet of water? In almost every case a six-foot draft cannot navigate safely in six feet of water. The only possible exception to this would be to ease your boat up a very protected channel, for a short distance, where you were certain no fall in water level would trap you and you would pass over a soft, oozy, mud bottom in which you were absolutely certain no hidden logs, rocks, or other hard things lurked to bend a wheel, break a shaft, or hole your boat. Of course, I too can recall getting all hands to hike out to leeward in a stiff breeze to carry a six-foot draft over a hard, five-foot sand bar. This is just not good navigation on a boat of any size. Getting away with such antics only proves God does love a sailor. Keep enough water under your keel.

But is seven feet of water enough? Maybe. A boat drawing six feet when dead in the water may squat by the stern if under power and making a lot of way. In shallow water her screws can suck enough water from under her hull to make her squat even more. You must know how much your boat draws at different speeds and under different conditions. A good navigator must know his boat. You cannot separate good navigation from good seamanship.

Even ten feet of water or twenty feet of water may not be enough for your six feet of draft, if breaking seas or deep troughs can drop your vessel on the ground. When a boat hits bottom like this, navigators usually turn pale, and people below hurriedly seek the air on deck. Shallow water may be deep enough to be essentially safe, but sea conditions found in shallow water may make running in such shallow water miserable. And, in the tropics, a stray coral head may be rearing up from otherwise adequate depths.

Another reason vessels of any size seek the deepest possible water is to find the best sea conditions. It is the steep and breaking seas of shallow water that cause heavy weather damage to large or small boats. An example of just this is found in studying the pilot chart of the North Atlantic. The western Caribbean is shown on this chart. At one time the steamer routes from the Yucatan Channel to Cristobal, Canal Zone, carried vessels west of Isla Providencia. This was the shortest feasible route, and there was adequate depth of water to carry almost any draft. But this portion of the western Caribbean is shallow as ocean depths are reckoned. Today, for this reason, the preferred route for all vessels passing between the Caribbean entrance to the Panama Canal and the Yucatan Channel is east of Isla Providencia, because the deeper water along this route reduces the chance of heavy weather damage in a boisterous sea. Remember this when selecting a route for a planned passage. The deeper the water, the better the sea conditions when all else is equal.

The good navigator knows his boat and assesses the conditions of the sea and sea bottom around his boat's position. He will then decide on a minimum depth he deems safe, and navigate his vessel to keep her always in water deeper than this. Navigators call such a minimum depth a *danger sounding*. A danger sounding may vary for the same boat depending on her position, bottom conditions, and sea conditions. In a 14-foot-draft deep-sea tug, you should stay off the 100 fathom curve, if possible, in some waters. The safety fairways between Mobile Bay Entrance and Gulfport run in only 8 fathoms. Ships drawing 30 to 40 feet use these safety fairways.

When navigating by soundings, the navigator frequently checks the depth of the water to see if his vessel is outside the danger limit much as he checks danger angles or danger bearings. Electronic depth finders, with automatic alarm signals, are wonderful for keeping outside your danger soundings. As navigator, you set the depth finder to sound the alarm when the water's depth decreases to the limit you set as the danger sounding. Then, if by chance you are distracted by other equally pressing observations, the alarm sounding off will warn you the water has shoaled to the danger limit. Do not place absolute reliance on the alarm's sounding. You should never allow yourself to be distracted for too long a period for any reason. Even with a depth alarm, frequent visual checks of the echo-sounder should be made. It goes without saying that you should select a danger sounding deeper than the true danger point to allow time for action. Always allow yourself plenty of leeway.

When considering the depth of the water as charted, remember charted depths are depths at datum of the chart. In areas, such as our Gulf Coast, where the tidal range hardly ever exceeds two feet, the height of the tide may not introduce significant error in soundings. On the other hand, if you are in an area where the tide range is considerable, you must consider the height of the tide to correlate the soundings you take with the height of the tide at the time the soundings were taken. In Chapter 18 you found that computing the height of the tide at any time, by use of Table 3 of the *Tide Tables*, is not too difficult. On the other hand, if you are, for some reason, unable to use Table 3, a rule-of-thumb procedure follows that should be far better than nothing:

• At high water deduct the whole range of the tide.

- At the first hour after *high water* deduct seven-eighths of the range.
- At the second hour after *high water* deduct three-fourths of the range.
- At the third hour after *high water* deduct one-half of the range.
- At the fourth hour after *high water* deduct one-fourth of the range.
- At the fifth hour after *high water* deduct one-eighth of the range.
- At the sixth hour after *high water,* or at *low water,* the soundings should agree with those given in the charts.
- At the first hour after *low water* deduct one-eighth of the range.
- At the second hour after *low water* deduct one-fourth of the range.
- At the third hour after *low water* deduct one-half of the range.
- At the fourth hour after· *low water* deduct three-fourths of the range.
- At the fifth hour after *low water* deduct seven-eighths of the range.
- At the sixth hour after *low water* or at *high water,* deduct the whole range of the tide.*

The above rules apply to semidiurnal tides. For diurnal tides, multiply the time in the rules by two, and your approximation should be right enough for rule-of-thumb purposes. Keep in mind these rules apply to *mean* tidal conditions. The behavior of the moon and the sun can cause tides to vary a good bit from the mean ranges. Nevertheless, if you ever find yourself in a part of the world where the lunar-tidal interval is your only means of tidal predictions, this little table of rules will help you predict the height of the tide at any time, not just at the times of high and low water.

Under conditions of good visibility, navigators use visual means to fix their position. But when distances involved are such that only one bearing on only one object is available, a sounding may well fix your position within a usable limit if the contour of the bottom is right. A fairly regular, sloping bottom with depths changing in one direction can almost give you a line of position. In Figure 14-3, the navigator found his position by a bearing and a distance off, and by two distances off. If the navigator had not been able to measure this distance, and had no way to get the distance off Mobile Point Light, a sounding at 49

feet would have told him something, although the small difference in depths in the surrounding area could make very close results difficult if he did not sound carefully.

On the other hand look at Figure 20-2. Suppose you are trying to find your way into Mobile Bay Entrance. You are coming from Pensacola. You have been creeping along in the fog at 4 knots for the past few hours. You estimate an easterly set of a 1-knot current is reducing your speed over the ground to 3 knots. By dead reckoning, your position is 12 miles east of Mobile Bay Entrance buoy number 1. Soundings at 0721 show you are in 33 feet of water. It is one hour past low water at Fort Morgan, Mobile Point. You continue on a course of 270°T, sounding at 10 minute intervals. At 0731 your lead reads less a quarter five, or 29 feet. At 0741 the lead reads less a half, around 27 feet. The yarn in your lead line lets you refine this to 28 feet. At 0751 you sound 33 feet again, and at 0801 the bottom jumps back up to 28 feet. At 0811 it is down to 35 feet, and at 0821 sounds back up to 29. At 0831 you are back in 34 feet of water. You have been running for one hour and ten minutes at three knots. Can you determine where you are? You sure can.

Your first step is to take a sheet of paper and scale out the distances run between soundings. At three knots you would run a half mile every 10 minutes. With your dividers, mark off half-mile intervals to the scale of your chart along the edge of this sheet of paper. Some navigators prefer to use a piece of tissue paper; they draw a line on the tissue, and scale the distances off on the line. Either way is good enough. Beginning at the first mark, label each mark with the time and the sounding. Then take your piece of paper, cut a strip about one inch wide off the edge with the marks, and place the first 0721 mark over your DR position. Align the edge of the paper, or the line on the paper, if you are using tissue paper, in the direction of your course. Then slide the line around, keeping it parallel to your course until the 0721 mark is in 33 feet of water. Keep the 0721 mark in 33 feet, and slide the paper around until the 0731 mark is in 29 feet of water. Lo and behold, these marks on your paper, and their accompanying soundings correspond to a series of ridges and valleys on the Gulf bottom about three miles offshore in the Gulf of Mexico and nine or ten miles east of the Mobile Bay Entrance Channel. By lining these soundings up this way you get a pretty good idea of your location. You obviously are about 2½ miles north of your rhumb line. You have lost speed, and you have been set north. Without this series of soundings, you may have never detected this set. Had you continued

*From *Navigation and Nautical Tables* (International Textbook Co., 1909).

162

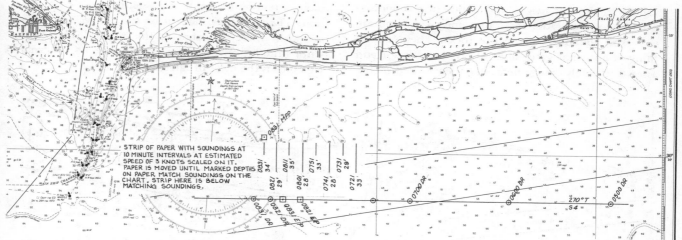

Figure 20-2. Using a chain of soundings to advantage.

on course you would likely have fetched up on the four-foot bar around buoy number 12.

You can't call this position at 0831 a fix, but you almost have to be about one mile inside the southeast corner of the fish haven shown on the chart. This is certainly your most probable position. Change course to 251°T until you can work up a course-to-steer current diagram to correct for the set and drift. Continue at four knots and keep on sounding. Set a danger sounding for your boat in these conditions at 30 feet. You should pick up the seabuoy.

The technique you used with this series of soundings is called *taking a chain of soundings.* Approaching Mobile you were lucky to run over distinctive bottom contours. On many coasts the bottom lends itself easily to the use of a chain of soundings. And too, don't wait an hour and ten minutes to start marking your chain of soundings on the paper. Do this as you go along. Make your first check on the chart as soon as you get your first two soundings. As time passes, and new soundings are scaled on the paper, you will see your track actually grow on the chart.

In restricted visibility, vessels use chains of soundings to find their course made good. I am not talking only about thick fog, but haze that may cut visibility to a mile or two. Time intervals and distances run are usually longer in these cases than the intervals you used in Figure 20-2. At 10 knots, take and log a sounding every 12 minutes, or every two miles run. Scale out a chain of soundings at two-mile intervals. Align them with your course. Or line them up reasonably near the direction of your course. You may not be making good the exact course you are steering, or the speed you are logging. If the soundings line up a

bit divergent with the course you are steering, and if the charted intervals between certain depths are consistently different from the scaled marks on your paper, your course and speed are being affected by a current. The difference in direction and difference in interval between actual soundings will indicate the course and speed your vessel is making good. I hope you have already corrected for leeway.

Soundings in navigation are so easy to use that some navigators just run the fathom curve in making an offshore coastal passage. This isn't a very refined way to navigate, but it works. When employed in conjunction with other techniques this can be a very good part of the navigator's procedures.

A bearing and a sounding may let you fix your position. If the depth of the water is constant, a bottom sample may be more important than the depth. In offshore navigation, where the order of accuracy is not as demanding, a radio bearing and a sounding may give you a very usable position. Look at Figure 20-3. A smack has been trying to beat a hurricane into Mobile. She has been unable to get her position for 24 hours. At 2340 she gets an RDF bearing of 348°T on Mobile Point. Her depth finder shows she is in 44 fathoms. This radio bearing and sounding have fixed her position as accurately as any other system could. The distance between the 40 and 50 fathom curves at this bearing is only about 2 miles. Had she been 10 miles closer in, and sounded between 21 and 22 fathoms, she would have been unable to fix her position closer than ten miles.

Again, the contour of the bottom has lent itself to the use of soundings. The topography of the ocean floor may be so flat that such exact position-finding would be impossible, or it may be a succession of ridges and

163

valleys so close in height and depth that soundings would be useless. And then, on some coasts, you are either off soundings or on the rocks. These are all things a good navigator must always be alert for and assess accurately. Judgement, experience, and meticulous attention to detail are essential to safe navigation. The crew may make it on the adage "never say die while there is a shot in the locker." The navigator's motto, on the other hand, must be, "eternal vigilance is the price of safety at sea."

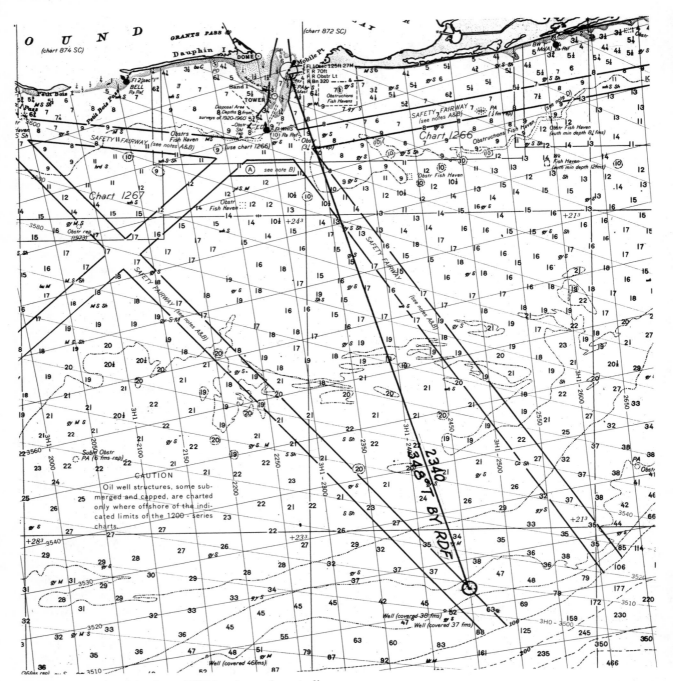

Figure 20-3. A position by an RDF bearing and a sounding.

21   RADIO NAVIGATION

Radio navigation is a facet of the art and science of navigation that is a study in itself. Yet, as the study of piloting is the traditional gateway to the study of celestial navigation, so, too, the study of piloting is the traditional beginning of the study of radio navigation. A work on piloting, to be complete, must cover the uses of radio direction finders — called RDFs — and loran, because this equipment is available on even very small vessels. Both are important tools of the navigator. I will leave the subjects of Decca, Omega, Consol, and Consolan for the specific study of radio navigation.

RADIO DIRECTION FINDERS

Proper results from any piece of equipment require equipment suited for the purpose and an operator sufficiently skilled in the operation of that equipment. Consider the radio direction finder. Those who have only a smattering of knowledge believe all you need do is turn the gear on, point it at a station, read the bearing, and plot it. There is a lot more to it than this.

A good RDF can be inexpensive compared to other equipment. For this reason you may find RDFs on outboard motorboats as well as ocean cargo ships. Very good portable RDFs can be obtained for use in small craft. Quality in RDF equipment does vary, and normally you get what you pay for. The inexpensive gear you rig on your 19-foot fisherman may be adequate for your needs, but it certainly will not give the performance a more sophisticated and more expensive piece of gear delivers.

At this time I am going to disclaim any technical knowledge, as such, regarding any electronic equipment. Unless you are an expert on electronic navigation gear, my recommendation is to buy your equipment from a reputable dealer, and buy equipment made by a reputable manufacturer. There are, however, several terms the rankest amateur should understand, if he intends to use RDF. One such term

is *sensitivity*. Sensitivity is the measure of a receiver's ability to receive a radio signal. The greater the sensitivity, the longer the range at which a set will receive a signal under a specific set of conditions. If your set does not have sufficient sensitivity, you may not receive the signal from a radiobeacon even within the beacon's effective range.

Another term is *selectivity*. Selectivity is the ability of a receiver to distinguish one signal — that is, one frequency — from others without interference. A receiver with poor selectivity will not give good results if other stations are on a near frequency. Such nearby, in frequency, stations will interfere with the reception of the signal you want.

Other desirable characteristics in RDF gear include sufficient moisture and saltwater resistance to permit the gear to survive aboard ship. The receiver should have a vertical sense antenna to preclude 180^0 ambiguity, and a null meter for the most accurate bearings.

RDFs work on the principle of directional sensitivity of a loop or horizontal antenna. The loop antenna was the common type used in early RDFs. Today, most RDFs have a built-in antenna consisting of a wire wound around a non-magnetic core. This antenna will be shaped like a round or flat bar. When the set or the antenna alone, if the antenna is rotatable, is positioned so its long axis is horizontal and points toward the transmitter, the sensitivity of the antenna is at its lowest. The weakest reception, or no reception, is experienced. The direction at which there is no reception is called the *null*. The null is used because the limits of the null direction are much easier to define than the limits of the maximum reception received when the axis of the antenna is 90^0 to the direction of the transmitter. The null may be determined by listening and judging in which direction the weakest signal is heard, or by reading the point at which the null meter indicates the weakest signal.

A problem with an RDF without a sense antenna is that you will receive a null no matter which end of the bar antenna points to the transmitter. Thus, as far as the RDF is concerned, the transmitter beacon may be either in the direction you are pointing the antenna or 180° opposite to this direction. This is the 180° ambiguity I spoke of previously. Unless you are really lost at sea and you are trying to get a bearing on Swan Island in the western Caribbean or some place like that, this 180° ambiguity is not often a serious problem. If you are off the Atlantic Coast, your station is going to be more or less west of you. In the Gulf of Mexico, the station will be on the west coast of Florida, east of you, or on the northern Gulf Coast, north of you. On the Pacific Coast, it would be hard to be east of a beacon unless it was on the Farallons or one of the channel islands. Even the rankest amateur navigator should have a DR that is accurate enough to tell him if he is getting a fair bearing or a reciprocal.

There are times, though, when taking bearings on lightship beacons, islands, or large navigational buoys, that 180° ambiguity can be a problem. For instance, you can lose all confidence in a DR if your boat has been hove to in a gale for several days. 180° ambiguity can be a real problem when trying to home on a low-power marker beacon in reduced visibility. To eliminate 180° ambiguity, some sets are equipped with a vertical sense antenna. In sets so equipped, a null is heard or seen only when the proper end of the antenna points to the radiobeacon. However, if your RDF does not have a vertical sense antenna, there is a way to tell the correct bearing of a radiobeacon. If your receiver cannot eliminate 180° ambiguity, simply wait long enough to detect a bearing change as you move along. If the bearing draws aft, it is the correct bearing. If the bearing draws forward, it is the reciprocal of the correct bearing.

At the moment, I am stating general principles that are relevant to all RDFs. When I next talk about homing or position-finding, I am going to assume you have reasonably good RDF gear, but we will take a quick look at some of the less sophisticated equipment. I am also going to mention the better than nothing — and not so bad — direction-finding potential of that darn transistor radio your kids have had blaring in your ear during the entire, otherwise pleasant, day.

Radiobeacons, and loran stations, too, are aids to navigation. Because of this, the *Light List* is an excellent source of information concerning radiobeacons, radio direction finders, and loran. In our study we will refer to the *Light List* for most of our information. For complete information concerning

radio aids to navigation, as well as other radio services available to the navigators, you should consult *H.O. 117, Radio Navigational Aids*. H.O. 117 A covers the U. S. Atlantic Coast, Gulf Coast, South America, Europe, the Mediterranean, and contiguous areas. H.O. 117 B covers the U. S. Pacific Coast, Pacific Ocean, west coast of South America, the Far East, and the Indian Ocean. You get these publications from the same place you buy charts.

A trick some of us who also fly airplanes use for rapid information concerning radiobeacons is to consult aeronautical sectional charts for marine beacon information. The best place to buy aeronautical sectional charts is from the fellow who operates the small plane hangar at your local airport. When you go to the airport, ask for the "general aviation fixed base operator," and someone should be able to give you the right directions. Marine beacons work well for airplanes, but *beware* of using *aeronautical beacons* for surface navigation. Both nautical charts and aeronautical charts list aeronautical radiobeacons, marine radiobeacons, and broadcast stations. But unless a beacon or station is calibrated for surface navigation, a serious error in bearing may be observed.

How accurate is an RDF for surface navigation? When good equipment, in good condition, is used by skilled operators to take bearings on radiobeacons properly calibrated for surface navigation, the order of accuracy is pretty high. Care should be taken to avoid bearings on radiobeacons or any station when a land mass intervenes between your receiver and the transmitter. Also, radio direction finder bearings may be unreliable around the times of sunrise and sunset, and to some degree these bearings are not reliable at night. Some authorities maintain that the resolution of RDF bearings is not fine enough to give results you can call a fix. Other equally competent persons claim you can get results closer than you can plot on a coastal chart, provided sea and atmospheric conditions are good.

Good conditions are essential to close resolution in any kind of navigation. For my money, RDF fixes are true fixes when the judgement of a competent navigator says his results are good enough to give a fix. After all, fixes are relative. A good celestial fix or a good loran fix may be several miles off. A good fix in pilot waters may tolerate only a few hundred yards of ambiguity, if that much. A radio direction finder bearing does have some lack of resolution. G. D. Dunlap in *Navigation and Finding Fish With Electronics* states that "the inherent accuracy of the system itself is said to be approximately plus or minus three degrees." A bearing on a beacon 150 miles off could be 3 miles on either side of the mean, even assuming operator, equipment, and conditions are excellent. This is within the bounds of realistic celestial navigation in small craft.

Skill in the operation of RDF equipment can be gained only through practice. Just as you should practice with your sextant in familiar water to gain the necessary confidence to use your sextant competently in strange water, you should also practice with your RDF in clear weather in waters where you can check your results. That is how skill and confidence are developed. Don't wait until a dark night when a dense fog catches you to turn on your RDF for the first time. Merely figuring out what all the knobs are for will distract you at a time when all your attention should be directed at the lead line, the lookout, and your prayer book.

No matter how good you are, and no matter how good your gear is, your RDF must be calibrated. Special radio direction finder calibration stations have been established for this purpose. Your *Light List* explains the use of these RDF calibration stations. To calibrate your RDF, install it in its permanent location on your boat. If it is a portable or hand-held RDF, place it and yourself where you are going to be when taking bearings. Select a radio-beacon, and run in a leisurely circle off the beacon. At every five-degree change in heading, take simultaneous pelorus and RDF bearings. Tabulate the pelorus bearings against the RDF bearings. With this information, make up a calibration table, and put it on or by your set (see Figure 21-1). In the table, note that the calibration error depends on the *relative bearing* of the beacon from your boat. The reason for this is that radio bearings are deflected by rigging, superstructure, and other magnetic influences. Normally RDF bearings from dead ahead will have the least deflection.

Some portable RDFs are equipped with a magnetic compass, and this arrangement removes the need for a calibration table. Bearings taken with such an RDF are much the same as visual bearings taken with a

RELATIVE BEARING	RDF BEARING	RELATIVE BEARING	RDF BEARING	RELATIVE BEARING	RDF BEARING	RELATIVE BEARING	RDF BEARING
000°	000°	095°	095°	185°	185°	275°	275°
005°	005°	100°	101°	190°	190°	280°	279°
010°	009°	105°	106°	195°	194°	285°	284°
015°	014°	110°	111°	200°	199°	290°	289°
020°	018°	115°	117°	205°	204°	295°	294°
025°	023°	120°	112°	210°	208°	300°	298°
030°	027°	125°	126	215°	213°	305°	303°
035°	031°	130°	133°	220°	218°	310°	306°
040°	037°	135°	138°	225°	222°	315°	311°
045°	042°	140°	144°	230°	227°	320°	317°
050°	048°	145°	149°	235°	233°	325°	322°
055°	053°	150°	155°	240°	238°	330°	328°
060°	058°	155°	154°	245°	243°	340°	333°
065°	064°	160°	161°	250°	248	345°	338°
070°	069°	165°	166°	255°	254°	350°	340°
075°	075°	170°	170°	260°	259°	355°	249°
080°	080°	175°	175°	265°	265°	360°	355°
085°	085°	180°	180°	270°	270°	365°	360°
090°	090°						

Figure 21-1. Radio direction finder calibration table.

hand-held bearing compass. You must correct such bearings for compass error. Careful compensation of the compass can remove much or all of the deviation error, but you must still apply variation to get a true bearing. Most RDFs, however, are equipped to take relative bearings. There is a dumb compass (see Chapter 12) incorporated into these RDF sets. Just as the dumb compass of a pelorus may be aligned with the boat's course, so may the dumb compass of the RDF be lined up with the boat's course. But, for the same reason relative bearings are preferred by most navigators when using a pelorus, you will most likely prefer aligning the dumb compass of your RDF so that 000⁰ is dead ahead and 180⁰ is dead astern. As with pelorus bearings, a relative bearing by RDF on a radiobeacon requires two people. The relative bearing must be corrected for calibration error, and then corrected to a true bearing. If the transmitter is over 50 miles from your DR position, you must also correct your RDF bearing for conversion angle.

Conversion angle is the difference between a Mercator bearing and a great circle bearing on an object. Radio waves travel the shortest distance between two points. On a sphere, this distance is the shorter arc of a great circle. The earth is a sphere, so radio direction finder bearings are great circle bearings. You are going to plot these bearings as a rhumb line on a Mercator chart. In the northern hemisphere, great circles curve toward the north pole, and in the southern hemisphere great circles curve toward the south pole. Thus radio bearings will be received at an angle tending more toward the pole than the angle at which the rhumb line bearing would plot. This difference in angle is the conversion angle. You get conversion angle corrections from conversion angle correction tables. To apply conversion angle corrections, there are four rules applicable:

1. In the northern hemisphere, if the radiobeacon is east of the ship, the conversion angle correction is added to the observed RDF bearing.
2. In the northern hemisphere, if the radiobeacon is west of the ship, the conversion angle is subtracted from the observed RDF bearing.
3. In the southern hemisphere, if the radiobeacon is east of the ship, the conversion angle correction is subtracted from the observed RDF bearing.
4. In the southern hemisphere, if the radiobeacon is west of the ship, the conversion angle correction is added to the observed RDF bearing.

Conversion angle corrections are applied only to bearings on stations over 50 miles from the ship. On a vessel equipped with a drafting machine for plotting, a first-rate RDF and an excellent compass to correlate relative bearings to this 50-mile minimum is realistic. On a small vessel, using parallel rulers to plot bearings taken with a bouncing RDF and compass, 150 miles may be more realistic. As your DR and/or the station's position approaches the poles, the conversion angle correction becomes greater at lesser distances. When the ship's DR and the radiobeacon are on the same meridian of longitude, no conversion angle correction is necessary, because the meridian is a great circle that also plots as a rhumb line on a Mercator chart.

Assume you are in *War Hat* on a passage from Panama City, Florida, to New Orleans via the Mississippi River Gulf Outlet. You do not have loran, and your soundings have been coming in at a monotonous 21 to 22 fathoms for several hours. An overcast sky prevents any celestial observations. You are steering 262°C at a speed of 8 knots. Your best source of position information is your radio direction finder. Your first job is to select at least two suitable radiobeacons in order to get two RDF bearings.

Open your *Light List*. In the general information section, radiobeacons are explained on pages xviii and pages xxi to xxiii. Read these pages carefully. Beginning on page xxi you will find a sequential list of the radiobeacons in the Atlantic and Gulf Coast Radiobeacon System. The list starts with the group of beacons sharing the lowest frequency, 286 kHz, and continues, by steps in frequencies, through 324 kHz. On page xxii you will see the radiobeacons for the area between Panama City and the mouth of the Mississippi River (see Figure 21-2). There are five radiobeacons listed, and they all share 320 kHz. Each of these radiobeacons broadcasts in turn for one minute. The beacon transmits a distinctive series of dots and dashes as an identifying signal for the first 48 seconds of the broadcast period, then a two-second pause followed by a 10-second dash. Although the dots and dashes are recognizable as single or double Morse code characters, the signals are not Morse code signals in that they are transmitted at a much slower rate than, and without the rhythm of, a Morse code keyed character. The signals are thus readable by an untrained ear. You are now ready for the first step in getting your RDF fix.

STEP 1

Bring your DR up to the time of observation. This is always the first part of the solution of any navigational problem. Assume the time is 1020 and your 1020 DR is latitude 29° 30.'0 N, longitude 88° 13.'3 W.

SEQUENCED

Freq. kHz	Group Sequence	Station	Characteristic	Range (miles)	Lat. (N) ° ′ ″	Long. (W) ° ′ ″
314	I	MOUNT DESERT	B (▬ • • •)	20	43 58 07	68 07 44
	II	MATINICUS ROCK	P (• ▬ ▬ •)	20	43 47 01	68 51 19
	III	MANANA ISLAND	OE (▬ ▬ ▬ •)	100	43 45 48	69 19 38
	IV	HALFWAY ROCK	O (▬ ▬ ▬)	20	43 39 21	70 02 15
	V	EASTERN POINT	RT (• ▬ • ▬)	20	42 34 50	70 39 54
	VI	PORTLAND L.S.	K (▬ • ▬)	50	43 31 37	70 05 31
320	I	SOUTHWEST PASS ENT.	OT (▬ ▬ ▬ ▬)	80	28 54 19	89 25 43
	II	SOUTH PASS WEST JETTY	M (▬ ▬)	125	28 59 25	89 08 29
	III	MOBILE POINT	C (▬ • ▬ •)	125	30 13 38	88 01 24
	IV	CAPE SAN BLAS	W (• ▬ ▬)	55	29 40 10	85 21 26
	VI	MOBILE POINT	C (▬ • ▬ •)	125	30 13 38	88 01 24
324	II	BUTLER FLATS	R (• ▬ •)	20	41 36 13	70 53 42
	III	NOBSKA POINT	G (▬ ▬ •)	20	41 30 58	70 39 20
	IV	CLEVELAND LEDGE	C (▬ • ▬ •)	20	41 37 51	70 41 42
	V	CAPE COD CANAL	U (• • ▬)	20	41 46 28	70 29 50

CONTINUOUS

Freq. kHz	Station	Characteristic	Range (miles)	Lat. (N) ° ′ ″	Long. (W) ° ′ ″
286	DRY TORTUGAS	OE (▬ ▬ ▬ •)	130	24 37 56	82 55 18
288	PUNTA TUNA	X (▬ • • ▬)	55	17 59 25	65 53 08
290	CHESAPEAKE LIGHT	P (• ▬ ▬ •)	70	36 54 15	75 42 47
296	ISLA MONA	O (▬ ▬ ▬)	75	18 05 19	67 50 48
306	ST. JOHNS	R (• ▬ •)	55	30 23 09	81 23 51
310	EGMONT KEY	H (• • • •)	170	27 36 02	82 45 39
314	BRAZOS SANTIAGO	PIL (• ▬ ▬ • • • • ▬ • •)	350	26 04 23	97 09 51
315	HATTERAS INLET	N (• ▬)	30	35 11 50	75 43 57
317	SAVANNAH	UT (• • ▬ ▬)	20	31 56 57	80 41 00
318	SAN JUAN	L (• ▬ • •)	55	18 28 14	66 07 03

MARKER

Freq. kHz	Station	Lat. (N) ° ′ ″	Long. (W) ° ′ ″
290	FREEPORT	28 56 27	95 18 04
292	BRENTON REEF	41 25 35	71 23 22
294	SANDY HOOK LIGHTED HORN BUOY 2A	40 26 31	73 55 01
294	OCEAN CITY INLET	38 19 30	75 05 18
294	MISSISSIPPI RIVER—GULF OUTLET APPROACH LIGHTED HORN BUOY NO	29 26 22	88 56 51
302	MANASQUAN INLET	40 06 02	74 01 58
308	INDIAN RIVER INLET	38 36 34	75 03 47
311	SHINNECOCK INLET	40 50 32	72 28 44
316	ABSECON INLET	39 21 57	74 24 37
317	JONES INLET	40 34 50	73 34 24
320	THE CUCKOLDS	43 46 46	69 39 02
320	SAYBROOK BREAKWATER	41 15 47	72 20 36
322	BARNEGAT INLET	39 45 28	74 06 30
324	CAPE MAY	38 56 38	74 52 20
324	(Wachapreague Inlet) PARRAMORE BEACH	37 34 24	75 37 03
326	ROCKAWAY INLET	40 33 07	73 56 22

Figure 21-2. Excerpt of the radiobeacon list in the *Light List*.

STEP 2

Select two or more suitable radiobeacons on which to take an RDF bearing. Your first consideration is to determine if there are any stations within range of your boat. The fifth column of the table in Figure 21-2 gives the range of radiobeacons in nautical miles. You select South Pass West Jetty at the mouth of the Mississippi River, identifier "M", two dashes and number two in the sequence. You select South Pass because this radiobeacon has a range of 125 miles. The only other radiobeacon with a range suitable for reception from your DR is Mobile Point, identifier "C", dash-dot-dash-dot. You get a little fringe benefit because Mobile Point has two places in the sequence, three and six. You can also hear Southwest Pass Entrance radiobeacon, but your DR is just within the maximum range of the Southwest Pass Entrance transmitter, and the bearing from your DR is very near the bearing of the South Pass transmitter. Keep Southwest Pass Entrance in mind, however, just in case South Pass is off the air for some reason. For your fix you select South Pass and Mobile Point.

STEP 3

You now must determine when each of these radio-beacons broadcasts. The *Light List* tells you that each one broadcasts for exactly one minute, with number one in sequence beginning precisely on the hour. Number two begins at the hour + 1 minute, number three at the hour + 2 minutes. The easiest way to find the time of broadcast of each radio-beacon is to make a table such as the one in Figure 21-3. From this table you can see that South Pass radiobeacon is on the air for exactly one minute after your 1020 ship's time at 1025, 1031, 1037, 1043, and on through the hour at six-minute intervals. Mobile Point broadcasts at 1020, 1023, 1026, 1029, 1032, 1035, and so through the hour at three-minute intervals, since it has two spots in the sequence.

STEP 4

Take RDF bearings on Mobile Point and South Pass. At 1023 you get a good, sharp null on Mobile Point bearing 115°R. At 1025 you get another one on South Pass bearing 334°R. These two bearings are relative bearings, and you must correct them exactly as you would relative bearings taken with a pelorus. But first extract the corrected relative bearing — corrected for calibration error — from the table in Figure 21-1. Interpolate by inspection, if necessary.

	Mobile Point	South Pass
Observed Bearing	115°	334°
Corrected Relative Bearing	117°	332°

STEP 5

Correct your compass course of 262° to a true course:

C 262°
D 8°W
M 254°
V 4°E
T 258°

STEP 6

Add your corrected relative bearings to your true course:

	Mobile Point	South Pass
Relative Bearing	117°	332°
True Course	258°	258°
	375°	590°
	-360°	-360°
True Bearing	015°	230°

STEP 7

Your 1020 DR at Latitude 29° 30.′0 N, Longitude 88° 13.′3 W is 60 miles from the radiobeacon at South Pass. You must correct the bearing on South Pass Jetty for the conversion angle. The conversion angle correction is applied to RDF bearings taken on stations over 50 miles away. As your DR is only 40.5 miles from Mobile Point, no conversion angle correction is necessary to the bearing on Mobile Point.

To obtain the conversion angle correction you can open *Bowditch* to Table 1. Table 1 is a dual-purpose table set up to provide conversion angle corrections to RDF bearings; it is also set up to be used as a means of finding great circle courses. Unless you are using RDF bearings on stations at great distances, the first part of Table 1 will suffice. But RDF bearings at distances beyond 4.05 degrees difference in longitude are feasible. In this case you must refer to the second part of the table; using it can be tedious. Fortunately, the *Coast Pilot,* which refers the reader to the *Light List* every time radiobeacons and radio direction finders are mentioned, changes its policy, and publishes an excellent radio bearing conversion table (see Figure 21-4). This table in the *Coast Pilot* can be used with differences of longitude as great as 10°.

STATION AND SEQUENCE	TIME IN MINUTES TO ADD TO EVEN HOUR									
I SOUTHWEST PASS	0	6	12	18	24	30	36	42	48	54
II SOUTH PASS	1	7	13	19	25	31	37	43	49	55
III MOBILE POINT	2	8	14	20	26	32	38	44	50	56
IV CAPE SAN BLAS	3	9	15	21	27	33	39	45	51	57
V VACANT	4	10	16	22	28	34	40	46	52	58
VI MOBILE POINT	5	11	17	23	29	35	41	47	53	59

Figure 21-3. Radiobeacon broadcast sequence.

Table of corrections, in minutes
[DIFFERENCE OF LONGITUDE IN DEGREES]

Mid. L.	½°	1°	1½°	2°	2½°	3°	3½°	4°	4½°	5°	5½°	6°	6½°	7°	7½°	8°	8½°	9°	9½°	10°
15°	4	8	12	16	19	23	27	31	35	40	43	47	50	54	58	62	66	70	74	78
16°	4	8	12	17	21	25	29	33	37	41	45	50	54	58	62	66	70	74	79	83
17°	4	9	13	18	22	26	31	35	39	44	48	53	57	61	66	70	75	79	83	88
18°	5	9	13	19	23	28	32	37	42	46	51	56	60	65	70	74	79	83	88	93
19°	5	10	15	20	24	29	34	39	44	49	54	59	63	68	73	78	83	88	93	98
20°	5	10	15	21	26	31	36	41	46	51	56	62	67	72	77	82	87	92	98	103
21°	5	11	16	21	27	32	38	43	48	54	59	64	70	75	81	86	91	97	102	108
22°	6	11	17	22	28	34	39	45	51	56	62	67	73	79	84	90	96	101	107	112
23°	6	12	18	23	29	35	41	47	53	59	64	70	76	82	88	94	100	105	111	117
24°	6	12	18	24	31	37	43	49	55	61	67	73	79	85	92	98	104	110	116	122
25°	6	13	19	25	32	38	44	51	57	63	70	76	82	89	95	101	108	114	120	127
26°	7	13	20	26	33	39	46	53	59	66	72	79	85	92	99	105	112	118	125	131
27°	7	14	20	27	34	41	48	54	61	68	75	82	89	95	102	109	116	123	129	136
28°	7	14	21	28	35	42	49	56	63	70	77	84	92	99	106	113	120	127	134	141
29°	7	15	21	29	36	44	51	58	65	73	80	87	95	102	109	116	124	131	138	145
30°	7	15	22	30	38	45	53	60	68	75	83	90	98	105	113	120	127	135	143	150
31°	8	15	23	31	39	46	54	62	70	77	85	93	100	108	116	124	131	139	146	155
32°	8	16	24	32	40	48	56	64	72	79	87	95	103	111	119	127	135	143	151	159
33°	8	16	25	33	41	49	57	65	74	82	90	98	106	114	123	131	139	147	155	163
34°	8	17	25	34	42	50	59	67	75	84	92	101	109	117	126	134	143	151	159	168
35°	9	17	26	34	43	52	60	69	77	86	95	103	112	120	129	138	146	155	163	172
36°	9	18	26	35	44	53	62	71	79	88	97	106	115	123	132	141	150	159	168	176
37°	9	18	27	36	45	54	63	72	81	90	99	108	117	126	135	144	153	163	172	181
38°	9	18	28	37	46	55	65	74	83	92	102	111	120	129	139	148	157	166	175	185
39°	9	19	28	38	47	57	66	75	85	94	104	113	123	132	142	151	160	170	179	189
40°	10	19	29	39	48	58	68	77	87	96	106	116	125	135	145	154	164	174	183	193
41°	10	20	30	39	49	59	69	79	89	98	108	118	128	138	148	157	167	177	187	197
42°	10	20	30	40	50	60	70	80	90	100	110	120	130	140	151	161	171	181	191	201
43°	10	20	31	41	51	61	72	82	92	102	113	123	133	143	153	164	174	184	194	205
44°	10	21	31	42	52	63	73	83	94	104	115	125	135	146	156	167	177	188	198	208
45°	11	21	32	42	53	64	74	85	95	106	117	127	138	149	159	170	180	191	201	212
46°	11	22	32	43	54	65	76	86	97	108	119	129	140	151	162	173	183	194	205	216
47°	11	22	33	44	55	66	77	88	99	110	121	132	143	154	165	176	186	197	208	219
48°	11	22	33	45	56	67	78	89	100	111	123	134	145	156	167	178	190	201	212	223
49°	11	23	34	45	57	68	79	91	102	113	125	136	147	158	170	181	192	204	215	226
50°	11	23	34	46	57	69	80	92	103	115	126	138	149	161	172	184	195	207	218	230
51°	12	23	35	47	58	70	82	93	105	117	128	140	152	163	175	186	198	210	221	233
52°	12	24	35	47	59	71	83	95	106	118	130	142	154	165	177	189	201	213	225	236
53°	12	24	36	48	60	72	84	96	108	120	132	144	156	168	180	192	204	216	228	240
54°	12	24	36	49	61	73	85	97	109	121	133	146	158	170	182	194	206	218	231	243
55°	12	25	37	49	61	74	86	98	111	123	135	147	160	172	184	197	209	221	233	246
56°	12	25	37	50	62	75	87	100	112	124	137	149	162	174	187	199	211	224	236	249
57°	13	25	38	50	63	75	88	101	113	126	138	151	164	176	189	201	214	226	239	252
58°	13	25	38	51	64	76	89	102	115	127	140	153	165	178	191	204	216	229	242	254
59°	13	26	39	51	64	77	90	103	116	129	141	154	167	180	193	206	219	231	244	257
60°	13	26	39	52	65	78	91	104	117	130	143	156	169	182	195	208	221	234	247	260

Example.   A ship in latitude 39°51′. N., longitude 67°35′ W., by dead reckoning, obtains a radio bearing of 299° true on the radiobeacon located in latitude 40°37′. N., longitude 69°37′ W.

Radiobeacon station_____ Latitude   40°37′ N.
Dead-reckoning position of ship_____ Latitude   39°51′

Middle latitude_____   40°14′
Radiobeacon station_____ Longitude   69°37′ W.
Dead reckoning position of ship_____ Longitude   67°35′

Longitude difference_____   2°02′

Entering the table with difference of longitude equals 2°, which is the nearest tabulated value and opposite 40° middle latitude, the correction of 39′ is read.

As the ship is east of the radiobeacon, a minus correction is applied. The Mercator bearing then will be 299° − 000°39′ = 298°21′. To facilitate plotting, subtract 180° and plot from the position of the radiobeacon the bearing 298°21′ − 180°, or 118°21′ (Mercator bearing reckoned clockwise from true north).

Figure 21-4.   Radio bearing conversion table from the *Light List.*

Another excellent radio bearing conversion table is found in H. O. 117. In most cases, however, the conversion angle correction is often so small it is beyond the limit of resolution you can measure with an RDF in a bouncing small boat in a rough sea. But, when conditions are good, applying even a small conversion angle correction can further refine an RDF bearing.

Page xxii of the *Light List* (Figure 21-2) gives the position of South Pass West Jetty radiobeacon as Latitude 28° 59.'25 N, Longitude 89° 08.'29 W. Note this position is to the nearest second of arc. For conversion angle corrections, you need work only to the nearest degree of arc for latitude, and only to the nearest half degree of arc for longitude. To find the difference of latitude, subtract the DR latitude from the latitude of the radiobeacon, and to find the difference of longitude, subtract the DR longitude from the longitude of the radiobeacon.

DR	Lat. 29°30.'0N	Long. 88°13.'3W
South Pass	Lat. 28°59.'4N	Long. 89°08.'5W

	Diff.		Diff.	
	Lat.	30.'6N	Long.	55.'2W
			or	1°0.'0W

Since you must use middle latitude as an argument to enter the table, divide 30.'6 by 2, and add this to 28°59.'4. Middle latitude is the latitude halfway between two latitudes on the same side of the equator.

$$28°59.'4$$
$$+ \ 15.'3$$
$$29°14.'7 \quad \text{Middle Lat.}$$

Middle latitude can also be defined as half the sum of two latitudes on the same side of the equator. You could have added your DR latitude of 29°30.'0 N to the latitude of South Pass, 28°59.'4 N. The sum would be 58°29.'4. If you divide this sum by 2, the result is 29°14.'7 N, the middle latitude.

Your arguments for entering the conversion table are: middle latitude 29°; difference of longitude 1°. From the table, a correction of 15' must be subtracted from the observed RDF bearing.

A 15' correction is hardly enough to plot with the tools you have aboard a small vessel such as *WarHat*. If you received a long range bearing on a station with a middle latitude of 27° and a difference of longitude of 6°, the conversion angle correction would be 82', or 1°.4. This correction is significant at a distance of several hundred miles.

STEP 8
Plot your 1025 RDF fix from a bearing on Mobile Point of 015°T and a bearing on South Pass Jetty

of 230°T. The 15' conversion angle correction is ignored in this case. If you want to be meticulous, you can advance the 1023 Mobile Point LOP one-third of a mile, but the inherent error in RDF bearings, plus the scale of the chart, make this really unnecessary.

In summary: If you familiarize yourself with your gear; practice enough to develop your skill; buy good equipment to start with and install the equipment properly; carefully make up a calibration table for the gear, after the gear is installed; be aware of the inherent error in your RDF; avoid too much reliance on bearings taken around sunrise and sunset and to some extent at night; correct your bearings properly; and plot your positions carefully, you can obtain quite good fixes with radio direction finders.

This isn't quite the same as turning the gear on and pointing it, is it?

Some boats are equipped with automatic direction finders, called ADFs. An automatic direction finder is a radio direction finder that automatically trains to the station being received. A needle on a dial points to the relative bearing of the station. This relieves the operator of the need to train the antenna to receive a null. If the ADF is properly located, one person can steer and observe a bearing with an ADF. An ADF is an excellent piece of gear, but ADFs usually cost a good bit more than RDFs.

Radiobeacons are also used for homing. A ship desiring to go to the beacon turns until the RDF bearing is 000°R, and steers to keep the station dead ahead. Be sure to eliminate any 180° ambiguity, or you may steer away from the station. You may find you have to change course from time to time to keep the radiobeacon dead ahead as a result of leeway or the set and drift of a current. When homing on a radiobeacon, care must be taken not to run your vessel on any rocks, reefs, or other hazards between your boat and the radiobeacon. If the radiobeacon is on a large navigation buoy or a lightship, you also must take care to avoid running the station down. Generally speaking, the best precaution in cases like this is to steer with the radiobeacon a few degrees on your bow.

If you can get a bearing on only one radiobeacon or one beacon at a time, you can advance RDF lines of position to get a running fix by RDF just as you can advance an LOP from a visual bearing. It is even possible to use the techniques of doubling the angle and other angles on the bow, if you want.

Some radiobeacons have a distance-finding capability and are listed as such. The use of such a radiobeacon is not limited to vessels equipped with radio direction finders. All you need is a radio to receive the radiobeacon. You must be close enough to the station to receive any sound signal emitted. All a distance-finding station does is broadcast a sound signal and a radio signal at the same instant. Radio waves travel at the speed of light, 186,000 miles per second, and are thus received instantaneously on board your boat. Sound travels at an average of 1,120 feet per second.

To compute your distance off a station, time the interval in seconds between the instant you first hear the radio signal and the instant you first hear the sound signal. You should do this timing with a stop watch. Divide the number of seconds in the time interval by 5.5. The result is your distance off. So, if you hear the radio signal from a beacon, and 28 seconds later you hear the sound signal, how far off are you? 28 divided by 5.5 is 5.09. You are 5.09 miles off the beacon. The *Light List* maintains that the order of accuracy with this method of finding distance off is within 10 percent.

The possibilities for applying the techniques of radio direction finding aboard any vessel are too well within the reach of any serious boatman not to be used. As I said earlier, good portable equipment can be bought at a very reasonable cost. On top of this a lot of very good radios, although not designed for radio direction finding purposes *per se,* have excellent direction-finding capability.

The radio in Figure 21-5 is a Zenith Trans-Oceanic Royall 3000-1. It is several years old. Of course, this is about as good a portable radio as you can get. Zenith does make a deluxe model of the Trans-Oceanic. Nevertheless, this radio was not bought for use as an RDF, but is used primarily for receiving time signals, weather broadcasts, navigation information, and entertainment. But, since this set can receive any frequency in the radiobeacon system, and the antenna is highly directional, it functions well as an RDF. I adapted the radio for RDF use by building the box and compass arrangement to fit over the antenna in the handle.

Credit for the idea of using the compass as in Figure 21-5 belongs to Mr. Hiram Hamilton Maxim and his article in the *National Fisherman* (January, 1972). Mr. Maxim very kindly sent me a copy of his article and detailed instructions, including sketches, on how to build this compass mounting assembly. Mr. Maxim did a workmanlike job of assembling his adapter, as evidenced by the illustration accompanying his article. He also used a much better quality compass than I did. With this arrangement on a Zenith Super Navigator (which is a portable RDF in its own right), Mr. Maxim gets results of finer resolution than it is possible to plot on a 1200 series chart.

Figure 21-5. A portable radio adapted for RDF use.

I must confess that my rig is not as well done as Mr. Maxim's. I used a very inexpensive compass to start with. The compass does have compensating magnets in it, however, and this is important. The box, which simply fits snugly over the radio's handle and antenna, is knocked together out of scrap plywood. My wife very kindly daubed a coat of red paint on the box to hide my sins and make it easy for me to find. The stanchion on which the compass is mounted is a piece of ¾-inch aluminum conduit. Aluminum is non-magnetic. The end of the conduit that goes into the plywood box is threaded and screwed into a hole bored in the wood. A piece of broomstick is driven into the top of the conduit, and the compass mount is screwed into the broomstick. I *was* careful to line up the lubber's line of the compass with the long axis of the antenna. With this rig, I can get lines of position within less than a quarter of a mile of accuracy on a radiobeacon 15 miles away. I can see how Mr. Maxim gets the results he claims with his set.

My point in all this is: you, too, can adapt any suitable radio in this manner. If you have a portable radio that can receive marine radiobeacons, you can convert it into an RDF with this assembly. If you have an RDF with a dumb compass, this rig will make taking RDF bearings a one-man job instead of a two-man job. But before you tackle the project of making and using a device such as this, I urge you to read Mr. Maxim's article.

Commercial broadcast stations are not calibrated for radio direction finding. Often the antennas of commerical stations are inland. Nevertheless, your charts will show the locations of the antennas of some commercial broadcast stations. Why? Because, when nothing else can be received, a bearing on such a station may be a lot better than nothing. I will never forget a Friday morning off the northwest coast of Africa when an RDF bearing on a Moroccan broadcast station and a sun line kept us from making a possibly fatal mistake. In your home waters, I urge you to take bearings on any station appearing on your chart. This goes for aeronautical beacons, too. Compare the fixes you get from these bearings with a known position, and you can get an index of the accuracy available. Information like this can be a Godsend later, if thick weather catches you.

That noisy, squeaky, scratchy little thing your son or daughter keeps blaring away in your ear all day can also get you out of trouble — maybe. Someday, when the youngster is distracted, purloin the little set and see what it can do. Even the cheapest of these little radios usually have directional antennas. They seldom receive anything but commercial broadcast stations, but, as I said before, this is better than nothing. Tune the set to a radio station appearing on your chart. Then turn the set slowly around the horizon. You will probably get a null when the antenna points to the station.

Before you try to take a bearing, you must know the way the axis of the antenna lies in the set, so you will know when the antenna is pointing toward the station. In almost every case, the antenna's long axis will be horizontal and parallel to the longest dimension of the radio's chassis. The easiest way to check this is at your mooring. If you have any business having a boat at all, you should be able to locate on a chart your marina and the best radio station to take a bearing on. Plot this bearing, and then turn on the little one's transistor radio, tuned to the station. Turn the radio around slowly, and see if you get a null. Notice which sides of the radio point to the radio station. These are the sides that parallel the antenna. You are now ready to take a bearing with this set, if you ever have to. But before you do, a couple of "don'ts" are in order. Don't turn the volume too high. The volume should be only high enough to hear the station with ease. With the volume too high the signal may override the null, and you won't be able to detect it. Practice with the set will tell you when the volume is high enough to get a good signal, but low enough to get a definite null when the radio is on the bearing. Also, don't try to take bearings on broadcast stations that are too close. The high signal strength of nearby stations will override any null.

I first saw the idea I am using in Figure 21-6 explained in *Rudder* magazine many years ago. Needless to say, your kid's transistor radio does not have a compass or pelorus on it. You can use the compass rose of your chart as a pelorus. Fold the chart, if

necessary, precisely along a meridian of longitude and a parallel of latitude so the compass rose is face up. Align the chart so the meridians are parallel to your boat's keel and the parallels of latitude are exactly perpendicular to the axis of the keel. The 000° of the compass rose should point dead ahead. The edge of the chart table or dinette may be a good reference point for lining up the chart. Place the little radio on the chart so that one edge of the set, an edge parallel to the bar antenna, passes through the center of the compass rose. Keep this edge passing through the center of the compass rose, and carefully turn the radio until you get a null. Sound out "mark." Read the relative bearing of the station off the compass rose. When the helmsman gives you the compass heading, convert the relative bearing to a true bearing and plot it. Check to see how accurate your results are.

Someday you and the family may be out fishing in the family runabout. Fog socks in. What do you do? How do you find your way home? You hear Junior's radio blaring softly away in the cuddy. Here is your answer. If you have done your homework, you are not licked yet. Of course, if, when you go below, you find that he has one of these little radios shaped like an apple or a pear, with no straight sides . . . well, everybody's luck runs out sometime.

LORAN

Loran is a hyperbolic system of electronic navigation. Two systems are available to the navigator, loran A and loran C. Loran A is by far the most frequently used by our fishermen, yachtsmen, and operators of small commercial craft. Loran C is a totally different system of greater accuracy and range than loran A. But loran C equipment is expensive and complex. We will devote our discussion to loran A.

There are a few basic principles involved with loran A that must be covered here. For a more thorough discussion of these principles, however, see *Navigation and Finding Fish With Electronics* by G. D. Dunlap and *Bowditch*.

Loran A is a hyperbolic system because the loran lines of position are hyperbolas. When points of equal *difference* in distance between two fixed points are plotted on a graph, or chart, these points plot as hyperbolic curves. This hyperbolic curve is a curved line of position. The two points, or foci, of the hyperbola that plot as a loran line of position are the locations of a pair of transmitter stations called a master station and a slave station. The master station transmits a pulsed signal, and, after a carefully timed delay, a signal is sent by the slave station. These stations may be separated by distances

Figure 21-6. Taking a bearing with a portable radio.

of 200 to 700 miles, and are called loran pairs. The loran A receiver aboard a vessel measures the difference in time required to receive the signal from the master station and the signal from the slave station. This *difference in time* is a function of the *difference in distance* between the master and slave station at your position or any position on the particular loran LOP resulting from the time difference measured. Thus, it is possible to compute or plot a hyperbolic curve on which this time difference is constant. And, as your set recorded this as the *time* difference at your position, your position must be somewhere on this curve. Lucky you, the navigator. You do not have to compute these curves. They are already computed and plotted on loran charts, such as Chart No. 1115, which we have been using, or they are tabulated in loran tables.

You are a navigator in the Gulf of Mexico, on a boat equipped with loran A. When you finish carefully turning the knobs on your set, and you get a satisfactory display, your loran set will give you a readout of, say, 3H0 3541. You go through this knob twisting routine again, and come up with a readout of 3H1 2273. What do all these number, letter, number combinations mean? What did you do to get this readout? And, now that you have these two combinations of numbers and letters, what do you do with them? When you can answer these three questions, you can call yourself a loran operator.

First, let's look at the meaning of the letters and numbers. You have two combinations, 3H0 3541 and 3H1 2273. The first number, 3, is the channel or frequency your receiver is tuned to. Channel 3 broadcasts on 1900 kHz. All loran pairs in the Gulf of Mexico broadcast on channel 3. Two other channels are available in other parts of the world. Channel 1 transmits on 1950 kHz, and channel 2 transmits on

1850 kHz. You must select a channel for the area your vessel is in.

The letter H, in the two cases above, indicates the *basic pulse repetition rate* at which the stations transmit. By varying this basic pulse repetition rate, it is possible for several stations to transmit on the same channel in the same reception area, without interfering with each other. H, for high, is the basic pulse repetition rate used by stations in the Gulf of Mexico. Other rates — L, S, SC, SH, SL, and SS — are used in other areas.

To broaden further the utilization of frequencies, basic pulse repetition rates are varied by a specific variation in the pulse rate. The third digit in the number-letter-number series, such as 3H0 or 3H1, indicates this *specific pulse repetition rate*.

To tune your loran A receiver, you must select a channel, a basic pulse repetition rate, and a specific pulse repetition rate. Figure 1302 A, page 332 of the 1962 edition of *Bowditch,* shows the channel, basic pulse repetition rate, and specific pulse repetition for loran pairs around the world. This same information is provided on pages ii and iii of the *Loran A Tables, H.O. 221,* which can be purchased from your Hydrographic agent.

The last group of digits, such as the 3541 of 3H0 3541 or the 2273 of 3H1 2273, are the number of microseconds of time difference your set measured in receiving the signals from the loran pair. To plot a loran line of position you must have this information. This, plus your channel and pulse repetition rates, tell you where your curved loran LOP plots. Navigators refer to this three-letter channel, base repetition rate, and specific repetition rate combination, such as 3H0, as a "rate."

How did you get this information? You got it by carefully selecting a rate, and tuning and turning knobs on your loran A receiver. And what is involved in this? Not too much, but enough to require your careful attention. To describe how you, as navigator of *War Hat*, got loran A readings of 3HO 3541 and 3H1 2273, let's reenact the procedure step by step.

STEP 1
Plot your DR up to the time of the observation. It is 1045 ZT on board *War Hat*, 29 Oct. 1972. Your DR is latitude 29° 38.'0 N, longitude 88° 01.'5 W. This is a hypothetical situation in that this DR is just made up for the sake of illustration. You will see, though, that a DR gives a little fringe benefit in tuning loran.

STEP 2
I am assuming you have thoroughly studied the

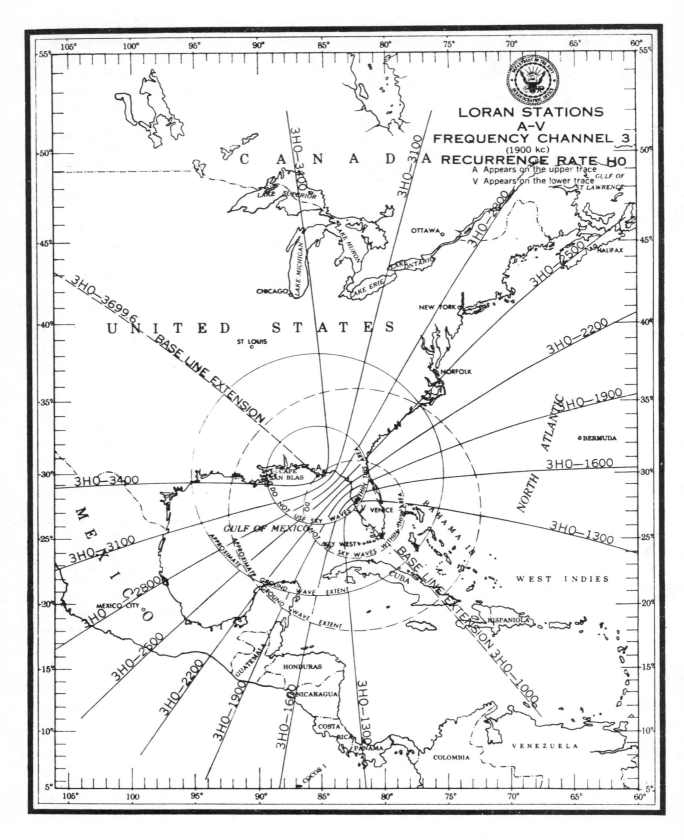

Figure 21-7. Extract from *H.O. 221 (127)*, rate 3H0, Loran A.

operator's manual that came with your loran gear. The procedure I am going to outline may vary from set to set, depending on manufacturer, but the fundamentals are the same. The manuals always tell you first to "turn the power on." Loran does work better when you do. So turn on the power, and let the set warm up. Be sure all knobs and switches are set at the proper place to start an operation. Then select the channel, the basic pulse repetition rate, and the specific pulse repetition rate you intend to use.

There are two means you can use to select these three essentials. Look at Chart No. 1115. At the top of the chart, just east of Mobile Bay, is a note that reads "rates on this chart 3H0, 3H1, 3H3." These figures are each in a different pastel color. These colors match the colors of the loran curves on the chart. Look at your DR plotted on the chart, and pick out two curves or "loran lines" that give you the best cross. 3H1 runs almost north and south, and 3HO runs almost east and west at your DR position. Rate 3H3 runs SSW by ENE and does not cross as well with 3H1 or well at all with 3H0. Rates 3H0 and 3H1 are your best choice. This is how you select loran rates, and also one reason why you want a DR.

You could have used loran tables to get the best rates, also. You get a little more basic information from the tables, and this information can be valuable. Loran rates are tabulated in the *H.O. 221* series of publications — *Publication No. 221 (127)* tabulates rate 3H0. *Publication No. 221 (128)* tabulates rate 3H1. Two more tables are on your shelf if you are using loran A tables in the Gulf of Mexico. These are *Publications Nos. 221 (129)* and *221 (130)*.

If you don't have a loran chart, you can select a rate by tables, first by choosing at least a pair of publications for the general area you are in.

STEP 1

Pull *H.O. 221 (127)*, *H.O. 221 (128)*, *H.O. 221 (129)*, and *H.O. 221 (130)* off the shelf. Open each set of tables in turn to page xi. On page xi is a chartlet showing the location of the master and slave stations. The chartlet also shows the general orientation of the loran lines of position and the *base line extension*.

For technical reasons, beyond the scope of this book, you should not use a loran pair when your position is near the base line extension.

STEP 2

The first set of tables you consider is *H.O. 221 (127)*, rate 3H0. The chartlet on page xi shows this loran pair is located with the master station at Cape San Blas, near Panama City, Florida (see Figure 21-7).

The slave station is at Venice, Florida. This is the eastern side of the Gulf of Mexico. The perpendicular bisector to the base line extension, the center loran LOP, is oriented NE to SW. The base line extension is oriented NW to SE. The station is close enough for good reception, and your DR is clear of the base line extension. Rate 3H0 is a good selection.

The individual tables are numbered in sequence. Pull *H.O. 221 (128)*, rate 3H1 from the shelf. A check of page xi of this set of tables shows the master station is at Cape San Blas, and the slave station is at Grand Isle, Louisiana (see Figure 21-8). The base line extension for this loran pair is oriented east to west. The loran LOPs are oriented nearly north and south. Again your DR is close enough to the transmitters for good reception. It is not too close to the base line extension, *and* the loran LOPs of 3H1 should make satisfactory crosses with LOPs from rate 3H0. Rate 3H1 is a good selection for use with rate 3H0.

A quick scouting of page xi of *H.O. 221 (129)* and *H.O. 221 (130)*, rates 3H2 and 3H3, indicates both of these stations are best situated to cover the western Gulf of Mexico. It could be possible to use these two loran pairs, but you would not do so unless one of the pairs in the eastern Gulf was unusable for some reason.

STEP 3

Tune your receiver to each of the rates, and get your readings in turn. As the procedure is basically the same for both rates, let's tune in on 3H0. Look at the loran receiver in Figure 21-9. The set illustrated is a Kelvin Hughes, Model LJ-11A, Loran A receiver.

On the left side of the front of the set are five knobs. The left three of these knobs, in a vertical arrangement, are station selectors. To select rate 3H0, turn the first knob marked "channel" on to the left to the position where the pointer on the knob is at 3. Turn the second knob from the top left marked "basic," to H, and turn the third knob from the top left marked "specific," to 0. You have tuned in rate 3H0.

In the center of the set is a cathode ray tube. The tube acts as an oscilloscope. The received signals are displayed visually in two horizontal traces. Each trace has a rectangular "bump" on it near the left called a pedestal. No sound signal is heard with loran. The upper trace, called the *A* trace, is the master trace. When the rate 3H0 is tuned in, the master station should appear on the upper trace as a vertical extension, or pip (see Figure 21-10).

To the right of the cathode ray tube are three rectangular buttons numbered 1, 2, 3, and arranged

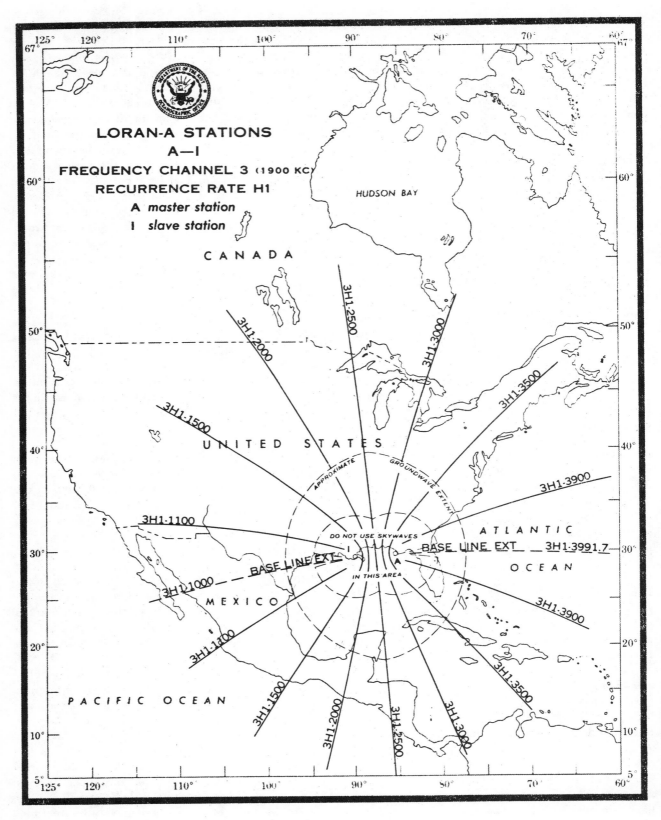

Figure 21-8. Extract from *H.O. 221 (128),* rate 3H1, Loran A.

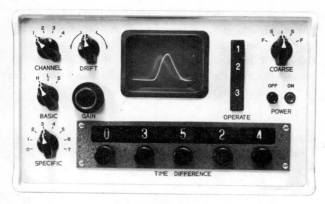

Figure 21-9. A loran A receiver (Kelvin Hughes).

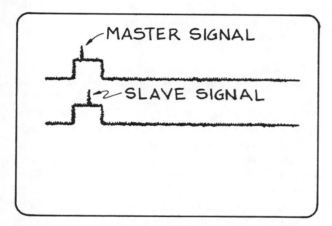

Figure 21-10. The display on a loran A scope at function 1. The returns of the master and slave stations are balanced, but not quite aligned.

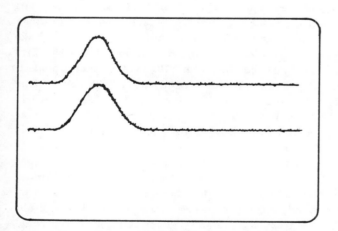

Figure 21-11. The *A* and *B* traces on a loran A scope aligned and balanced at function 2.

vertically with the number 1 the uppermost. The number 1 button should be depressed when you first begin operating the gear. This is the operation setting necessary to get the display shown in Figure 21-10.

To the right of the channel selector is a switch marked "drift." If the master pip does not appear on the scope, or if it appears off the pedestal, holding the drift switch to "L" for left, or "R" for right will cause the pip to move to the left or right. Put the master pip on the left edge of the pedestal. If the master pip cannot be seen at all or is very faint, turn up the gain, by turning the master gain knob, just under the drift switch, until a good pip appears. The gain knob is really two knobs mounted concentrically in this set. One knob controls the master pip and the other knob controls the slave pip.

STEP 4

Begin the aligning, balancing, and matching of the traces from the master and slave station. Here again a good DR comes in very handy. You could approximate the time delay for the rate 3H0 at your DR by trial and error. But your DR puts you between the lines 3H0 3540 and 3H0 3550 on Chart No. 1115. You can get a good start by cranking 3540 into the time delay dials on the set. The five knobs across the bottom of the set control the time difference reading. Turn the left-most knob to 0, the second knob from the left to 3, the third knob to 5, and the fourth knob to 4. Leave the fifth knob at zero. Your slave pip should appear on the *B* trace of the oscilloscope. If the slave pip does not appear, or is faint, or is not even the same size as the master, turn up the slave gain by turning the slave knob of the combined master-slave gain knob.

If the pip does not appear on the scope after turning up the gain, or if the pip is off the pedestal, pressing the drift switch to the right or left will cause the pip to move accordingly. Put the slave pip on the pedestal.

When the slave pip appears, it may be drifting slowly to the left or right. The drift knob now may be turned slightly to the left or right to halt this drift. Do not be concerned if other pips keep marching across the scope. These are traces from loran pairs on the same channel, but of different pulse repetition rates.

When you have stabalized the pips on the pedestals, and balanced the gain on each so that the master and slave pips are the same size, you are ready for the next step.

STEP 5

Press the function button, marked "operate" on the receiver at 2. You should get a display similar to the display in Figure 21-11. At this point, refine the balance and alignment of the pips by manipulating

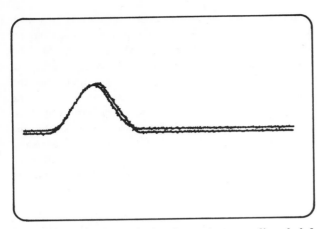

Figure 21-12. The *A* and *B* loran A traces aligned, left edge, at function 3. At this point the time difference reading is taken.

the gain knob and drift switch very carefully. When the pips are balanced and aligned with the *B* trace exactly under the *A* trace, go to Step 6.

STEP 6

Press the operate button number 3. Now the *A* and *B* traces are superimposed as shown in Figure 21-12. By turning the fourth and third knobs of the time difference reading, bring the left or leading edge of the pips into exact coincidence. When the pips are matched, read the time difference. This time difference reads 3541 microseconds. Your reading is 3H0 3541; 3H0 is the rate or station, 3541 is the time delay.

Repeat the procedure for your reading on rate 3H1. You get 3H1 2273.

STEP 7

You have two loran rate readings: 3H0 3541 and 3H1 2273. What do you do with these readings? You plot them. If you have the correct loran charts, you can plot your 1045 position right on the chart. If you do not have a loran chart, you can plot these readings on any chart of the area or on a plotting sheet by the use of a loran table. Let's plot *War Hat's* position on Chart No. 1115, a loran chart.

When you examined Chart No. 1115 to get a time delay to start with in Step 5, you found your DR was between lines 3H0 3540 and 3H0 3550. The line of position for 3H0 3543 must lie between these two pointed lines. You have to interpolate the difference between 3540 and 3550 against 3540 and 3543. No arithmetic is required. You make this interpolation graphically with the linear interpolator on the chart (see Figure 21-13).

180

In the upper right-hand corner of Chart No. 1115 is a triangular-shaped, lined diagram labeled "Loran Linear Interpolator." A similar diagram appears in the lower left-hand corner of the chart. To interpolate for the time difference of 3543 between the printed loran lines of position:

STEP 1

Take your dividers and measure the exact distance between the loran lines of position 3H0 3540 and 3H0 3550 on the chart at your DR. Without changing the spread of your dividers, find the points where the distance between the base of the triangular diagram of the interpolator and the topmost sloping edge of the interpolator matches the spread of the dividers. These two points are connected by the vertical dashed line drawn in Figure 21-13.

STEP 2

Inspect the vertical edge of the interpolator. On the linear interpolator on Chart No. 1115 are the numbers 0, 1, 2, 3, 4, 5, 6, 7, 8, 9, 10, beginning at the base and reading up. Each of these numbers marks an intermediate sloping line on the interpolator. As the difference between 3550 and 3540 is ten, and the difference between 3540 and 3543 is three, select line 3.

With your eye, follow line 3 to the vertical dashed line. Again take your dividers, and this time measure the distance between line 3 and the base of the diagram. Be careful not to change the spread of the dividers, and measure this same distance away from, and perpendicular to, the line 3H0 3540 on the chart at the point nearest your DR. The direction in which you measure must be toward line 3H0 3550. Take your parallel rulers and draw a line parallel to 3H0 3540 at this point. Your 3H0 3543 reading is plotted. Repeat the procedure to plot 3H1 2273 between the printed loran lines of position 3H1 2250 and 3H1 2300. Where these two plotted lines of position cross on the chart is your 1045 loran fix. Label this fix "1045 Loran."

If you do not want to plot and erase all over your chart, or if you do not have a loran chart to plot on, the loran tables published in the *H.O. 221* series tabulate the data necessary to plot the LOPs resulting from your loran readings. Of course you could use these tables to plot loran LOPs on any chart, too. Early in this work, you may recall, I told you good navigators often avoid plotting on their charts because the writing and erasing sooner or later may remove vital information. One solution is to plot loran fixes on a plotting sheet.

What is a plotting sheet? Plotting sheets are Mer-

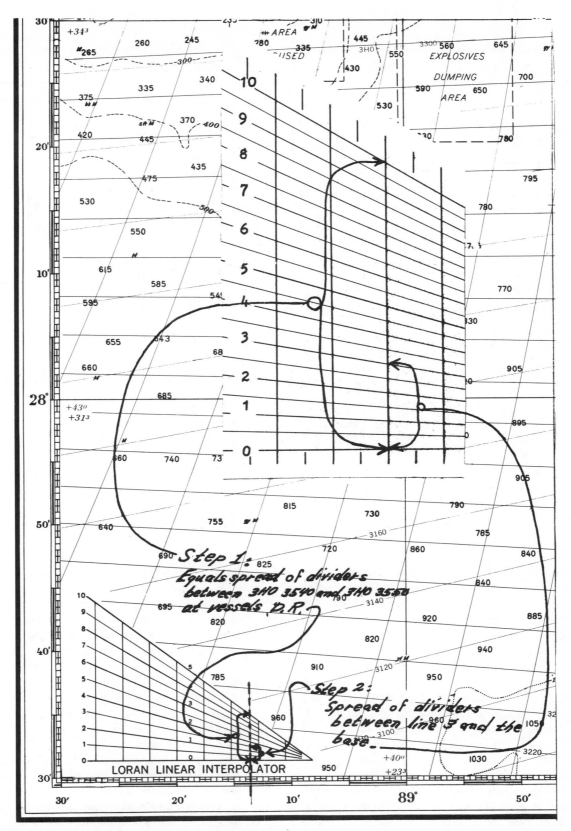

Figure 21-13. Using the loran linear interpolator.

T	3HO-3500		3HO-3520		3HO-3540		3HO-3560		3HO-3580		T
Lat	L	Δ	L	Δ	L	Δ	L	Δ	L	Δ	Long
° ′	° ′		° ′		° ′		° ′		° ′		° ′
	29 24.2 N + 31		29 30.5 N + 32		29 37.1 N + 35		29 44.3 N + 37		29 52.0 N + 41		88 W
	29 28.2	35	29 35.3	37	29 42.9	39	29 51.0	42	29 59.8	46	88 30
	29 32.4	39	29 40.3	41	29 48.7	44	29 57.8	47	30 07.6	52	89
	29 36.6	43	29 45.3	45	29 54.6	48	30 04.6	52	30 15.5	57	89 30
	29 40.9	46	29 50.4	49	30 00.6	53	30 11.5	57	30 23.3	63	90
	29 49.4 N + 54		30 00.5 N + 57		30 12.3 N + 62		30 25.1 N + 67		30 38.9 N + 73		91 W
	29 57.7	62	30 10.4	66	30 23.9	70	30 38.4	76	30 54.2	83	92
	30 05.7	70	30 20.0	74	30 35.1	79	30 51.4	85	31 09.1	93	93
	30 13.4	77	30 29.2	81	30 45.9	87	31 04.0	94	31 23.5	103	94
	30 20.7	84	30 38.0	89	30 56.4	95	31 16.1	103	31 37.5	113	95
	30 27.6 N + 92		30 46.4 N + 97		31 06.4 N +104		31 27.8 N +112		31 51.1 N +122		96 W
	30 34.1	99	30 54.4	105	31 15.9	112	31 39.0	121	32 04.1	132	97
	30 40.2	106	31 01.9	112	31 25.0	120	31 49.8	129	32 16.6	141	98
	30 45.8	113	31 09.0	120	31 33.6	128	32 00.0	138	32 28.7	151	99
	30 50.9	120	31 15.6	127	31 41.8	136	32 09.8	146	32 40.2	160	100
	30 55.7 N +128		31 21.8 N +135		31 49.5 N +143		32 19.1 N +155		32 51.3 N +169		101 W
	30 59.9	135	31 27.5	142	31 56.7	151	32 28.0	163	33 01.8	177	102
	31 03.8	142	31 32.8	149	32 03.5	159	32 36.3	171	33 11.8	186	103
	31 07.1	148	31 37.5	157	32 09.7	167	32 44.1	179	33 21.3	195	104
	31 10.0	156	31 41.9	164	32 15.5	174	32 51.5	187	33 30.3	203	105
	31 12.5 N +162		31 45.7 N +171		32 20.8 N +182		32 58.3 N +195		33 38.8 N +212		106 W
	31 14.5	169	31 49.1	178	32 25.7	189	33 04.7	203	33 46.7	220	107
	31 16.0	176	31 52.0	185	32 30.1	197	33 10.6	211	33 54.3	229	108
	31 17.1	183	31 54.5	192	32 34.0	204	33 16.0	218	34 01.2	237	109
	31 17.7	190	31 56.5	199	32 37.4	211	33 20.9	226	34 07.7	245	110
	31 17.9 N +196		31 58.0 N +206		32 40.3 N +218		33 25.3 N +234		34 13.7 N +253		111 W

Figure 21-14. Excerpt from *H.O. 221 (127).*

cator projections. They are essentially blank pieces of paper with a true compass rose and the parallels of latitude and the meridians of longitude printed on them. No other navigational data is provided on a plotting sheet except a logarithmic scale printed on the edge of the sheet to help solve the speed, time, distance problems of dead reckoning. Parallels of latitude, north and south, are printed on the plotting sheet, and numbered for both north and south latitude. Meridians of longitude are *not* numbered. Thus, you must select a plotting sheet to cover the latitudes your vessel is in, but not the longitude. If your DR is between 29° and 30° north latitude, you must select a plotting sheet that has 29° and 30° of latitude on it. You would use the same plotting sheet if your DR was 29° or 30° south latitude. A word of caution is appropriate here: to use a plotting sheet in south latitude, you have to turn the

sheet upside down. Notice the compass rose; the inner scale is for north latitude, the outer scale is for south latitude and is opposed 180° in direction.

The meridians of longitude are not numbered on a plotting sheet, so you must write the values of longitude in to suit the longitude of your DR. If you are in 88° W longitude, you select a meridian to be 88° W, and number the meridians to the left of it 89°, 90°, and so on, increasing in longitude as you go west if you are in the northern hemisphere. You number the meridians to the right as 87°, 86°, decreasing in the west longitude as you go east. If your DR is 88° E longitude, just the opposite applies. You select a meridian and number it as 88° E, and number the meridians to the right 89°, 90°, and so on, increasing in east longitude as you go east. In east longitude, you would number meridians to the left 87°, 86°, and 85°, decreasing in east longitude as you go west. In the southern hemisphere the situation is reversed. East longitude increases to your left and west longitude increases to your right as you face the south pole.

This basically explains a plotting sheet. Plotting sheets come in several scales and series at your local hydrographic agent's shop. It is even possible to make your own plotting sheets. For more detailed information on plotting sheets, see *Bowditch* and my own book, *Celestial Navigation Step by Step*.

You have taken a loran reading on rate 3H0, but instead of plotting this reading on Chart No. 1115, you decide to work from the loran tables and plot your results on a plotting sheet. We will assume you are at the same DR as before, and your reading is the same, 3H0 3543. This will give a good comparison of the two methods, chart or tables, of getting loran fixes.

Break out *H.O. 221 (127)* of the loran tables. The pages are numbered, and the time difference columns in the tables are in increments of 20 microseconds of delay. Without referring to page number, it is quite simple to thumb through the tables, and find the column headed 3H0 3540 on page 57 of the

tables (see Figure 21-14). Always select the tabulated time difference nearest the actual time difference you read on your loran set.

You will notice that there are two sub-columns under each of the columns headed with a rate and time difference. The left sub-column is headed Lo, for longitude, or L, for latitude. The heading of this left sub-column depends on whether the loran line of position represented in the table tends in an east-west or north-south direction.

The right-hand sub-column of the loran tables is headed with a symbol consisting of a small triangle. This triangle is called "delta" or "increment," and the data tabulated in this column is the factor for the increment of change in latitude or longitude between each latitude or longitude in the left-hand sub-column and the difference in time delay between the tabulated time difference and the observed time difference.

Column "T" is in the right and left margins. If longitude is tabulated in the left-hand sub-column of the time difference column, latitude will be tabulated under T (see Figure 21-15). And vice versa, if latitude is tabulated in the left-hand sub-column of

AI 27

T	3H1-2200		3H1-2220		3H1-2240		3H1-2260		3H1-2280		T
Lat		Δ		Δ		Δ		Δ		Δ	**Long**
° ′	° ′		° ′		° ′		° ′		° ′		° ′
28 45N	88 03.7W –	9	88 01.8W –	9	87 59.8W –	9	87 57.9W –	9	87 55.9W –	9	
29 N	88 04.5W –	9	88 02.6W –	9	88 00.8W –	9	87 58.9W –	9	87 57.0W –	9	
29 15N	88 05.7W –	9	88 03.9W –	9	88 02.0W –	9	88 00.1W –	9	87 58.3W –	9	
29 30N	88 07.4W –	9	88 05.5W –	9	88 03.7W –	9	88 01.8W –	9	87 59.9W –	9	
29 45N	88 09.5W –	9	88 07.6W –	9	88 05.7W –	9	88 03.8W –	9	88 01.9W –	9	
30 N	88 12.0W –	9	88 10.1W –	9	88 08.1W –	9	88 06.2W –	9	88 04.2W –	9	
30 15N	88 15.0W –	10	88 12.9W –	10	88 10.9W –	10	88 08.9W –	10	88 06.8W –	10	
30 30N	88 18.3W –	10	88 16.2W –	10	88 14.0W –	10	88 11.8W –	10	88 09.6W –	10	
31 N	88 26.0W –	12	88 23.5W –	12	88 21.0W –	12	88 18.6W –	12	88 16.2W –	12	
32 N	88 44.0W –	16	88 40.7W –	16	88 37.5W –	16	88 34.2W –	16	88 31.0W –	15	
33 N	89 04.2W –	21	89 00.0W –	20	88 55.9W –	20	88 51.7W –	20	88 47.6W –	20	
34 N	89 25.9W –	26	89 20.7W –	26	89 15.5W –	25	89 10.3W –	25	89 05.2W –	25	
35 N	89 48.6W –	31	89 42.3W –	31	89 36.0W –	31	89 29.8W –	30	89 23.6W –	30	
36 N	90 12.2W –	37	90 04.8W –	37	89 57.3W –	36	89 50.1W –	36	89 42.8W –	36	
37 N	90 36.7W –	43	90 28.0W –	43	90 19.5W –	42	90 10.9W –	42	90 02.6W –	41	
38 N	91 02.0W –	49	90 52.1W –	48	90 42.3W –	48	90 32.6W –	48	90 23.0W –	47	
39 N	91 28.1W –	56	91 16.9W –	55	91 05.9W –	54	90 54.9W –	54	90 44.1W –	53	
40 N	91 55.1W –	62	91 42.6W –	62	91 30.2W –	61	91 18.0W –	60	91 05.9W –	60	
41 N	92 23.0W –	69	92 09.1W –	69	91 55.3W –	68	91 41.8W –	67	91 28.4W –	66	
42 N	92 51.8W –	77	92 36.5W –	76	92 21.3W –	75	92 06.4W –	74	91 51.6W –	73	
43 N	93 21.7W –	84	93 04.8W –	83	92 48.2W –	82	92 31.8W –	81	92 15.6W –	80	
44 N	93 52.6W –	92	93 34.2W –	91	93 16.1W –	90	92 58.2W –	89	92 40.5W –	88	
45 N	94 24.7W –	100	94 04.7W –	99	93 45.0W –	97	93 25.6W –	96	93 06.3W –	95	
46 N	94 58.1W –	109	94 36.4W –	107	94 15.0W –	106	93 53.9W –	104	93 33.1W –	103	
47 N	95 32.8W –	118	95 09.4W –	116	94 46.2W –	114	94 23.4W –	113	94 00.9W –	111	
48 N	96 09.0W –	127	95 43.7W –	125	95 18.7W –	123	94 54.2W –	122	94 29.9W –	120	
49 N	96 46.7W –	137	96 20.2W –	135	95 52.6W –	133	95 26.2W –	131	95 00.1W –	129	
50 N	97 26.1W –	147	96 56.8W –	145	96 28.0W –	143	95 59.6W –	141	95 31.6W –	139	
51 N	98 07.4W –	158	97 35.9W –	155	97 05.0W –	153	96 34.5W –	151	96 04.5W –	149	
52 N	98 50.7W –	170	98 17.0W –	167	97 43.8W –	164	97 11.1W –	162	96 39.0W –	159	

Figure 21-15. Excerpt from *H.O. 221 (127)*.

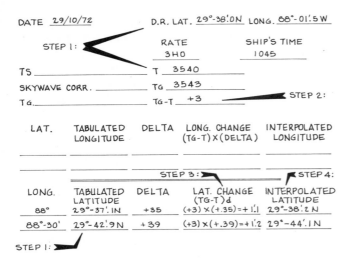

	RATE	SHIP'S TIME
STEP 1:	3H0	1045
TS _____	T 3540	
SKYWAVE CORR. _____	TG 3543	
TG. _____	TG-T +3	STEP 2:

LAT.	TABULATED LONGITUDE	DELTA	LONG. CHANGE (TG-T) X (DELTA)	INTERPOLATED LONGITUDE
			STEP 3:	STEP 4:

LONG.	TABULATED LATITUDE	DELTA	LAT. CHANGE (TG-T)d	INTERPOLATED LATITUDE
88°	29°-37.'1 N	+35	(+3) x (+.35) = +1.'1	29°-38.'2 N
88°-30'	29°-42.'9 N	+39	(+3) x (+.39) = +1.'2	29°-44.'1 N

STEP 1:

Figure 21-16. A form for working loran lines of position by the loran tables, which is used here to interpolate for latitude. It can be used to interpolate for latitude or longitude, depending on how the data is tabulated in the loran tables. It goes without saying that you should draw in your notebook only the portion of a form needed to do the interpolation required.

the time difference column, longitude will be tabulated under T (see Figure 21-14). With this information, the coordinates in the T column and the coordinates in the left-hand sub-column, you can plot a series of points on a plotting sheet or chart through which the loran line of position 3H0 3540 passes. Fair a curved line through these points, and you have a plotted loran LOP for 3H0 3540. With loran tables you can construct a loran chart, and this is precisely what you are going to do. But, because the part of the loran LOP you are going to plot represents such a small portion of the entire curve, you can plot the LOP obtained from the tables as a straight line, and you will not introduce any serious error.

You are not going to construct a chart of the entire area covered by the tables. You are going to construct in effect a chartlet of the area right around your DR. And you are not going to plot LOP 3H0 3540 and LOP 3H0 3550 and interpolate between these two LOPs with a linear interpolator to find LOP 3H0 3543, as you did when plotting directly on the loran chart. You are going to interpolate and plot LOP 3H0 3543 right from the tables, and it is going to be so easy you will be amazed.

STEP 1

Open *H.O. 221 (127)* to column 3H0 3540. This is the time difference in the table nearest your actual loran reading of 3543. Find two lines in the T column bracketing your DR longitude of 88° 01.'5 W (see

Figure 21-14). You find this column on page 57 of H.O. 221 (127). Under 3H0 3540, and opposite 88° W in the T column, extract latitude 29° 37.'0 N from the left-hand sub-column, and + 35 from the right-hand "delta" column. Drop down one line to 88° 30.'0 in the T column, and opposite this longitude extract 29° 42.'9 from the left sub-column of the 3H0 3540 column. Under the right-hand sub-column headed with the delta, extract + 39. Be sure to note the sign. At this point you should be using a form as in Figure 21-16. This form is the same as the one used by the Loran School, Gulf District, Maritime Administration, U.S. Department of Commerce, New Orleans, Louisiana, and closely follows the format used in the examples accompanying the loran tables. It is an excellent form, and one that can be ruled neatly into your navigator's notebook as you need it. Put your DR, the ship's time, the loran rate observed, the loran reading, and the data you extracted from the tables into the form as indicated.

STEP 2

Subtract the time difference of 2540 from 2543. The remainder is plus 3. If your reading of the time difference were 3537, the remainder would have been minus 3. Again, it is essential to apply the correct sign.

STEP 3

Multiply the delta factor of + .35 by 3. This is the interpolation of the latitude factor for a longitude of 88° W. and now note the decimal in front of the 35 that makes it + .35. The tables do not show a decimal in the sub-column, but the decimal is required.

Multiply: $(+ .35) \times (+ 3) = +1.05 = 1.'1$
Multiply: $(+ .39) \times (+ 3) = +1.17 = +1.'2$

The results of this multiplication are rounded off to the nearest tenth.

At this time, a refresher course in algebra is in order. In multiplying algebraic expressions, such as $(+ .35) \times (+ 3)$, or $(+ .35) \times (-3)$, or $(-.35) \times (+ 3)$, or $(-.35) \times (-3)$ the following rules apply to determine the sign of the product (answer):

1. When a figure whose sign is plus is multiplied by a figure whose sign is also plus, the sign of the answer is plus.

2. When a figure whose sign is plus is multiplied by a figure whose sign is minus, the sign of the answer is minus.

3. When a figure whose sign is minus is multiplied by a figure whose sign is plus, the sign of the answer is minus.

4. When a figure whose sign is minus is multiplied

184

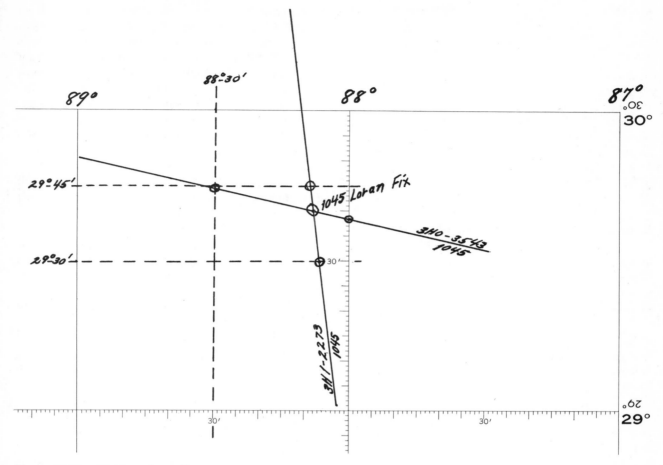

Figure 21-17. Plotting a loran fix.

by a figure whose sign is also minus, the sign of the answer is plus.

It is possible to have any of these combination of signs when working with loran tables. Hence the short course in algebra.

STEP 4

Add +1.1 to the latitude of 29⁰ 37. '1 N in the form. Your interpolated latitude is 29⁰ 38. '2 N at longitude 88⁰ W.

Add +1.2 to latitude 29⁰ 42. '9 N. The interpolated latitude at longitude 88⁰ 30. '0 W is 29⁰ 44. '1 N.

STEP 5

Plot the position of latitude 29⁰ 38.'2 N, longitude 88⁰ 00.'0 W on your plotting sheet. Plot the position latitude 29⁰ 44.'1 N, longitude 88⁰ 30.'0 W on your plotting sheet (see Figure 21-17).

Draw a straight line connecting these two positions. This line is your loran LOP. Label it "3H0 3543, 1045."

Because words are limited, it takes pages to explain a process like this, when in fact the whole problem can be worked in minutes. Let's work and plot a loran LOP for 3H1 2273.

STEP 1

Put the time, your DR, and the rate that you are using in the form. Open *H.O. 221 (128)* and find the time difference column nearest your actual time difference reading of 2273. This will be column 2280 on page 27 AI of the tables (see Figure 21-15). Your DR lies between 29⁰ 30.'0 N and 29⁰ 45.'0 N in the T column. From the 29⁰ 30.'0 N line of column 2280, extract longitude 87⁰ 59.'9 W and a delta of –9. From the latitude 29⁰ 45.'0 N line extract longitude 88⁰ 01.'9 W and a delta of –9. Put all this data in the form (see Figure 21-18).

DATE _29/10/72_ D.R. LAT. _29°-38'.0 N_ LONG. _88°-01'.5 W_

		RATE 3H1	SHIP'S TIME 1045
TS _____		T _2280_	
SKYWAVE CORR. _____		TG _2273_	
TG. _____		TG-T _-7_	

LAT.	TABULATED LONGITUDE	DELTA	LONG. CHANGE (TG-T) x (DELTA)	INTERPOLATED LONGITUDE
29°-30'.0 N	87° 59'.9	-9	(-7) x (-.9) = +6.3	88°-06'.2 W
29°-45'.0 N	88°-01'.9	-9	(-7) x (-.9) = +6.3	88°-08'.2 W

LONG.	TABULATED LATITUDE	DELTA	LAT. CHANGE (TG-T) d	INTERPOLATED LATITUDE

Figure 21-18. Interpolating for longitude.

STEP 2
Subtract the actual observed time difference of 2273 from the tabulated time difference of 2280. The remainder is -7.

STEP 3
Multiply (-7) by (-.9) = + 6.3. Note that as a coincidence the delta factor -.9 applies to both longitudes.

STEP 4
Add + 6.3 to longitude 87° 59.'9 W. The interpolated longitude is 88° 06.'2 W at latitude 29° 30.'0 N.

Add + 6.3 to longitude 88° 01.'9 W. The interpolated longitude is 88° 08.'2 W at latitude 29° 45.'0 N.

STEP 5
Plot the position latitude 29° 30.'0 N, longitude 06.'2 W (see Figure 21-17 again). Plot the position latitude 29° 45.'0 N, longitude 88° 08.'2 W. Draw a straight line through these two positions, and label it "3H1 2273, 1045." Your loran fix is the intersection of LOP 3H0 3543 and LOP 3H1 2273. Not difficult at all is it?

Some more sophisticated loran sets are equipped with automatic tracking devices. To operate automatic tracking loran, all you need to do is select a rate. The set will automatically seek a time difference, if a strong enough signal is received. At the completion of the function 3 operation -- the final matching of the signals — a set capable of automatic tracking will "lock in" on the matched signals. As the ship's position changes the loran reading for time differences will also change automatically to conform to the time difference at the ship's new position. No further tuning of the set by the operator is normally required.

Automatic tracking loran is designed to be left on while at sea. If you turn the set on only when you want a reading, you are sacrificing the automatic tracking ability of the gear. Of course, if you want two rates from two LOPs to get a loran fix, you must tune the set to receive the second rate by going through the entire tuning and matching process. If you have only one automatic tracking loran set aboard, a good practice is to select a rate to give you a LOP that makes a good cross with your course. This LOP will give you a continuous indication of your speed over the ground. By comparing this actual speed with your logged speed, you can correct your DR. Then every hour or so, depending on how close you may be to land or another point, you can switch over to another suitable rate for a fix. The ultimate in automatic loran is to have your vessel equipped with two automatic tracking receivers, or at least one automatic tracking receiver capable of tracking two loran rates simultaneously. Then you can tune each receiver to a different rate, and instant fixes can be obtained at any time — providing you can get two loran pairs. In commercial or fishing operations, where time is money, the cost of two such sets on one boat may be justified.

Up to now no mention has been made of some of the special problems associated with loran. Everything has been presented as if all you need to do is turn the set on, manipulate a few knobs and dials, and get your time difference. Under good radio conditions, during daylight hours, this is often all that is required. Unfortunately, when a radio operator speaks of daylight, the term includes the time of about an hour, or even more, before sunset and an hour or more after sunrise. In the winter, in high latitude, this may leave a very short day.

What is the problem with loran between sunset, or several hours before, and sunrise, including sometimes several hours after sunrise? The problem is a phenomenon called *skywaves*. This is the same phenomenon that makes RDF unreliable near sunset and sunrise, and to some extent during the entire night.

Radio waves in the low frequency spectrum propagate (travel) in two ways. They are projected in a straight line in all directions, and they also follow the curvature of the earth. During good daylight conditions, it is these latter waves, called ground waves, that your radio receiver picks up. The other type, skywaves, are lost in space, or at least come in as much weaker signals. With the approach of sunset, and again at the approach of sunrise, the upper atmosphere becomes electrically charged, or ionized. Scientists refer to this charged layer of upper air as the ionosphere. This charged condition prevails to some extent throughout the night, but falls off to a much lower level of ionization during the day. When the skywaves are so charged, as at sunset or sunrise, and at night, skywaves are reflected back to earth. During daylight, when the charge is lower, most of the skywaves escape into space.

Skywaves bouncing off the ionosphere have several properties that make their use to some degree more difficult than ground waves for loran position finding. Skywaves can be difficult to read because they vary in strength. Just when you are ready to match a skywave, it may just fade away. Since they travel in a zig-zag path by skipping back and forth between the earth's surface and the ionosphere, skywaves take longer to travel a given distance over the earth's surface. For this reason a correction must be applied to the time difference readings your loran gear produces when observing skywaves. Because the height of the ionosphere varies, this correction is an average correction. Consequently there is an inherent inaccuracy in skywave readings, even after the correction is applied.

In loran A navigation, only the first reflection, or "hop", off the underside, or "E", side of the ionosphere is usable. Thus, you hear navigators say they got an observation of a one-hop E skywave. As if this were not enough trouble, skywaves cannot be used within 250 miles of a station.

You should learn to use skywave readings from your loran gear. Don't be like so many would-be navigators who plot skywaves by acting as if they were ground waves. These chaps apply no skywave correction, and their results are usually way off, sometimes dangerously so. Another group of would-be navigators just turn their receivers off when skywaves appear as the dominant signal. As this means no loran for over fifty percent of the time, it is not a very good system either. I must admit, however, that not using skywaves, when you don't know how, sure beats using them improperly. The best approach to skywaves is to learn to recognize them, and then use them. Skywaves do extend the nighttime range of loran to 1,220 to 1,400 miles. The maximum range of ground waves in daytime is 700 to 750 miles.

I told you at the start of this chapter that radio navigation is a phase of navigation in its own right. An entire book could be written on this subject, and written for the user, not the technician. For a good discussion of the characteristics of ground waves and the usable one-hop E skywaves, as well as the unusable two-hop E and F skywaves, I again refer you to *Bowditch* and *Navigating and Finding Fish With Electronics* by G. D. Dunlap. But, as before, a few

words on recognizing skywaves are appropriate here. What to do about skywaves we will cover in more detail.

Appearance on the scope is the only way to tell a skywave from a ground wave. Yet skywaves, when fully developed, may look identical to a ground wave. It is the relative lack of uniformity of signal strength, plus the time of day you are making your observations, that give the best means of knowing you are receiving skywaves. Another clue is that often, when a strong one-hop E skywave is being received, an equally strong one-hop F skywave will appear on the scope immediately to the right of the one-hop E wave. Ground waves are steady, and they remain steady. Skywaves may remain steady in strength for short periods, but they characteristically fade, or even disappear, and come back with a different intensity. *Bowditch* tells you that experience in watching the various presentations throughout the 24-hour day is the best way to learn to recognize the various waves you will see on a loran scope.

As the day fades, and skywaves begin to appear, the skywave is first seen as a small bump or 'pip' on the base of the *right* leg of the ground wave. As the skywave gains in strength with the onset of night, the ground wave fades, and the skywave pip becomes larger and assumes the size of the ground wave. At some point, usually in the late afternoon, the ground wave and skywave will be about the same size as this transition in relative signal strengths occurs. Before disappearing entirely, the ground wave appears as a small pip on the *left* leg of the skywave. As morning approaches, and the skywave begins to strengthen again, the cycle is repeated. It is the several hours before and after sunset and sunrise that skywave reception is the most likely to cause problems. The distance from your DR to the stations can be your best guide to wave identification. The critical range lies between 500 and 700 miles by night, and between 600 and 900 miles by day. Inside these ranges, the first wave seen can be considered to be a ground wave. Beyond these ranges, the first wave to the left is likely a skywave. It is between these critical ranges that identification becomes crucial. For additional information I refer you to the chapter on hyperbolic systems in *Bowditch*, and Figure 21-19, which is taken from *Bowditch*.

It will help to know that the sequence from left to right across the scope, when all types of wave reception are present, is: ground wave, one-hop E skywave, two-hop E skywave, one-hop F skywave, and two-hop F skywave.

How do you correct and plot skywaves? Assume you are deft at reading and matching skywaves on your

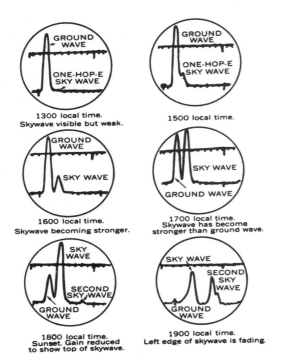

Figure 21-19. Skywave formations on a loran scope as the afternoon progress (from *Bowditch*).

loran receiver. What do you do with them? How do you find and apply the required skywave corrections? The best way to answer all these questions is to work an example as if it were real:

At 2143 on the evening watch, you compute your DR to be latitude 23° 19.'7 N, longitude 85° 39.'8 W. You take a loran A observation and get the following readings by skywave matching: 3H0 1762 and 3H3 2172. Apply the skywave corrections, and plot your 2143 loran fix.

Your first job is to determine these skywave cor-

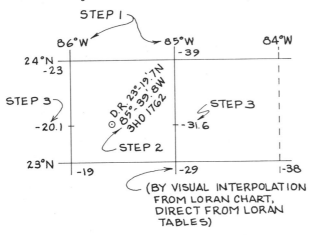

Figure 21-20. Diagram for interpolating skywave corrections.

188

rections. You can get them from either your loran chart or your loran tables. Almost invariably you will have to interpolate. The procedure for making this interpolation is *almost* identical for charts and tables. The skywave correction is always applied to your initial time difference reading.

You want to correct the reading 3H0 1762 by reference only to your loran chart. Remember the loran rates are color coded on loran charts. Rate 3H0 is a light purple or lavender. At your 2143 DR position you would likely be navigating on Chart No. 1007. This is a small-scale chart of the entire Gulf of Mexico. Meridians of longitude and parallels of latitude are drawn in every other whole degree. At the intersection of each meridian and parallel are groups of several numbers — at the position of latitude 23° 00.'0 N, longitude 86° 00.'0 W are the numbers -19, +15, -16, and +02. Each of these numbers is a different pastel color. And each color corresponds to the color code of a loran rate appearing on the chart. These numbers indicate the skywave correction to be applied to loran readings taken by vessels at latitude 23° N, longitude 86° W. The correction is only applicable to the rate of the same color. This means -19, the lavender-colored number, is the skywave correction to the lavender-colored rate 3H0. The minus sign means the correction is to be subtracted from the time difference of loran skywave readings of rate 3H0 at that position. If lighting makes the color of the numbers on the chart hard to distinguish, each skywave correction also has a small number, an exponent, such as -19^0, with it. This exponent corresponds to the specific pulse repetition rate of the rate to which the skywave correction applies.

But your DR is latitude 23° 19.'7 N, longitude 85° 39.'8 W, and not latitude 23° 00.'0 N, longitude 86° 00.'0 W. Since skywave corrections may vary for each position on the chart, it is apparent that you must do some interpolating. How do you do this? The best way to make this interpolation is by the use of a diagram (see Figure 21-20). The diagram should be drawn in your navigator's notebook. Here is what you do:

STEP 1
Bring your DR up to the time of the loran observation. Draw a square diagram, about two or three inches on each side in your navigator's notebook. Each corner of this square represents the whole degree coordinates of latitude and longitude immediately surrounding your DR. These are the positions for which skywave corrections are usually given on the chart, and in the tables, too. On Chart No. 1007,

these coordinates are latitude 23⁰ N, longitude 84⁰ W; latitude 23⁰ N, longitude 86⁰ W; latitude 24⁰ N, longitude 85⁰ W; latitude 24⁰ N, longitude 86⁰ W. On Chart No. 1007, no skywave correction is given for latitude 23⁰ N, longitude 85⁰ W, but on the 23rd parallel the skywave correction for rate 3H0 is –38 at 84⁰ W, and –19 at 86⁰ W. Visual interpolation will supply the correction of –29 for this last position. (–38) minus (–19) = –19; –19 divided by 2 = –9.5; (–9.5) added to (–19) = 29. You now have skywave corrections for the four whole-degree coordinates of latitude and longitude nearest your DR.

If you were using loran tables instead of the chart, you could have taken the skywave corrections right from the tables (see Figure 21-21). The use of tables for skywave corrections is much quicker and easier than picking the corrections from the loran chart.

SKY WAVE CORRECTION AV 3

LONGITUDE WEST

LAT	95	94	93	92	91	90	89	88	87	86	85	84	83	82	81
53						0	0	0	0	0	0	0	0	0	0
52		0	0	0	0	0	0	0	0	0	0	0	0	0	
51	0	0	0	0	0	0	0	0	0	0	0	0	0	0	
50	0	0	0	0	0	0	0	0	0	0	0	0	0	0	
49	0	0	0	0	0	0	0	0	0	0	0	0	0	0	
48	0	0	0	0	0	0	0	0	0	0	0	0	0	0	
47	0	0	0	0	0	0	0	0	0	0	0	0	0	0	
46	0	0	0	0	0	0	0	0	0	0	0	0	0	0	
45	0	0	0	0	0	1	1	1	1	1	1	1	1	1	1
44	0	0	1	1	1	1	1	1	1	1	1	1	1	1	1
43	1	1	1	1	2	2	2	2	2	2	2	2	2	2	1
42	1	2	2	2	3	3	3	3	4	4	3	3	3	3	3
41	2	2	3	4	4	5	5	5	5	5	5	4	4	4	4
40	3	4	4	5	6	6	6	7	7	7	7	6	6	5	5
39	4	5	6	7	7 *ADD*	8	9	9	9	9 *ADD*	9	8	8	7	6
38	5	6	7	9	10	11	11	12	12	12	11	11	10	8	7
37	7	8	9	11	12	13	15	15	16	16	15	14	12	11	9
36	8	10	11	13	15	17	19	20	21	21	20	18	16	13	10
35	9	11	13	16	18	21	24	27	29	29	28	25	21	16	12
34	11	13	15	19	22	27	32	37	42	43	42	37	29	21	14
33	11	14	17	21	27	34	43	53				55	41	27	16
32	12	15	19	24	31	41	55		DO NOT USE			56	31	14	
31	12	15	20	25	34	47			SKY WAVES				27	3	
30	12	15	19	25	35	49			IN THIS REGION					24	
29	11	14	18	23	32	45									
28	10	12	15	20	26	36	50								
27	9	11	13	16	20	25	31	38	38	22	25				
26	7	8	10	11	14	16	17	16	8	13	54				
25	6	6	7	8	8	9	7	3	6	23	50				
24	4	5	5	5	5	4	1	3	11	23	39	57			
23	3	3	3	3	2	1	2	6	11	19	29	38	46	49	46
22	2	2	2	2	0	1	3	6	10	15	21	26	31	32	32
21	1	1	1	0	1	2	4	6	9	12	16	19	22	23	23
20	1	1	0	0	1	2	4	6	8	10	12	14	16	17	17
19	0	0	0	1	1 *SUBTRACT*	2	3	5	7	8 *SUBTRACT*	10	11	12	13	13
18	0	0	0	1	1	2	3	4	5	7	8	9	9	10	10
17	0	0	0	1	1	2	3	4	4	5	6	7	7	7	8
16	0	0	0	1	1	2	2	3	3	4	5	5	5	6	6
15	0	0	0	0	1	1	2	2	2	3	3	4	4	4	4
14	0	0	0	0	1	1	1	1	2	2	2	2	3	3	3
13	0	0	0	0	0	0	1	1	1	1	1	1	2	2	2
12	0	0	0	0	0	0	0	0	1	1	1	1	1	1	1
11	0	0	0	0	0	0	0	0	0	0	0	0	0	0	0
10	0	0	0	0	0	0	0	0	0	0	0	0	0	0	0

LONGITUDE WEST

Figure 21-21. Skywave correction table.

STEP 2

From this point the process of finding and applying the skywave correction for your DR position is identical whether you are using loran charts or loran tables. Put your DR in its approximate position in your diagram. This will aid you in visualizing the relative position of your vessel and the effect your vessel's position should have on the skywave correction.

STEP 3

Begin interpolating. You will make three interpolations. You may interpolate for difference of latitude *along* two meridians of longitude *between* two parallels of latitude, and then interpolate for difference in longitude along the latitude of your DR. Or you may interpolate for difference in longitude *along* two parallels of latitude, and then interpolate for difference in latitude *between* the two meridians of longitude along your DR longitude. It makes absolutely no difference. Let's interpolate for a difference in DR latitude of 19.'7 along the meridian 85° W and the meridian 86° W, and then interpolate for the difference in DR longitude between the parallels of 23° N and 24° N along the DR latitude of 23° 19.'7 N.

(A) Interpolation at 85° W for difference in latitude:

Lat. 24° N	Skywave correction −39
Lat. 23° N	Skywave correction −28

Diff. 1° or 60.'0   −11
DR Lat. 23° 19.'7
        23° 00.'0
Diff. Lat.   19.'7
Round off 19.'7 to 20.'0
Multiply 20/60 by (−11) = −3.6
Add (−28) and (−3.6) = −31.6. This is the skywave correction at latitude 23° 19.'7 N, longitude 85° 00.'0 W

(B) Interpolation at 86° W for difference in latitude:

Lat. 24° N	Skywave correction −23
Lat. 23° N	Skywave correction −19

Diff. 1° or 60.'0   −4
Multiply 20/60 by (−4) = −1.1
Add (−19) and (−1.1) = −20.1. Skywave correction at latitude 23° 19.'7 N, longitude 86° 00.'0 W

(C) Interpolating for difference in longitude along the DR latitude of 23° 19.'7 N.

Long. 86° W	Skywave correction −20.1
Long. 85° W	Skywave correction −31.6

Diff. 1° or 60.'0   −11.5

DR Long. 85° 39.'8
        85° 00.'0
Diff. Long.   39.'8
Round off 39.'8 to 40.'0
Multiply 40/60 by (−11.5) = −7.6
Subtract (−31.6) and (−7.6) = −24.0. This is the skywave correction to rate 3H0 1762 at your DR

STEP 4

Add algebraically the skywave correction of −24.0 to the time difference of 1762 you read off your loran gear. 1762 + (−24.0) = 1738. Your corrected loran reading is 3H0 1738.

STEP 5

For all practical purposes, your corrected loran reading of 3H0 1738 is a ground wave reading. Proceed now with either a loran chart or loran tables as already explained. Then compute and apply the necessary skywave correction to 3H3 2172. Plot the corrected reading. The resulting cross of these two lines of position is your 2143 loran fix. And you did it with *skywaves!*

From the example it is apparent skywave corrections can be quite important. If you do not apply skywave corrections to skywave readings, you cannot rely on your results. If you do not use skywave readings in loran navigation, you are not getting full use of your loran equipment.

A word of caution. Skywave corrections depend on your DR for accuracy. If, after plotting your position by loran, your DR is found to be way off, you should recorrect your skywave readings by using the first loran fix as a DR. Plot a second fix from the resulting second loran LOPs. The second fix should be the most accurate.

Master the techniques I have explained, and you should be on your way to becoming a competent loran navigator. Keep in mind, however, that this treatise only scratches the surface of the subject. Get copies of the works I referred to previously, and any other good texts on radio navigation. Study these books carefully, then practice with your equipment.

Before leaving the subject, a few additional remarks on the use, accuracy, and some dos and don'ts about loran A are in order. As in all systems, loran navigation has its signs and symbols. *Tg* signifies a ground wave, and *Ts* signifies a skywave. Use these symbols to label all your work. Others can then follow what you have done.

The effective range of loran: Loran A depends on ground wave reception during daylight. The effective range is 700 to 750 miles during daylight. At night ground waves may be received up to 450 miles from a station. During daylight the range of skywaves is zero miles. At night loran A depends primarily on skywave reception. The effective range of skywaves at night is between 1,200 miles and 1,400 miles.

As to accuracy, the best claim I am aware of is about 1½ miles. This does *not* approach the resolution obtainable with celestial navigation under good conditions. On the other hand, good celestial conditions on very small boats are almost impossible to achieve. In very small craft, loran could well exceed the resolution obtainable by celestial means. Remember, though, the limited range of loran.

As in any system worth using, radio navigation requires some effort to develop the knowledge and skill to use the system to its best advantage. The *proper* use of loran is no harder and no easier than the proper use of celestial navigation. Celestial navigation is certainly not too difficult for any intelligent person to learn, if that person knows how to add and subtract. To use loran you must know how to multiply and divide.

Loran is manmade gear. Receivers go out at the most inconvenient times, and master and slave stations may get out of order too. When they are out of order, these master or slave stations may still send signals. Results from such signals will be erroneous. A typical malfunction between a master and slave in a loran pair is for the stations to get out of synchronization. When this happens, both the master and slave stations *blink*. This blinking consists of a shifting of the signals, right and left, across the scope.

Avoid matching skywave and ground waves, if possible. If you must match a ground wave from one station in a loran pair with a skywave from the other station in the pair, be sure to follow the procedure outlined in the operator's manual that came with your gear.

22   HOW TO GET IT ALL TOGETHER

I have tried to convey several attitudes and approaches to you in the course of this book, as well as show you certain fundamental things a navigator must understand and be able to do. My first general premise is: don't wait until you cast off on your first passage into strange waters before you practice what you have learned. Be sure you have practiced enough to gain the skill to apply this knowledge. Don't go out one time and take a bearing or vertical sextant angle, and, when luck makes this sight come out good, say "well, I know how to do that." Practice the same thing over and over and over again. Then practice some more. You must develop your ability to the point where you can do these things by reflex when you are under pressure. This will also cause you to gain that all-important confidence that makes you believe in yourself, and trust your instruments when the going gets heavy. Without this confidence, the only alternative is panic or oriental stoicism.

True, you have read of people who claimed they set out without any knowledge of navigation, and sailed around the world. William Albert Robinson claims he knew no celestial navigation when he left to sail around the world in *Svaap*, except what he had learned by self study ashore. He had never used a sextant. *But* Robinson was already an excellent seaman and an experienced sailor, and he headed for Bermuda, offshore, off soundings where he could get the practice he needed while in familiar waters on the first leg of his voyage. You have also read of untrained people who landed an airplane when the pilot suddenly dropped dead. In the case of our globe-circling friends, each and every one of them follow their first statement with an account of how hard they worked and studied to learn to navigate as soon as they got underway. Those who made it back to tell of this are the ones the Lord smiled on.

Please do not think I am telling you that you *must* practice the entire routine of formal navigation every time you go out in your boat. I can run hun-

dreds of miles along the Gulf Coast, and never look at a chart or a compass. Yet I know my position accurately at all times. Still, I use my navigation's because precise navigation is more efficient. Perhaps you can navigate by the seat of your pants in home waters, but where else other than your home waters are you familiar enough with the aids and landmarks to check the results you get with piloting, and thus develop, along with your knowledge, the skill and confidence you also need to be a competent navigator.

Another thing you must bear in mind is that no competent navigator depends solely on one means of position finding to guarantee the safety of his vessel. Again, the navigator making a passage along a well-marked coast, in good weather, would not have a man in the chains heaving the lead and another on the RDF taking bearings. No, in a case such as this, the navigator could rely on visual bearings and sextant angles. The same navigator, on another type of day, on the same coast, or on a good day on some less familiar coast, would use every trick in his bag to confirm his position.

Keep in mind, if you can't get a line of position one way, try another. There is no reason why one good loran LOP cannot be crossed with an RDF bearing, if no other loran pair can be received. You may not always get a fix, but you will get something far better than a guess.

Before you shove off on any voyage you should be sailor enough and navigator enough to take care of yourself and your vessel. But no man, no matter how good he is, is bigger than the sea, and even the best boat, the best judgement, and the best seamanship may not always be enough to carry you through. Remember though, that you are not in the same boat as Columbus or Magellan, unless you are far at sea on your world cruise. Along the coasts of the United States and in our inland waters, too, are organizations like the U. S. Coast Guard and your state's

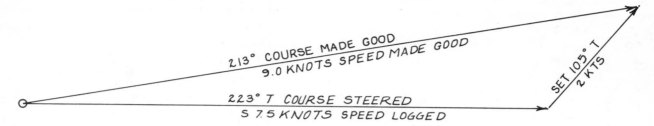

Figure 22-1. Vector diagram to solve for course made good on the cruise from Horn Island Pass to Gulfport.

marine police. One of their main jobs is to help you help yourself. Don't call these folks unless absolutely necessary, even though you are a bit frightened, but by the same token, do not wait until disaster is unavoidable before you ask for help when assistance is needed. Not even the U. S. Coast Guard or the marine police of your state can work miracles.

We left *War Hat* beating out to sea from Mobile Bay Entrance while we went in her in other times and places to study RDF and loran. It is time for us to continue our cruise to Gulfport.

After completing her excursion out into the Gulf of Mexico, *War Hat* touched at Pascagoula, Mississippi. She departed Pascagoula seabuoy, HIP, at 0512 the morning of 26 October, 1972. She set sail with a light westerly wind, expecting an easy reach to the seabuoy, the number one whistle buoy, at Gulfport Ship Channel. Her departure course out of Horn Island Pass is 229°C. After fairing away on course, you observe your wake is making an angle of 3° on your starboard quarter. As you passed buoy HIP departing Horn Island Pass, you noticed the current around the buoy. You estimated the set of this current to be 105° and the drift to be 2 knots. Your speed is 7.5 knots, under sail. At 0640 the wind lays. What is your course to steer, under power, if you use your 0640 EP as a departure, to lay the whistle buoy at Gulfport Ship Channel?

Your DR would normally be your departure for this 0640 course change under the conditions I just described, and, no matter what, you should also continue to plot from your 0640 DR, too. But, for the sake of our example, assume a round of RDF bearings tended to confirm the 0640 EP as your vessel's most probable position. With caution, it is logical to plan from your 0640 EP. In the area of your 0640 DR or EP, you should get RDF bearings on South Pass West Jetty and Mobile Point. Although the range is extreme, it is possible to read the marker beacon at Mississippi River Gulf Outlet. The range of these marker beacons is normally ten miles. If for some reason the beacons listed above could not be

heard, bearings on WLOX at Biloxi, Mississippi; WVMI at Ocean Springs, Mississippi, and WPMP at Pascagoula could well put you in a triangle around your 0640 EP. If you have no RDF aboard, you could borrow the cook's transistor radio to take these bearings. Each of these commercial broadcast stations is accurately located on Chart No. 1267.

The situation I am describing here is certainly routine. I hope you will actually work out this exercise with me as we proceed. My purpose is to combine several of the things we covered separately in a way they may actually be used by you some day. The solution to each part of the problem is given as we go, but try to work out each plot or example before looking at the solution.

When you depart Horn Island Pass, the first thing you should do is correct your compass course to find *War Hat*'s true course.

C_s	229°
L	3°W (She is being set to port)
C	226°
D	7°W (From deviation table)
M	219°
V	4°E
T	223°

With a true course of 223° and a speed of 7.5 knots, construct a vector diagram to see what a current with a set of 105° and a drift of 2 knots is going to do to *War Hat*'s course and speed. From the vector diagram in Figure 22-1, you see you should make good a course of 213°T and a speed of 9 knots. Take this information, and advance an EP to 0640. At the same time also advance your DR along a course of 223°T to 0640.

Figure 22-2 is a reprint of Chart No. 1267 with the entire passage that is covered in this chapter plotted. This consists of the dead reckoning plot and the estimated plot, along with the ensuing courses and plots resulting from information the navigator developed during the passage.

To plot your 0640 EP, plot your course made good and distance run since 0512. You have sailed for 1

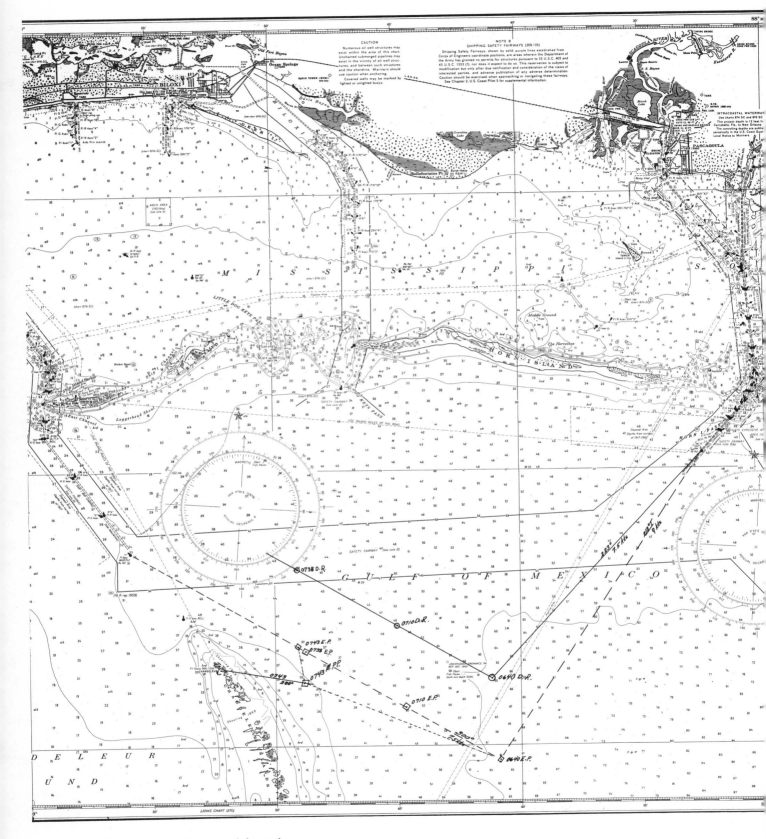

Figure 22-2. The end of the cruise.

hour and 28 minutes at 9 knots. The distance *War Hat* made good is 13.2 miles along the estimated track on course 213°. At a logged speed of 7.5 knots, she should have sailed a distance of 11 miles along her DR course of 223°. At 0641 your EP is latitude 29° 59.'4 N, longitude 88° 40.'8 W. Your DR position at 0640 is latitude 30° 02.'4 N, longitude 88° 41.'0 W. Because of the flat bottom, soundings will not tell you much. The chart shows "M" for mud as the bottom material for miles around. No need to arm the lead now. Your RDF bearings are your best choice.

You consider your 0640 EP as your most probable position. Since the wind has died, you furl your sails, and head directly for the whistle buoy off Gulfport. You have no reliable current information now. What is the true course to the whistle buoy from your 0640 EP? What course should you steer for the whistle buoy?

Lay a rhumb line from the 0640 EP to the whistle buoy, and with your parallel rulers and the compass rose of the chart, measure the true course as 300°. Uncorrect the true course for the course to steer:

T   300°
V   4°E
M   296°
D   4°W
C   300°
L   0° (No wind)
Cs 300°

Only by coincidence does your compass error equal zero, and your compass course to steer equal your true course. You change course to 300°T/300°C at 0640. Continue the estimated plot from the 0640 EP. Also be sure to maintain a plot, now along the true course of 300°, from your 0640 DR.

Visibility is under two miles, with occasional rifts in the haze permitting prominent objects up to five miles away to be seen. You turn on the depthfinder. At 0710 the depthfinder shows a depth of 47 feet. At 0738 the depth suddenly decreases to 29 feet! If you are like a lot of our less fortunate souls who go to sea, you may say, "heck we only draw six feet, keep on trucking. What is there to worry about?" If you are a competent navigator, you will say, "something is wrong here!" Your chart shows a depth of 34 feet to 37 feet at your 0738 EP, and a depth of 47 feet at your DR. It is pretty darn obvious you are not at either place. You slow to 3 knots, and heave the lead, armed with a fresh hunk of cold butter. A bottom sample shows clean, hard, white sand. What is your most probable position?

An examination of the chart shows a sudden shoaling over to the west off the Chandeleur Islands. You must be nearer to the Chandeleurs than your plots

show. You must be inside the 30-foot curve east of these islands. But where are you? The varying visibility has suddenly closed to less than a mile. You can see nothing of the low-lying Chandeleurs to the west of you. You are obviously being affected by a current. At this point it is difficult to tell how much set and drift you are experiencing.

A course change is certainly in order. At 0740 you change course to 315°C. An examination of chart 1267 shows a really abrupt shoaling from 14 feet to *no water* at the northern end of the Chandeleur Chain. You decide a danger sounding of 25 feet is advisable. You are setting the alarm on your depthfinder to 25 feet, when a cry from the lookout tells you Chandeleur Light is visible through a rift in the haze. A quick bearing on the light cuts in at 324°R. The time is 0743. The depthfinder shows 28 feet. Plot your MPP.

To plot your most probable position you must first correct and plot the bearing on Chandeleur Light:

C   315°   (Your compass course)
D   2°W
M   313°
V   4°E
T   317°
    324°R   Bearing
    641°   Sum
    -360°
    281°T   Bearing (the bearing of Chandeleur Light)

With a visual bearing on Chandeleur Light of 281°T and a sounding of 28 feet, you can fix *War Hat*'s position within 0.2 miles! (See Figure 22-2). For my money, this is a fix. I would certainly abandon my earlier DR and EP plots with information this firm.

You now have enough knowledge of your actual position to figure the set and drift you experienced since 0640. Measure the distance from your 0640 EP to the 0743 MPP. This distance is slightly more than 7.4 miles. In an hour and three minutes, your vessel traveled 7.4 miles plus. You must have been making a speed of about 7.1 knots.

With your parallel rulers, measure the course from your 0640 EP to your 0743 MPP. This course is 293°T. You have been making good a course of 293°T.

Now plot your 0743 EP along the original estimated track. Surely this seems hardly worthwhile. You know *War Hat* cannot be anywhere along this track. Your 0640 EP was pretty valid, however, so look. By connecting the three points made up of your 0640 EP, the 0743 EP, and the 0743 MPP, you construct a vector diagram. The line from the 0743 EP to the 0743 MPP is the set and drift vector of this diagram. The vector diagram resulting from this plot is shown by dotted lines in Figure 22-2. Measure the direction of the line from the 0743 EP to the 0743 MPP and you have an indicated set of 170°T. The distance between the two points is 1.3 miles in a time of one hour and three minutes. The drift is 1.3 knots.

With this information it is no problem to set a course to steer, at 7.5 knots, for the whistle buoy. Maintain your danger sounding. Keep a sharp lookout. When Chandeleur Light is abeam, if you can still see the light, you may want to check your distance off by a vertical sextant angle. In due time a buoy appears bearing 005°R. With your binoculars, you read a great big "1."

As navigator, you cannot help but feel a tinge of pride.

BIBLIOGRAPHY

Dunlap, G. D. *Navigating and Finding Fish With Electronics.* Camden, Maine: International Marine Publishing Co., 1972.

This work describes the principles of operation and uses of the several popular systems of electronic navigation available to the navigator today. Described also are the sonic devices used for depth finding and locating fish.

Dunlap, G. D., and Shufeldt, H. H. *Dutton's Navigation and Nautical Astronomy.* 12th ed., Annapolis, Maryland: United States Naval Institute, 1969.

The standard Navy navigation text. This work covers all types of navigation, from the simplest to the most complex.

International Marine Textbook Co. *Navigation and Nautical Tables.* Scranton, Pennsylvania, 1909.

An older text containing treatises on the elements of navigation; the chart, lead, and log; deviation and compass compensation; piloting; dead reckoning and nautical tables.

Norville, W. *Celestial Navigation Step by Step.* Camden, Maine: International Marine Publishing Co., 1973.

Primarily a work on celestial navigation, but it contains examples of the dead reckoning plot and advancing (celestial) lines of position, as well as a description of the construction and use of plotting sheets.

Shufeldt, H. H., and Dunlap, G. D. *Piloting and Dead Reckoning.* Annapolis, Maryland: United States Naval Institute, 1970.

This is the official United States Coast Guard Auxiliary text. The work is an excellent introductory text for beginners, yet it is also sufficiently complete to give a well-rounded and useful presentation of all the basic subjects of piloting and dead reckoning.

Maxim, H. H. "Simple Hand-Held RDF Method Can Plot Positions Within 200'." *National Fisherman,* January, 1972.

An article on the precise use of radio direction finders for navigating in confined waters.

United States Government Publications

Defense Mapping Agency, Hydrographic Center. *American Practical Navigator,* Bowditch, HO 9; 1962 ed., U. S. Government Printing Office, Washington, D. C., 1966 (corrected printing).

The standard reference for all American navigators. This work covers the entire subject of marine navigation with additional information on aeronautical navigation, land navigation, hydrographic surveying and related subjects. The work is supplemented with twenty-eight appendices and thirty-four tables.

Defense Mapping Agency, Hydrographic Center. *International Code of Signals (visual),* HO 103.

A code of one, two, or more letter signals or combination letter/number signals. These signal groups may be transmitted by flag hoist, sound, semaphore, or flashing light. Each participating nation prints a version of this code in its national language so vessels from different nations may communicate. The decode for a specific signal group is written in the language of the particular holder's nation. Thus, the signal "B", a single letter signal meaning "I am loading, discharging or carrying (as appropriate) dangerous cargo," would be understood by foreign vessels of nations supplying their vessels with this signal book.

Defense Mapping Agency, Hydrographic Center. *Sailing Directions,* various HO numbers.

These publications provide information concerning coast lines, hazards to navigation, climatic conditions, ocean currents, weather, tides, coastal and ocean routes, approach and entering instructions for ports and harbors, port services and facilities, pilotage regulations, and other details of the areas covered.

Defense Mapping Agency, Hydrographic Center. *List of Lights,* HO 111-116.

These publications cover foreign aids to navigation. They provide information on navigational lights, light structures, radio beacons, and fog signals.

Defense Mapping Agency, Hydrographic Center. *Radio Navigational Aids,* HO 117 (A & B).

This publication lists the many different types of radio services essential to safe navigation such as radio beacons, loran stations, omega stations, stations broadcasting time signals, and other radio information.

Defense Mapping Agency, Hydrographic Center. *Radio Weather Aids,* HO 118.

This publication lists sources of radio weather information for the mariner.

Defense Mapping Agency, Hydrographic Center. *Loran A Table(s),* HO 221 (with individual parenthetical numbers for tables for each rate).

These tables contain the necessary data to plot loran A lines of position, including skywave corrections, for the areas and rates covered by the particular table. With these tables loran A lines of position can be plotted on any suitable navigation chart, including plotting sheets, without the loran A overprint appearing on loran charts.

National Oceanic and Atmospheric Administration, National Ocean Survey. *Coast Pilots,* Numbers 1 through 8.

These publications cover the territorial waters of the United States. They provide information concerning coast lines, hazards, wind, weather, climate, currents, coastal and ocean routes, tides, approach and entering information for harbors, port facilities, port services, and other information of interest to the navigator.

National Oceanic and Atmospheric Administration, National Ocean Survey *Tidal Current Tables,* several volumes.

These publications provide the predicted time of slack water, time of maximum flood, time of maximum ebb, and velocities of the tidal currents. Predictions are provided for each day of the year covered by these annually published volumes. The tables also provide information to compute the velocity of the current at any time, and the duration of slack water at ebb and flood. Rotary current tables for strategic points along the coasts are given as well as other related information.

National Oceanic and Atmospheric Administration, National Ocean Survey. *Tide Tables,* several volumes.

These tables provide high and low water predictions for the areas covered by each volume for each day of the year for which they are printed. The tables also provide information to determine the height of the tide at any time, the local mean time of sunrise and sunset, and the local mean time of moonrise and moonset.

National Oceanic and Atmospheric Administration, National Ocean Survey. *Distances Between United States Ports.*

This publication assembles under one cover the distance tables in the eight volumes of the *Coast Pilot.* Distances are given between ports and points in the Intracoastal Waterway, coastwise routes, inside routes, and inland waters of the Atlantic, Pacific, and Gulf Coast, as well as the waters of nearby foreign countries.

Department of Transportation, U. S. Coast Guard. *Light List*, numbers vary for areas covered.

These publications provide information concerning navigational lights, light structures, radio beacons, and fog signals of the waters of the United States.

Department of Transportation, U. S. Coast Guard. *Aids to Navigation,* CG 193.

This booklet describes the appearance and function of all types of aids to navigation established and maintained by the U. S. Coast Guard and aids employed in the Uniform State Waterway Marking System.

U. S. Navy, Naval Observatory. *Nautical Almanac.*

This publication tabulates the positions of celestial bodies for each second of the year published, the times of sunrise and sunset, the times of morning and evening twilight, the times of moonrise and moonset, sextant altitude corrections, and other astronomical data of interest to the coastal navigator as well as the offshore navigator.

INDEX